Praise for *Lost Bird of Wounded Knee*

"[A] moving chronicle of one American woman's life and a perceptive study of white racial ambivalence. . . . [Flood] is a passionate advocate with a great story to tell."
—*San Francisco Chronicle*

"The work gains its power from the remarkable story of Lost Bird. . . . Flood writes history with style and tells an informative, affecting tale." —*Kirkus*

"[A] passionate book: a hybrid of domestic history, western history, women's studies, and the study of U.S.-Indian relations. . . . [*Lost Bird of Wounded Knee*] is a fascinating and important contribution to the field of history. . . . [A] detailed, engrossing and extremely well-written exploration of the life of a remarkable woman." —*Western Historical Quarterly*

"Well-documented, powerful and chilling. . . . Flood's narrative grippingly illustrates the clash between Indian and white cultures." —*Publishers Weekly*

"Engaging. . . . [The author's] extraordinary research brings this biography to life with such energy that readers must share the bitter despair and sheer hopelessness of Lost Bird's 29 years of life. . . . Flood provides a refreshingly sharp perspective." —*Denver Post*

"No details of the atrocities prior to, during, and after the Wounded Knee Massacre are left undescribed. Given from both the Indian and the white perspectives, the story has a depth rarely found in [other books]. . . . Flood is a first-rate scholar with extraordinary research skills." —*Tulsa World*

"A fascinating story that will appeal to a wide range of readers. Highly recommended." —*Library Journal*

Brigadier General Leonard W. Colby holding his adopted Lakota daughter
Lost Bird in 1891. Colby took the infant from the Pine Ridge Reservation
after the December 29, 1890 Wounded Knee Massacre.

(Photograph courtesy of Bea Kendall.)

Lost Bird of Wounded Knee

SPIRIT OF THE LAKOTA

Renée Sansom Flood

DA CAPO PRESS • NEW YORK

Library of Congress Cataloging-in-Publication Data

Flood, Renée S.
 Lost bird of Wounded Knee: spirit of the Lakota / Renée Sansom Flood.
  p.   cm.
 Originally published: New York: Scribner, c1995.
 Includes bibliographical references and index.
 ISBN 0-306-80822-6 (alk. paper)
  1. Wounded Knee Massacre, S.D., 1890. 2. Lost Bird, d. 1920. 3. Dakota
 youth—Biography. 4. Dakota youth—Cultural assimilation. 5. Dakota youth—
 Ethnic identity. I. Title.
 E99.D1L773   1998
 978'.004975—dc21
 [B]   97-34902
                                                                           CIP

First Da Capo Press edition 1998

This Da Capo Press paperback edition of *Lost Bird of Wounded Knee* is an unabridged
republication of the edition first published in New York in 1995,
with minor textual emendations. It is reprinted by arrangement with
Scribner, an imprint of Simon & Schuster, Inc., and the author.

Published by Da Capo Press, Inc.
A Subsidiary of Plenum Publishing Corporation
233 Spring Street, New York, N.Y. 10013

I am proud to dedicate
this book to my eldest son,
Dominic Anthony Figueras, M.D.

Contents

Preface
The Recurring Dream

From January 1980 until November 1987, I was a social worker in southeastern South Dakota. I soon learned that social workers were (and are) underpaid and overworked. I was white and married to a Yankton Dakota and had an Indian child. Because of my marriage, I was often the target of prejudice in my office. One man in particular, a fellow social worker, plagued me in front of coworkers with stinging remarks and hurtful gestures. When he saw me coming, he pretended to Indian dance around me, clapping his mouth, singing "Dumb dumb dumb dumb! Dumb dumb dumb dumb!" It amused everyone, and not one person ever tried to stop him or step to my defense. Seeing my helpless disgust, he jumped around, making sounds of swishing arrows penetrating his chest, pretending to be hit. "Swish! Thunk! Swish! Thunk!" I took it for a long time, looking away so that my tears were private. Four or five years later, after he had been promoted to a better position in Child Protection at the state capital, he visited my office. The minute he saw me he made a degrading sexual remark, and suddenly the years of prejudice against my husband, child, and everything good in Indian life—and now even my own womanhood—came together, and I flared up. "What did you say to me?" I snapped, staring directly at him. A look of utter astonishment crossed his face. I immediately reported his abuse to my supervisor, and she stood by me, but she said that I should have reported him years before. There was a joint meeting between his supervisor and mine, and my bigoted attacker and I faced each other across the table, equal at last. This time my perfectly aimed arrows of pent-up fury found their mark with an unmistakably loud *swish* and *thunk!* I must not have been the only one who complained, because not long afterward he resigned.

But prejudice in its blatant form wasn't the main reason I was concerned about continuing in my job. I had watched while many Indian children were placed in foster and adoptive care away from their tribes. Due to ignorance and lack of funds there were inadequate services offered to Indian children in foster care, and some were lost for years in the legal system, lobbed from one foster home to another like battered tennis balls. Many had been taken from their families because the social worker, lawyer, or judge did not understand Indian ways, or automatically judged a family unfit based on his or her own middle-class Christian values. Ignorant of extended Indian family kinship patterns, workers truly believed they were "saving" children by placing them in white homes where they would have material and educational advantages. The common reason for removing Indian children was usually not the sadistic physical and sexual abuse seen more frequently in white homes. More often, it involved an Indian mother or father with a drinking problem, people ashamed to face a judge who would criticize their parenting skills, blasting them with accusations they were too humiliated to deny, so they wouldn't show up for the court hearing. They knew the white people would take their children anyway. To the state and to the legal and social services systems, absence from a hearing meant only one thing—lack of parental devotion.

One day I went to a local hospital with another social worker. On the maternity ward, we found a young Lakota mother holding her baby boy. She had him wrapped up tightly in a warm blanket, and he was asleep. When the social worker barged in on the mother, she didn't look up. A nurse came and pulled the curtain around us.

"Are you having trouble finding a place to stay?" the worker began sympathetically. She gave me a knowing look and she thought the Indian girl hadn't noticed.

The girl was scared. Without looking, Indians can read body language like radar. "We just need a ride back to Rosebud," she said softly, still without looking up.

Now began the barrage of questions, each unconsciously calculated to destroy the young woman's self-esteem. "How will you raise your child without money?" the worker asked. "What kind of life can you provide for him on the reservation? If you really love your boy, you'd give him a chance in life. We have a long list of good people who can never have children of their own. They have money, beautiful homes. Your baby would have everything—a good education, nice clothes, loving parents, opportunities you can never give him. Don't you want to finish school? Later on you can have more children. Think of what's best for your child, don't just selfishly think of yourself. You can write him a letter telling him why you had to give him up, and it will be a part of his legal record, so that when he's twenty-one he'll be able to read your letter and understand why you let him go. Tell him you want a better life for him than you can possibly give him now. Tell him how bad life is on the reservation."

The mother looked at her newborn son. Tears ran down her cheeks and dripped from her chin. I couldn't stand to hear any more, so I eased out of the room to wait in the hall. But that was even harder to take. As I stood there, I saw plump, smiling white mothers wearing striped hospital gowns, holding hands with excited husbands as they headed for the nursery. Proud grandparents and happy siblings stood at the smudged nursery window gleefully admiring their new family members. Laughter filled the hallway and close family love, love that surrounds newborn babies and their relatives, touched my heart and echoed through my soul.

It seemed like hours before the social worker finally came out carrying the signed papers and the tiny baby, who was blinking his dark brown eyes in the harsh fluorescent lights.

She looked at me scornfully. "Where have you been? I needed you in there."

The nurse followed us to the elevator, smiling as she passed the nursery where little pink and blue bundles were tagged and left alone in their bassinets, side by side behind the glass window.

"She did the right thing," the worker told the nurse.

"They usually do," the nurse sighed. "Once they realize their children have no future if they keep them." I looked up at the elevator ceiling and prayed for the child. How I wished I could help the mother find a relative to take them in and teach her how to care for the baby. I could help her find a job, a sitter, baby clothes, and be there to answer her questions. With the right supportive services, she probably would have made a good start at motherhood. Or maybe she already knew all about babies and didn't need any help, only a bus ticket back to her reservation home.

When we got to the state car in the parking lot, I looked back up at the hospital window. There stood the young Lakota mother, her open palms on the window above her head. The worker handed me the baby, and I held him, still looking up at the Lakota girl watching us helplessly as we drove away with her precious child.

On the way to the foster home, the worker talked incessantly of the negative aspects of reservation life, things she knew nothing about, exaggerated opinions she had probably learned at the dinner table, in a college classroom, or from a book written by some "Indian expert" who had never known a Lakota woman in his life. I looked down at the sweet babe and I knew in my heart that taking this healthy child from his natural mother was a sin, like cutting down a tall ponderosa pine in order to improve a mountain view.

Before we pulled into the driveway at the foster home, I had heard ten minutes of bigoted generalizations about Indians. "They never go to college. Their houses are filthy. They all drink. They dress in rags and never bathe. They all get big government checks every month."

I tried to argue. "If you take one block in a white neighborhood and compare it to one block on a reservation, you will have clean and dirty houses, but in the white neighborhood there will be fifty times more child abuse. On both blocks there will be problems with alcoholism and drugs. By the way, have you ever been inside a reservation home?" That got her.

I leaned back and remembered a similar conversation I had had with my Dakota husband not six days before:

"All white people destroy the environment," he had generalized. "They're all serial killers and perverts. They beat and torture their children. They bomb innocent countries. They go to church and the next day they're sleeping with the next door neighbor. *Money* is their only God."

I tried to argue. "Well then," I said, "if you think everything about white people is so bad, I think you should stop watching 'Monday Night Football'!" That got him.

Sometimes, I received calls from adult Indians who were searching for their real families, and the stories were often the same—many had lived restless, unfulfilled lives and had lost their identities. I had also seen Indian children sold illegally, despite the Indian Child Welfare Act of 1978, which was often circumvented by shrewd lawyers and doctors. Countless Indian children were taken by well-meaning religious agencies and I had no way to find out what became of them. But I did follow up on state placements, and I noticed that during pre-adolescence Indian children seemed most at risk. They had not bonded with their adoptive parents, although the parents loved them and provided for their needs as best they could. But love wasn't enough, and often the parents blamed themselves and each other while their marriages crumbled. The Indian children were unable to identify with being either Indian or white. They drifted in and out of white society, sometimes ending up in prison, where they were likely to receive longer prison terms than whites, even though the crimes were the same. I felt compassion for Indians looking for their roots, but could not help them. As a state employee, I was not allowed to discuss past adoptions. I could only refer them to legal services for help.

Statistics were frightening. Thirty-five percent of Indian children nation-wide were not living with their own families, and teenage suicide rates among Indians were the highest of any group in the country. Generations of these misplaced children grew up unable to nurture their own children effectively.[1] They had become victims of a powerful society that believed swans could raise eaglets. Thousands upon thousands of misplaced Indian children, generations of tribal people from all over the United States, including Hawaii and Alaska, bore silent witness to a moral tragedy of major proportions.[2]

I was at my desk one Friday afternoon when Bea Kendall, a gentle homemaker working for Adult Services, leaned against my door. "Renée, I know you like Indian history and old photographs, so I brought you something." I can still recall that moment in slow motion. She handed me a faded photograph she had found at the bottom of an old trunk in her late father's attic. I took the Victorian picture in my hand. It was a general in full dress uniform holding an Indian baby. I turned the picture over, and on the back was written: "Zintkala Nuni, Lost Bird, found on the field of Wounded Knee on the fourth day after the battle by the side of her dead mother and adopted by me. Yours, L. W. Colby." I turned the picture over again and at the bottom corner in small letters were the words "Beatrice, Nebraska." I looked at the child's face and saw there the same expression that I had seen many times on the faces of Indian children who had been taken from their parents and placed in foster care. I stared at the piercing, hypnotic eyes of the handsome General Colby. That look was a dare.

The next day, I packed my son Shane, his teddy bear, and his favorite blanket in the car and we drove five hours to Beatrice. I had decided to investigate the story to see if the child had lived a happy life. Perhaps by studying this one adoption, I might find answers for the eaglets and the swans.

I became hopelessly intrigued and spent my spare time during the next five years tracking down the details of Lost Bird's life. Finally, I ran out of funds. Two Beatrice residents, Marlene Snyder and Senator Pat Morehead (Morris), suggested I look for a grant so that I could quit my job to concentrate on research. Many foundations don't give research money to individuals, so I went to the Gage County Historical Society in Beatrice, and with help from the director, Kent Wilson, they backed me. Through their non-profit organization, we applied to the Burlington Northern Foundation for a research grant.

Nearly a year later, I was surprised to receive notice that the grant was funded. Meanwhile, I remarried a Yankton Dakota scholar, Leonard R. Bruguier, who was working on his doctorate in history. (He later became the director of the Institute of American Indian Studies at the University of South Dakota.) Passing his doctoral exams, writing his dissertation, teaching, and babysitting while his wife flew off on research trips for weeks at a time were not easy tasks. The grant allowed me to travel coast to coast to major archival depositories, gathering letters, diaries, and photographs. I found General Colby's family in Oregon and his wife Clara's family in Wisconsin, along with a large collection of exciting artifacts and revealing private correspondence between Mrs. Clara B. Colby, a devoted suffragist, and her close colleagues, Elizabeth Cady Stanton and Susan B. Anthony, as well as letters from Leo Tolstoy, Carrie Chapman Catt, William Jennings

Bryan, and many others. It took years of constant begging to convince descendants to release the material into the care of the State Historical Society of Wisconsin.

I finally traced Lost Bird to California, with the help of my oldest son, Tony, always my biggest supporter, who took time off from his medical studies at UCLA to drive his mother to a little town in the hot San Joaquin Valley. There we pored over old newspapers on microfilm and found her obituary and, finally, the cemetery in Hanford where Lost Bird had been buried.

The caretaker took us to her gravesite. There was only grass, nothing more. "It has to be here," I told the man. "Her grave is listed in your cemetery records!" He took a long metal rod and poked down two or three feet into the earth—nothing. He probed again, but this time he hit something solid. He shoveled down and pulled up a round gravestone with Lost Bird's name on it. I started to cry.

"I'm going to throw that old plug away," the caretaker muttered, covering up the hole. "This is what poor people got in the old days. Nobody must have come and cleaned off the grave, so it just sank in." I memorized the placement of the gravestone. Years later, I was glad that I remembered the exact location of the stone.

"You're going to throw it away?" I stammered. "If you are, I'll take it."

"You might as well," he said, "I'm not puttin' it back there. It looks bad."

Tony went to his car and pulled out a roll of medical gauze used to wrap wounds. He carefully bundled the precious stone that I was to keep for years, and then he put his arm lovingly around me. "You okay, Mom? Don't feel bad. We found her, didn't we?"

I flew home to South Dakota with the gravestone in my lap. It was after I took the round marker that I began to have a recurring dream that haunted me:

I walked through a green park with neatly trimmed hedges and large trees. It wasn't misty or mysterious, it was just a park. I saw an old-fashioned carousel going around, and I walked over. There was nothing special about it, except that it was a silent merry-go-round—no calliope music or sound of any kind. I saw an Indian girl about ten years old riding side-saddle, ankles crossed demurely, on the back of one of the carved wooden horses. The stallions had powerful heads with windblown manes, flaring nostrils, shiny, jeweled bridles, and saddles covered with spangled stars and golden wings. Their frozen, galloping hooves went past me in slow motion, without sound, around and around. The child was the only person on the carousel; in fact we were the only people in the park. She was always dressed in the same perfect white dress, lace at the sleeves, with opaque black stockings and black high-top shoes. Tightly curled dark ringlets hung down her back, and there was a large white bow on the top of her head. She never looked at me as she went around, even though I smiled and waved to get her attention. She was completely absorbed, watching herself in ornamented mirrors in the center of the carousel. As I watched the gallant horses, she rode around again. The dream always ended the same way. As she went past, I jumped on the carousel and held onto one of the carved poles beside her. I looked in the mirrors to see what she was observing so closely. To my astonishment, her reflection was a Lakota girl in a fringed buckskin dress, with beaded leggings and moccasins. She galloped on a real horse, her long, straight hair flowing freely behind her. I could feel the wind blowing against my face. She looked at me, recognized me, smiled and laughed, and I laughed, too. Then I glanced over at her sitting on the jeweled carousel horse and I saw that she was still the sad child in the white dress with ringlets and lace. I called to her, "Lost Bird! Lost Bird!" But she couldn't see or hear me. Her reflection saw me, but Lost Bird could not.

Then I woke up and a wonderful feeling stayed with me for a long time afterward. I had the dream twice, but it didn't disturb me until I interviewed an old man in Beatrice, Nebraska, where Lost Bird had lived as a child with General Colby. He told me that "Zintka," as he called her, did not fit in, had no friends, and was always alone. "She had this odd habit," he said, "of riding the carousel in the park. She rode it all day long, hour after hour, and they had to drag her off and bring her home at night."

After many years of exploration and inquiries, I was invited to Wounded Knee for a meeting with the Wounded Knee Survivors' Association on August 8, 1990. I hadn't gone to Pine Ridge or Cheyenne River to interview members of the Wounded Knee Survivors' organizations because it seemed so brash to ask personal questions of people I didn't know. My niece, Dorothy Kiyukan, a student at the University of South Dakota, accompanied me on the eight-hour drive to Wounded Knee.

When we arrived, the meeting was already in progress under an arbor made from tree branches. It was almost a hundred degrees in the August sun. Most of the people present were Lakota elders speaking in their own language. When it came my turn to speak, I was so nervous my knees were shaking and I felt like a fool. Although they already knew about Lost Bird, they asked specific questions about my research. One thing seemed especially important to them—where she was buried. I finished what I had to say and was just about to sit down when I felt a strong tug on the hem of my shirt. "Renée, tell them *why* you are writing the book!" Dorothy whispered emphatically. She had experienced the "Lost Bird Syndrome" herself, having been moved from one foster home to another, and she wasn't going to let me leave without explaining.

"Oh no, this is it," I thought to myself. Excluding my in-laws, I'd never met an Indian yet who trusted a state social worker. The last thing I wanted was to admit that I'd been one for nearly eight years! For a second my throat got very dry and I took off my glasses so I wouldn't have to see the looks on their faces. Then I stared at the ground. After a little while, I put my glasses back on and glanced into their eyes. I saw they weren't judging me; they understood. There was a long moment of mournful silence. I stood there unable to move. "We should bring Lost Bird home," someone said. "We'll bury her with her relatives at Wounded Knee." I could hear my heart pounding.

Claudia Iron Hawk Sully, president of the organization, put Marie Not Help Him, secretary, in charge of the fund-raising to bring Lost Bird home. They wanted her to be buried at Wounded Knee as a symbol of the thousands of Indian children lost from their tribes, a symbol for all people of the world who had been violently deprived of their heritage.

Marie then prophesized, "She's buried in a layer of white sand. We'll find her bones in the sand." I remember thinking skeptically, "Is there white sand in central California?"

With help from Oglala attorney Mario Gonzalez, also a Wounded Knee descendant, Marie started the difficult search for funding. A year later, on July 11, 1991, the Pine Ridge Wounded Knee Survivors Association's painstaking efforts to return Lost Bird to her homeland became a profound and sacred reality.

Acknowledgments

Takunal waglusnan nains ipayeh ecamun heci wakanki amiyeciktunjapi wacin. Wanagi Wacipi ki he tohani iwowaglakin kta kecanmin sni. Wicasa Itacan Hehaka Gleska nains Cankpe Opi el wicakasotapi ki he oblaka wacinsni. Taku un ecamu ki he Zintkala Nuni waniyetu wikcemna mihakab un. Tohani miheyab iyaye sni. Takuwe miyelahci toun ki le oweciyakin kta un makahnige he slolwaye sni. Le un iyokipisni nains amayacanzekapi wacin sni. Hecegla epa wacin ye.

The author wishes to thank those many people who helped for ten years to bring this book to publication.

Marie Not Help Him, husband Luke Lone Elk, her mother Celene Not Help Him, daughter Summer, and grandson Wasu at Pine Ridge never gave up on me. I will always remember you with respect and gratitude.

Arvol Looking Horse, Carole Ann Heart, Mario Gonzalez, and Ann R. Roberts made the return of Lost Bird possible. Arvol's prayers sustained us during that long journey home.

A special debt of gratitude to Marjorie "Hoppy" Weeks and her husband, Martin. My association with Hoppy has led to many stimulating conversations concerning the spirituality of my work. There were times when I really thought I could not continue. She was always there to give me the strength to go on.

Although Margaret "Maggie" Lemley Warren and I don't always agree on the facts of history, I have learned a great deal from her. Her ongoing advice to me when everything else fails: "Vamp hell out of 'em!" Thanks, Maggie.

I also acknowlege the advice, support, and encouragement from the following friends and relatives: Avis Little Eagle, Sam Eagle Staff, Tim Giago, Irene Dillon, Doris Robertson Polley, Alex White Plume, Dorothy "Scootie" Kiyukan, Pat and Jerrod Tate, Claudia Iron Hawk Sully, Dick and Betty Cline, Richard Garnier, Robert Cline, Bill Flood, Lorraine Papin Cline, Carmel Flood, JoAnne Muir, Curtis Carroll, Corrine Stump, Earl Flood, Rita Flood, Warren Flood, Marie Sargeant, Nona McGaa, Julie Joseph, Carmen McMillan, Francis Hart, Helen Colby, Benny Gonzalez, Muriel Anderson, Joan and Jerry Indermark, Alice Smith, Helen Bewick,

Cathe and Crystal Walker, Robert G. Hanson, Jim Gillihan, Kaye Gustofson, Burdell Blue Arm, Frances, Shirley and Malita Bernie, Steve Emery, Arthur Short Bull, Sidney Keith, Galen and Hope Drapeau, Marlene, Lee and Kevin Snyder, Goldie Iron Hawk, JoAnn Angel, Max Breslauer, Gertrude Zephier, Parnel, Gracie, Martina, Danny and Sam (Buffalo Boy) Necklace, Pat and Dick Morris, Robert Stead, Marilyn Runs After, Moses N. Big Crow, Martin Brokenleg, Dora Shoots Off Bruguier, Sharon (Bruguier) Wichner, Charlene Stuhlmacher, Josephine Rooks (Goes After Her Horses), Marty and Linda Two Bulls, Victoria Siers, Robert Stewart, Herbert T. Hoover, Verna Hultgren, Vic Runnels, Elaine Melior, Sadie Hail, Karen and Larry Zimmerman, Connie Hoover, Gloria Heart, Russel Barsh, Verna Gannon, JoAnn and Larry Guckert, Ben Gullikson, Alan Hare, Mr. and Mrs. Michael Hogan, Shelia Dunn, Bernard G. Flood, Jr., and Josie C. Manternach.

My special thanks to those librarians and archivists whose knowledge and efficiency expedited this task in many ways: Harry Miller and Jack Holzhueter of the State Historical Society of Wisconsin; George Miles, the Beineke Rare Book and Manuscript Collection, Yale University; Margaret Quintal, the Institute of American Indian Studies and the South Dakota Oral History Center at the University of South Dakota; Max Leget, Florence Muller, and the staff of the I. D. Weeks Library, University of South Dakota; Rita Klepec, Craig Hannasch, Jimmy Rush, and Richard Fusick, the National Archives; Paul Fees, Sylvia Huber and Tina Stopka, the Buffalo Bill Historical Center, Cody, Wyoming; Laureen Riedesel, Beatrice Public Library, Beatrice, Nebraska; Kent Wilson and staff, Gage County Historical Society, Beatrice, Nebraska; the staff of the Circus World Museum, Baraboo, Wisconsin; Harry Thompson, the Center for Western Studies, Augustana College, Sioux Falls; Staff of the Colorado State Historical Society, Denver; D. Steven Corey, University of San Francisco, Richard A. Gleeson Library; Joseph Samora, the California State Archives at Roseville; James Van Stone, the Field Museum of Natural History, Chicago; Jill Holmes and John Phillips, Edmun Low Library, Oklahoma State University, Stillwater; Fred Boman, Library of Congress; Mark Thiel, Marquette University Archives, Milwaukee; Marty Miller, Gail D. Potter, Eli Paul, and Dick Jenson, Nebraska State Historical Society; the staff of the Western History Collections, University of Oklahoma, Norman; Lori Emison, the Bancroft Library, University of California at Berkeley; the staff of the Gilcrease Museum, Tulsa; Amy Hauge, Sophia Smith Collection, Smith College, Northampton, Massachusetts; Suzanne Zack, the Stowe-Day Foundation, Hartford; the staff of the Arthur and Elizabeth Schlesinger Library on the History of Women in America, Radcliffe College, Cambridge; the staff of the New York City Public Library; Pat Holland, the Papers of Elizabeth Cady Stanton and Susan B. Anthony, University of Massachusetts at Amherst; Laura Glum, Marveen Riis, LaVera Rose, and Lynda Sommers, the South Dakota State Historical Society; the staff of the University of Rochester Library; Abigail Scott Duniway Papers, David Duniway custodian, Salem, Oregon; Harriet McLoone, the Huntington Library, San Marino.

I owe a debt of gratitude to my Dakota husband, Leonard R. Bruguier, Ph.D., who assisted me with historical research and edited my work while earning his doctorate in history. I respect you for all your achievements.

Thank you Barbara and Tom Sansom, my wonderful parents, my aunt Ruth E. Arms, cousin Corrine Stump, and my brother, Tom R. Sansom and wife Doreen, my son Dominic Anthony Figueras, M.D., and my Dakota son Wambdi Tokahe, Shane Sundance Flood. I am sorry that I spent so much time on this book and that you had to make so many sacrifices for the Lost Bird.

A special acknowledgment to Carolyn Blakemore, Jody Hotchkiss, Ted Lee, my agent Sterling Lord, and my very patient editor at Scribner, Bill Goldstein.

This book was made possible by the Gage County Historical Society of Beatrice, Nebraska, and by a grant from the Burlington Northern Foundation.

This is a spiritual journey, a turning point for our people. This journey, for years to come, will mean a better life for our children, so that things don't happen to them like they did to Lost Bird.

> —Arvol Looking Horse, 1991,
> nineteenth-generation Keeper
> of the Sacred Calf Pipe
> of the Lakota Nation

A Spirit Journey Home

Arvol Looking Horse, the nineteenth-generation Keeper of the Sacred Calf Pipe of the Lakota Nation, towered six feet three inches above Lost Bird's grave under a broiling 94-degree California sun. His great height, the intense spiritual strength surrounding him, and his refined bearing gave us courage and held us spellbound. He knelt on the grass on one knee as sweat poured down his face onto masculine, expressive hands, his skin a rich red-brown. His long hair gleamed in the merciless sun. Arvol was dressed in black pants with concho belt and a white shirt, which had a hole in the front that was hidden by a beaded buckskin vest. Poor materially, the spiritual leader was to us at that moment the richest and most regal person on earth, and we were proud to stand around him in a circle as he prepared his pipe to pray to Tunkanshila Wakantanka (Grandfather Great Spirit).[1] Still resting on one knee, Arvol reached inside his pipebag and took out a rabbit-skin pouch, the fur black on one side and white on the other, containing specially prepared tobacco and other sacred plants. As he filled his personal pipe, he prayed aloud in Lakota to each of the four directions. He burned sage and purified the pipe by passing it over and through the smoke, his elegant hands gesturing in humble prayer. After he connected the bowl to the carved wooden stem, it was ready to use. Arvol Looking Horse stood up, a giant among us. He explained to the California Indians present, newspaper people, cemetery staff, and grave diggers why the four of us—Marie Not Help Him, secretary of the Wounded Knee Survivors' Association at Pine Ridge and founder of the Lost Bird Society; Avis Little Eagle, reporter for the *Lakota Times*; Carole Anne Heart, a Rosebud Lakota; and Renée Sansom Flood, a descendant of the Papin (Pappen) fur-trading family—had accompanied him on the long journey from the northern plains of South Dakota to this lonely cemetery in the San Joaquin Valley of California. In English, sincere and eloquent, he said:

> This is a spiritual journey, a turning point for our people. This journey, for years to come, will mean a better life for our children, so that things don't

happen to them like they did to Lost Bird. We can have a better respect for each other and understand where we came from to create a positive environment for our children. We're going to return the remains of Lost Bird to Wounded Knee, to put everything back in place, in balance with nature. In 1890, during the time of the Wounded Knee Massacre, our great leaders were killed and today alcoholism affects large numbers of families. Our people are being misled. They need a spiritual way to connect with Mother Earth. This is one way of bringing unity. We will take Lost Bird back, rebury her, and do the Releasing of the Spirit Ceremony. As Lakotas, we believe if this ceremony is not done, then the spirit is still wandering this earth.

Arvol began to sing a prayer to guide us through the emotionally difficult exhumation and reburial of a woman who as an infant had survived the Wounded Knee Massacre of December 29, 1890. She was then taken away from her tribe by force and had suffered for twenty-nine years trying to find her heritage.

Representatives from several California tribes, plus Indians from Mexico, were purified with sage smoke as we individually made tobacco offerings, sprinkling the shreds over the untouched grave. When it was my turn I knelt down, hands on my thighs, and started to cry. I talked silently to Zintkala Nuni, the Lost Bird, as I had done during the many years I had spent in researching her life, whenever I felt her lonely spirit hovering close to me. "Be patient a little longer," I told her. "We've come to take you home to the Lakota. Your mother and father and your relations are waiting for you at Wounded Knee. It won't be long now."

Marie Not Help Him, great-granddaughter of Dewey Beard (Iron Hail), the last survivor of both the Battle of the Little Bighorn and the Wounded Knee Massacre, stood next to me, her tears falling softly into the grass. She was crying not only for Zintkala Nuni but also for the thousands of "Lost Birds" who had been deprived of their heritage through adoption and foster care over the last one hundred years. She prayed for all her relatives who were slaughtered at the Wounded Knee Massacre. I couldn't lift my head up, couldn't stop looking at the spot where I knew her bones lay. Others stood huddled in groups, mourning. One man raised his arms up to the sky and wailed like a wounded deer. California tribal members gathered around us and sang soothing sacred songs and drummed in unison on their palms with clapsticks.

Avis and Carole Anne walked among the television and newspaper reporters who had crowded around us. Clicking cameras and repeated questions bothered me until finally I had to tell a reporter walking beside me to "please leave me alone!" I was totally focused on the grave, and I knew Arvol wouldn't want anything sacrilegious or undignified to occur.

There was no wind, no movement of air during the two and a half steaming hours that it took to exhume the remains. The first grave digger cut his shovel into the earth and it hurt me as though my own body had been torn. He sectioned and took up all the grass in perfectly square pieces. I cringed when next came the bizarre yellow backhoe, strange because the modern earth-moving convenience seemed like a rumbling, clangorous alien, totally out of place at this sorrowful spiritual gathering. The machine clawed the earth and dumped the dirt into a pile three feet high. We watched every load anxiously, expecting at any moment to see a human bone. After removing several feet of earth, the noisy backhoe, which had drowned out the melodious sounds of the sacred songs, stopped tearing the earth and I was glad. I didn't want it to scrape or break her bones.

Two grave diggers, one an old man who shouldn't have been working so hard in the hot sun, jumped down into the gaping hole and again it hurt as if they had landed on the body of my own child. They shoveled down three more feet and suddenly came up with pieces of decayed redwood, a common coffin material in 1920, the year Lost Bird was buried. Next, there were the metal coffin handles, corroded so badly they crumbled in our hands when we tried to pick them up. Now we all grew worried because we could see that the entire coffin had collapsed.

Sweat dripped from the men's noses. The tension, coupled with the broiling sun, made the moments unbearably long when suddenly they dug into a thin layer of white sand, just as Marie had prophesied over a year before.

"There is the sand!" we whispered to each other. "She'll be in the sand!"

Now the exhausted grave diggers switched from shovels to small spades and carefully dug into the coffin. Someone bent down close to my ear and whispered, "Renée, they've found the skull!" Suddenly Arvol loomed above the grave and in a strong low voice, said, "Turn off the cameras! No photographs of the remains." Indian security men walked silently toward the cameras. The newspaper and TV people were stunned for a moment, but they obeyed the spiritual leader and packed up their equipment. The Wounded Knee Survivors' Association at Pine Ridge had kept the location of the grave a closely guarded secret, because they feared desecration of the grave by artifact hunters. Even reporter Avis Little Eagle hadn't been told the location until the night before, although we had grown to love and trust her. Later Avis wrote: "My inner self was torn in two. My Lakota heritage told me that this was history happening and I was proud to be a part of it. As a reporter, I was part of a media acting like piranhas in a feeding frenzy. I held myself in the outer ring of people and watched. . . . Most reporters and photographers departed, leaving us to a quiet, dignified ceremony."[2]

Before they left, a woman reporter came up to me and pleaded, "Can't I just take a shot of them holding up their hands in prayer? I promise I won't take any photos of the remains!" I looked at her and thought of all the broken promises, broken treaties, broken bodies, broken families of Lakota people.

"No! Didn't you hear Mr. Looking Horse? He said no cameras. You just don't get it, do you?" She stalked away. Among insensitive non-Indians, as in all races, ignorance is learned and passed on to future generations.

We had been in touch with the People's Funeral Chapel and the Hanford Cemetery for years. They handled the arrangements discreetly and professionally. They placed a white sheet close to the grave, and the skull was gently handed up out of the moist, pungent earth and placed on the sheet. I knelt down next to it, but when one man put his thumbs into Lost Bird's skull cavity to clean out the sockets of her eyes—eyes that had gone blind in life—I felt as though I couldn't take it. My head started to spin, and I thought I was going to throw up. But I did what I usually do in a sweatlodge ceremony when the heat becomes intense: I shut my eyes and remembered why I was there. I prayed for strength and for Lost Bird's wandering spirit, and the weakness passed.

Her skull was beautifully formed, with high cheekbones. I had expected the bones to be white but only bones exposed to air bleach in the sun. The bones were dark brown, the color of the earth and of her soft skin when she was alive. Next, they handed up the long femurs, the leg and arm bones of her tall frame, followed by fingers, ribs, and toes.

Just then, Carole Anne came over and told me that she thought one of the arm bones was missing. Shocked, I stared down into the open grave. I wanted to jump in and thrust my hands into the pieces of coffin to find out if there might be another bone, beads from her dress, something more. But Arvol had said only the bones were to be removed, and the grave diggers assured me they had gotten everything that had not decomposed. I was worried by the thought that we might have missed fragile pieces of her buckskin dress or the bracelet she always wore, because she had it on when she was found under her mother's dead body at Wounded Knee. For a moment I imagined myself in the hole, digging through the coffin like a greedy artifact hunter, but I couldn't do it. I backed away from the deep chamber of living earth, the disturbed home of many plant and animal organisms.

The remains were placed in a rough coffin covered with a star quilt in various shades of lavender. In our anxiety we had forgotten flowers, but Arvol put sage into the coffin and that was enough. He then called for pall-bearers, and six Indian men came forward while the singing continued to comfort us.

We asked for overnight security at the funeral home until the coffin could be taken to our Delta flight early the next morning. We were relieved, but the long plane trip to South Dakota and the poignant reburial the next day lay before us. The Big Foot Memorial Riders would be waiting at Porcupine Butte to escort the remains by horse-drawn wagon to the mass grave. Lost Bird would be placed to rest above the peaceful valley where a century before hundreds of Lakota men, women, and children were left to freeze to the ground in their own blood after they were massacred at Wounded Knee by the United States Seventh Cavalry under a white flag of truce.

As we walked away from the grave, we thanked the grave diggers. When we got to the wrinkled old man who had worked so hard in the hot sun, he grasped my hand and I saw that he had tears in his eyes. "Now I understand the importance of history," he said. At least one white man had realized the purpose of our mission. Perhaps others would also, if only they knew the story of the Lost Bird.

CHAPTER 1

The Massacre at Wounded Knee

On the bitterly cold morning of December 29, 1890, Alice Ghost Horse rode her *śunka wakan,* the horse she had raised from a yearling, through the U.S. Army camp at Wounded Knee Creek in southwestern South Dakota. The thirteen-year-old Lakota girl was looking for her father, one of the Indian men who had been rounded up earlier that day.

A sudden shout in English riveted Alice's attention to the center of camp and she stood up in her stirrups, stretching as far as she could, trying to see what was going on. That yell meant only one thing to Alice: Someone was about to be assaulted, arrested, and dragged away by the soldiers. The military demanded not only obedience, not only compliance, but also cringing submission from Indians.

Less than fifty yards away she could see her father sitting on the ground with other disarmed men from Chief Big Foot's band, surrounded by more than 500 heavily armed soldiers of the Seventh Cavalry. A young girl was not supposed to mingle among strange men with her head and face uncovered, yet Alice rode toward her father through long lines of infantry standing at attention—grim-faced men wearing muskrat hats and heavy woolen coats. She looked north up the hill where four "guns on wheels" pointed in her direction. Mounted troopers watched silently on each side of the Hotchkiss battery.[1]

Moving among the tipis, soldiers lifted women's dresses and touched their private parts, ripping from them essential cooking and sewing utensils and a few old, battered rabbit guns. The men sitting in the council heard the angry shrieks of their wives and mothers.

Several young Lakota, offended by the abusive arrogance of the cavalry, stubbornly waited to have their weapons taken from them. It was a show of honor in front of their elders, for few of them were old enough to have fought in the "Indian wars" fifteen years before.

To one side Alice noticed a familiar figure standing with hands raised above his head, his palms turned upward in prayer. She later recalled:

A medicine man by the name of Yellow Bird . . . stood facing the east, right by the fire pit which was now covered up with fresh dirt. He was praying and crying. He was saying to the spotted eagles that he wanted to die instead of his people. He must sense that something was going to happen. He picked up some dirt from the fireplace and threw it up in the air and said, "This is the way I want to go back—to dust."[2]

The Ghost Horse family knew this Holy Man. Alice's translation of his eagle prayer refutes historians who have relied solely upon the translation of Sun Gi ("The Fox"), Seventh Cavalry interpreter Philip F. Wells, whose knowledge of the Lakota language (let alone the Hohwoju dialect spoken by Big Foot's band) was poor. Wells later told military investigators that a man named Yellow Bird stood up at Wounded Knee and deliberately incited the Lakota to fight. But Colonel James W. Forsyth, commanding the Seventh, reported that Yellow Bird had not bothered him at all until Wells made an issue of it:

One Indian separated a little from the rest, and in ghost dance costumes, began an address, to which I paid no attention. . . . After a short while, how-ever, the interpreter told me that he [Yellow Bird] was talking of wiping out the whites.[3]

Wells had repeatedly mistranslated the Lakota language and lost his tem-per during important tribal meetings. Headmen complained vigorously to agents and War Department officials until their protests made news on December 8, 1890, in an article saying that Wells had "failed to explain the meaning of many idioms which, when . . . not fully explained, leave . . . an impression entirely the reverse of that intended to be conveyed."[4]

But complaints against the blond, blue-eyed, mixed-blood interpreter were ignored. "The Fox" had all the right connections. An in-law of pow-erful Standing Rock agent James McLaughlin, Wells had been McLaugh-lin's chief of police and intimate friend for twenty-six years.[5] When cornered about his alleged dishonesty, Wells bragged: "Count the blades of grass between here and the Missouri River, and when you finish, I will start counting the lies I have told."[6]

The only interpreter present at the center of the disturbance on Wounded Knee Creek was Philip Wells. Moments before, Forsyth had ordered John Shangreau, a well-trained government scout and interpreter, to search the camp for guns. The day before, Shangreau protested vigor-ously when officers tried to disarm the Lakota: "Look here . . . if you do that there is liable to be a fight here; and if there is, you will kill all those women and children and the men will get away from you."[7]

With Shangreau out of the way, Colonel Forsyth gave a bizarre order: Each soldier was told to aim his unloaded gun at an Indian's forehead and to pull the trigger.[8] After Wells translated the demeaning (or drunken) order to the astonished Lakota, Iron Hail, later known as Dewey Beard, ". . . could not comprehend this foolishness."[9] Looking from one to another, he saw the faces of his companions grow "wild with fear."[10]

Alice realized a serious fight was looming, but her view was now blurred as soldiers advanced and passed by, their Springfield carbines ready. Dewey Beard saw "two or three sergeants" grab a deaf man named Black Coyote who had yet to be disarmed.[11] His friends had been so busy talking, they had left him uninformed.[12] The soldiers tore off his blanket, roughly twirling him around. He raised the rifle above his head to keep it away from them. In the midst of yelling, jerking, and twisting, the struggle ended unexpectedly when the rifle pointed upward toward the east and discharged into the crisp morning air.[13]

The sharp crack resounded and echoed across the rolling hills and prairie grasslands on the Pine Ridge Reservation. Lieutenant W. W. Robinson, Jr., the only mounted cavalryman in the center, shouted: "Look out, men. They are going to fire!"[14] The headmen jumped to their feet just as Lieutenant James Mann screamed: "Fire! Fire on them!"[15] On command, Troops K and B opened fire in an explosive volley, enclosing both attackers and victims in a curtain of dark, pungent smoke.

Years later, on frigid winter evenings around the woodstove, Alice Ghost Horse related her Wounded Knee experience, punctuated with expressively eloquent hand gestures, movements that brought her story vividly alive to grandchildren listening beside her. On one such night, while Alice recalled her private account of the Wounded Knee Massacre for her son, John War Bonnet, he penciled her Hohwoju words on ledgerbook paper. She told him about a religious ceremony called the Wanaǧi Wacipi, the "Spirit or Medicine Dance," referred to by reporters as the "Ghost Dance," a term sensationalized and distorted to sell newspapers. She did not call it a "religion." It was, and remains today, a ceremony as sacred as a Sun Dance or a Holy Communion.[16]

The purpose of the Ghost Dance was to communicate with dead relatives.[17] Attuned to the earth's all-absorbing, all-encompassing molecular energies, Ghost Dancers realized other dimensions. The Lakota thought it might even have been possible to call back the great herds of buffalo, the antelope and black-tailed deer. Perhaps together in sacred circles, purified, clasping each other's hands, they might empower the roots to grow, to harness their senses to revitalize the world. The Ghost Dance was an attempt to save the earth and bring back the original creatures to live upon it. Spiritual Lakota beliefs were and still are fearsome concepts to most non-Indians.

Instead of accepting the Ghost Dance as a religious ceremony, Christian missionaries harassed Ghost Dancers unmercifully. The dance was branded as a curious, frenzied "craze." Non-Indians would enter the Ghost Dance camps unmolested, and sometimes stole artifacts from the sacred trees. They interrupted sweatlodge ceremonies with loud laughter and they mocked people who had reached an altered state of grace. Even Father John J. Jutz, much loved by the Lakota, went uninvited to a Ghost Dance:

> During the dance I took up my position in the middle of the circle, dressed in my religious habit, and from my place of observation I could see everything that went on. I went over to those who were "resurrected from the dead" and asked them if they had spoken with their deceased friends. I offered them a dollar if they would tell me their experiences, but they would not answer me. I offered them two, three, four, five dollars, but they only looked at me and said not a word.[18]

The Lakota did not step forward to the altar in the middle of Communion services at Holy Rosary Mission and offer to pay Father Jutz one, two, three, four, five dollars if he would tell them how it was possible to eat the body of Jesus Christ and drink His holy blood.

Throughout time, Lakota religious belief involved the search for God and self through visions, dreams, trance, and intensely profound sacrifice and prayer. Before white contact, holy men were attuned to the rhythms, the harmonious patterns of all life forms, including earth's creatures and plant organisms and their respective magnetic fields. They understood and used inherited senses that even today scientists employing techniques of neuroscience, microbiology, and biotechnology cannot duplicate or explain.[19]

Imagine a holy man alone on a hill, purified by steam, washed internally of all waste by fasting, cleansed mentally of all impure thoughts with the Sacred Pipe. Raising his arms into the sky, he addressed the directions of the world, singing a song linked to the magnetic sounds of the earth:

> I send a voice:
> *Hee-ay-hee! Hee-ay-hee! Hee-ay-hee! Hee-ay-hee!* Here me, four quarters of the world. A relative I am! Give me the strength to walk the soft earth, a relative to all that is! Give me the eyes to see and the strength to understand, that I may be like you . . .
> Great Spirit, Great Spirit, my Grandfather, all over the earth the faces of living things are all alike. With tenderness have these come up out of the ground. Look upon these faces of children without number and with chil-

dren in their arms, that they may face the winds and walk the good road to the day of quiet. This is my prayer: Hear me![20]

Using well-developed senses and ancient herbal medicines, holy men healed the sick. Some possessed the power to call the buffalo, the eagle, and the deer by their singing, while others communicated with the spirits of their ancestors: as did the monarch butterfly and the chinook salmon and the green sea turtles on their migratory journeys home. In so doing, medicine men exerted remarkable physical and mental sacrifices for the good of their people, eventually depleting their strength. When they died, they rejoined the same magnetic field, absorbed into the mysterious power they could merely touch in life. Such was the power of the Lakota holy men before the coming of the white man.

After the whites came—some good, some evil—they cut up the land to take out minerals, vital sources of energy the earth had always used for the good of all. Diseases and plagues then entered the life paths of organisms and pollution evaporated into the skies and leaked down into the waters of the earth. Holy men began to have a difficult time. Some of their powerful senses had been weakened, yet, miraculously, many remained strong.

Traditional Lakota people worshiped in highly complex sacred ceremonies, and by 1890 the ceremony they called for most often was the Ghost Dance. Government officials and the white population generally regarded the dance as menacing, perhaps because it made them uneasy to see large groups of united Lakota doing something they could not understand. It is ironic that a spiritual ceremony frightened so many people. Newspaper reporters focused their anxiety on what they called "ghost shirts," made from muslin or cotton cloth and decorated with crescents, crosses, and birds—ceremonial clothing they claimed thousands of Indians wore to render them impervious to bullets. In 1906 author Natalie Curtis interviewed Short Bull, a Ghost Dance leader, for her publication, *The Indians' Book*. She asked him if the Ghost Dance was warlike, and this was his reply:

Who would have thought that dancing could have made such trouble? We had no wish to make trouble, nor did we cause it of ourselves. . . . We had no thought of fighting. . . . We went unarmed to the dance. How could we have held weapons? For thus we danced, in a circle, hand in hand, each man's fingers linked in those of his neighbor. . . . The message that I brought was peace.[21]

Alice Ghost Horse had not yet been influenced by non-Indians. Her parents and relatives, indeed her entire *tiospaye*, or extended family, were Ghost Dancers.[22]

We were camped at the mouth of Cherry Creek last part of December 1890, where it empties into the Cheyenne River, home of "Big Foot's Band"—the band we belong to. I was 13 years old at the time. These people are all Hohwoju, just as we are all Minneconju. [Both words mean "Plants by the Stream."] They live up and down Cherry Creek and . . . the Cheyenne River clear to Takini ["Barely Surviving"], the farthest district on the [Cheyenne River] reservation.

My people usually do the Ghost Dance above the Plum Creek, straight east of Cherry Creek across the Cheyenne River. It's a big, flat area up there. When they have it, most of the Cherry Creek people go up there to experience the ceremony.

The ceremony starts toward evening. The purpose of the Ghost Dance was to see their dead relatives and converse with them. When it is announced, all the people that are going to dance go down to the creek to swim and they take a bark of chokecherry stem and chew it or eat some chokecherry. Some have sweatlodge—they sweat that way. The Ghost Dance was like a Sun Dance [sacred], but in the Ghost Dance they form a circle, holding hands, and they sing and dance. They do this till someone falls or several fall. [They have] some visions of going to heaven and back with a good feeling of having seen their dead relatives, but God does not permit them to look at you because you are not dead.

They wait till they tell what they saw or hear during their trance. The dances usually last for four days, and quite a few camp up there during that time. Children are not allowed to go near the ceremony, so my brothers and I play near the wagons or along the hills or go pick cherries while this is going on. It usually lasts after dark and that is it.

The military leaders send scouts out to the dance to go around asking questions. The military was very suspicious about this ceremony.[23]

An officer at Fort Bennett once tried to bribe Alice's father to spy on Chief Big Foot, called Spotted Elk by his people. Ghost Horse refused. For a time he went daily to the fort to buy newspapers and have a good look around. His behavior finally riled authorities, who brought his visits to an end with a newspaper story entitled "Indians Who Read." The article reported "a spy named Ghost Horse" and others (who) "regularly . . . buy copies of each daily paper on sale, which they took back and read to the council composed of chiefs and leading braves, interpreted in the Sioux tongue."[24] The article about Ghost Horse delighted his friends and relatives in camp, who took pleasure in teasing him. Dakota anthropologist Ella Cara Deloria described such a lighthearted event:

In the evenings congenial men gathered in a tipi of some person of prominence whose personal charm drew others to his company. There they sat sometimes long after midnight, smoking and talking and lunching occasionally amid much laughter and gaiety over funny stories and jokes. All kinds of talent came out. There were those who clowned cleverly on purpose, and those whose behavior, comical by nature, unintentionally sent the company into roars of laughter.[25]

Alice remembered the day that laughter in Big Foot's camp changed to grief when exhausted survivors of Sitting Bull's band reached Big Foot:

> Some people came from Standing Rock and told Big Foot that Sitting Bull was shot and killed at his place by Indian policemen. This killing was provoked by the agent (James) McLaughlin.[26]

It was said that Sitting Bull and Big Foot were related and called each other "brother." Alice heard particulars of Sitting Bull's death recounted over and over by crying relatives who had seen him die. Another eyewitness account, written by a Standing Rock policeman named John Loneman, details Sitting Bull's arrest and assassination:

> One morning, the 14th day of December, 1890 . . . Policeman Charles Afraid of Hawk of Wakpala District came to me with the message that all of the . . . entire Reservation Indian Police had been ordered to report immediately to the Lieut. Henry Bullhead's place. . . . My wife hearing the news became rather nervous and excited for she seemed to realize that there was a serious trouble coming. . . . On the way up we notified several police— Bad Horse, Armstrong, Little Eagle, *Wakutemani*—Brownman, Hawkman and Good Voice Elk and others that, by the time we arrived at Bullhead['s] place there were about 12 of us from our way and the rest of the 37 were all from different districts in the reservation. Of course, we had quite a lot to say on the way among ourselves knowing full well that we were called to take a final action to suppress this ghost dance which was becoming a menace to the tribe. I'm simply expressing my viewpoints as one who had reformed from all heathenish, hostile and barbarous ways . . .
>
> The order being for us to act about daybreak and as the night was rather long, we tried to pass the intervening time in telling war stories. The Indian Police who were on this campaign were a class of Dakotas who had enviable achievements and attainments . . . having highest estimation in the minds of government officials, missionaries, traders, as well as possessing good influence in their respective communities. . . .
>
> We rode in a dogtrot gait till we got about a mile from the camp, then we galloped along and when we were about a quarter of a mile, we rode up as if we attacked the camp. Upon our arrival at Sitting Bull's cabin, we quickly dismounted and while the officers went inside we all scattered round the

cabin. I followed the police officers and as per orders, I took my place at the door. It was still dark and everybody was asleep and only dogs, which were quite numerous, greeted us upon our arrival and no doubt by their greetings had aroused and awaken[ed] the ghost dancers.

Bullhead, followed by Red Tomahawk and Shavehead, knocked at the door and the Chief answered *"How, hiyu wo,"* [or] "All right, come in." The door was opened and Bullhead said, "I come after you to take you to the Agency. You are under arrest." Sitting Bull said, *"How,* let me put on my clothes and go with you." He told one of his wives to get his clothes. . . . After he had dressed, [he] arose to go and ordered his son to saddle up his horse. The police told him that it was already outside waiting for him. When Sitting Bull started to go with the police . . . one of Sitting Bull's wives burst into a loud cry which drew attention. No sooner had this started, when several of the leaders were rapidly making their way toward Sitting Bull's cabin making all sorts of complaints about the actions of the Indian police, *Mato Wawoyuspa.* The Bear That Catches, particularly, came up close, saying, "Now, here are the *ceska maza*—'metal breasts' [meaning police badges], just as we had expected all the time. You think you are going to take him. You shall not do it." Addressing the leaders, [he said] "Come on now, let us protect our Chief." . . . Lieut. Bullhead got a hold on the Chief's right arm, Shavehead on the left arm, and Red Tomahawk back of the Chief—pulling him outside. By this time the whole camp was in commotion—women and children crying while the men gathered all round us— said everything mean imaginable but had not done anything to hurt us. The police tried to keep order but [it] was useless—it was like trying to extinguish a treacherous prairie fire. Bear That Catches, in the heat of the excitement, pulled out a gun from under his blanket and fired into Lieut. Bullhead and wounded him. Seeing that one of my dearest relatives and my superior shot, I ran up toward where they were holding the Chief, when Bear That Catches raised his gun, pointed and fired at me, but it snapped. Being so close to him I scuffled with him and without any great effort overcame him, jerked the gun away from his hands and with the butte [sic] of the gun, I struck him somewhere and laid him out. It was about this moment that Lieut. Bullhead fired into Sitting Bull while still holding him and Red Tomahawk followed with another shot which finished the Chief . . .

The rest of the police now seeing nothing else for them to do but to defend themselves became engaged in a bitter encounter with the ghost dancers. It was daybreak and the ghost dancers fled to the timber and some already started running away into the breaks south of the Grand River.

Hawkman . . . was sent to carry the news of the fight to the Military Forces. . . . Running Hawk said to the police: "Say, my friends, it seems there is something moving behind the curtain in the corner of the cabin." The cabin, instead of being plastered, the walls were covered with strips of sheeting, sewed together and tacked on the walls making quite a bright appearance within. All eyes were directed to the corner mentioned and without waiting for any orders I raised the curtain. There stood Crow Foot [Sitting Bull's fifteen-year-old son] and as soon as he was exposed to view, he cried out, "My uncles, do not kill me. I do not wish to die." The police asked the officers what to do. Lieut. Bullhead, seeing what was up, said, "Do what you like with him. He is one of them that has caused this trouble." I do not remember who really fired the shot that killed Crow Foot—several fired at once. . . .

The soldiers having dismounted rushed to the camp—ransacking anything worth keeping. . . . About this time, some of the relatives of the police killed arrived and such lamenting over the dead was seldom known in the history of my race. Taking a last look on my dead friends and relatives, I, in company with Charles Afraid of Hawk, started for home. On the way, we past [sic] several deserted homes of the ghost dancers and felt sorry that such a big mistake was made by listening to outsiders who generally cause us nothing but trouble.

I reached home and before our reunion I asked my wife, brothers, sisters and mother to prepare a sweat bath for me, that I may cleanse myself for participating in a bloody fight with my fellow men. After doing this, new or clean clothes were brought to me and the clothes I wore at the fight were burned up . . .

The next day I took my family into the Agency. I reported to Major McLaughlin. He laid his hand on my shoulders, shook hands with me and said: "He alone is a Man. I feel proud of you for the very brave way you have carried out your part in the fight with the Ghost Dancers." I was not very brave right at that moment. His comment nearly set me a crying.[27]

As soon as Chief Big Foot heard of Sitting Bull's death, he fed and clothed the refugees from Standing Rock and then held a council to decide what to do next. During this time Big Foot received an invitation from Chief Red Cloud to come to Pine Ridge for talks. Alice Ghost Horse remembers the decision:

Big Foot's followers decided they should flee to Pine Ridge for protection. They thought that Sitting Bull was killed because of the Ghost Dance, and they were afraid for their leader Big Foot. On short notice, it was decided to move out the very next day, so they all staked out their horses close by and all went to bed.

Early . . . we packed up in a hurry and headed out, crossing the mouth of

Cherry Creek, staying on the west side of the Cheyenne River, following an old wagon trail that was pretty well used. This trail led to Takini. We kept to the low land in case the military was sending out scouts. We ran all the way like this, stopping halfway for lunch. My mother had some [food] for us to eat.

Late afternoon, we pulled into Takini amid clusters of lean-tos, tents, and small cabins. Most of them were getting ready for winter by looking at the wood piles. . . . After we got settled in our tent, my mother started cooking, the kids were at the river playing, so we joined in. My father was called to a meeting at the chief's tent. After we ate, there was little time to visit, so we hung around outside till they told us to go to bed, as we had to leave pretty early.

Next morning, I heard my father hitching up the horses, so I got up and saddled my horse, as I plan to ride all the way to Pine Ridge. In a little while they all started out single file. First wagon to leave was Big Foot's wagon, followed by all his relatives. We fell in about the middle of the wagon train and we headed up this long hill we had to climb east side of the Cheyenne River. I looked back and I could see more wagons joining in and coming and many children were on horseback, too. It was a sight to see. Some of the local boys went with us for a while and they turned back. My father sat in front driving the team, sitting with my older brother, and my younger brother sat in the back with my mother who kept an eye on me. I was on my favorite horse. We had extra horse tied to the team in case we need to change horses. . . .

Some of the riders would fall back to check on the people to see if they are okay, or if they need anything. This is at the request of the chief. We were not allowed to start a fire. . . . [28]

As Chief Big Foot's band and some thirty-eight Hunkpapa refugees from Sitting Bull's camp were traveling to Pine Ridge on the cold late afternoon of December 25, they came upon a log church. Long before they reached the structure, Alice and her mother heard singing.[29] Christmas hymns beckoned the tired people to come in: "Silent night, holy night / All is calm, All is bright, / Round yon Virgin, mother and child. / Holy infant, so tender and mild. / Sleep in heavenly peace. / Sleep in heavenly peace."

The cavalcade stood in silence listening to the gentle carol. They watered their horses as a red-gold winter sunset spread across the western horizon and brought an end to the wearisome day. When cold and darkness engulfed them, Big Foot sent a woman to the church door to ask if they might bring their babies and old people in to warm themselves by the fire. She knocked and when the door opened, exhausted travelers caught sight of a glowing fireplace covered with woven cedar boughs and a tree strung with many colored ribbons. Small candles shimmered on each bough. The draft from the open door caused the flickering dipped-wax flames to beam

dancing shadows on the snow outside. Several mothers with hungry, whim-
pering infants in their arms jumped down from wagons and crowded close
together, shivering in the frigid night air. They lowered their heads, blinking from behind blankets into the holy place the white men called "the
house of God." Suddenly, a man's threatening voice and raised fist startled
Alice and the other women, making them step backward.

Verbal abuse struck the women like blows and then the door slammed
shut. Humiliated, they ran back to the wagons to tell Chief Big Foot they
were not welcome. In a menacing voice the minister had growled: "Go
away, outlaws!"[30] On Christmas Day pregnant women, babies, and elderly
people were denied the warmth of an open fire. Turned away from the
"house of God," the long caravan passed silently into the darkness. They
discussed this inhuman rejection, an evil example of the white man's
strange religion.

Alice and her band continued onward, suffering from hunger and cold
throughout the night:

> The going was tough but we were now below the Porcupine Butte. Some-
> times . . . there was no trail.
>
> [The next day] the head wagons stopped on a hill overlooking a creek.
> My father got off and went over there to see what they were looking at. In
> the meantime, my mother came over and tighten[ed] my cinch. She said in
> case we might have to run for it. There was a cavalry camp below. That's
> what they were looking at.
>
> Pretty soon my father came back and said the chief was sick and is lying
> in the back of the wagon all bundled up. My father said they picked some
> young men to go down and talk to the military as they [the cavalry] are in
> the way of our path. I saw four [Lakota] riders riding down toward the cen-
> ter of the camp, where they have big guns on wheels. One of the riders had
> a white flag, a white material tied to a stick, riding in front of the other three
> riders. Soon as our riders crossed the creek, the soldiers layed down and
> aim[ed] their rifles at them, but they kept on going. They dismounted at the
> center and they were talking for a while and a lone rider galloped up the hill
> to Big Foot's wagon. He said they wanted the chief at the center for talks,
> but the family said no, because he was very sick, so the rider went back to
> tell them. Mother told me again to keep close in case we have to make a run
> for it.
>
> Later they sent a buggy up with a doctor, who checked the chief. The doc-
> tor said he had pneumonia. He gave him some medicine, and they loaded
> him in a special wagon and took him down. Pretty soon a rider came back
> and told us to camp along the west side of the creek [Wounded Knee]. So

we drove down there and pitched our tents as ordered. An old army wagon was going around passing out bacon, flour, coffee beans, army beans, and hard tacks.

By sundown we were completely surrounded by foot soldiers, all with rifles. My mother and I went down to the creek to pick up some wood and to go to the bathroom, but two soldiers followed us . . . so we hurried and came back with some sticks.

At this time everyone went to bed because we were all tired out from this hard trip. Some of the young men were up all night to watch the soldiers. Some of the soldiers were drunk, saying bad things about the Lakota women.[31]

Alice bedded down next to her little brother. As the children slept, the adult Lakota watched Colonel James W. Forsyth ride in to take command with reinforcements from Pine Ridge. Accompanying Forsyth was James Asay, the well-known Pine Ridge/Lodge Creek trader and whiskey runner, driving a wagon containing supplies and a ten-gallon keg of whiskey.[32]

Among the officers assembled for the reunion were seven who had been with the Seventh Cavalry since General George Armstrong Custer's ill-fated Battle of the Little Bighorn on June 25, 1876: Captains George D. Wallace, Myles Moylan, Charles A. Varnum, Edward S. Godfrey, Henry J. Nowlan, Winfield S. Edgerly, and Lieutenant W. W. Robinson, Jr. Auburn-haired Lieutenant Robinson (son of a Seventh Cavalry colonel) transferred to the Seventh one day after Custer fell.[33]

That evening Colonel Forsyth sent a courier to find Philip Wells. The interpreter joined the officers in what Robert M. Utley called "a jolly time. . . . [T]he officers celebrated the capture of Big Foot."[34] Richard C. Stirk, former scout for the late Major General George Crook, owned a horse ranch and freighted for James Asay. Instead of returning to Pine Ridge after dropping off a load of food, he decided to stay the night. Interviewed later by Nebraska historian Judge Eli Ricker, Stirk said:

The officers were passing from tent to tent and drinking and congratulating Forsyth on his capture of the Indians. He [Stirk] says he did not see that the officers were boozy the next morning, but he knows that whiskey was plentiful.[35]

While the party continued, a few laughing officers "staggered" toward Chief Big Foot's tent. They tried to get the leader to come outside but were stopped by the captain of the guard, Myles Moylan.[36] Inside the large army tent eight soldiers guarded the dying Big Foot, along with six of his headmen, including Dewey Beard and Spotted Thunder. While the headmen sat around Big Foot's cot with eight soldiers guarding them, the chief spoke to Beard in a voice so weak "that he could barely hear him." The dying chief whispered, "Remember that I'm sick . . . humble yourself."[37]

Dewey [Iron Hail] died in 1956 at the age of ninety-eight. He often told his granddaughter, Celene Not Help Him (Marie's mother), about that night in Big Foot's tent. One hundred years later, on September 25, 1990, Celene Not Help Him testified before the Select Committee on Indian Affairs of the United States Senate. She related the story that her grandfather Beard told her:

> They wouldn't let us go to sleep. . . . All night they tortured us by gunpoint. They asked us who all was in the Battle of the Little Big Horn, the battle with Custer. . . . "Were you there?" . . . We told them we don't know. They were saying things to us in English, but we can't tell them what we don't know. Besides, the interpreter is not that good. . . . Maybe he tells them something else or is afraid to say anything.[38]

Segregating older headmen in Big Foot's tent away from the younger men was not inappropriate behavior. But keeping them awake, jabbing them with gun barrels, and asking questions about the Bighorn Battle violated the rules of military conduct afforded prisoners of war—if indeed it was a war, as the military later claimed. The Lakota have asked themselves ever since, who gave the order to keep Chief Big Foot and his Headmen awake all night, and why?

The next morning, December 29, 1890, Alice Ghost Horse was startled awake by a bugle call:

> I went outside and I noticed all the soldiers were gone. There was [a] lot of activity in the army camp. Some kind of excitement going on. . . . We ate in a hurry because everyone was loading up their wagons and my father had the horses and he was saddling my horse.
>
> At the time a crier was making his way around the camp announcing that all the menfolks were to report to the center for talks, so they all left, but the women folks continued to pack their belongings in the wagons.

When they were ready to leave, Alice mounted her pony and went to look for her father:

> I was on my horse. . . . I noticed that they were arguing and some were shouting. Pretty soon some cavalry men rode in from the center at a fast gallop and they started to search the wagons for axes, knife, guns, and awls. They were really rude about it. They scattered their belongings all over the ground. The guns the Lakota have were for hunting and they were not that

good. Few bow and arrows, too. These they took to the center and piled them up in the middle. They also searched the men at the center.

At this time there were cavalrymen all on bay horses . . . lined up on top of the hill on the north side. One officer rode down toward the center at a full gallop. He made a fast halt and shouted something to his commanding officers and retreated back up on the hill, and they all drew their rifles and long knife. And you can hear them load . . .

In the meantime, some more cavalrymen lined up on the south side. A big gun was also aimed down towards the center and towards where we were. I heard the first shot coming from the center, followed by rifles going off all over, occasionally a big boom came from the big guns on wheels. The Lakota were all disarmed, so all they could do was scatter in all directions. The two cavalry troops came charging down, shooting at every one who is running . . .

My father made it back to our wagon and my horse was trying to bolt, so he told me to jump, so I got off and the horse ran for all its worth towards the creek. We fled to the ravine, where there was lots of plum bushes and dove into the thicket. The gunfire was pretty heavy and people were hollering for their children. With children crying everywhere, my dad said he was going to go out to help the others. My mother objected, but he left anyway. Pretty soon, my father came crawling back in and he was wounded below his left knee and he was bleeding very bad. He took my youngest brother, who was six years old, and he said he was taking him further down the river to a better place and he would come back after us.

A while later he came crawling back in and said, "*Hunhun he, micinksi kte pelo!*" ("They killed my son!") He had tears in his eyes so we cried. . . . There was no time to think.[39]

"*E'yaye'ye'! E'yaye'ye'!*"
It is my own child.
It is my own child.[40]

My father said we should crawl further down, but my mother said it's better we die here together, and she told me to stand up, so I did, but my father pulled me down. With a little effort, we were able to crawl to a bigger hiding place. Bullets were whistling all around us but my father went out again to help.[41]

The Lakota made desperate attempts to reach their captured weapons stacked nearby. After the first unaimed shot, a thunderous volley from the soldiers mowed down nearly every man in the center, including Captain George D. Wallace, who only moments before had turned to Joseph Horn Cloud (Dewey Beard's brother) and warned, "Joseph, you better go over to the women and tell them to let the wagons go and saddle up their horses and be ready to skip, for there is going to be trouble, for that officer is half shot."[42] There are no autopsy records to prove whose bullets killed and wounded the soldiers, but it was immediately assumed that Indians must have fired the shots. Abundant evidence now suggests a military cross-fire—the soldiers killed each other. A private in the Seventh Cavalry wrote a graphic account from Pine Ridge to his brother in Philadelphia:

> Every one was shouting and shooting, and there was no more order than in a bar-room scrimmage. . . . I shot one buck running, and when I examined him, he had neither gun nor cartridge belt. . . . From beginning to end I don't think I saw two dozen bucks, and it is a mystery to all where the bullets came from that killed and wounded one-third of my regiment. My left arm felt sore, and I found that a bullet had cut my sleeve and grazed the flesh. It was bleeding freely, and I have no doubt that I was shot by one of my comrades. . . . Colonel Forsyth looked very white as he gave orders to see if any of the women who lay thick around were alive. . . . But we had got it "in the neck." My captain, Wallace, was dead and eight of my company, and when we mustered in, it looked as if half the regiment was gone. I had my arm dressed, and we returned to Pine Ridge. . . . Of course the camp-liar was in his glory, but who shot the [women] was not known, at least no one boasted of it.[43]

Another letter from Private Eugene Caldwell to his father, who was a member of the Philadelphia police force, adds documented evidence that the first volley came from the troops:

> Dear Father and Mother:
>   . . . We have had some hard times since I wrote to you last, which you all know of by the papers. . . . It was a very poor plan, the way they laid out the fight. They had four troops dismounted and formed a square around the Indians, and they were so close together that they could touch the Indians with their guns. . . . At the first volley we fired, there were about twenty or thirty Indians dropped, and we kept it up until we cleaned out the whole band. . . . After it was all over, it was an awful sight to see. It made me sick to look at it. . . . Some of the men went wild; they would shoot men or women. The commanding officer is going to get a raking over the coals for the way that he managed the fight. If he had done what was right, we would not have lost one-fifth of the men that we did.[44]

One of the four Hotchkiss mountain howitzers, manned by a German immigrant, Corporal Paul H. Weinert, advanced into the mouth of the ravine where screaming groups of women and children were slaughtered within a few feet of each other by exploding two-pound, ten-ounce cartridges with a range of 4,200 yards. When he stopped firing, soldiers ran up to congratulate him. Knowing what he had done, he said:

> I expected a court-martial, but what was my surprise when gruff old Allyn Capron, my captain, came up to me and grasped me by the shoulders and said to the officers and men: "That's the kind of men I have in my battery."[45]

Instead of a court-martial, Weinert received the Congressional Medal of Honor, the highest military award given for heroism in the United States of America. Eighteen Medals of Honor were given to officers and enlisted men for engagements at Wounded Knee.[46] More were given for the mismanaged Drexel Mission fight the next day.

Dewey Beard lost seven family members in the Wounded Knee Massacre, including his mother, Brown Leaf Woman; his father, Horn Cloud; two brothers, William and Sherman; his sister, Pretty Enemy; his wife, Wears Eagle; and his baby son, Wet Feet. Beard was shot four times: in the back, the hip, the calf, and in his "lap." Enraged, he killed a soldier and took the trooper's gun, then limped toward a ravine, where he fell:

> While I was lying on my back, I looked down the ravine and saw a lot of women coming up and crying. When I saw these women, girls and little girls and boys coming up, I saw soldiers on both sides of the ravine shoot at them until they had killed every one of them. [I] saw a young woman among them coming and crying and calling, "Mother! Mother!" She was wounded under her chin, close to her throat, and the bullet had passed through a braid of her hair and carried some of it into the wound, and then the bullet had entered the front side of the shoulder and passed out the back side. Her mother had been shot down behind her. . . . Going a little farther, [I] came upon [my] mother, who was moving slowly, being badly wounded. . . . When [I] got up to her, she said, "My son, pass by me: I am going to fall down now." As she went up, soldiers on both sides of the ravine shot at her and killed her. I returned fire upon them defending my mother.[47]

Further on, Second Lieutenant Sedgwick Rice, Troop E, plowed through the melee. To the end of his days he remembered running up to a woman standing near a group of bodies, which may have included her entire family. The last person left alive, she had apparently decided she could not live alone without them. Lieutenant Rice was shocked to see "[she] . . . had cut her own throat and was in the last throes of death when I went up to her."[48]

Meanwhile, gunfire exploded around the thicket where Alice and her mother waited in vain for her father to return:

> Some people crawled in. . . . The young ones were whimpering. One of the wounded died right there, but there was nothing anybody can do about it.
>
> A man by the name of Wawoslol Wanapin, or "Breast Plate," came in and told us that my father was killed instantly. We all cried but for a short time lest we be heard. Charge In Kill and Nistuste, or "Back Hip," came in later, but they left again. I thought they were brave. It seemed like eternity but it didn't last that long. It was getting late in the afternoon as more people straggled in. It got dark, and the shooting stopped all of a sudden and we heard a wagon moving around, probably to pick up their dead, killed in the crossfire . . .
>
> We all got up, those who could, and walked or limped to the north, tiptoeing our way through creek beds and ravines. . . . We stumbled over dark objects which turn[ed] out to be dead animals or even a dead Lakota. We heard a child crying for water somewhere but we couldn't do anything about it. It was so dark and it was cold. Many more wounded were crying for help.[49]

> Michi'nkshi tahe'na ku'piye.
> Michi'nkshi tahe'na ku'piye.
> Mako'che wan washte aya'gali'pi-kte.
> A'te he've lo'. A'te he've lo'.
> My child, come this way.
> My child, come this way.
> You will take home with you a good country.
> Says the father, says the father.[50]

We walked in the creek bed always north. It must have been Wounded Knee Creek. . . . We met up with some of our relatives and friends who were also trying to escape.

Next morning when we got ready to leave, they found that Dog Chasing, with two women, had come in sometime during the night. The men who rode out must have sent them. . . . So, now there is sixteen of us. We left bright and early, the men walking ahead. A little ways, very good fortune it was, for I was again riding a horse with my little brother, and mother led the horse walking ahead.

Along the way, I must have dozed off and on, half asleep, half awake. I didn't know anything for a while. When I became clearheaded again, we were going down a hill. At the bottom of the valley stood a log house with even a wooden floor, and a fireplace which they fired up and we rested and got warmed up. After we warmed up, we started to shake. Some daylight left, we started off again, covering some miles before dark. It started to cloud up, . . . cloud waves seeming to roll over the hills and valleys like water, from misty fine drops, somewhere closer to a drizzle. Then, the wind came. Some minutes later it turned into a blizzard. . . . One of the men steered us towards a cabin which he spotted from atop a butte some miles back. This blessed haven we reached along a creek, so we stopped there all glad. We sat out the storm . . . [51]

Later that night Alice was awakened by voices, men and women talking urgently about the possibility that they had heard approaching cavalry. She was frightened then for the first time, her heart pounding in her chest, and moved nearer to her mother in the darkness. "Squirming close to Mother's body was as natural as a cottontail jumping from danger into its lair."[52] Soon she heard one of the men whisper in a low voice:

"It is time to go." No one complained, all acted on instinct to survive. It was still cloudy and a little dark yet when we left the cabin. Again my brother and I rode double. Sometimes the snow would blow, but we kept on moving into a deep draw where the wind wasn't that bad. Finally, we stumbled into a camp of Oglalas.[53]

Alice and what was left of her family were safe, but other women and children running to escape the massacre did not fare as well. Days later, the bodies of a woman and her children, who had been hunted and slaughtered like quail, were found three miles from Wounded Knee Creek. A newspaper reporter accompanying the burial party described the first body they found as that of a male about twelve years old. The boy had been shot

beneath the right eye, tearing open the cheek and leaving a bloody hole as large as a silver dollar. There must have been at least a few seconds of agony before death came, for the right arm was thrown up to and across the forehead and the fingers of the left hand stiffened in death while clutching the long, jet-black hair near the powder-burned orifice in his skull.

And the mother. Gentle hands loosened the frosty bands which bound her to the soil and fingers which tingled with the hot flow of blood from indignant hearts tenderly removed from her flattened and distorted face the twigs and leaves and dirt. Her strong arms were bare and her feet were drawn up as the natural consequences of a wound which commenced at the right shoulder and ended in the lower abdominal region. From the wounded shoulder a sanguinary flood had poured until her worn and dirty garments were crimson dyed; the breasts from which her little ones had drawn their earliest sustenance were discolored with the gory stream. It was an awful sight. . . . Who were these murderers? There is where the shame comes in.

They were and still are soldiers in the army of the United States. . . . [N]ot one of the men who fired those shots can say that he was unaware of the character of his victim, for each wound shows that the rifle muzzles were within a few feet of the person at whom they were aimed.[54]

The man in charge of burying the bodies, Captain Frank D. Baldwin, wrote to the Assistant Adjutant General, Headquarters Division of the Missouri, Pine Ridge, South Dakota:

> I am certain that these people were killed on the day of the fight, and no doubt by the troop of the 7th Cavalry, under Command of Capt. Godfrey. Tracks of horses shod with the Goodenough shoes were plainly visible.[55]

Many of the wounded survivors later died or were secretly carried away in the night by Lakota from other bands. In temperatures of forty degrees below zero, they endured suffocating snow and wind so strong that when they opened their mouths, teeth froze to lips, and icy wind rasped their throats and lungs like burning fire. The dead were buried in hidden locations, carefully concealed from federal officials who later underestimated the Indian death toll at 146, over two hundred less than the actual number who were butchered on their own land. Sick and unable to walk or defend himself, Chief Big Foot (Spotted Elk) was first shot while he lay on the ground in front of his tent. Later, he tried to raise himself up but was seen by one of the officers, who shot him again. When the chief's daughter ran to protect him, she was shot in the back.[56]

> Run slowly, for Spotted Elk has been
> killed and laying there.
> Your friends say this and stand there.
> Run slowly, for Spotted Elk has been
> killed and laying there.
> Your friends have come saying this.
>   DORA HIGH WHITEMAN,
>   a survivor (died June 16, 1964)[57]

Not all the survivors were found by the Lakota. Less than a mile from the center of the camp, one young mother had tried to hold her baby out of the wind. The terrified woman pulled the infant over her head and ran one-eighth of a mile away from Wounded Knee Creek before she was chased down by a mounted soldier. Perhaps when she saw that it was too late to run, she begged the man for her child's life, as the other women had done, by holding the infant up to him. *"Michin chila! Michin chila!"* (My baby! My baby!) But the plight of a child brought no mercy. She was shot twice in the breasts at point-blank range and left for dead.[58] Wind had slammed her against solid ground under a cut bank. The Lakota mother and child may never have been separated during life, but in death they were divided. Yet before the woman was released from all in her life that was unjust—from religious persecution, from fear, pain, starvation, and grief—she must have wrapped the baby beneath her own body in a last attempt to save her little one.

Under the frozen corpse, the baby could neither move nor see in the darkness. Three lonely nights and four days later, the blizzard passed, leaving mother and child covered by a light snowdrift. The child cried out miserably, cried out in the frozen stench of her mother's blood and her own defecation. Miraculously, ice did not form over the child's nostrils to smother her. High winds and cold caused loss of body heat, while hunger and thirst dehydrated the small body. But trapped and protected, the Lakota spirit within lived on during the long nights and frigid days that followed the Massacre at Wounded Knee Creek. If the baby girl screamed, there was no one alive to hear her.

CHAPTER 2

The Lost Bird

As quickly as the blizzard had appeared out of the dark-gray northwest sky, it passed at dawn, leaving behind an eerie, empty silence. In pain and grief, the Lakota Nation awoke after the horror of the preceding days. While mutilated women and children, refusing the touch of an army surgeon, lay dying in a nearby Episcopal mission chapel, many others suffered from mortal wounds in Lakota camps not far from Wounded Knee. For them, death came in the grieving arms of relatives and friends, the Ghost Dancers, or so-called hostiles who had risked their lives during nights of lashing winds and blinding snow to drag away as many survivors as possible from the frozen ground.[1] Chiefs, headmen, and medicine men counseled patience to those still anxious to find their slain or missing relatives. Decisions had to be based on what was right for all, not just one band, regardless of the loss. It was nearly an impossible task to control the warrior societies, so long inactive, now that grief had driven them to violence beyond despair. Mounted among them, young Black Elk the visionary, destined for immortality, eagerly "wanted revenge; I wanted to kill."[2] He sang his courage song, a forceful pledge to ignite within himself the power to fight, a tribal man's ancient instinct to protect the women and children in order to survive:

> A thunder being nation I am, I have said.
> A thunder being nation I am, I have said.
> You shall live.
> You shall live.
> You shall live.
> You shall live.[3]

Black Elk knew Chief Big Foot was dead but he didn't know that, three weeks before the Wounded Knee Massacre, Chief Big Foot had sent a peaceful hunting party consisting of fifty people, mostly women, to Buffalo Gap across the Cheyenne River into non-Indian territory. They never returned.

When Big Foot accepted Chief Red Cloud's invitation to go to Pine Ridge "for talks," he and his people had left their village without waiting for the missing hunters to return. An oral traditional story, recalled by a young female member of the hunting party, tells why the hunters had disappeared:

> The government took away our food and the people were weak. The men had to hunt for food so we wouldn't starve. . . . We started out from Big Foot's village, taking our time. We finally got to the place where we liked to hunt. This was the same place Big Foot's men went hunting many times before during the same season of the year. The men drove ten wagons and the women sat in the wagons and joked.
>
> I sat beside my husband while he drove the team. We stopped at the ranch of a white man who had always been our special friend. He was a good man. His wife was always kind to our people. She baked bread and had a smiling face. When we were going to be around the rancher's place, we would go to him and let him know first. This was to show respect and it was always done like this.
>
> The hunting party pulled up in front of the ranch and I jumped down from the wagon. I didn't speak too good in English but I could understand some words because I went to school. My husband said to me, "Wife, go to the door and tell the white man we are here on his land. Ask where his cows are so that we can hunt away from them." So I did that. I went up to the door and knocked. Nobody answered and all was quiet. I knocked on the door again. I waited. I was waiting to see the rancher's wife, my friend. I thought nobody was home so I looked out at my husband in the wagon and he signed [pointed at the door with his mouth] to wait . . .
>
> Suddenly, the door opened! The rancher grabbed me by the hair and twisted me around and put a gun to my head! I couldn't cry out. The white woman screamed and begged, "Don't kill her! Please! In the name of God, don't kill her!" The wife grabbed her husband and tried to push his arm down. When she did that, I twisted free, ran to the wagon, and jumped in. We got out of there fast and everyone was very confused. My husband yelled to the others, "Something is wrong! This white man was our good friend and now something has happened to change him! We must get away fast!"
>
> The horses ran a long ways and got tired. The men didn't want to stop. . . . Everyone was so afraid, but the horses were going to die without water and rest. We made camp on a creek.[4] We were all so afraid and thinking about what had happened, we couldn't sleep much. All of us huddled together and talked. It was decided to break camp at daylight and get out of there because strange things were happening and we didn't know what.

Before daylight, our people packed up the camp and went to get into the wagons. At that first moment of daylight, many ranchers attacked and shot us all down! I felt a bad pain in my thigh and when I looked down at myself, there was my blood coming out. I laid down as if dead.

I didn't move. When the ranchers were gone, the people who were still alive started to moan and cry out. All of my family, my good mother, my father, everyone was dead or crying in terrible pain. All the rest of my life I could hear their moaning and coughing up blood, their pleading for help.

I crawled to where my poor husband was. He was still alive but hurt bad. He said to me, "Wife, are you badly wounded?"

"No, I'm hit in the thigh but I can walk."

He could barely speak but he told me, "Make believe you are dead until dark comes, then go for help."

I stayed there for a long, long time. All day long I was there next to my dead husband. It was agony to lay there, listening. One by one, the moaning stopped, the people died, everything was quiet, and the darkness came. When I tried to get up, more blood came out of my thigh. I tore off the bottom part of my dress and wrapped it around my leg to stop the bleeding. I got up and started to walk. At night, the coyotes howled and I cried and was very afraid they would smell my blood. But I kept looking for my people to get help, to warn them. I walked many days until my feet were raw.

When I came to Chief Big Foot's village at Takini, I saw my cabin and all the other cabins were empty. I knew my people had gone away fast. There on the ground were signs that many horses with metal shoes came and went. The Lakota didn't have iron shoes on their horses. White men had come and taken everything out of the cabins. My dishes were all broken up. The food, clothing, and chickens, all that Big Foot had was raided and taken away. I found little scraps of food. I was very tired and sick at heart.

I kept on Big Foot's trail, walking and walking. My leg stopped bleeding and it was numb . . .

When I was going on the trail I watched cowboys raiding a farmhouse.[5] They rode past me where I was hiding and I was thankful they didn't see me. The cowboys were raiding cabins all along the trails, leading off horses packed with many things.

The days passed and I forgot how many. I kept on walking and walking. A blizzard came up with high winds and I came to an old shack and crawled in. It was very cold. When the snow passed, I kept going until I got to the hill above Wounded Knee Creek. I was so tired, there was no use to walk anymore.

I looked down by the creek and I could see a big bonfire with soldiers and some government Indian scouts walking around. Everything looked burnt up and there were dead people on the ground. I cried because I found Chief Big Foot too late to warn him the whites wanted to kill us all . . .

A soldier saw me, but I couldn't run away. He talked to me but the words were strange. Then he came back with a boy and I told the boy I was wounded in my thigh and couldn't walk. The soldier thought I was shot in the massacre. He picked me up and carried me to a wagon, where I passed out.

When I woke up, the soldier was carrying me into a long building. I stayed there with my relatives who survived the massacre. Most of them died in terrible pain.[6]

The heroic woman had walked approximately 250 miles in twenty-two days to warn her chief that his hunting band had been ambushed by cowboy vigilantes without provocation.

The only barrier that had separated the Ghost Dancers from ranchers and setttlers in the Black Hills was the long winding Cheyenne River bordering the Pine Ridge Reservation. Directly on the other side of the river from Indian land lay the huge, valuable grasslands of ranch kings, men who played a deliberate and devious role in the violent events that culminated in the Wounded Knee Massacre of December 29, 1890.

A sea of waving grass as high as a tall man's waist was worth dying for, but ranchers did not have to pay such a high price. Aside from the traders, ranchers were the first white men to move into the area after the gold miners came in 1874. They squatted on thousands of acres that fed huge horse herds and provided pure profit. There was the breathtaking beauty of unspoiled land as far as the eye could see, backed by the magnificence of the Sacred Black Hills, kept clean and natural for centuries by generations of Lakota people.

Ranchers ran horses on lands they had always considered free for the taking. Some were tough, mean men who worked their wives to death in the kitchens and fields for an inch of sod, pilfered stock and hay from their neighbors, and trampled or burned the crops of unwary settlers. An Indian treaty meant next to nothing to the rancher. The one exception was the 1889 Agreement between the government and the Lakota that opened millions of acres for settlement in and around ranch barons. Stockmen had no intention of giving up this land to new settlers.[7]

The young men they hired were cowboys and drifters. A few honest cowhands might realize their dreams with prayer and backbreaking work. Others made it by killing everything and everyone who stood in their way. Some had big dreams but few brains, and more than a little liking for liquor. One thing most cowboys had in common: They were young and would do anything just for the hell of it. When the punchers were laid off from ranches in October, they went looking for pocket money and a little fun.

In the fall of 1890 ranchers had provided their boys with brand-new guns, adding a lethal element to the combination.

Colonel Merritt H. Day, a rancher and old friend of South Dakota's first governor, Arthur C. Mellette, petitioned the executive for hundreds of rifles and ammunition to protect the settlements from the supposed Indian uprising threatening at Pine Ridge.[8]

It is difficult to justify Mellette's sudden belief that an Indian uprising was imminent in November 1890, when less than two months earlier, he and L. H. Baily of the Pierre Land Office and two other sportsmen had been hunting on choice Indian land and got lost. They wandered around for three days until a cowboy found them staggering, sick, and half starved.[9] Had the Ghost Dancers been warlike and threatening, it is unlikely that the land-speculating governor and his sporting friends would have made it out of Indian country alive.

Nevertheless, one month later, with Mellette's full cooperation, Colonel Day organized a two-part militia consisting of fifty-one men under the command of Captain George Cosgrove and another company of forty-nine men under Captains Gene Aiken and J. B. McCloud.[10] As soon as the Home Guard was a sanctioned organization, Governor Mellette encouraged and praised Colonel Day for stirring up the Lakota. Mellette's dispatches to Day show a cover-up devised so that military officials and citizens would not find out about the deliberate attempts of the Home Guard to provoke an uprising:

> I was pleased to get your message stating that in a skirmish three Indians had been killed by "our men" without loss to the whites. Be discreet in killing the Indians.[11]

Ranchers, hoping for action that would scare settlers away, attacked the Lakota throughout December while the Ghost Dance leaders held their young men back from retaliation.

An Indian called Dead Arm (whose name indicated he had a paralyzed arm), a nephew of Ghost Dance leader Kicking Bear, went to the M. D. Cole Ranch on the Cheyenne River, where Cole kept a small trading store. The rancher had always appeared friendly and Indians were his frequent customers, but the moment Dead Arm appeared at Cole's ranch, he was shot dead.[12] His decomposing body lay in the dirt for more than three days while cowboys poked sticks at it and a photographer took numerous photographs of the bloated corpse. As relatives watched from a nearby hill, Dead Arm was scalped by a white man. A newspaper report said the scalp was "secured" by John R. Brennan, a respected, churchgoing, and prosperous Rapid City businessman, who ironically later became agent at Pine

Ridge.[13] The *Hermosa Pilot* published an account of the killing entitled "A Really Good Indian," which characterized the sentiment of the majority of non-Indian South Dakotans in 1890:

> A report that seems entirely reliable says that on Sunday night [December 14] a couple of Indians were about to enter the stable of a rancher named Cole at the mouth of Spring Creek, when that gentleman opened fire and brought one of the Reds to the ground. . . . The dead Indian . . . may be viewed by those who are curious to see how a really good Indian looks.[14]

Dead Arm had been a Christian baptized by Episcopal Bishop W. H. Hare.[15] From a hill nearby, the dead man's relatives sang for him while the cowboys hooted loudly and tried to mimic the sounds of the anguished death songs. J. B. McCloud wrote to Doane Robinson, director of the South Dakota State Historical Society, describing the Home Guard's actions against "thousands of insanely desperate ghost dancers."[16] He then admitted that the Guard had scalped an Indian.[17]

> Have you ever heard an Indian death song?—Well—no white man can produce anything like it, at least we could not. Rage—despair—sorrow—all combined seemed to be included in the awful wail . . . .[18]

Pete Lemley, later known as "the Badlands Fox," was one of the young cowboys who witnessed the killing at the Cole ranch.[19] Pete became a millionaire rancher and lived to be ninety-one years old. In 1959, at the request of his son (Dr. Ray Lemley), Pete tape-recorded details of his participation in the attacks against Ghost Dancers during the month of December 1890.[20] His account of the Home Guard Ambush on December 16, 1890, is a cowboy's unashamed narrative of the day he considered one of the most exciting in his life:

> There was a bunch of men there. We went over [Cheyenne River] and stirred them [Lakota] up and a lot of our fellows laid in at the head of a gulch. We went over to the Stronghold and got 'em after us and they chased us down Corral Draw. Riley Miller was at the head of it and layin' up there behind the trees and rocks. This Riley Miller was a dead shot, and he just killed them Indians as fast as he could shoot. Francis Roush, Roy Coates, George Cosgrove, Paul McClellan was with us. We killed about seventy-five of them. Riley Miller and Frank Lockhart went back there and got some pack horses and brought out seven loads of guns, shirts, war bonnets, ghost shirts, and things. Riley took 'em to Chicago and started a museum. He made a barrel of money out of it.[21]

Pete was a twenty-year-old daredevil, a renowned horseman who wasn't afraid of anything or anyone. He was just the kind of fearless rider Colonel Day wanted to lead the Home Guard Ambush. Day and other ranchers, including Magnus Thompson, Charlie Allen, and Frank Hart, sent Lemley and others galloping in upon a band of Ghost Dancers with orders to shoot directly into them.[22] The Lakota ran to their tents for weapons. They mounted and chased the cowboys, falling directly into a well-planned ambush at the head of the Corral Draw, three miles south of Heutmacher Table.[23] Then Pete and the younger boys were sent home.[24]

It is possible that some of the cowboys believed they were helping to protect white settlers, but most members of the Home Guard were out for the sport of killing Indians and nothing more. In Rapid City, Colonel Day became a local hero and young boys and reporters followed him around. Only one individual came forward to protest. Dan Cushman, an instructor at what is now the School of Mines, told a newsman at the *Rapid City Journal* that he suspected Merritt Day had other more sinister motives for provoking an Indian war:

> He is not giving his services for his health or glory alone, but in order to ingratiate himself with the farmers who will have claims against the government in the future for raids committed by the Indians. These, Day will propose to engineer through at Washington and collect for his farmer friends, of course for a consideration.[25]

Sure enough, less than one month later on February 19, 1891, thousands of dollars in fraudulent Indian depredation claims were filed by farmers and ranchers and nearly all of them were paid.[26] Colonel Day's subsequent career included an 1896 indictment on embezzlement charges in Cincinnati, where he was extradited from Boston in chains.[27]

Riley Miller, Colonel Day's marksman during the Home Guard Ambush, had survived the notorious death camp at Andersonville Prison during the Civil War, and there was practically nothing left of him when he was released. From that time on, Miller killed for pleasure and anything moving was fair game.[28]

After the Home Guard killed the Ghost Dancers, Miller and Frank Lockhart scalped, stripped, and left the corpses (men, women, and children) where only wolves could find them. Miller shipped his fresh Indian artifact collection to Chicago during the 1893 World's Columbian Exposition and went into partnership with "Omaha Charlie" (D. Charles Bristol). They opened a 500-piece Indian relic sideshow on the midway.[29] The principal attraction in their exhibition: a dried Indian baby. The grisly relic attracted hordes of people, who filed past the unfortunate child, nestled in a glass box. Thousands of curious people pressed their hands and noses to the scratched glass, and parents lifted children to catch a glimpse of what the billboard called the "Mummified Indian Papoose, the Greatest Curiosity Ever on Exhibition."[30]

After Miller's partnership with Omaha Charlie soured, he sold Bristol all of his Home Guard artifacts and then left for the Klondike gold rush, abandoning his wife and eight children on a South Dakota homestead. Bristol's Indian artifacts went on display at the Nebraska State Historical Society in 1906, but the final purchase occurred in 1935, and as of 1992, several objects were still on display at the Museum of Nebraska History.[31]

Although the Home Guard committed most of the atrocities against the Lakota in 1890, the United States military also bears responsibility for an outrage prior to the massacre at Wounded Knee. Troops A and B of the Eighth U.S. Cavalry under Captain Almond B. Wells had been stationed at Oelrichs, South Dakota, since April 1890. Under orders from General Miles, they moved closer to the Badlands in December to keep a more vigilant watch on Ghost Dancers.[32] The general's plan was to place a cordon of troops around the reservation with posts from ten to twenty miles apart.

Lieutenant Joseph C. Byron, an 1886 West Point graduate and classmate of General John J. Pershing, nursed a ruthless ambition for promotion, usually a slow process during peacetime, but much less difficult during war. Artist and writer Frederic Remington accompanied Lieutenant Byron and the Eighth Cavalry on several reconnaissance missions into the Badlands, sketching them for future publication in *Harper's Weekly*. Remington wrote that the Badlands were "full of savage Sioux."[33]

During the week of December 12, 1890, Captain Almond Wells gave Lieutenant Byron permission to reconnoiter into remote sections of the forbidding countryside, close to the Lakota Stronghold, a high plateau where the Ghost Dancers were conducting ceremonies. Remington followed along, describing for his readers the stark Badlands surrounding him as a "place for stratagem and murder, with nothing to witness its mysteries but the cold blue winter sky."[34]

There were other civilians with the troops including rancher Ed Lemmon, who rode along with the Eighth Cavalry to see if the Lakota were really on the verge of an uprising. From the beginning, Lemmon ". . . didn't believe the Lakota were hostile at all."[35] Lemmon provided an eyewitness view of Lieutenant Byron and military discipline during the "Indian Campaign" of December 1890:

> Wherever possible these [military] camps were off the reservation, and the troops had strict orders to stay off, too, but the orders were often disobeyed

by both the troopers and the [home] guards. One day . . . Byron asked
Major Wells for permission to reconnoiter with a dozen men. With Gus
Haaser as guide, they went out toward the west end of Cuny Table. Byron
wanted to see if he could get cannon within range of the Indian village, out
there on the flat. On the way back they came onto a small band of Indians.
Byron and his men intentionally cut the band off from their own village and
killed them all. If this had been known at headquarters, it would have been
a court-martial case, so it was kept a secret.[36]

Lieutenant Byron's troops searched the corpses, removed all the guns they
could find, and buried them in a separate pit from the bodies. The West
Point graduate then lined up his men and swore them to secrecy.[37] Byron's
troop returned to camp very late that night—much to Remington's relief,
as he rushed out of his tent to meet them as they came in. In the darkness,
Remington heard Lieutenant Byron's low voice: "We have been on the
Stronghold; they are all gone. Rustle some coffee."[38]

General Nelson Miles was ultimately responsible for crumbling discipline among his troops, and he maintained little or no supervision over the
Home Guard.[39] His officers apparently ignored orders with impunity. The
general had political aspirations and was a clever manipulator of the western press, knowing a successful expedition against Indians was certain to
elevate him in the eyes of his fellow citizens. The attention he paid to his
image in the press took time—perhaps time he should have been using to
oversee his officers before they committed unconscionable atrocities
against the Lakota.

When Miles first heard about the confrontation at Wounded Knee, he
set out immediately by train to survey the death and destruction. After
raising the fears of a nation in the press, after amassing the largest troop
buildup since the Civil War, and after badly orchestrating military maneuvers by telegraphic dispatches from Chicago and Rapid City, Miles had lost
control of his "Dakota Campaign"—with embarrassing and disastrous
results. He felt his orders had been ignored or willfully disobeyed and he
turned his wrath on the Commander of the Seventh Cavalry at Wounded
Knee Creek, Colonel James W. Forsyth.

On January 4, 1891, by direction of President Benjamin Harrison, General Miles relieved Forsyth from his command until a full investigation of
Forsyth's placement of troops, the orders he gave and received, and the
reported atrocities against defenseless women and children were evaluated
by a hastily organized military court of inquiry.[40]

Stunned, the Seventh Cavalry rallied behind Colonel Forsyth. One
night in a bar, interpreter Philip Wells's loud accusations against General

Miles were heard by all.[41] The interpreter was especially angered by a newspaper report calling him the "mascot" of the Seventh Cavalry, who would lie to protect them.[42] Wells was ready to beat up the reporter, when he was stopped by Seventh Cavalry veteran Captain W. S. Edgerly, who came up with a better idea:

> Sit down awhile. There are lots of things you don't know. . . . That reporter can hit you harder with his pen than you can hit him with your fist. Fight him by all means, but do it with his own weapons, and you can knock him out in the first round. Get Mr. Cook, the clergyman, who is well thought of and a master of the Indian language, to go with you to secure a statement from the wounded Indians, and it will knock him out . . . [43]

Wells took Edgerly's advice as he later recalled:

> We went to the hospital and got a statement from the wounded Indians. . . . Miles at that time had been ordered to hold a court of inquiry respecting the battle and the conduct of the Seventh Cavalry. . . . Meantime the statements procured by Cook and myself were forwarded to the War Department, following which it reprimanded Miles and reinstated Forsyth.[44]

Since Wells considered himself a white man (his white father had been killed by Indians), he found nothing wrong with vindicating Forsyth at the expense of the Lakota Nation. Wells's suspiciously articulate reports (he had only six days of schooling in his life) became the pivotal point in the investigation that ultimately reinstated Forsyth and cleared the colonel of charges stemming from the massacre.[45]

On January 1, 1890, angry Ghost Dancers watched from hills and ravines as burial details arrived at Wounded Knee. Lieutenant George W. Kirkman had tried everything to keep from going. He was ordered to return to the scene where four days earlier the bodies of slain and wounded Lakota had been left on the ground. Kirkman took part in the massacre he would always call "a battle," believing that all Indians were "as murderous, treacherous a lot of villains as ever went unhung." Before leaving Pine Ridge, he picked up Paddy Starr, a half-breed scout, William Peano, and F. McWilliams, men whom the arrogant Kirkman referred to as "dirty half-breeds and squawmen." The lieutenant had no intention of touching dead bodies, and for that reason he said he "had them along to do the burying."46

As the wagons clattered along, the burial troop kept a sharp lookout for Ghost Dancers, afraid at any moment they might be attacked: "We kept going at a lively gait, with "flankers" ahead of us on the hills to guard against ambush." Finally they came over a hill and there lay the field at

Wounded Knee in a flat over 200 acres wide, "amid the low desolate hills, strewn with the terrible wreck of the fight . . . shattered tepees, the still black patches that here and there darkened the peaceful snow . . . over all hung the gray sky and the heavy clouds."[47]

More than 100 Lakota wagons had been destroyed, now mingled with blackened mounds of rags—small red squares of cloth used to make sacred tobacco bundles. Freezing winds lifted and scattered the crimson material over dead horses, humans, and dogs, frozen in the last agonies of death, eyes turned to ice, gaping mouths pushed open by bloated, frost-fringed tongues.

Lieutenant Kirkman sent Eighth Cavalry private August Hettinger with a wagon to gather more corpses. At first sight of the twisted, mangled faces of the dead, Hettinger leaned over and vomited into the snow.[48] When the harnessed cavalry mules smelled human blood, they shied, reared up, and fell sideways, snapping their frozen jerk lines like dried twigs. Hettinger tried to grab the spooked animals, but they bit and kicked him, throwing the stubby German immigrant backward into the snow. Cursing, he got to his feet, but the sharp-shod mules flattened their ears and bared menacing teeth. The Kentucky mules had been tied all night to a wagon wheel in the blizzard without hay. The stench from the dead made them bolt for Wounded Knee Creek, only to stumble over more bodies, frozen into ghastly forms in the snow. Still kicking and biting each other, the terrified mules finally entangled themselves in plum bushes along the creek.

Kirkman's burial party worked a day and a half in the bitter cold. Miraculously, four days after the massacre and blizzard, they still found people alive and suffering at Wounded Knee. Now and then, a living man or woman was found and Hettinger helped load them on wagons, on top or alongside dead friends and relatives. One woman was shot five times through the body. Hettinger remembered that "to the last they were defiant and our reward for making them comfortable were looks of the blackest hate. You could not help but admire such courage in the face of the dead."[49]

The frozen bodies of Big Foot's band were taken to the top of the hill overlooking the valley where they had died. Grave diggers carved a gaping hole from the earth, six feet deep, ten wide, sixty long.[50] Others stood around, leaning on their long rifles, ignoring the scene of horror, yet alert in case of ambush. Steaming horses chomped their icy bits, snorting uneasily. The scratch of spades against rocks and the screams and moans of mourners below in the valley broke the silence. The huge grave was finally finished, and the diggers climbed out to look down at their work.

When the order was given to bury the first load, Starr, Peano, and McWilliams jumped into the grave and each corpse was thrown down to them one at a time. They stripped all salable articles from the bodies as if they were skinning rabbits. The clothing was sold piece by piece to the many spectators. Bloody garments brought more money, and interpreter Philip F. Wells was among the highest bidders for Ghost Shirts that he later sold to the Bureau of American Ethnology.[51] Unlike Wells, Starr was ashamed of his role in the grave robbing: "I feel," he said, "that I owe an apology to my tribe. These soldiers seemed to discard all civil and moral respect, and [were] inspired with a malicious mania to kill dispatched human lives by the scores. . . . I speak with regretting terms in expressing my atonement."[52]

Photographer George E. Trager of Chadron, Nebraska, hauled his bulky equipment up to the grave just in time to capture the line of soldiers at the edge as they began to unload the first bodies. Trager shuffled back and forth, setting up his tripods and camera. Troopers clustered around to help him find the most interesting dead Indians. Someone recognized Chief Big Foot, and Trager hurried over to get a good shot before the burial detail got to him. The chief was in a half-sitting position, a look of bewilderment on his face. Next, Yellow Bird, the medicine man, who had prayed to the eagles before the massacre, was found lying in the snow on his stomach. Not satisfied with the camera angle, Trager, with help, turned the corpse over on his back, exposing the man's frozen genitals. Someone propped a gun up alongside the body, which gave the finished photo just the right fearsome touch.[53] Yellow Bird's private parts were later etched over on the photograph, so as not to offend the ladies. The Yellow Bird and Big Foot pictures, along with the clothing and belongings of the dead, became valuable to collectors, and the endless exploitation of Ghost Dance artifacts has continued to the present day. (In 1992 Ghost Shirts were selling for more than $40,000 each.)[54]

Without prayer services of any kind, the Lakota dead were "layered in the mass grave, first one naked row across the bottom of the trench, and old army blankets were placed over them, then another layer of bodies lengthwise. And so they continued until the dead were nearly level with the ground," and the dirt was shoveled on. James Pipe on Head, Big Foot's grandson, recalled:

> One of them was shot in the eye but he was still alive and helpless but [they] buried him with the rest of the dead. . . . We feel that this act is not human.[55]

As the burial continued, Dr. Charles Eastman, a Dakota physician, led another detail out from Pine Ridge. Dr. Eastman's motives were entirely humanitarian. He was looking for survivors.

At the rear of his solemn cavalcade rode eighty Lakota, including American Horse, all looking anxiously into every gully and bush. The day before, wagons had been fired upon by the angered Ghost Dancers and there was no reason to believe this day would bring less danger. Eastman described the journey:

> We feared that some of the Indian wounded might have been left on the field, and a number of us volunteered to go and see. I was placed in charge of the expedition. . . . Fully three miles from the scene of the massacre we found the body of a woman completely covered with a blanket of snow, and from this point on we found them scattered along as they had been relentlessly hunted down and slaughtered while fleeing for their lives. . . . It took all my composure in the face of this spectacle and of the excitement and grief of my Indian companions, nearly every one of whom was crying aloud or singing his death song. The white men became very nervous, but I set them to examining and uncovering every body to see if one were living. . . . All this was a severe ordeal for one who had so lately put all his faith in the Christian love and lofty ideals of the white men.[56]

Eastman looked for places he would have hidden himself had he tried to survive the massacre. By noon, his men found ten more living people, most of whom endured an agonizing death within twenty-four hours. One man asked only to have his pipe filled before he died.

Exhausted and shaken by the ordeal, the doctor worried over the ten wounded survivors waiting to be taken to Pine Ridge, afraid that he had missed some who had crawled away to the gullies and plum thickets and were now too far gone to move.

While resting for a moment on his horse near Dr. Eastman, George E. Bartlett "heard a noise which I took to be the cry of an infant. I turned but could not place the sound. My men also thought they had heard the cry and we listened again. In a few seconds another moan reached our ears . . ."[57]

The men could tell in which direction a person might go for shelter against the wind from the position of frozen prairie sand reeds, brittle yet always surviving the strongest forces of nature, with roots that grip the soil like curved eagle claws. Men fanned out, walking and riding toward the sound.

And that is how they found the dead and mutilated Lakota mother, burrowed and frozen into a cut bank, where the dying woman had scraped a shallow hole. Hiding the baby under her body, she drifted into a slumber from which she never awoke. Four other women had joined her, in a huddled group, sharing death as they had shared life.

Dr. Eastman and his men chipped around the woman's frozen body and lifted her stiff corpse like a heavy slab of ice. Entrapped in a cold embrace, they found the source of the muffled cries—a baby girl. Bartlett knelt down to pry the mother's frozen arms loose from the gasping infant: "To my surprise, I found her all right." The child's frostbitten head was barely visible under a hide cap distinctively decorated in beads with red, white, and blue American flags. When Bartlett lifted the child away from her mother's body, the infant managed a weak scream. Bartlett took charge of the child, wrapping her for the trip back to Pine Ridge.

Among the nearly 100 men in Eastman's party were interpreter John Shangreau and Little Bat Garnier. Years later, Shangreau, Garnier, and Bartlett, as well as other men riding with the burial detail, each claimed to have found a child—and their stories were all true. Confusion developed over the children because at least five babies under a year old, as well as several older orphans, were brought in alive to Pine Ridge by men from various burial parties. Other infants lived through the ordeal, rescued during the blizzard by men from the Ghost Dance bands. Black Elk and Red Crow rode out from Pine Ridge after they first heard the muffled gunfire in the direction of Wounded Knee. Looking for survivors, each man found an infant alive and brought the children into the Ghost Dance camp where "women who had milk fed the little babies."[58]

Of the infants who survived the massacre, one went to Pine Ridge with Bartlett, several others were given away to reservation families, and still another was taken to the Holy Rosary Mission where priests and nuns were waiting to help survivors. The mission was located about five miles north of Pine Ridge and throughout the troubles of 1890–91, it remained a haven for Indians and non-Indians alike. Because of Father John Jutz's reputation for unfailing kindness, and despite his ignorance and insensitivity, Ghost Dance leaders assured Jutz that his mission would not be burned, and the Lakota kept their word.

At Holy Rosary, Mary White, wife of scout Frank White, reached up to take the baby girl who was sheltered inside a man's coat. The child rasped with burning lungs, but her little arms moved with quick jerks like a boxer's—a good sign. She kicked out, toes and fingers curled, then opened, and jabbed the air. Mrs. White moved quickly to save the child and took her into the warm mission kitchen. A wet nurse was called while several nuns inspected the child for injuries. "Look at her!" cried one. "The poor child is painted!"[59] The infant's face was daubed red and black on her forehead and on her cheeks. The women were horrified, not realizing the paint was mixed with grease, an age-old protection against frostbite. They gasped when they saw the child's blood-soaked clothing, a crusted woolen dress with bloody leather leggings. Mrs. White peeled the leggings off carefully, expecting to find a wound, but the child was uninjured. The blood that soaked her clothing and matted her hair may have been that of a relative who clutched the child in the last terrified moments of life.

The baby was eager to suckle from the breast of the Lakota wet nurse. But first the woman gently forced her warm breast milk into the infant's nose to soften the clogged mucus there. The baby coughed and sneezed, expelling the mucus, so that she could now drink comfortably. The nurse used drops of milk to flush the baby's eyes as well.

This little survivor of Wounded Knee gulped her first sustenance in four days, gripping the breast of the wet nurse with fingers like tiny icicles. Then Mrs. White bathed the infant.[60]

The women took turns watching the sleeping child. Everyone was hushed and tiptoed quietly, as is often the custom of non-Indian mothers in the nurseries of their children. "Mrs. White, what will we do with the child?" one woman whispered. "Will you keep her?"[61]

"I cannot," Mrs. White answered quietly, "but we shall ask until we find an Indian woman who wants a child. It will be better for the baby if she has an Indian mother." The women looked at each other in amazement.

The Lakota wife of Manuel Thomas, a man from White Clay, was asked if she wanted the baby. She came at once and took the child within the folds of a blanket, rubbed her cheek against the sleeping face, and disappeared out the door as silently as she had come in. The babe was suckled, carried, slept with, and cared for by an Indian surrogate mother who knew instinctively that her own body warmth and smell would reestablish a special bond, a secure and genetically familiar replacement. The Thomases named their adopted baby girl Neglicu, or Comes Out Alive, and the child was baptized in the Catholic faith as Mary Thomas. Neglicu was to live her entire life on the Pine Ridge Reservation, unlike the baby girl found with the cap decorated with stars and stripes, whom George Bartlett had taken to Pine Ridge.[62]

Because of her beaded patriotic headgear, this child at once became a curiosity. She had lived through the massacre and then a three-day blizzard in temperatures forty degrees below zero. Her life was more than a miracle—it was a manifestation of an heroic little spirit, preordained with an unusual destiny from the moment she was taken from her mother's icy grasp.

The first two weeks after she was found shaken by her ordeal, men who would be heroes took charge of her life and decided her fate. She received four different names; at least one man wanted her enough to christen her, then she was stolen and retrieved, yanked from comforting arms and stolen again, until finally one man was willing to risk hundreds of lives to carry her home as his prize.

When George Bartlett reached Pine Ridge with the baby, he found the agency under siege. Frightened settlers and a large band of mixed-bloods living there expected at any moment to see hundreds of revengeful warriors attacking them from all directions. Rumors of burned houses and murdered settlers filled the believing ears of most inhabitants. The inexperienced and erratic Indian agent Daniel F. Royer was as frightened as the rest.

Alarmed citizens rushed through the streets of Pine Ridge to find material to barricade their homes, while more than twenty newspaper reporters converged on the settlement to write lurid exaggerations of danger, which they telegraphed to newspapers around the country. Special Agent E. B. Reynolds, called the reports "the most stupendous rot ever printed."[63] In the midst of this confusion, Bartlett gave the infant survivor of Wounded Knee to a Lakota named "Long Woman, the wife of Feather on Head."[64] Bartlett's sincere concern and subsequent requests for information about the child's welfare continued until 1904.[65]

But Long Woman did not keep the baby that Bartlett had entrusted to her. During the mayhem, the child was probably taken by several people seeking a wet nurse. A Lakota named Chester White Butterfly came across an old woman holding an infant and he asked if he could take her to his brother's home.[66]

White Butterfly then brought the baby to his half-brother, John Yellow Bird, a trader and John's gentle wife, Annie.[67] (John Yellow Bird was not related to the medicine man Yellow Bird, who died at Wounded Knee.)

Annie named the infant Okicize Wanji Cinca, or "the Child of the Battlefield," and in her capable hands the baby recuperated from her painful ordeal.[68] John Yellow Bird's trading post filled with people buying supplies for what they imagined might be a food shortage as a result of Indian troubles. Among the customers was Buffalo Bill Cody, accompanied by his press agent, Major John Burke. The major saw the little waif from Wounded Knee and hit upon the idea of securing the child for a wealthy socialite in Washington, D.C., Mrs. Allison Nailor, whose husband was Buffalo Bill's old hunting partner.[69] Details of the transaction are unknown, but Burke stood godfather as the little girl was baptized Maggie C. Nailor in a Christian ceremony.[70] It is doubtful that Annie Yellow Bird ever knew the particulars of the arrangement, for she had grown so attached to the baby that when her own children gathered around, she told them, "This is your new baby sister."[71] Within three days Annie would defy her husband and the United States Army to protect the innocent child from abduction.

CHAPTER 3

A Trophy of War

Brigadier General Leonard Wright Colby, the handsome commander of the Nebraska National Guard, arrived in Rushville, Nebraska, on January 5, 1891.[1] He headquartered in the land office there, twenty-six miles south of Pine Ridge, but spent a good deal of time setting up outposts along the South Dakota border, primarily an encampment on Beaver Creek, next to Lieutenant Edward W. Casey's Cheyenne and Oglala scouts.[2] (Ironically, Philip Wells was assigned to Lieutenant Casey's troops to recuperate from a severe facial wound he received during the massacre.[3])

General Colby was bringing regiments here, en route to Pine Ridge, on his own initiative. A political mess dubbed "the Nebraska Muddle" had prevented him from calling up troops earlier.[4] After a heated election, Democrat James E. Boyd had just won the governor's chair by a narrow margin. Governor John M. Thayer, the Republican incumbent, had not run for reelection, but when he found that the newly elected governor was not a citizen of the United States, he refused to vacate his office, saying Boyd was legally unqualified for the office because he was an Irishman. In the state with a motto of "Equality before the law," Governor Thayer barricaded his office and refused to leave for seventy-two hours, while newspaper headlines in Lincoln declared the situation "Red Hot!"[5] Governor Thayer finally collapsed from nervous prostration, but not before the Supreme Court had disgraced itself in a bloody free-for-all. A general riot broke out among the junior senators with fists and chairs flying, while the elderly legislators looked on. Suddenly, one of the oldest members, a staunch Thayer supporter, stood up and bashed an elderly Democratic senator on the head with an ornamented cane of the latest fashion, setting off an uproar and forcing Thayer to call in the state militia. The embarrassing scrap made national headlines, with eastern newspapers poking fun at brawling midwestern politicians.[6]

General Colby did not find the situation at all humorous. The state lacked leadership authorized to call up National Guard troops to the scene of a possible Indian uprising on the northern border of Nebraska. Colby visited Governor Thayer, himself an old Indian fighter, to show him daily dispatches from frightened settlers demanding protection. Thayer allowed Colby to put his men on alert on December 21, 1890.[7] But after the massacre at Wounded Knee on December 29, days passed without word from the governor. Colby could wait no longer. In character with his hero Andrew Jackson, who reacted with the same audacious force during the bloody Redstick wars, General Colby summoned the National Guard to the front claiming:

> The danger to the lives and property of the citizens of our state was imminent. There being no funds provided for the state available for the support and maintenance of the National Guard in the field, I tendered the services of my command to the state in its emergency, free, without consulting officers or men; believing that I expressed the patriotic sentiments which have always pervaded my command, and relying upon the Legislature when it convened to do justice to those who were willing to risk their lives in defense of the property and homes of the citizens of Nebraska . . .[8]

On Colby's order, two regiments of infantry, ten companies each, one troop of cavalry, and a battery of light artillery left crowded Nebraska train depots amid brass bands, parades, cheers, and waving lace handkerchiefs.[9] In Beatrice, where Colby lived, almost the whole town turned out to see the Company C, First Regiment boys leave from the Burlington depot, described by one bystander as "a perfect jam of humanity."[10] Civil War veterans squeezed into old uniforms and "were warmly affectionate in their words of good cheer."[11] Guardsmen left jobs, studies, and family farms, as townswomen stuffed their duffel bags with pies, cookies, and bread for the journey north.

Delighted Nebraska border merchants, on the verge of ruin for months, now capitalized on rumors of Ghost Dance uprisings. Nothing bolstered business like the threat of an Indian war. One Rushville miller bragged that he had "contracted 68,000 pounds of flour for the troops."[12] The "Ghost Dance Craze" pulled Nebraska out from under one of the leanest economic decades of the nineteenth century.[13]

On January 5, a lithe but muscular General Colby stepped down from the train at Rushville wearing fringed gilt epaulettes and black Spanish leather knee boots with jingling spurs. An engraved gold-and-ivory sword, its hilt in the shape of an open-mouthed lion, hung by long tassels from his waist.[14] This was not regulation wear.

The general's forefathers had fought valiantly in the Revolutionary War with the same ease and disregard for authority. A relative, James W. Colby, explained the proud family heritage: "Warfare seems to have been its hereditary disposition and frequently its constant vocation."[15] Colby men broke rules and loved war, a dangerous combination.

In the Civil War, Colby had become a hero during the siege of Mobile, and "in front of the charge of the skirmish line at Fort Blakely . . . he mounted cannon under fire and stormed the fort. While on a dead run fifty yards in front of a rebel cannon, it fired, throwing him down hard with grape and canister. He took a blow on his head which fractured his skull and nearly ended his life . . . and [was] left bleeding and powder-burnt for dead."[16] But it took more than that to kill a Colby. He jumped up, and was among the first to scale the walls, capturing a Confederate flag and two prisoners. He stood guard over them holding his musket with one arm. With the other hand, he reached around and jerked out a rebel bayonet thrust in his side.[17]

After the war ended in 1865, Colby mustered out, but war suited him, so he looked around for another one. Luckily, excitement was not far off. He joined Emperor Maximilian's forces in Mexico, fully aware that most Union forces and the United States government sided with the Mexican leader Benito Juárez against the puppet Maximilian, a pawn of Emperor Napoleon III of France.[18]

Mexican propaganda lured young mercenaries like Colby with promises of free land if American fighting men would join them. Demonstrating shrewd military skills, the nineteen-year-old was made a captain among Maximilian's 40,000 elegant French forces.[19] In later years he often relived his fierce war exploits, calling them "the high points of [my] life."[20]

Other mercenaries did not recollect the Mexican experience so glowingly. Thomas Reynolds, a former governor of Missouri, "found he could not forget the rawhide whippings, the [Indian and Mexican] prisoners made to kneel between their coffins and their graves before they were slain, and particularly the sight of a sixteen-year-old boy shot by a dozen executioners who hit him in fifty places as his blood went dribbling through the Mexican dust . . ."[21]

Colby recalled none of the carnage remembered by Governor Reynolds. With ownership of his Mexican orchards secured, he left the war-torn country, resigning his commission, or so he said.[22] If he had simply turned his horse northward, no one would have known the difference in the midst of the emperor's chaotic reign of terror against the Mexican people. But with fighting heritage in his blood, it is unlikely Colby turned tail during any military battle.

At Rowel Colby's comfortable home in Freeport, Illinois, Leonard Colby had grown up hearing his father's thrilling war stories, tales not only of his grandfather's exploits, but deeds of valor going back to the Crusades, when the Colbys earned a coat of arms featuring a brutal right arm covered with armor raised victoriously above the emblem. A steel point protruded from the elbow while a tightly clinched fist held aloft a broken sword dripping with blood.[23] For as long as he could remember, the colorful coat of arms had hung above the fireplace and Leonard Colby grew up hearing the menfolk say, "It has always been accounted a great honor to descend from a crusader."[24]

The elder Colby was a strict father, and wrongdoing brought swift punishment. Nor was weakness tolerated. When Leonard was seven years old, his father, who placed great value on education because he himself had never had "the advantages of a higher course of knowledge," sent his fifth son off to school during a blizzard.[25] The child struggled through drifts until he fell into the snow and was found semiconscious by a neighbor. Regaining himself, Leonard walked on to school, but the kindly farmer followed behind at a respectful distance.[26]

When the attack on Fort Sumter began the Civil War on April 11, 1861, Leonard was fourteen years old. Patriotic fervor swept northern Illinois. Flags waved from church pulpits, from women's hats and men's lapels.

Leonard Colby stood up tall and tried to enlist, but was turned away with an insulting wave of the hand. "Run along home now, sonny," the officer advised.[27] Men waiting in line laughed. The wiry youth stalked away with a gleam in his eye. Five months later, now fifteen, he enlisted after placing two pieces of paper printed with the number 18 into his boots. He then swore faithfully before God and country that he was over the age of eighteen.[28] (Andrew Jackson had joined Revolutionary forces at the age of thirteen using a similar technique.) Private Colby served four months at Rockford, Illinois, but "was sent home by order of the Governor (Yates)."[29] His third successful try landed him in Company B, Eighth Illinois Volunteer Infantry under Colonel Sheetz, who knew the boy was underage but looked the other way. Colby went on to a distinguished military career.

After the Massacre at Wounded Knee in 1890, the prospect of more glory must have tempted Leonard Colby into action again. He led Nebraska National Guard units to Rushville, Nebraska, about thirty miles south of Pine Ridge. The troops disembarked from trains in the cold, their frightened horses bolting from boxcars during the worst season of the year to face the possibility of an Indian war. As the cars unloaded, General Colby "bestirred himself," galloping from one car to the next with morale-building yells of encouragement to his men.[30]

Nebraska guardsmen idolized their commander. He displayed few of the military affectations he had observed among the French in Mexico—in his stride or in the way he communicated with his men. He walked informally among the troops, allowing them to approach without saluting (he ignored the military rule except during inspections), to clap him on the back, whisper in his ear, or tell a joke. But when angered, he commanded respect with an unblinking, hypnotic stare, the penetrating gaze of an eagle watching its prey. Few dared push him beyond that look.

Confidence in a military leader when lives are in jeopardy is essential, and Colby's men had supreme confidence in him. Trooper William R. Hamilton described Colby's magnetism as he sat astride a smooth gray-white Arabian stallion named Linden Tree, originally a gift from the sultan of Turkey to President Ulysses S. Grant:[31]

> Of dark complexion, with piercing eyes, full of strength and vigor, a mind as strong and well balanced as his body, with a thorough and absorbing love for his military life, he is the beau-idéal of the citizen soldier. Such men make the position of a guardsman full of honor, while serving as a constant example to be followed . . . [32]

Catching a glimpse of the gallant general, young boys ran alongside and fought to take his reins when he dismounted. Rushville schools lost more than half their male students whenever the troops were in town. Thirteen-year-old schoolboy B. J. Petersen recalled the thrill:

> We used to play hookey from school and go down among the soldiers. . . . It was great sport for us boys to watch the soldiers, to pick out the most beautiful horses as they stood in double rows tethered to a heavy ground rope. . . . The picturesque blue uniforms, with the various insignia of rank, and their great capes with yellow or red linings thrown back over their shoulders as they stood around the campfire. Each company had its guidon or company flag, set up in its place, and its regimental bands, with their gray horses, made a gay and interesting scene. . . . Through all this came wild rumors of bloody battle, which were printed mostly in the big eastern dailies, and of course were false.[33]

For the children of Rushville—indeed for all the nearly 500 inhabitants—the so-called Indian uprising was the most exciting experience of their lives. The town became an overnight attraction on the northern border of Nebraska.

Buffalo Bill Cody, aide-de-camp on Governor Thayer's unstable staff, and his portly "prince of press agents," Major John Burke, reported to General Colby at the train and escorted him to Pine Ridge.[34] Buffalo Bill and the general were competitive friends. They had been known to whip out pistols to see who could hit the most birds overhead. Once, they took turns shooting out gas street lamps on a wager.[35]

The trip to Pine Ridge took three and a half hours over a good road lined here and there with tipis. The trio passed through narrow valleys leading to the crest of a ridge. There the road plunged in a wild descent, and beneath sprawled the grandeur of a western military encampment, perhaps the last of its kind. A writer for the *Illustrated American* described his impression of Pine Ridge:

> Far in the distance are the agency buildings, and clustered around them the tents of the soldiers, carefully arranged in rows, with teepees flanking them on every side. The agency is situated near the center of a broad plain, with hills sloping backward all around. As one approaches, an indistinct mixture of noises attracts the attention of the rider. You can distinguish bugle notes, shouts of young children at play, the loud and discordant bray of the ever-present government mule, and the continuous hum of a busy camp. . . . White tents of the infantry and the posts of the 100 Indian police completely surround the Agent's home, the General's quarters, and the warehouses. You see tons and tons of hay—great stacks of sacked oats and corn for the horses, the offices of the Agency are filled with extra rifles and boxes of cartridges—hundreds of barrels of flour and bacon, crackers and biscuits. . . . Enormous quantity of food provided the men sent to hold in check the handful of Sioux who, on account of hunger, have ventured farther away upon their own land.[36]

Buffalo Bill and Major Burke had already been to Wounded Knee on January 1, assisting Major General Nelson Miles while the bodies of the Lakota were buried. Now they guided Colby through Pine Ridge and continued on to Wounded Knee, less than twenty miles east. From a hill, they looked down upon a forlorn valley of death still occupied by scavenging artifact hunters. In his widely published report Colby wrote of the slaughter, which resulted, he said, "in the wanton murders and cruel massacres of hundreds of unoffending people, [that] has passed into history as one of the stains upon the national honor of the United States."[37] Colby reasoned that true valor in battle resulted when armed men faced an armed enemy in declared combat. When he saw that no war had existed, he blasted the army. Whatever else was said of Wounded Knee, the fact remains that 500 heavily armed American soldiers killed a band of tired men, women, and children and an old chief dying of pneumonia on the frozen ground in front of his tent. To well-trained soldiers like Colby and Captain Frank D. Baldwin, military investigator of the massacre—two men with real war experience—the sight of dead women and children hunted down and slaughtered at close range three miles from the scene was an abomination.[38] Baldwin's wife failed to mention her husband's important presence at Wounded Knee in his biography.

Colby, Major Burke, and Buffalo Bill rode back to the popular Pine

Ridge trading post and bar belonging to Jim Asay. The Asay clubhouse had become a favorite meeting place during the dangerous troubles. Mrs. Jim Asay, Margaret or "May" as she was called, was a black-haired Chicago woman who presided over the trading post like a queen. Her husband, Jim, the spoiled son of a wealthy lawyer, was an attractive, witty man whose daily life dissolved into drunkenness by midday. He slept all afternoon until May dragged him out of bed in the evening to oversee the illegal bar in the backroom, described by one guest as a place where "jugs, bottles, and demijohns, and cases of liquors were constantly on tap. . . . [S]ome of the orgies indulged by officers, newspaper correspondents and civilians would disgrace a not very respectable doggery in a frontier mining town."[39]

May still made the most of the unhappy union, becoming a business-woman with an eye for profit any way she could get it. General Miles spent a good deal of time there, as did all the officers and men. Agent Daniel Royer's wife recalled years later that she and the other "women were then afraid to stay [at Pine Ridge] . . . for they did not feel safe as General Miles was dining and drinking at the Asay house. General Miles drank most of the time and every one felt like they were left insecure."[40]

When sober, Jim and his brother Edward charmed their guests. They charged outrageous prices at both their Lodge Creek store and at Pine Ridge. Between treaty annuity payments from the government, the Lakota suffered for want of the basic comforts of life: food and blankets. A week before the money was due, traders became generous with maximum credit. Poverty-stricken, the Lakota accepted this illegal extortion. Those in authority—chiefs, headmen, and Indian police living at the agency—did nothing to stop the illegal exploitation many knew existed.

In this unhealthy atmosphere, the Asay brothers made easy money compared to Chicago, where Edward Asay was accused of embezzlement in 1885.[41] Edward and brother Jim managed to obtain a trader's license for Pine Ridge, South Dakota, after their father paid off the creditors from his own pocket. Ed Asay's contemporaries expressed amazement that a man with his questionable record should have been allowed to trade with Indi-ans. One newspaper headline read: "WHY CHICAGO PEOPLE THINK HE SHOULD NOT BE POST TRADER."[42] Nevertheless, the well-heeled brothers arrived at Pine Ridge with more than enough money to set themselves up in a lucrative whiskey trade fronted by a trading post at the agency.

Buffalo Bill played serious poker and drank serious whiskey at the Asay club-house. His bellowing baritone, much like the buffalo he was named for, infused conversations with a sense of the dramatic, the larger-than-life.[43] It was enough to be in the same room with the man to feel his flowing enthusiasm.

For more than ten years, May Asay and Buffalo Bill had scandalized northern Nebraska with their open love affair.[44] They often rode out on warm afternoons in a splendid buggy, carrying wicker baskets of picnic fare and an ice bin of chilled wine. Local citizens wondered who was at home minding the store. Nebraskan Charley O'Kieffe remembered seeing Cody

> in the yard with Mrs. Asay, or sitting on the porch with Mrs. Asay, or out driving with Mrs. Asay. It was always Mrs. Asay, never her old man.
>
> [W]hen the lovely lady herself climbed into the front seat [of the carriage] wearing a large picture hat and long gauntlet gloves, and Buffalo Bill was royally seated by her side, the result was a vision of dashing loveliness and class. . . . Her husband was just the opposite in about every respect— nearly always partly, if not entirely, soused.[45]

John M. Burke, possibly the greatest publicity agent of all time, often drank with Buffalo Bill at Asay's post. He was profane and boisterous, but underneath the showy exterior he was William F. Cody's faithful friend.

Burke had acquired an infant survivor of the massacre, a baby girl, from a storekeeper in Pine Ridge named John Yellow Bird. He kept the details of the transaction to himself, but he undoubtedly paid a good price for the child and probably had plans to exhibit her in Cody's Wild West show, even though he had ostensibly allowed the Nailors, friends of Cody's in Washington, to adopt her.[46]

General Colby probably saw the little survivor for the first time on January 5, 1891, and heard her story from a most convincing storyteller. Burke's tale fascinated Colby and the child inspired him. He said he was moved by "the pathos," and mesmerized by the baby's seemingly immortal spirit.[47] The man who saved this "Child of the Battlefield" would be a hero, much like Andrew Jackson, who had adopted a full-blood Creek orphan, Lincoyer, during the Creek Wars, an act so appealing to the voting public that one biographer said, "American hearts shall throb with tearful pleasure at such a story."[48] The boy died early but the heartwarming tale gained Jackson considerable political clout, despite the fact that "he was the single figure most responsible for Indian destruction in pre–Civil War America."[49]

Like Jackson, Colby also desired a keepsake—a live, not dead, reminder of war's exploits; "an instrument whose mainspring is memory, that, like a clock, shall ring out his hour with musical chimes of recollection . . ."[50] The infant was a living symbol of white victory.

As soon as Burke sensed Colby wanted the baby girl, the bargaining became heated. Buffalo Bill, Colby, and Major Burke sat by the warm woodstove in Yellow Bird's store and bartered for the child. They wrangled while the Yellow Bird family sat by and listened, especially Mrs. Annie (Lone Horn) Yellow Bird, holding the infant she loved at her breast.[51]

Colby made the winning bid and late that cold night, January 6, 1891, the general took Annie (with John Yellow Bird's permission) and his newly acquired baby to his tent, where they would stay until he arranged for transport to Rushville the next day.

Colby made them comfortable, providing a warm stove, bunks with woolen blankets, and hot food. The meal was probably served on a white monogrammed linen tablecloth. (The initial C was embroidered on all of Colby's personal items.)[52]

Colby planned to show off the "most interesting Indian relic" to his soldiers along the Nebraska border before sending her home to Beatrice.[53] Members of his staff were as excited about the child as he was. In the past, the general had frequently surprised friends and family with living tokens: rare birds, pedigreed hunting dogs, and Arabian colts.[54] The child would make an interesting gift for his busy wife, Clara, although he had not bothered to send her a wire asking her if she wanted an Indian child. It was to be a surprise—and what could be better than to "give a piece of throbbing life . . . an immortal excitement."[55]

Although Annie was five months pregnant, she did not want the white general to take this orphan. As soon as the sounds of camp life hushed, she crept from her bed, opened the tent flap and ties and slipped easily past guards stamping back and forth on cold guard duty, and the outpost sentries standing around small crackling fires. On her way back to her husband's store, no dogs barked and no sounds frightened the horses. She led her pony from the corral, mounted, and rode away to the "hostile" camp carrying the infant survivor.[56]

Early reveille and the accompanying morning sounds and smells of army camp life awoke the general, and he lit a fire in the campstove. Mrs. Yellow Bird and the child appeared to be still asleep in the bunk, so he left them while he conferred with his staff over breakfast.

After coffee, the general asked an orderly to take a breakfast tray to Annie, and it was then that the ruse was discovered. The orderly found nothing in the bunk but rolled-up blankets.[57] News spread quickly among Colby's disappointed aides, and the Beatrice newspaper reported that "the entire staff of the brigadier general engaged in the search for Colby's papoose."[58] The general rode to the Asay trading post to ask Buffalo Bill for advice.

The Asay bar overflowed with officers, reporters, and freighters. After Colby arrived and told Mrs. Asay that his baby had been stolen, May jumped at the chance to help Leonard Colby. The foster mother of two children, she sympathized with his determination to obtain the child and pitied his childless marriage.[59] Besides, Buffalo Bill supported the scheme to recover the infant and enjoyed the evolving plot. May called a private

meeting away from the gossipmongers. The group consisted of her husband, Jim, his brother Edward and wife Elizabeth, an unknown interpreter,
and the mixed-blood trader John Yellow Bird.

Colby was willing to go to the Ghost Dance camp immediately to parley for the child, but General Miles had issued strict orders for the military
to stay away from the camps while he negotiated fair surrender terms.[60]

John Yellow Bird had to find out where his wife had taken the child
before they made further plans, but he flatly refused to participate in any
negotiations. After Wounded Knee, angry Ghost Dancers had struck back
at him for past grievances. Besides, if he attempted to enter the camp, his
presence would endanger his wife.[61] It was decided that before any further
plans, a spy would find out who had the child. Colby finally "induced" John
Yellow Bird to cooperate in the scheme, probably with a threat or an offer
to recoup the trader's heavy losses.[62]

The next day, on January 7, 1891, Lieutenant Edward W. Casey, a popular officer and Philip Wells's commander, rode with scouts on a dangerous and unexplained mission to the Ghost Dance camp. Historian Robert
M. Utley describes Casey's reckless action:

> The Lieutenant asked Bear-Lying-Down [his scout] to ride back to the
> Indian camp and request one of the chiefs to come down for a parley. If none
> would do so, he was to ask Red Cloud himself to come. At the camp, Bear-
> Lying-Down told his story to He Dog, who went to Red Cloud's lodge.
> There, a number of Oglala chiefs were in the midst of a council. They had
> just decided to try to slip out of camp . . . and go to the agency for a talk with
> General Miles. He Dog relayed Casey's message, and Red Cloud called
> Bear-Lying-Down into the tepee to tell his story personally. . . . [Then] Red
> Cloud instructed him to . . . [tell] . . . the officer . . . that he must leave the
> area immediately for there were hot-headed young men all around who
> might try to kill him.[63]

The Lakota courier brought the urgent message back to Casey, but by this
time angry Indian scouts had spotted him:

> Casey reluctantly agreed to give up his plan . . . when Plenty Horses, astride
> his horse four or five feet to the left and rear of Casey, raised his Winches-
> ter and shot the officer through the back of the head. Casey fell to the
> ground dead.[64]

After the horrors of Wounded Knee, many had suffered mortal wounds in
the so-called hostile Ghost Dance camps. A collective grief swept over the
people, with the accompanying responses of shock, anger, reproach, guilt,
and depression. Plenty Horses, fresh from boarding school in Pennsylvania,

had found himself a social outcast. Told by his teachers to return to the reservation and help his people, he was shocked that he would be ostra-cized by his own relatives and friends. The white man's knowledge meant nothing if Plenty Horses could not find work to use what he had learned. He later testified that he saw in the murder of Lieutenant Casey the chance to appear heroic to his comrades.

No documented proof exists that Lieutenant Casey intended to parley with Red Cloud for Colby's stolen infant, but it is a possibility. Philip Wells had plenty of time to interest Casey in the child before the lieutenant took this highly unusual risk. Later, at Plenty Horses' murder trial, Wells arrived as a witness for the defense, a peculiar action considering that Casey was Wells's commander. Why would he testify for the man who had killed his friend in cold blood?

Enticed by Wells (who became a chief of scouts after the lieutenant's death), Casey might have taken a ride for a stolen waif, a child whose story softened the hearts and minds of the hardest would-be heroes and made her a military trophy worth dying for. But no one publicly implicated Lieu-tenant Casey in any kind of plot.

Casey's death on January 7 set back peace negotiations with the Ghost Dancers and terrified the inhabitants of Pine Ridge.[65] The dreadful news made Leonard Colby and May Asay more cautious. May wanted to delay their attempts to find the child. Colby could wait, but he was willing to risk death and the possible incitement of an Indian war to find "the infant heroine."[66]

Casey's gory demise did not deter Colby. He had never been reasonable in avoiding risk. On the contrary, there were numerous instances in his life when his incredible behavior bordered on lunacy.

As a struggling young lawyer in Beatrice, he had been asked to defend a widow accused of killing her rich husband by poisoning him with arsenic. There was a public trial:

> The evidence was practically conclusive and there was hardly a flaw in the case presented by the prosecution. The husband's body had been exhumed, the poison found and placed in a bottle. There was indubitable proof that the woman had administered the poison and Colby did not contest this point. He merely laid stress on the contention that the man had died from natural causes and that the poison found in his stomach was not sufficient to cause his death.[67]

Colby's law office was in a building adjoining the courthouse. He spent his lunch hour there, and when he reentered the courtroom after the noon recess, he gave an eloquent and dramatic summation for the defense:

"Gentlemen of the jury . . . I contend that the poison my client is said to have administered to her husband was not enough to kill any man, to say nothing of one possessing his constitution. He died from some other cause."[68]

Colby walked to the judge's bench and then turned sharply toward the jury.

"If this poison would have killed him, it would kill me." He picked up the bottle of poison. "There is not enough poison there to kill a kitten," he said. "I will prove to you that there is not enough to kill a man."[69]

Before anyone could stop him, Colby pulled out the cork, threw back his head dramatically, and drank the contents of the bottle.

Then he stood before the jury, his black eyes flashing and thundered out: "Gentlemen of the jury. If this poison kills me you can convict my client, but if I live—as I shall—you will have to bring in a verdict in her favor."[70]

He then bowed low to the twelve jury men. Pandemonium broke out and the judge pounded the gavel: "Order in the court! Order in the court! There will be a twenty-minute recess!"[71]

Colby walked nonchalantly out of the courtroom and over to his office, where he locked himself in. Twenty minutes later, he was back in the courtroom—confident, smiling, and ready to hear the verdict. People were already on their feet applauding:

It took the jury about three minutes to bring in a verdict of acquittal. A few days afterward it leaked out that . . . Colby had a doctor in his office and that the physician removed the poison—enough to have killed ten men— with a stomach pump. Of course there was an uproar, but the law says that a prisoner's life cannot be twice placed in jeopardy and Colby had destroyed the only evidence upon which conviction would be obtained in event of another trial.[72]

For his extraordinary efforts in her behalf, the widow paid her lawyer handsomely and not long afterward married a younger man. Colby had yet another story to tell his friends, who thought of him as amusing, outrageous, and exasperating—in short, wonderful company.

With his usual disregard for personal risk, General Colby soon plotted to "rescue" or scheme the baby away from the Ghost Dancers. Dangerous, yes, but he loved the challenge. Better to die a hero than disappoint the boys under his command.

January 13 brought an important dispatch from General Miles, who assured the Nebraska commander that the Indian negotiations were well in hand and "nothing has occurred that makes it desirable to delay the removal of your troops."[73]

That day, Buffalo Bill wired Colby that General Miles had just freighted out "several thousand pounds of flour and several hundred pounds of coffee and sugar" to the "hostiles" as a gesture of good will.[74] It was the break Colby had been waiting for. He immediately stalled his troop pullout:

> At about noon of January 14th I received a message from Pine Ridge Agency[May Asay?], asking if the troops of my command could be held until something more definite could be ascertained in regard to the intentions of the hostile Indians; and I at once wired information that the same could be held and immediately instructed Major C.O. Bates, my Assistant Adjutant General, to have Regimental Commanders hold their companies until further order, after which I proceeded to Pine Ridge Agency, where I arrived about three o'clock.[75]

An air of intrigue surrounded the Asay trading post that afternoon. May and her sister Elizabeth dressed Colby to look like a mixed-blood Indian, as the ladies prepared themselves and the general for the adventure. Timing was critical. The Ghost Dancers had packed up and some had already joined the long caravan moving toward the agency for the formal meeting with General Miles. A military officer stood on the crest of a hill and watched the scene he called "a spectacle worth beholding:"[76]

> They moved in two columns up White Clay Creek, . . . about 5,500 [closer to 4,000] people in all, with 7,000 horses, 500 wagons, and about 250 travois, and in such good order that there was not at any point a detention on any account. . . . [T]he rear and right flank of this mass was covered during the movement by a force of infantry and cavalry deployed in skirmish order, and moved with a precision that was a surprise to all who witnessed it.[77]

The officer failed to see one dangerous "detention." General Colby, May, Elizabeth, and her interpreter were being escorted close to the Ghost Dance camp. Riding in front was John Yellow Bird, a man in mortal danger.

Somehow, Colby "induced" Yellow Bird to take part in the scheme to retrieve the orphan, even after the trader had steadfastly refused. Yellow Bird found his wife but Annie declined to help Colby kidnap the child. The Lakota had just come through psychological and physical hell. John Yellow Bird knew that to deliberately provoke the Indians, to ride directly into the camp of the men who hated him, would have been suicidal. He agreed to guide Colby to the edge of the camp, and then he would turn back.

May, Elizabeth, and the general sat on the high wagon seat. Outside the camp, scouts stopped the wagon, but let them proceed when they recognized May. People passed slowly by—grieving, cold, and hungry. May's familiar wagon overflowed with delicious food conspicuously displayed: bags of sugar and coffee, boxes of crackers, candy, and fruit. The three jumped down and walked from tent to tent distributing supplies to grateful mothers whose children were crying for food. This gesture of goodwill was excellent for business, even though May was not paying for the provisions. These gifts of badly needed rations were the single most important step—the only possible step—in showing good faith by giving.

The general's presents of food in great quantity opened a path that led to the Wounded Knee orphan. When they found the child, the disguised general stepped forward. Black-haired, dark-complexioned, standing erect, eyes hypnotic with conviction and pride, Leonard Colby spoke through an unknown interpreter:

> I am a Seneca Indian—my grandmother was a full-blood Seneca. I have brought food on behalf of my tribe for your children. I rescued the child who survived the massacre at Wounded Knee. Take pity on me and my wife. We have no children of our own. I want to give this child to my wife. We will take good care of her.[78]

As Colby spoke, women wept. He later recalled those seemingly endless moments a time of "considerable difficulty," probably the Colby way of saying he was scared to death.

A strange, mixed-blood Indian asking for a full-blood baby was unusual, but after the murder of Sitting Bull and the pain of Wounded Knee, nothing was beyond belief. The child may not have been a member of the Ghost Dance *tiospaye* (extended family) protecting her at the time, but she was spiritually one of them.

Suddenly the crowd of Lakota surrounded Colby. Had he flinched or recoiled, the matter might have ended abruptly. He remained calm and he saw that he was not threatened. No one spoke, for to the Lakota, words were not an advanced form of communication. Finally, a man stepped toward the old woman who was holding the infant:

"I am her brother," he said, reaching out for the baby.

"I am her aunt," pleaded another. "I have nothing, but I will take her."

"I am her grandmother," announced a woman, extending her arms.[79]

When others pressed forward, May's interpreter intervened. We do not have her exact words, but she must have appealed to them with sincerity and reason; otherwise, they would never have accepted Colby's request.

When Colby reached for the child in the grandmother's arms, she resisted and cried out, *"Zintkala Nuni! Zintkala Nuni!"* ("The Lost Bird! The Lost Bird!")[80] But she finally released her hold on the sleeping child. Colby looked Indian. He did not appear frightened and ill at ease like a white man with one eyebrow raised. And perhaps it was better to let her go with a mixed-blood for the moment, just to make sure she had food and clothing. Besides, they knew where to find May Asay. The grieving people turned away.

The Asay women boarded the wagon, followed by Colby, still holding the infant. May cracked the whip over her team and they pulled out, heading for the infantry line. By the time they reached John Yellow Bird's store, the unhappy baby girl looked to Colby "like a frozen frog."[81] If we are to believe Philip Wells, he was either present at the infantry line or at Yellow Bird's store, where the general's horse waited. "The Fox" gave away his intimate involvement when he mentioned in his autobiography that he was there formally to interpret her name as "Zintkalanuni," the Lost Bird.[82] If on-the-spot as he claimed, his involvement—and thus Lieutenant Casey's entanglement in the plot—assumes greater probability.

An eyewitness, Thomas Tibbles, recalled:

> I saw . . . Colby come riding rapidly into Pine Ridge with that baby on his saddle pommel, and I watched him handle the little Sioux child as tenderly as he would have handled one of his own flesh and blood. They gave the tiny girl some hot beef extract for her first feeding.[83]

Hot beef extract, just what she needed to sustain life. Or was it? The Lakota baby was unprepared for an entirely new way of feeding, not to mention a radical difference in the way she was being handled. Her previous life in Big Foot's band had consisted of being constantly held, slept with, and cuddled. Not only women but many male relatives carried her around gently. (Lakota men were often just as good with children as women, sometimes better.) Men shared child care with their wives and sisters willingly, and when they became grandfathers, their grandchildren took care of them in turn. Lakota educator Pat Locke describes Lakota children:

> The Lakota word for child is *wakan heja* or *wakaj yeja*, which means "sacred one," "consecrated one," "the being endowed with a spiritual quality." The *wakan heja* is viewed as a gift from the Creator.
>
> Throughout the life of the *wakan heja*, he or she was beloved by the parents and the *tiospaye*. The parents' role was to convey unconditional and genuine love to the *wakan heja* . . . Such love is the foundation of life. Unconditional love means that the child is loved no matter what, that is,

whatever mistakes, age, weight, appearance, performance or handicaps might be manifested, the child is loved. The way unconditional love is transmitted is by focused attention, physical contact, playfulness and gentle discipline . . . Birthing is a calm and gentle time. . . . The baby is not permitted to cry and is carried about by family. . . . It is a myth that Indian parents are solemn, stern and stoic with their children. On the contrary, laughing, smiling, and playfulness were and are the Lakota norm for parents and the extended family. . . . [A]ll of the adults in a community are responsible for the safety and happiness of the collective *wakan heja*. The effect of this love on the children is a feeling of security and self-assurance. Children are put first in all things.[84]

Acclimated to the cold, Lost Bird probably never had anything hot in her stomach, save the slight warmth of breast milk. Here was a Lakota *wakan heja* who was spiritually, psychologically, and physically bound to her biological mother and relatives.

Was extra love and affection all that was needed when a Lakota child— even an infant—went from firm racial roots to a transracial adoption? The Lost Bird was cut off not only from her biological parents, but from a whole race and culture that was her heritage.

The Lakota feel the kinship of brother and sister to all other "red" native peoples. If there are two Indians—not necessarily Lakota, but two Indians—in a crowd of one thousand people of different origins, those two will find each other. An instant psychic bond will occur, a conscious neural capability. Biochemist Donald Carr called it "transcendental memory," as inexplicable as how fish predict earthquakes or how colonial bees possess a vivid sense of how to get home, or how trout and red lake salmon return hundreds of miles to the exact place where they were born. Lost Bird was taken from that memory, a oneness with the universe, which centered and made her a whole person.[85]

General Colby had no inkling of these considerations. He thought his "humanitarian" rescue had worked well—until something unexpected happened. A Lakota named Felix Crane Pretty Voice and his wife Rock Woman came to Yellow Bird's store. Felix said they had lost a daughter during the massacre and they wanted to see if Yellow Bird had their baby. Since Lost Bird had been held for more than a week in the Ghost Dance camp, why had the family decided to come to Yellow Bird's store now?

Rock Woman looked at the baby and began to cry, not an unusual response for a survivor of Wounded Knee. (Published photographs of the dead taken after the Wounded Knee Massacre still cause grief among the Lakota.)[86]

Colby grew suspicious when Rock Woman did not touch the child or react toward her like a relieved mother. He felt it was a scam, and he the target. The general did not believe Rock Woman was the mother or Felix Crane Pretty Voice the father of Lost Bird. But he was seeing the event from a white man's view, so he could have been wrong. It was possible but highly unlikely that a Lakota mother would "throw away" her own child to a soldier just days after the slaughter at Wounded Knee. Rock Woman may have cried because she saw the child was not hers, but the couple finally accepted provisions because they were desperately in need after the massacre.[87] Scam or not, fifty dollars sent Crane Pretty Voice and his wife on their way.

Colby wired his staff in Rushville to proceed with the troop removal. He would catch up with them later.

Just as Colby was leaving for Rushville, he was shocked when Lakota women at Pine Ridge came forward to say that they recognized Lost Bird as "the daughter of Black-Day Woman, last and youngest wife of the Chief, Sitting Bull."[88] This information deeply worried the general. What if the baby were really Sitting Bull's daughter? Eventually, the medicine man's relatives might come after her. To guard against that possibility, Colby boarded the first available train to Beatrice and adopted Lost Bird in a court of law on January 19,1891.[89]

He was still worried a year later when he obtained legal documentation proving she was not Sitting Bull's daughter. (Colby protected his trophy with certified records, much like the prize Arabian pedigrees he preserved in an office safe, next to the collection of ancient hieroglyphics kept locked in a tin box.)[90] Recordkeeping, not necessarily accurate or genuine, saved Colby's hide on a number of future occasions, even though the general preferred face-to-face meetings. He rarely wrote a letter. Spoken words evaporated into air. Written words of any kind, especially personal missives, left an undeniable trail.

Colby asked government census-taker Archibald T. Lea to check Indian Agency lists. The general wanted tangible proof that Lost Bird was not related to Sitting Bull in any way.

Mr. Lea's reply came December 15, 1892:

Dear General:

. . . Ascertaining the parentage of your little Indian girl . . . I have gone through the old rolls containing the names of those killed in Wounded Knee fight, and find but two families reported killed with little girl babies or where the babies were not accounted for to wit: Black Fox, father, 32 years old, Brown Hair, mother, 28 years old, Brings White Horse, infant, daughter. The other family was Male

Eagle, father, 43 years old, Short Woman, mother, 41 years old, Runs After Her, daughter, infant. Now Black Fox and his wife Brown Hair were killed near each other, with the dead body of an infant by the side of its dead mother. The description of the mother and babe correspond with rolls for wife of Male Eagle and child. Hence I can arrive at but one conclusion, and that is, that Black Fox and Brown Hair, were the parents of Brings White Horse, and that Brings White Horse is none other than the little Indian girl you now have.

The exact age of the little girl is not given, only infant, "under one year." When a child is born, as soon as a mother can get to the agency, she goes and has its name placed upon ration rolls, and in making such entry, date of birth is not given, only "under one year," or infant giving the sex . . . [91]

General Colby wrote a rare note of reply to Lea on December 27, 1892:

My dear Sir:

I have your esteemed favor of the 15th instant, and you will please accept my thanks for your courtesy and for the information contained in your letter in regard to Zintka Lanuni. The evidence referred to by you seems to be quite convincing that our little Indian babe . . . (is) Brings-White-Horse.

You do not say that you have examined records in regard to Sitting-Bull's band. You doubtless will recollect that Big-Foot's band was composed not only of his own people but also partly of the members of Sitting-Bull that escaped for the Bad Lands after his death. . . . I wish, if possible, that you could look this matter up and see what record there is as to a babe being with that tribe—Uncpapas.

Yours very truly,
L. W. Colby[92]

Along with this note, Colby sent a form:

I inclose a statement in accordance with your letter, which you will please copy off in your own hand-writing, and sign and return to me . . .[93]

The document was obviously meant to substantiate Lea's findings. If Sitting Bull's family ever came looking for the child, Colby had covered his tracks. In the years to come, the nagging question of Lost Bird's relations continued to haunt Leonard Colby. The strong, interwoven threads of

Lakota kinship led from one family to another, always ending with an intriguing question mark near Sitting Bull's home on the Standing Rock Reservation.

Lea was known for questionable reporting of the 1890 Lakota census and for warmongering among government officials regarding the Ghost Dance.[94] Rosebud trader Charles P. Jordan described Lea as "manifestly an Indian hater."[95] Soon after Lost Bird's recapture, Colby named the girl Margaret Elizabeth in honor of Margaret and Elizabeth Asay, the ladies who helped him take her from the reservation. The general got what he wanted, but his accomplices did not fare as well. Less than a month later, an intoxicated Jim Asay fell afoul of the law. At Holy Rosary Mission, Father Emil Perrig wrote in his diary on February 21, 1891:

> Mr. Asay, whose store had been closed some days, seems not to have succeeded in clearing himself of the accusations of selling whiskey and allowing gambling in his store. Hence the store was reopened Feb. 19th for disposing of all its contents within 60 days, when Asay will have to leave the reservation.[96]

Not wishing to face a federal indictment, the Asays left Pine Ridge, but May Asay was much too clever to leave the area completely. The Asays bought a store in Rushville and reopened with business as usual.

For years afterward, May and Buffalo Bill Cody carried on their notorious liaison, giving Rushville residents a scandalous diversion. It was not until May 17, 1897, that Oglala leaders were able to bring more damaging charges against James Asay in a Memorial Petition to the 55th United States Congress, 1st Session:

> James F. Asay, a white man, who was expelled from the Pine Ridge Reservation for misconduct in 1891, has a deep rooted scheme, and the Indians are coerced and it is made compulsory for them to trade at Asay's store in Rushville, Nebr., and pay for goods they purchase the most outrageous charges. . . . Asay is permitted to be present and collect bills against the Indians while final payment is being made, and in some instances Asay handles the cash and presides over the payment. Mr. Asay's conduct was such that he was . . . removed from the Pine Ridge Agency . . . but was still permitted to use the reservation at his convenience and defraud the Indians by charging them exorbitant prices for goods sold under the Buffalo Bill trading combination, which seems too strong for the officials at Pine Ridge to break, in face of Asay's persuasive powers of pleasing those whose favoritism he seeks. . . . Asay should be kept off the reservation altogether . . . [97]

A sad reminder of Jim Asay's fatal ten-gallon keg of whiskey at Wounded Knee occurred in 1906 when Mr. W. A. Luke dug up the remains of buried cavalrymen who had died at Wounded Knee. He penned this description:

> Sixteen years later, as a student undertaker in the employ of E. Mead of Chadron, Nebr., who had been awarded the contract signed by William Howard Taft, Secretary of War, the writer was sent to Pine Ridge to exhume the remains of the military deceased [from the massacre] and prepare them for shipment to national cemeteries.
>
> We found the remains in very shallow graves, some in coffins inside of rough boxes, others because of the frozen condition of the body could only be placed in rough boxes. They were buried in the clothing they were wearing at the time when they fell, including uniform, gloves, overcoat, spurs, with personal effects including signet ring, watch, and other possessions such as small amounts of money.
>
> [W]e found one grave empty; possibly relatives or friends had been there first. The 29 cases containing the remains of the 29 deceased of the Seventh Cavalry were shipped to Fort Riley, Kans., to be reinterred in the Post Cemetery, and the case containing the remains of the one member of the Ninth U.S. Cavalry (negro) were shipped to Fort Robinson, Nebr., to be reinterred in the Post Cemetery.
>
> The contract assumed that after 16 years in the grave, all the remains would be reduced simply to bones. In certain of the graves was the mute evidence of too heavy a use of liquor in life—which in death tends to preserve or embalm the body. This brought to mind the criticism leveled at Colonel Forsyth, before he was relieved of his command, that liquor was one of the main causes of the wanton massacre of the women and children at Wounded Knee.[98]

General Colby's association with the Asays came to an end on January 17, 1891, when he hurridly boarded a train to Beatrice with the Lost Bird and a "half-breed" nurse named Mrs. Going(s). On the way to Beatrice, they stopped overnight in Lincoln at the popular Capital Hotel. The imposing three-story brick building had 100 "splendidly furnished" rooms and the first floor boasted dining rooms for 125 guests, the hotel office, a large kitchen, barber shop, billiard rooms, telegraph office, and a newsstand and cigar store.[99] The English-born hotel manager, R. W. Johnson, "one of the most popular managers in the West," had his hands full when General Colby and Zintkala Nuni caused a sensation in one of the dining rooms: "The little heroine of Wounded Knee sat in the lap of its nurse . . . and received for three hours the attention and caresses of hosts of ladies and gentlemen . . ."[100]

The attention was intoxicating. No sooner had the general returned to Beatrice than he opened the doors of his home to introduce the Lost Bird to Beatrice society and "not less than 500 persons called at his house to see it."[101] Colby's remarks about the child received attention in the national press: "She is my relic of the Sioux War of 1891 and the Massacre of Wounded Knee."[102] (In his official military reports he called it a "battle," but in all subsequent statements he referred to the tragedy as a "massacre.")

The general and his guardsmen were honored with a large banquet and reception the evening of January 20, 1891. The Beatrice Auditorium was too small to hold the crowds waiting in jostling lines to jam through the door:

> When Company C marched from their armory to the auditorium, headed by the band, they were led to seats, surrounding two long tables on the main floor. . . . The supper was enlivened with more music. . . . At the close of this, a prominent feature of the evening, General Colby appeared at the front door accompanied by the half breed nurse, Mrs. Goin(gs) and the General's protege, Margaret Elizabeth Colby, reclining in her arms. A shout went up from every one near and it was with difficulty the party managed to reach the stage through the crowd which pressed around and peered at the bright faced baby. Mrs. Goin(gs) and the baby were given seats in the right hand box and continued to attract general attention through the evening, the baby seemingly being interested in everything going on about it.[103]

When General Colby was introduced as the "father of the Nebraska National Guard and of the Sioux orphan," someone in the audience "proposed three cheers for General Colby, which were given with a will."[104]

The cheering people of Beatrice must have had short memories. It had not taken them long to forget they had once tried to hang Leonard Colby. When he first came to Beatrice in 1872, lawyers were scarce in Nebraska. Fresh out of law school from the University of Wisconsin, where he had graduated as valedictorian, Colby judged Beatrice a backward community of pioneers. He found out the hard way that the founding fathers of the small town were honest and unified. They did not always agree with one another politically, and there were occasional public spats, but the men were generally fair in their business dealings. These were frontiersmen, and frontier justice brought swift punishment to a city slicker making fast deals. Leonard Colby underestimated Beatrice and quickly learned his lesson. Fordyce Graff, onetime Beatrice city clerk, remembered:

> Colby thought he'd pull a fast one. He went down Court street with that devilish look in his eye—he could charm the pants off you—had merchants sign

quit claim deeds! Luckily, they found him out before he did much damage. A bunch grabbed him. About a hundred men with more joining in, dragged him down to the wooden bridge on Market Street to hang him, but he was cool as ice. He let them put the noose around his neck and then he said real calm, "Now, gentlemen, this won't do you any good. Your property will go to my heirs when I die. You will lose everything you own." The boys looked at one another. He had 'em. They took the rope off and he agreed to sign the properties back to them. Even after what he did, he made them so mad they ended up liking him. People always said afterwards that "Leonard Colby stole Beatrice," in more ways than one, and they'd laugh about it. But you couldn't hate the man. He got to you. He'd do somethin' downright underhanded and he'd do it right under your nose, and you'd end up giving him a second chance. He was a scoundrel alright, but Beatrice liked the man and took him in. I think a lot of it had to do with his wife—she was goodness itself.

Another time he defended a bank robber and got the man off. The courtroom was full of angry people who didn't like the verdict. I was right there. They stormed over the railing and Colby knocked down a few before the sheriff stepped in. A few minutes later somebody told Colby his client had headed out. Colby jumped on his horse and followed the man to his house way out in the country. After Colby nearly banged the door down, the man proceeded to pull up the floor boards and paid him for his services right out of one of the stolen bank bags![105]

Since those early days, the general must have settled down and walked a straighter line. When he returned a hero from the 1891 "Indian Wars," he proudly took the stage to speak amid thunderous applause:

> "Mr. Chairman, Ladies and Gentlemen and members of Company C, Nebraska National Guard . . . I don't know as a speech is needed unless upon the paternal side and that is in my line [*applause*]. . . . I knew the boys would do their duty and that the place for them was at the danger line . . ."[106]
>
> He closed his talk by saying that Beatrice should always have the best of everything and that was why he secured and brought home the baby. He said, "It belongs to the Nebraska National Guard, its commander and to the citizens of Beatrice."[107]

Colby failed to add that the state of Nebraska paid for Crane Pretty Voice's provisions, substantial bribes, clothing and food for the recapture, medicines, and the nurse's wages, Burke's bargaining fee, and all accommodations for the Nebraska National Guard delay at Rushville—plus the Capital Hotel bill in Lincoln. The Lost Bird from Wounded Knee was an expensive trophy.

The reception ended at a late hour. A little girl with a doll in her arms stopped at the door and looked at the sleeping Lakota infant, now "the daughter of the regiment." In a loud voice she said, "I wish I could have it, Mama."[108]

Stared at and breathed upon by nearly 2,000 curious souls within four days, it was no wonder that on January 21, 1891, Lost Bird developed a sudden fever and each breath came in labored gasps. It was pneumonia, the first virus she had known.[109] In the confusing atmosphere of hot and cold rooms, strange milk and water, handed from person to person in a dizzy whirl of loud bands, applause, and harsh laughter, she began her precarious new captivity, observed on all sides by well-meaning people, one of whom wrote after the reception:

> "Zoe"—Life—I might have called thee,
> Infant of the battle-field.
> No one but the dead was with thee,
> Thou alone didst never yield.
> Kingly nature must be thine,
> American of ancient line.
> "Lost Bird" so they call thee, baby?
> Ah, my child, once lost now found.
> Now a new life lies before thee,
> Up and onward and be crowned.
> Nobly live that all may see,
> Indian girl of "Wounded Knee."
>
> ARA LOVE AMOS COBURGH,
> Nebraska, Dec. 27, 1891[110]

And where was the "mother" of the newly adopted Indian child? In the sensation of the moment, her absence apparently went unnoticed. Nationally known suffragist, lecturer, educator, and newspaper editor Clara Bewick Colby was in Washington, D.C., with her mentor, Susan B. Anthony. Leonard Colby had not yet informed his wife that at the age of forty-four, she had abruptly become the mother of a full-blood Lakota *wakan heja*, a sacred child from Wounded Knee.[111]

CHAPTER 4

The Suffrage Mother

On January 19, 1891, the general petitioned the Gage County Court in Beatrice to adopt Zintkala Nuni, and on January 20 the adoption was made legal in session with Judge W. S. Bourne. Although General Colby had not discussed it with his wife, Clara Colby's name appeared on the legal document:

> Leonard W. Colby & Clara B. Colby, husband & wife . . . filed his duly verified petition praying that said infant might be legally adopted . . . alleging that the parents of said child are both dead.[1]

On January 23, Clara received her husband's letter telling of the adoption. Her astonishment can only be imagined.

The Reverend Olympia Brown described Clara as "an honored advocate of woman suffrage, a co-worker with Elizabeth Cady Stanton and Susan B. Anthony, a devoted reformer in many lines, a consecrated church-worker, a writer of marked ability, an interpreter of poets and philosophers, and amid all an exceptionally fine house-keeper and excellent cook."[2]

Clara had founded the *Woman's Tribune* in Nebraska in 1883, and by 1888 it was the recognized newspaper of the National Woman Suffrage Association. During the 1888 International Council of Women in Washington, Clara published the *Tribune* for two weeks, probably the first instance of a daily woman's paper being published by a woman.[3] After her notable success, and with her husband's approval, she removed her office to the nation's capital and made it her headquarters six months of every year while Congress was in session. During the summer months, she published the paper from the family home in Beatrice.

Miss Susan B. Anthony, her mentor and cherished friend, came often to see her in Washington, and Clara was a familiar figure on the streets and avenues as she scurried from place to place loaded down with suffrage petitions. Clara was always in a hurry. She could have waited for a horse-drawn cab or taken an electric trolley, but she loved to walk in the brisk air, no matter the weather. While the capital slept, she was up before dawn, feeding her pet songbirds, answering letters, and writing articles for the newspaper.

For ten years Clara had idolized Susan B. Anthony and her motherly colleague, Elizabeth Cady Stanton. Mrs. Colby had met both women after they were asked by the library committee to give a series of lecture courses in Beatrice. Before the lectures began, the two speakers had to be introduced, but the person designated for that honor had not yet arrived. Mrs. Stanton turned to Clara in her usual straightforward way and asked her to present them to the membership, a gesture that began Clara's transformation from director of small-town community activities to internationally recognized woman educator. Stanton would later write to her, saying: "What a merry supper we had that night . . ."[4] Years later, Clara fondly described the evening after the Beatrice lecture: "They were guests in my house and this little service brought me the . . . great reward of companionship with these illuminated souls who looked at life out of human eyes and not merely out of woman's eyes."[5]

A naturalized American citizen, Clara was one of ten children (three died in childhood) and the eldest daughter of Thomas Bewick, a railway contractor, and his wife, Clara Willingham, of Gloucester, England. She was born there on August 5, 1846.[6] Mr. Bewick was related to the celebrated naturalist and engraver Thomas Bewick, and Clara Medhurst Chilton was the niece of Walter Medhurst, D.D., pioneer missionary to China.

As a young child, Clara was left behind in London with her devout maternal grandparents, Stephen and Clara M. Chilton, while her parents immigrated to the United States. "The very earliest recollection of my life [was] kissing my mother good-by," Clara remembered.[7] Her fragile mother married for love and had chosen a man known as the most advanced scholar in his township, having mastered geometry, trigonometry, and the French language in a private school. "He made such advancement that at the age of eleven years, the teacher sent him home because he had advanced as far in his studies as the teacher could take him."[8] There was every reason to believe Thomas was on his way to good fortune—especially in America, the land of opportunity.

Held up in her grandfather's arms in the doorway at 11 Waterloo Place, the girl in the embroidered India linen dress could barely see the back of a statue of the Duke of York. During wet, gloomy London winters with coal fires burning in nearly every room, Clara played in the comfortable home furnished in the latest Victorian fashion, with soft flock wallpaper—dark green in some rooms and red in others—among potted palms, cozy chairs, and dark walnut furniture topped with marble.

Winter in London was bearable for the rich and the middle classes, but the working poor suffered miserably in Victoria's capital. Historian Cecil Woodham-Smith said the British possessed a "characteristic of indifference to cold." Even Queen Victoria, perhaps the most beloved queen in the history of England, gave birth to her third daughter (and fifth child in six years), Princess Helena, on May 25, 1846, while living in the "icy magnificence" of Buckingham Palace.

Clara was spared the horror of poverty in her native land. Although the British were in the midst of the Crimean War against Russia, Clara's only remembrance of it were the stories she heard about a young woman named Florence Nightingale, a national heroine who single-handedly revolutionized nursing, a legendary figure whom the troops called "the Lady with the Lamp" because she walked the hospital halls at night with an old-fashioned lamp.

Spring days were spent with a headful of fancies on carriage rides around majestic parks, amid ponds full of miniature yachts, on paths rimmed with boxwood and quince hedges and thousands of riotous tulips, daffodils, and hollyhocks bending in the breeze.

There were picnics in the countryside, baskets packed with Devon honey cakes or white chocolate muffins, strawberries, and tightly wrapped enameled jugs of tea. Of course, every self-respecting family had a proper white lace tablecloth to place over a larger quilt. The fields were full of fresh lavender, and one could easily bring home its sharp scent by dampening a handkerchief and letting it dry on a lavender bush.

But there was another side of London that Clara loved; the excitement of noisy meat markets with stalls filled with an array of cooked and uncooked foods, heavenly smells of roast lamb and cornish hen, with meat vendors competing for the attention of the multitudes. Clara remembered looking up at a scheming bargainer selling a Christmas turkey at Smithfield Meat Market:

" 'Ere's a fine bird, sixteen pounds if it's an ounce. We've been arskin' sixteen bob [shillings] for it all day and now you may 'ave it for eleven. Eleven bob," slapping it vigorously on the breast.

"Wot, eleven bob too much, then 'ave it for ten and six." (Slap) Ten bob, and that's giving it away"—while his resonant slapping was drawing the crowd around him.

"Who knows a good bird when he sees it? You do—and you may 'ave it for nine and six." (Slap) Another moment's hesitation while the auctioneer picks out his man, and fixes his eye upon him.

" 'Ere. It's yours, mister, for nine bob (slap). Sold."[9]

On meandering walks down cobblestone streets with grandmother Chilton, a beautiful woman impeccably dressed and coiffured, Clara learned by heart the 119th Psalm, all 176 verses, at the age of five.[10]

Clara jumped up and down and clapped her hands when Grandmother took her on her first train journey she called "riding on the cars." Looking out arched train windows, thatched, whitewashed cottages rushed by, church spires, rapid drifts of colorful garden walls, and steep-roofed Tudors. Clara was so excited that Grandmother told her that her eyes looked "like sparkling diamonds."

The pretty child learned to sew, tat, embroider, and set tea in the English tradition. She was a joy to care for. These carefree days spent with her attentive grandparents were the only pleasant moments of childhood that Clara would ever know. When she was nine years old, her parents sent word they wanted her to join them in America.

Tired of railroad work in a country where his working-class accent placed him forever in a caste system from which he could never rise, the adventurous Thomas Bewick and family had sailed for America without knowing the great hardships that lay before them. They slept on cots in the steerage and breathed rank air for six long weeks. "Unpalatable food, sea-sickness, and squalling children bore heavily" upon Mrs. Bewick, who had left behind a comfortable upbringing, her parents, relatives, and numerous beloved friends.[11] The mother's worst fears became reality on the wearisome trip when her son Tom fell overboard and nearly drowned in the foaming sea.[12]

After reaching the shores of their new country, the family traveled to Ohio, but Thomas soon left for Wisconsin to find better land. During the separation, the youngest boy, Ebenezar, died in his mother's arms. The grieving family returned to England, but came back again to America in 1849.

In poverty Clara Bewick moved to Wisconsin over bad roads, through sloughs and boggy places. There were few bridges, and when wading or fording, travelers often came into unpleasant contact with underwater "bloodsuckers"—leeches—which had to be found and pulled off every night, leaving itchy welts.

From the ordered hedgerows of the English countryside, Mrs. Bewick came to Wisconsin and endured with nothing but a washboard to call her own. Frontier life for a woman accustomed to London milliners, tearooms, and a greengrocer within a servant's walking distance can hardly be imagined. A pioneer family did not merely clear land, plant fields, and sit back. Plants, insects, and creatures of the forest constantly moved in and tried to surround the small cabin, to steal food, water, and crops. Unlike Indians, who had lived in harmony with nature for thousands of years, leaving little trace of their continuous habitation, pioneers felt compelled to battle nature, to fight the creeping vines reaching out from the forest and the forbidding beasts with glowing eyes lying eagerly in wait. The pioneer woman, often left weeks at a time to manage alone, beat back the forest instead of trying to domesticate it.

Backbreaking manual labor in the house and fields, made harder by the care of seven stair-step children, wore on Mrs. Bewick's nerves. "Her patience," remembered son Stephenson, "was much in evidence, though severely tried by the conditions in which she was placed, which were so different from what she had been used to in England . . ."[13]

The religiously devout and loving mother bore seven children who lived, and mourned three who died. During the last year of her life in 1855, and just before the family moved into a much larger stone house five miles from Windsor, Wisconsin, little Clara began her journey from England to join her parents, accompanied by the Chiltons.

Traveling to a new romantic land seemed a grand experience from the moment Clara stepped on board the beautiful *Queen of the Sea* clipper ship, a jungle of five rows of thirty sails and three huge masts, crissed-crossed riggings with a heavy iron anchor resembling the lifeless tailfin of a whale strapped alongside the slender hull. The long engraved prow pointed toward the shores of America. Years later, Clara remembered the voyage:

> We have been tossing on the ocean for three weeks. Most of our number have become heartily tired of it during that time, but I, possessing a natural fondness for the water, and having escaped the disagreeable sensations generally attendant upon sea-life, have thought every day too short.
>
> The boundless expanse of water was a mystery to me; and children . . . love mysteries. So with a feeling something akin to that with which, in our pensive moods, we gaze towards the horizon, I have stolen away from my companions, and, leaning far over the side of the ship, tried to learn the secret of the deep. We became pretty well acquainted in those days, the old ocean and I, considering the disparity of our years; my aged friend would listen patiently to the story of my childish griefs, and soothe my troubled spirit . . .
>
> But most of all I loved the ocean in a storm. Setting aside the gratification of tumbling from one side of the ship to the other, of watching the terror-stricken faces, of listening to the noise and confusion of those running hither and thither there is something awe-inspiring in the manifestation of so much power.
>
> For even at this moment, I hear a sailor from his look-out cry, "Land aho." The words are echoed by every tongue, and all eagerly strain their eyes to catch a glimpse of the desired haven. . . . We go on deck, and . . . we can

see, faintly looming up before us, as a cloud in the horizon, the lovely island of Staten.

The air is balmy this morning; it is like the breath of sweet tempered June, rather than that of impulsive, irritable May. We have suffered very much with the cold while passing the banks of Newfoundland. Only a few mornings ago, we could hardly stand on the deck for the ice; and now, how changed the face of the great ocean sparkles with joy, and reflects undimmed the radiance of the sun. . . . I can not tell how Staten Island may appear on nearer examination, but certainly it is of surpassing beauty as the first object which welcomes us to the new world.[14]

The Chiltons took their granddaughter by train and carriage to Wisconsin. Clara was overjoyed to see her parents after so many years, but the naïve English girl was unprepared for the difficulties awaiting her. She spent the next few months working beside her mother. They were inseparable, talking and laughing, often going off together to read poems aloud and giggle over mother-daughter secrets and dreams.

On a summer morning in 1855, Clara was helping her mother carry water from the cistern. Details were etched in her memory forever because it was the last long day and evening of her mother's pregnant life. In later years Clara Colby told her niece, Sadie, the terror of that fateful day. Thinking to write a biography of her Aunt Clara, Sadie took sketchy notes of Clara's story:

Mother [was] working, getting ready to do a huge washing, young Clara & William helping to pull bucket by bucket . . . then filling great boiler on wood stove. Tiny [mother]; beautiful auburn curly hair—gold brown & blue eyes—tiny hands & feet. Unhappy face.

She calls Clara to come to help her lift [the] boiler off the stove—Clara says it is too heavy—[Mother said] "I'm sorry, child. It was more than you could lift." Tears came to [her] eyes. She was numb with weariness. Impatiently she lift[ed] the boiler herself, seized it with both tiny arms—She began to rub the heavy pieces. Clara helped her wring the bulky shirts & trousers.

By the time Thomas [Father] and his four sons came in from the field, the big pine table was covered with a white cloth & there were heaping plates of food waiting. Thomas lowered his head and solemnly said grace . . .

[After supper] Thomas picked up [a book] and turned a few familiar pages when he heard [his wife] give a sharp little cry. She had sat down, her head resting on the table. Thomas went to her side. "What is it, Clara?" She clutched the edge of the table. "The pain," she whispered, "The unmistakable pain." . . . [With] stern voice he said, "Brace up, Clara." She [went] to bed in agonizing pain—cry of pain—3 older boys knew what it meant. Thomas (Jr.)

and Father hitched horses to go for the doctor—Piercing cries. Children would drop off, and be wakened by cries. Dr. finally brought in. William . . . prays to God for help . . . sees inside that [the] doctor is really drunk. Screams stop in silence. She is unconscious. Boys wait, wondering. Dr. sitting there now sober, trying to keep her from bleeding to death—around 3 or 4 in the morning she died. Thomas in his own heart knew that he had killed her—sobbed with his head on the table. They took her to the lonely . . . cemetery.[15]

Watching her mother's painful death in childbirth left a profound impression on Clara. From then on, she deeply distrusted "drugs" and the medical profession, waged unceasing war on alcohol, and worked diligently for the relief of women whose lives were destroyed by toil, too many children, and family drinking problems. Her mother never saw the completion of the new stone house that her hard work had helped make possible.

Grief-stricken, Thomas Bewick was left with seven hungry children and heavy farm work. He depended on young Clara and her grandmother and grandfather (now both over sixty years old) for a year until Grandmother put her foot down and began looking for a new wife for Thomas.

Older brother Stephenson recalled the old folks' dilemma: "The noise and confusion of seven healthy active children soon became irksome to them, and the attempted restraint also to the children, . . . tired of the constant urge for quietness."[16] Grandmother, in her forceful but well-intentioned manner, picked out a young lady she thought would do nicely, but Thomas refused and there was trouble at once. Sadie's notes continue:

Grandmother . . . her one thought—how terribly her daughter had been treated. After a week [of] her bitter quarrel . . . Thomas would blaze with wrath. Grandmother took Clara. Thomas could not kill Clara as he had killed his wife. Clara [had no] feeling of fierce loyalty . . .

It was the men and boys who must be served . . . the food for them & their beasts. Their meals must be cooked, their [clothes] made, washed, mended—all their house must be made comfortable—yes & more boys must be born to help in the fields![17]

Thomas went to town one day and married a "sturdy beauty," Jane Boynton Cox, a widow with five children. None of the Bewick children liked their new stepmother, and there were hard feelings on both sides.

Thomas Bewick had a large trunk filled with books from England and his children loved it—they called it "the knowledge box."[18] But none of the Cox clan took to book learning. Accustomed to his refined and gentle mother, brother Stephenson was offended at his father's choice for a bride and the numerous untutored newcomers:

If I should say they [the Cox children] were regarded as undesirable, it would be but giving expression to our feelings at that time. . . . Yes, there was some friction, but Father's stern attitude toward any offenders, who were guilty of disrespect towards the wife, kept any such manifestations in the background. It may have appeared to some outsiders that our father was at times unduly strict, and even severe. It was the only successful course to pursue under such trying circumstances. A less capable man could not have controlled the situation for a day. He was a most affectionate man, who his children loved very dearly; and whom all his neighbors respected and honored.[19]

Jane Bewick moved all of the brood into the spacious new home and the exhausted grandparents returned to England, leaving Clara, the nine-year-old—the brilliant well-bred daughter—to help care for the eventual seventeen children!

Clara attended a one-room country school with sixty other students but her scholarly interests were cut short when she was asked to care for her father and stepmother's firstborn child, Sarah Elizabeth. The pretty little girl was made "Clara's special charge," but Sarah caught typhoid fever and died after a protracted illness. It was a great grief to all, "especially so to Clara who had so fondly cared for her from infancy."[20]

Perhaps blaming herself for reading when she should have been watching the little girl more carefully, Clara never wrote or spoke the child's name again.

When sister Mary, eight years younger than Clara, was old enough, she hired out as a domestic, desperate to get away from home. Clara, on the other hand, was too proud to take menial work. She taught school for a while, but she wrote in her diary that teaching children was "one of the greatest strains upon the nervous system. . . . It is hard to keep 54 pairs of hands and feet and 54 little tongues in perfect order . . ."[21]

Clara wanted to attend the University of Wisconsin, but her father was against it. Stephenson explained that his devout father "objected because of the religious views held . . . by some of the faculty. Their teaching was similar to what is . . . known as Modernism, Rationalism, New Thought; discrediting the most vital parts of the Bible; accepting only such parts as appealed to the natural course of reasoning."[22] Surely, he also wanted Clara to stay at home to help with the heavy workload of her noncomplaining stepmother, who remained endlessly pregnant, the one condition she shared with her devoted predecessor.

Determined to escape the brutal farm work and nerve-racking care of numerous whining children at home and the "54 little tongues" at school, Clara appealed to her grandparents in London to save her from an early grave. Having lost their only daughter to pioneer life in America, the Chiltons sacrificed to make sure the same fate did not await their favorite granddaughter.

Mrs. Chilton would harbor bitter feelings toward Thomas Bewick for the rest of her life. Later, she wrote Clara: "Your father is reaping what he has sown, and so not having any other resting place has grown into himself, his children [by the stepmother] are most ill mannered and hatefull & hating one another. I was told . . . he was a stumbling block to his children . . ."[23]

The old couple again left England, family, and lifelong friends, sold everything they owned, and moved back to the Wisconsin farm to take over Clara's duties at home. Despite her father's objections, she entered the University of Wisconsin in Madison at the age of twenty-one. It was a welcome adventure for the grateful young scholar.

Wisconsin University
April 14, 1867

My dear Grandfather & Grandmother,

I had Latin, Mental Philosophy and geometry—only three studies. I asked Prof. Pickard what else I should take and he said "Nothing," but I felt as if I ought to do more and so . . . I decided to go into the advanced Latin class which was reading Cicero. Mr. Matson is going to preach here next Sunday. I do wish you could hear him. I would not miss it for anything. . . . [A]s you will see from the account I send you, I shall no doubt get along very well. And now let me say for the fiftieth time, "Do not under any circumstances worry about me." Don't get lonesome . . . and may God bless and keep us for each other. With 1,000 kisses, I remain your loving granddaughter,

Clara Bewick

Tuition	9.00
Books	1.50
Hat	2.00
Hoop Skirt	1.00
Chimneys	.27
Tax	.25
Belt	.40
Stamps	.15
Corset string	.07
Pencil & paper	.13
—and vinegar	.13
Cash in hand	.10
Sum total	$15.00[24]

Later she wrote:

> Dearest Belovedest Grandfather and Grandmother,
>   We all like the Preceptress very much, but I do not like the new arrangement yet. We do not go up to school til a quarter of ten. (That's so we shan't meet the young gentlemen. They go at nine.) And then we can't come down til one o'clock. We . . . attend Chemistry lectures with the young gentlemen but then a teacher goes with us to see that we don't come to any harm. There are about 70 girls at school.[25]

After receiving a letter from Clara saying that she was having a midnight suitor after having gone to bed ("Somebody sent his card, so I had to fix up again quick as lightning"), Grandma decided it was definitely time to move to Madison, leaving the Bewick family to fend for themselves. Having now a limited income, the Chiltons bought a boarding house in Madison and Clara moved in with them. The old folks were gratified when Clara finally rebuked her suitor, saying: "You must always remain bad, as long as you are not a Christian."[26]

Most university classes were held in Bascom Hall, a splendid four-story, white-columned brick building topped with an elegant dome, with large southern and northern dormitories on either side, situated on a high hill overlooking Lake Mendota. The grounds and wide paths were rimmed with flower gardens and huge apple trees that showered blossoms along the paths in spring to form a fragrant white carpet. From classrooms, students had a panoramic view of sailboats gliding on the lake amid flocks of swooping gulls. At dusk, twinkling lamps and guitar music from the boats lured young people to the narrow footpaths of the lake to smell the moist earth, to hear the rhythmic lapping waters along the shores, an ideal setting for lovers. In her diary for 1868, Clara recorded five suitors.

Clara studied vigorously but also found time for winter sports such as well-chaperoned tobogganing, and she was popular with her classmates. In 1869 she was graduated valedictorian of her senior class of six young ladies—the first graduating class of women from the University of Wisconsin female college—and Phi Beta Kappa.[27]

An unforeseen snag developed at the last moment before graduation when a college official refused to present diplomas on the grounds that "never will I be guilty of the absurdity of calling young women bachelors."[28] He was prevailed upon to change his mind by six irate scholars and the university staff. The graduation ceremony went on as planned.

Clara wore a garland of fresh white rosebuds in the long hair cascading down her back as she proudly took the podium. Her valedictory essay prophesied her future:

> ... Dear companions of by-gone days ... A broader and nobler life lies before us. Let us hasten to make it our own. Solemn responsibilities await us, let us not evade them ... and what you do, do quickly. Work today— your fellow creatures are everywhere dying around you. Their souls are starving for the bread of life.... [S]et your face sternly against wrong in every shape; in devoting yourself to the service of others ... [w]e ought to have constantly before us the thought that we are not living for the moment merely, but that everything we do is done for eternity.[29]

Among the curious spectators sat the popular captain of military cadets, a Civil War hero dressed in a smart uniform that set off his dark good looks. Leonard Colby had only recently moved into the Chiltons' boarding house, and now his piercing eyes fastened on the young valedictorian as she returned to her seat after a well-earned ovation.

Clara was astounded when Dr. Chadbourne called her aside at the reception following the ceremony and offered her a position on the faculty for the coming year, with the clear understanding that in future her salary would be raised. He agreed to pay her $400 the first year "for teaching four classes, and $100 for any additional class it might be necessary to assign ..."[30] Clara was to teach courses in History, Latin, and chemistry. Her friends and family were proud—all but her father, who still felt the instructors were nothing but heathens and his daughter was about to join them on their journey to hell.

The summer of 1869 was a busy one for Clara as she prepared class plans and sewed her wardrobe for the coming fall semester, but it was also a romantic one. "Leon," as she called her grandparents' new boarder, went home to Freeport, Illinois, for a brief vacation but returned suddenly in July. On August 5, 1869, Leonard and Clara discovered they were coeval—they shared the same birthdate. From then on, his attentions to Clara became obvious, and Grandmother Chilton had all she could do to keep her eyes wide open in a home now filled with emotional tension and covert glances. Grandfather slept peacefully at night, but Grandmother listened for the slightest footstep, the softest knock.

Scented lace handkerchiefs joined books and pencils, and the once simple home for young students now erupted room by room with vases of fresh tulips, roses, and wildflowers.

Two things bothered Grandmother Chilton about Colby: He did not go to church and he was vague and mysterious about his comings and goings.

Clara's brother William, two years older and her closest sibling and dearest friend, was informed about the sly suitor. William had been his mother's favorite son and Clara's confidant. He dearly loved his sister and felt duty-bound to protect her. Had his mother lived, she would have been concerned above all with Clara's spiritual welfare. Brothers were constantly reminded at home that "Woman is so formed as to be dependent on man. The woman who is considered the most fortunate in life has never been independent, having been transferred from parental care and authority to that of a husband . . ."[31]

William's career as a farmer and Baptist minister of a small congregation gave him deep satisfaction. A well-respected member of his community and a solid family man, he did not possess his father's brilliance, but inherited a profound Christian belief that stabilized his life and made him a sincere and trusted minister of his faith. To some he may have seemed a bigoted, narrow man, but his anxieties came from genuine concern for his sister's welfare.

William did not mention Leon to Clara, but waited for her to confide in him. But that day did not come. William resorted to hovering about, trying to find out what Colby was up to with his innocent sister. Father Bewick had little time for her after she disregarded his advice not to enter the university.

William's suspicions grew to alarm when he found his sister meeting Colby secretly for a long walk, hand in hand, around Lake Mendota on a balmy summer afternoon. He watched them through a spyglass as they rowed out on the lake unchaperoned. William even appeared in disguise, following by boat under the bending branches along the shore to within earshot, only to snag on an underwater root. The lovers, preoccupied with each other and oblivious to the world, soon rounded a bend and rowed out of sight.

Clara said nothing about Colby to her grandparents. They all sat down for meals together—Grandfather at the head, charming and witty, and Grandmother at the far end of the table, with the two young people sitting directly across from one another. Not a word was spoken between Clara and Leon, while Grandfather tried to engage them in conversation. Neither would look at the other, but there were many secret smiles. Grandmother yearned to grab Leonard Colby around his evasive neck and wring the life out of him, but her religious convictions made even the thought of it a sin.[32]

The fall term at the university brought more boarders and gave Grandmother plenty of work to keep her busy, but she kept one eye on Colby, nonetheless. Clara's classes were a sensation, well attended, and "she greatly endeared herself to her pupils."[33] The only notice of disquiet was the striking captain of cadets, who appeared too often before and after classes. Despite Grandmother's vigilance, Clara found velvety rose petals sprinkled in her bedcovers and poems slipped under her door.

Clara's behavior contained contradictions she had to resolve: Should femininity win over self-fulfilling achievement? During the summer of 1870, Clara asked for a raise to the same wage level paid to male instructors. She wrote to the University Executive Committee but got no reply. After classes began, she continued to try to reach the committe with her request: " . . . relying on the encouragement given me by Dr. Chadbourne," she wrote, "I take the liberty of requesting an increase of salary."[34] In the middle of the semester she received a letter from the vice president: "There is very little probability that such an exigency will occur next term. It is important that I should know immediately, what, in this state of the case, your decision is? Cordially, J. W. Sterling."[35]

Clara was disappointed and insulted. She had been asked to teach at the university directly after graduation—a singular honor—yet she was paid less than beginning male instructors. The wage was based solely on gender—not on her work. Instead of seeking a compromise, she proudly resigned. The university regents sent her a hastily written note: "Your resignation under date of 8th inst. received. It will be regarded as taking effect at close of this term. . . . Regretting the necessity of you thus terminating your connection with our institution, I remain Your Obedient Servant, N. B. VanSlyke."[36] Clara's prestigious career as a university instructor ended almost as soon as it began.

In December 1870 Clara accepted a position teaching at Fort Atkinson, a town about forty-five miles east of Madison. She went there the first week in January, much to the consternation of her grandparents, who did not want her to live away from home. Captain Colby, still boarding with them, finished his senior year in December, with honors as valedictorian of his class. He received a degree in civil engineering and mechanical engineering and the recommendation for a lieutenant's commission in the United States Army. Within six months, he had also obtained a law degree.[37]

After Clara left Madison, Grandmother Chilton wrote to her often, expressing how much they missed the granddaughter they nicknamed "Pie," and revealing Colby's continued interest in her.

January 9, 1871

My Beloved Child,

After you left I felt as if someone had beat me. . . . GF would not trust himself to speak of you at first, but now almost every meal he has something to say. "I wonder how Pie is getting on!!" . . . I think of you as usual almost every hour in the day. I need not say as times are hard, be careful of your money. You need not fear we shall easily neglect or forget you, so cheer up. . . .[38]

January 22, 1871

My Beloved Child,

Today at dinner Jones [a boarder] said "Let me see, Clara has been gone 2 weeks."

"Yes," I said. "It seems more like 3 months." C. looked as if he would shove his plate over the table. G.F. said he would like to take a sleigh and go to see you. I said if he did I must [looking down the table] enlist Mr. C. to take care of him which, in spite of his solemn face, made him laugh—the others too. I think C. might be a little more sociable. God bless you my Dear Child.[39]

By January 25 a slight change had come over Grandmother as she watched Leonard restless and unhappy at Clara's absence:

I was glad when C. said he should write and ask you to come home. He sat down and wrote here. . . . I should like to have asked C. to go to church for I wish he would, but I did not like to appear to use my influence, and he is not very communicative. Perhaps 'tis bashfulness, perhaps 'tis fear.[40]

On January 29 Grandmother sorely missed Clara and Grandfather went into a depression:

My dear child we do think of you as our own dear little girl and hope tho' now for the present separated it may not be for long. There is nothing here worth living for if we cannot be with those we love. . . . I am sorry GF is so poorly and is obliged to go to bed—he says he feels as if all his limbs fail him. God is our refuge and strength.[41]

On February 8, Grandmother was trying to convert Leonard:

C. has stayed an hour tonight. . . . His cough is rather bad so I have prescribed for him. I told C. if he was not so much engaged I should wish him to read it, [Bible teachings] he said he would. I believe it would do him good, it appears to me the right way to get the gospel before the sinner and to leave the Spirit to work His own work in the heart. My dear child pray keep from picking your nose—just put Glycerine at night.[42]

[no date]

My Beloved Pie,

What is the reason you did not send me my usual letter on Saturday? Also there is another disappointed as well as myself for he came to me in the kitchen this morning to ask if I had had a letter. When I said no, he said, neither have I, since Monday. G.F. . . . coughed full an hour last night. I thought he would be choked. I hope he will be spared until you come home to stay. C. has been bad too. All my doctoring failed, although I believe he took it faithfully. He has a constant hacking cough, so yesterday he stayed for prayers and wrote your letter. G.F. prescribed camphor for he saw the lungs needed warming and that did him good. After he came from the post office we persuaded him to lie down and I gave him some broth. He was much better and remained so today. . . . C. gave me $20.00 last week, and I have been able to lower my heavy bills.[43]

Soon after, Leonard received a poem from Clara, which lifted his spirits and made him bolder.

> When I talk with other men
> I always think of you.
> Your words are keener than their words
> And they are gentler too.
> When I look at other men
> I wish your face were there
> With its grey eyes and dark skin
> And tossed black hair.
> When I think of other men
> Dreaming alone by day
> The thought of you like a strong wind
> Blows the dreams away.[44]

In February brother William stomped into his grandparents' home after hearing that Colby was secretly visiting Clara at Fort Atkinson. Grandmother Chilton wrote:

William came in yesterday in order to have some understanding with Colby as he had heard you were engaged etc. and they had a long conversation on the subject. William spoke pretty freely to him and as a Christian brother should do. Mr. C. said his intentions were perfectly honorable etc. and that when the time arrived to be married they would all know it; . . . and now may the Lord have compassion on you both and for Jesus sake forgive. Your loving Grandmother.[45]

William wrote Clara soon after his talk with Leonard:

> Clara there is a rumor afloat that you are married, but of course I don't believe it. Unless you told me yourself I would not believe that you would consent to a clandestine marriage but one thing I do believe that you and Colby are engaged, but why you are so opposed to saying a word about it to me I have yet to learn. Now if you will bear with me and hear a little what I must say. I shall feel better and seeing it is down in black and white you will have to hear it or throw this letter in the fire. [I] dread to think of what may be the consequences to you, when you have put yourself in his power. When his will is your will and he controls your actions and to a great extent your thoughts. Perhaps you think this is strong language but I cannot find language strong enough to suit my thoughts. Perhaps you take shelter where many a loving, trusting one has before you, in the strength of your faith and in the power of prayer, but if your prayer was earnest and your faith strong enough would you not expect a more immediate result, that is, in the conversion of Mr. Colby ere marriage was entered into. You surely expect that he will be saved at some time and why not now? Does this seem too hard a thing for the Lord? Is not your love for him strong enough that the thought of him being eternally damned is harder to bear than that of losing him in this life? If a man really loves a woman—and if he does not she does not want him—and she . . . in obedience to the word of God and the dictates of her own conscience, tells him that she can not become the wife of a man who has not in his heart believed unto righteousness and with his mouth confessed unto salvation . . .[46]

William went on to quote chapter and verse from the Scriptures to support his warning, and then ended the letter saying:

> So I cannot blame myself for not having spoken. I do not wish to say anything against Mr. Colby for I know nothing against him, that is as a man. The objection I have is that one of the Lord's children that is a part or member of the Lord's body should be joined to a man who does not believe the Bible which is making God out a liar. This one flesh which was formerly two is going where? part of it to heaven and part to hell—is not the one sure to drag the other with it? I am as ever your very affectionate and loving Brother, William Bewick.[47]

In March Clara wrote that she was ill, and Grandmother Chilton replied: "I am sorry you had those pains again."[48] Knowing Colby was sneaking off to Fort Atkinson, Grandmother noted:

> I suppose you were very pleased at your visitor. Mr. Colby is yet arrived, but we guess you know . . . you cannot make a Christian of him, you may as well try to change the Leopard's spots . . . I should like to have some talk with C. about his and your future but unless he begins I have no right to interfere tho' I have many thoughts about you. . . . Be careful of yourself . . .[49]

In May Clara was still sick, and Grandmother wrote that she had resigned herself to a marriage:

> My daughter is a prize for any man altho she wore Gingham and her house humble. . . . I am more in the dark than ever, but 3 weeks more and then I suppose Mr. C. will explain. It is not in your interest to keep quiet so long, but I am not going to speak. . . . I hope he will love and care for you as I have, then I will willingly give up my charge to his care—and say my work is done.[50]

On May 29 Reverend Richards, Clara's minister since childhood, wrote a curious letter, as though he had learned or suspected something. Clara had always trusted Reverend Richards, a sensitive and devoted friend:

Dear Friend Clara Bewick,
      . . . I wonder if you will forgive me if I say a word about something which is "none of my business?" Of course you will, for you know me well enough to trust me, I hope, & to believe that I am no meddlesome gossip, & am only anxious for your welfare. All I am going to say is this: Why don't you tell me all about a certain matter (which I need not name), & let me advise & help you? I wish you would, for I have seen that you have fought trouble enough alone in your own mind, & I think you would find relief & help in sympathy & counsel. I am not curious & I know how to hold my tongue. I suppose I know of the matter sooner than anyone in town, perhaps, being told by a gentleman abroad who was anxious for you. But I said nothing to you, nor to anyone about it because I tho't it was your private affair, & if you chose to keep it entirely a secret, I would not seem to intrude. I tho't I would wait till you should say something of it to me yourself. But now, as you are aware, it has become generally

known . . . I had not lisped a syllable of it till it became publicly spoken of. I have since dared what I could privately to stand up for you,
& stop the tongues. Now I am only anxious in the future for your
happiness & usefullness & success. And if you want to talk with me
about it, I think I can help you. . . . But not unless you choose. I am
no priestly confessor, only your Pastor & friend. Think it over & let
me know. . . . Ever Cordially, Your Pastor, C. H. Richards.[51]

Pastor Richards may have been worried about a possible pregnancy, or that
Clara was having a scandalous liaison with a man who was not a Christian,
a concept that three years earlier would have been wholly repugnant to
Clara herself. Ignoring her brother, to whom she had always been devoted,
Clara and Leonard were married by Reverend Richards on June 23, 1871.
A local newspaper noted:

> The groom and bride made their pledges to each other in beautiful language
> of their own. . . . After the ceremony . . . [they] started for the home of the
> husband at Freeport, Illinois. A few classmates and friends attended them
> to the depot, sending after them their heartfelt "God-speed."[52]

Neither Clara's brother William nor her father and many other siblings were
mentioned as being among the wedding guests, or present at the unusually
brief reception and hasty departure, even though nuptials of the time usually included a merry wedding dinner arranged by the bride's father.

The name "Ada Mary" is recorded in the Bewick family records. She is
listed as the "adopted" daughter of Leonard and Clara Colby, who died
when she was less than a year old.[53] No correspondence has been found
regarding Ada Mary from the first full year after the wedding, despite the
fact that Clara was a prolific and faithful correspondent. Nor does the
name Ada Mary ever appear in any of Clara's subsequent writing.

Clara believed that motherhood was divine, but she had a lingering
loathing of pregnancy and the sometimes dangerous aftereffects of childbirth—no doubt reinforced by the memory of her mother's piercing screams
and tragic death in her tenth pregnancy. Of a young woman bearing a
child, Clara wrote:

> The complete physical changes incident to a wife and mother, experienced
> at an immature age, often break down her health and lay the foundation of
> nervous disorders which cause her lifelong suffering. Development of mind
> and body is arrested; the judgement is warped; cheerfulness gives way to
> complaint, or silent endurance increases the strain on the nerves.[54]

CHAPTER 5

The Nebraska Frontier

A year later, Clara left Madison after convalescing from an undefined illness, and joined husband Leonard in Beatrice, Nebraska, where he had gone to set up a law firm.

Oct. 11. 1871

Dear Grandfather & Grandmother,
   I arrived here safe & sound at 5:50 P.M. . . . I never felt better in my life—have not had the headache in the least. . . . This is only to let you know I arrived safe—Leon is a happy boy. Good-by dear ones for the present. I have hardly dared to allow myself to think of you yet. Love to all, Your very loving girl, Clara B. Colby. Hurrah for Nebraska!!! I think I will get along all right now. You must both make calculations to come.[1]

Clara wrote at least three times a week during her first months in Nebraska:

   Beatrice is a very pleasant place and I think you will like it very much. . . . [It] has some very good buildings . . .
   The plants looked very well when I set them out & I put them in a shady place out-of-doors & went out for a walk—While I was gone the wind rose. . . . I found them scorched to death by the hot winds. . . . I suppose if you could see me now you would at last acknowledge that the "realities of life" had come to me. . . .
   Wednesday we found a little house which we could have for just a month & no longer for 12 1/2 dollars. It has 2 rooms & a cook room, all along in a string & not a sign of a closet or shelf in the whole thing. . . . The windows are curtained with Harper's Weeklies which make very picturesque & improving blinds. . . . I must also introduce you to the bedroom & kitchen for here alas! most of my time is

passed. Our poorest clothes are strung round the room & conse-
quently it looks like a rag shop. . . . My safe is invaluable as affording
my only refuge from the horrid mice & flies . . . [2]

Despite her temporary hardships, Clara wanted her grandparents to move
to Beatrice. They were old and ailing, and she knew that eventually they
would need her constant care. She rarely mentioned unpleasant experiences, which was her way, always expecting the best from every situation.
Clara's enthusiasm and intense interest in life appealed to her friend and
fellow suffragist Reverend Olympia Brown (the first American woman
ordained a minister), who later recalled:

> She was optimistic in the extreme and her aspirations lifted her into an
> atmosphere of ideality and exaltation. . . . [A]nd forgetful of the difficulties
> to be encountered . . . she always saw the promised land ahead. Discour-
> agement was a word which had no meaning for her.[3]

Brown exaggerated. Although Clara's spirit always seemed ebullient, there
was another side to her that she shared with no one. She was inclined to
worry, had slight depressions, and tended to cover up her real feelings.
Basically, Clara was intensely private, and in later years she would bury her
heartaches so deeply that few close friends knew she was suffering.

During the first year in Beatrice, Clara's one worry was her grandparents' health. They had willingly sacrificed their comfortable lives in England to make higher education possible for her when few women had had
that opportunity.

> Dear Grandfather,
> . . . Oh! I was so sorry to hear last night that you were sick. You
> must get right well quick . . . I have thought about you lots & lots
> today. You know I love you awfully, and it makes me real blue to think
> of your being sick and I am so far away.[4]

Leonard added a few lines to Clara's letter with his usual wit and peculiar
handwriting, the last letter of each sentence ending in a flamboyant downward spiral:

> Clara has told me to finish her letter to you. And so here goes.
> Well . . . . If you will come out and be a good citizen—law-abiding of
> course—I will give you a present—3 lots to build on. . . . So you must
> make up your mind to come. . . . I am your grand son in law. L. W.
> Colby.[5]

Leonard had gone into law partnership with an old friend, L. B. Sale, in a rented office that had formerly housed a barbershop. The law firm of Colby and Sale specialized in real estate, soldiers' claims, taxes paid for nonresidents, and tax collections.

Leonard immediately began construction of a $600 home, favorably described by a local newspaper as a "medium-sized house, a story and a half high. The right kind of citizens are those who build as soon as they decide upon locating. That's 'business' every time."[6]

Mr. and Mrs. Chilton sent money and Clara wrote:

> I received your note this morning with its welcome contents, welcome because very much needed. . . . You are true blue every time, aren't you! It most makes me cry just now to think how good you are. Some time I hope to be good to you. Leonard thinks that in a year he will have a good business, but of course we could not expect to make money right off. And we have had to constantly pay out. . . . Leonard has been quite bothered but we hope to hear from his father soon & meanwhile your kind loan will keep our heads above water, enable us to go to the Thanksgiving supper, me to hire a woman to help clean the house, etc. I shall have a fire in my bedroom, so you must not worry about my taking cold. . . . The first pennies came in on Saturday, some more to-day, total $1.46. Hurrah Leonard.[7]

Although Clara had watched her mother worked to death and saw her father's labor provide only the barest essentials for his large family, her grandparents furnished the means by which she was able to afford some of the niceties of life. Clara never lacked refinement, even during the first few months when she and Leonard were living in rented rooms.

From the first week, Clara began paying calls in the community to make friends and help publicize her husband's new law firm. With the prodigious strength and energy inherited from her father, she easily made ten visits a day, in good weather and bad. Her efforts paid off. In late November 1872, the Colbys moved into their first real home.

After much coaxing, Clara's grandparents sold their home in Madison and moved to Beatrice in 1874, too frail by this time to care for a home of their own. Clara lovingly watched over them until Grandfather Chilton began to talk more and more about "going home." After a short and painless illness, his vital forces gradually weakened, although his jolly nature never left him and his mind remained clear. On February 13, 1877, Grandfather passed away peacefully in the presence of his wife of fifty years and his devoted stepgrandaughter, who had loved him as a father. Clara wrote his obituary and noted that "on the coffin was a wreath of pure flowers prepared by loving hands," no doubt the hands of "Pie." Leonard planted a tree at the head and foot of Grandfather's grave in remembrance of a man he greatly admired, a proper Englishman who had given him "wise counsels and unselfish affection."

Two years later, in 1879, Grandmother Clara Medhurst Chilton died, expressing a great desire "to be reunited" with her husband. One of her grandsons, in writing her eulogy, might well have been describing Clara Colby instead: "Had Dickens met grandmother he would have made her all his own. Her clear intellect, her determination, her brusque comments on the follies and vices of the day, her wit . . . would have delighted the great student and painter of character. . . . It would be impossible to associate with such traits the faintest shadow of hypocrisy. She ever bore with her the pure diamond of truth."[8]

After the loss of her grandparents, Clara became restless. The adventure of her early days in Beatrice had settled into the monotony of each windswept prairie day. After eight years of marriage, she realized that she might never have children. It is possible that after the death of Sarah, and then Ada Mary, Clara would not risk the possibility of another infant's death.

With a housemaid, a nice home, and with friends among the wealthiest people in town, Clara had little in common with her poorer pioneer sisters who endured untold misery, living in shanties or houses made from sod, called "Nebraska marble." Clara had little use for "dugout" living: "These places [are] unhealthy and gloomy at the best, are ruinous to mind and body if long inhabited. Yet there are men and women degenerated into mere animals, who dwell in these holes . . . [and] even learn to like them."[9]

Poor families sometimes subsisted on hominy—boiled corn or wheat—for a week at a time, but the Colbys ate meat twice a day. Coffee and teas were beyond the means of many, while Clara served a daily English high tea, "strong & fragrant, with cream & sugar, bread and butter . . . and jam & cheese—maybe a bit of cold meat, & little raisin tea cakes or poundcake."[10] Some women on the frontier lacked the few pennies necessary for postage, but Clara wrote as many as fifteen letters a day. With the advantages of an extraordinary education, travel experience on two continents, a refined appearance complemented by a British accent, and a clever lawyer for a husband, Clara's life differed greatly from that of the average pioneer woman's.

Nebraska in the 1870s was not without its terrors. Lurid tales of Indian raids, especially against white intruders in Lakota country, understandably terrified newly arrived white women, who lived in constant dread of the Indian.

When Indians found settlers taking over their land, cutting down trees and clearing large areas of protective vegetation, leaving ugly wagon tracks, piles of burned trash, and filthy makeshift outhouses on the prairie, they retaliated by making themselves as annoying as possible. They stared into windows, rudely barging into cabins without knocking to demand food (something an Indian would never do in his own village, where tribal etiquette was strictly observed). Constant needling, like begging, often resulted in a handout from a frightened householder. Bloodshed occurred when the buffalo were slaughtered for their tongues and left to rot in piles, or when living conditions became intolerable for Indians—usually after much provocation on the part of settlers, miners, or military intruders. Atrocities happened on both sides, but the barbarity of whites went unreported while the slightest threat from an Indian would make front-page news.

Neighborly relations between settlers and Indians were not sensational enough to sell newspapers. Norwegian pioneer Amanda Olson's experience with Indians is remembered only through oral tradition:

> Amanda was alone with her children one day while her husband was away for a fortnight. As she stood outside her sod home hanging clothes, fifteen or twenty Indians approached on horseback. Although they did not display hostility, Amanda was frightened. A man dismounted and walked toward her. Amanda stood her ground, afraid to show fear as her young children played around her skirts. The man gave the "sign" that his people were thirsty and needed water. After they had taken water, he looked over at her much-used wooden washtub and washboard. He "signed" that he wanted to take them, and Amanda was too terrified to refuse. After they had gone, she sat down on the ground and burst into tears. She thought she had surely seen the last of her washtub. A week passed. Early one morning, Amanda was awakened by clinking noises in the yard. When she looked out, she could see nothing except the washtub and washboard placed conspicuously in front of her sod home. She ran over to it, looked down, and was amazed to find the tub filled with enough meat jerky [wound carefully around sticks] to feed her family for months.[11]

Another pioneer wife had a heartening experience:

> A Yankton [Ihunktonwan Dakota] woman wearing a new dress of trader's cloth approached a farm wife. They exchanged greetings. The Indian woman came directly to the point, saying "Man [husband] . . . bad hunt." Then she pointed to three chickens and then to some beadwork she had brought to trade. The farm wife shook her head and made her own bid. "Man [husband] . . . no money," she said, looking down at her faded dress.

She pointed to the three chickens and then to the Indian woman's new dress. Silently, the women exchanged garments without embarrassment, and the Yankton took the chickens home to feed her hungry children. This rapport was genuine; practical needs were met, and the outcome was not determined by treaty negotiations.[12]

Clara never knew an Indian, never traded with one, and if she saw any, it was only in passing. She was a well-meaning reformer, typical of the late-nineteenth century, and believed in "civilizing" the Indians through Christianity. Like most reformers, she truly believed she was a "friend" of the Indians. Historian Frederick E. Hoxie wrote that such reforms "proved disastrous for Indian people."[13] Clara had no way of knowing this. She had not the slightest fear of Indians, and apparently thought highly of the Lakota people, yet she saw them as most whites did—as a dying race.

She had once written a long narrative poem while in college, one that was riddled with errors about Lakota religion, entitled "The Song of the Plains" and dedicated to the "pioneers of the prairies."

> And white men from beyond the dawn have come
> And bought our lands and paid for them with blood.
> Among my people they sowed seeds of woe.
> And e'en my power to their service yoked.
> My children hear and heed my voice no more:
> But as some giant oak, into whose heart
> Disease has crept, will flourish for a time.
> Then, one by one, the branches fade and fall.
> Until a bare and withered trunk it stands
> For the first storm to fell—e'en so decay.
> With slow and certain blight has seized upon
> The Red Man: and the nation which agone
> Flourished with branches wide and rootlets deep.
> Now tottering stands, and in it leafless age.
> Casts but a shadow of its coming doom.[14]

Reformer and newspaper publisher Horace Greeley, who made popular the saying, "Go West, young man," died in November 1872, the same year that Elizabeth Cady ("Kate") Stanton made front-page news across the nation lecturing for woman suffrage, a subject remote from the busy lives of Beatrice's women. Clara's daily routine and those of her wealthy friends centered around religious and civic duties, but she had been trained as a college professor. When she saw that Beatrice lacked a public library, where women as well as men might better themselves through knowledge, she and others began a community drive to collect books. Leonard supported her efforts, and the collection was temporarily housed in his law office.

The women tried all sorts of experimental projects to make money, including what the local newspaper called "the original, world renowned, genuine and only Mrs. Jarley's Hydrostatic, steam-dried, Reversible Wax Works. The above entertainment to be given under the auspices of several of the enterprising ladies of Beatrice and it is something entirely new."[15] At the same time, Clara was reportedly selling "Seward's famous book of travels . . . and her lengthy list of subscribers would indicate that she is meeting with good success."[16]

Clara appreciated the kind people of Beatrice, and thought of herself "before all . . . a western woman," but in the 1870s there was little intellectual stimulation for an educated woman living in this quiet, conservative village known as "the Queen City of the Blue." Farmers came to town to sell grain, hogs, and other produce, driving slow-moving teams of oxen, stirring up dust that rose and drifted away. The Pacific House on Second Street was the only hotel, and its rooms were rarely filled. The sole lender, the Smith Brothers Bank, was located in one half of a shack; the other half housed a watchmaker. The "sports" of Beatrice, including Leonard Colby, spent a good deal of time at the racetrack and at cockfights, hardly places for a decent woman.

But in 1876 Clara found the intellectual excitement she had craved. Leonard bought the *Beatrice Express,* and for the first time Clara realized the power that came with having her own words in print. Busy editing the newspaper and researching her own well-written articles, she was fulfilled and happy, but Leonard was not. He decided that his own fulfillment would only come with political power. He needed money to run for the Nebraska State Senate, and selling the *Beatrice Express* would provide it. Always supportive of her husband's endeavors, Clara relinquished the paper and saw her husband elected in 1877.[17] A woman was supposed to find her highest glory in the shadow of her husband's career. Although Clara must have felt a great sense of loss, she had gained valuable writing and publishing experience.

In 1883 Leonard ran for judge of the First District against Jefferson H. Broady. At first, the attacks against his candidacy were good-natured and Clara rather enjoyed them:

> There are strong probabilities that Mr. Colby will not be elected district judge in which event the town site of Beatrice will be perfectly safe.[18]

It was amusing, considering that years before Leonard had talked his way out of nearly being hanged from a bridge after trying to trick the town fathers. But as the campaign progressed, Clara was shocked at the growing charges made against her husband during a heated political campaign. Leonard became the target of powerful newspaper editorial attacks:

> Colby is declared by those who know him best to be given to immorality and base habits.
>
> No man living is inclined to dive deeper or can hold his breath longer in the dirty pool of politics than Mrs. Colby's husband.
>
> . . . Mr. Colby, a married man, now a candidate . . . on the R. ticket, visited the Arlington Hotel at Lincoln in company with a prostitute, and there took lodging for the night. The landlord . . . ordered Colby and the woman to leave. Mr. Colby got down on his knees and begged pitifully to be allowed to remain overnight.[19]

Clara did not believe Leonard would go down on his knees to any man. She dismissed this as merely a political slur and a desperate one. Nonetheless, sordid attacks on her husband's morality must have hurt Clara. Although Leonard was sure the county was "red hot for me," he lost the election.[20]

Leonard traveled a great deal when he was campaigning, but in his spare time he helped organize a company of state militia called the Paddock Guards.[21] An impressive orator, he was called upon to speak at holiday celebrations and lead his men in every parade. On one occasion the Guards were called to the northern border of Nebraska to intercept Chief Red Cloud, reportedly moving south during the "Indian Wars," but the Guards could find no trace of the Indians. The Lakota were masters of the use of light to camouflage and conceal. They preferred to defend themselves or attack in the daytime and move their camps through enemy territory at night. During the day, warriors faded into shadows, through infinite grades of light, space, and dimension—a high art that most white men found impossible to understand, especially large groups of soldiers riding in orderly columns, carrying clattering equipment and bright-colored flags, and shiny swords flashing to signal their whereabouts for miles in every direction, like a lighthouse beacon sweeping over a prairie sea. The Paddock Guards may have looked magnificent, but they never saw one Indian. They were undoubtedly surrounded by invisible Lakota warriors, standing motionless in the shadows of trees along the creek banks or blending into the varied hues of swaying prairie grasses.

Left alone for long periods of time when Leonard was away on business, Clara grew increasingly weary of the tea circuit, restless with the humdrum conversations and predictable Sunday sermons. She wrote her husband often: "Leon—you are the blessedest darling alive & I want to see you awfully—Good night my own boy—God bless & keep us." Leonard responded jokingly, "You are a real nice good dear loving darling girlie wifie. . . . God bless you & keep you for your dear husband (that's me)."[22]

Life was so boring that Clara was more than willing to care for Sara ("Sadie") and Eva, her sister Mary's girls, when Mary went to medical school after her first husband died. Still yearning for more educational stimulation herself, Clara helped arrange lecture courses on various subjects for the "library committee," with the hope of educating women in Beatrice to issues in the world around them.

In the late 1870s, it was Clara's inspiration to invite Susan B. Anthony and Elizabeth Cady Stanton, controversial leaders of the woman suffrage movement, to speak on the role of women in America. They spent the night in Clara's home. Stanton later wrote of her friendship with Clara as one of "confidence & sympathy: For this is the settled state of my mind towards you & always has been since the first day we met in Beatrice."[23] Anthony wrote a four-page thank-you letter referring to Leonard as "your non-believing husband. . . . I long to see women be themselves—not mere echoes of men."[24]

Susan B. Anthony, whom William Henry Channing called the "Napoleon of the movement," had endured public humiliation when she was arrested in 1872 for having voted in a presidential election. Margaret Truman, in her book *Women of Courage,* explained in two words the angry male response surrounding Anthony's terrible deed: "Mustaches twitched."[25]

Clara would later ally with Stanton against Anthony on a number of critical issues, but Anthony was always her personal favorite no matter how hurtful their disputes: "There was nobody like her for encouraging young women each to do her best in her own line. . . . They fell at once under her personal charm, and caught the spirit of her work and doubled her power . . ."[26]

Like Grandmother Chilton, Stanton and Anthony saw the "diamonds" in Clara's eyes that, once directed, caught the rays of hope glimmering dimly in the hearts of thousands of uneducated, abused, and poverty-stricken women. Clara had found her lifelong calling—woman suffrage—in a "free" country where in most states a husband could legally seize his wife's earnings; where a spouse could not testify against her husband; where she was not allowed to own land or enter into a business partnership without his consent; where a mother had no rights to her children. In many places men could not be prosecuted for forcing sexual relations with preadolescent girls.

After total immersion in the woman suffrage movement, Clara's feminine voice became a potent and commanding force against injustice to womankind:

> Man can not be both father and mother in society and the State any more than in the home. Woman suffrage is in harmony with the growth of the idea of the worth of the individual, which has its best expression in our Republic. Our nation is heir to all the struggles for freedom that have been made. In all these achievements women have borne their share. . . . Women love liberty as well as men.[27]

By 1891 Clara was at the height of influence with Susan B. Anthony, spending six months of every year in Washington, D.C., while Congress was in session. Her newspaper, the *Woman's Tribune,* was regarded as the organ of the suffrage cause. While lobbying congressmen on January 23, 1891, Clara received an astonishing letter from her husband, Brigadier General Leonard W. Colby, instructing her to come back to Beatrice at once, as she was now the adopted mother of his "living relic," a full-blood Lakota baby girl taken "from the Pine Ridge reservation after the Massacre at Wounded Knee, . . . and who living, will be one of the most interesting historic figures in the progress of that unfortunate nation, which in the winter campaign of 1890–91 brought four thousand warriors into the field; and who, dying, will close the tribal inheritance of Big Foot's heroic band, whom valor has made immortal and whose blood should make forever sacred the murmuring waters of Wounded Knee."[28]

Clara must have wondered why her husband would have adopted a child without consulting her. True, this was not their only child. In 1883, an orphan train had pulled into Beatrice with a carload of homeless children taken from the streets of New York—wild urchins of various ages, who through the benevolence of eastern humanitarian societies would find clean air and better homes in the West. Some would end up slaving as cooks and fieldhands until they could run away, while some of the girls were taken as "daughters" to provide sexual services for the men who had "saved" them; others found excellent homes with pioneer families.[29]

They had walked from the train hand in hand along the streets to the Beatrice courthouse, where they were inspected by townspeople and farmers. After all the other children had been selected, one curly-haired three-year-old boy sat forlorn on the courthouse steps. No one wanted him. Either Leonard or Clara happened to pass by then and noticed the silent boy. He was taken home, washed up, and named Clarence. It did not take long to discover the boy was developmentally slow. Clarence would never reach the mental age of thirteen and could follow only simple directions. The boy was a "keen disappointment," but Leonard taught him to groom horses. He finally learned the skills necessary to care for his father's majestic Arabians, although he needed to be looked after "to keep him from vicious and demoralizing companions."

Clarence was eleven years old in 1891, and Clara had taken him with her to her winter headquarters in Washington. There she unexpectedly became the surprised mother of an Indian baby. The sudden responsibility seemed more complicated than Clara could imagine. She took her husband's letter directly to her mentor, Susan B. Anthony.

Clara climbed the steps to Miss Anthony's room at the Rigg's House, gathering courage enough to tell her what had happened. How could Clara hold her head up as an outspoken advocate for women if she refused to care for a "pitiful" orphan girl, when the protection of women had been her main goal? It must have been a long walk down the hall to Anthony's room, with the elderly sage's words echoing through Clara's mind: "If I had had a husband and children, or opposition in my own home, I never could have done it. How much depends on the sympathy and co-operation of those around us!"[30] Since the child had been thrust upon her, without preparation or discussion, Clara now questioned how much "sympathy and co-operation" she could expect from her husband. Long accepting of his reckless ways, she left him with the benefit of doubt, but Anthony thought the adoption was an outrage.[31] One of her most important rules was that public scandal or private problems must never take away from the main goal—the vote for women—the enfranchisement of half the population of America.

On the afternoon of January 24, after Clara left the Rigg's House, Miss Anthony collapsed and was at once taken to the home of Mr. and Mrs. William Lloyd Garrison's son, where she remained bedridden until February 2. It was one of several attacks of depression she experienced throughout her long, courageous life.[32] When visitors came to see her or she was asked to attend meetings, Ida Husted Harper noted that Susan "was so prostrated . . . she was unable to attend . . ."[33] Anthony kept a diary for years, but 1891 is unaccountably missing.[34] For the first time in forty years, she chose to rest at home.[35]

Clara disregarded the advice of the woman she most admired in the world. She decided to obey her husband, to do her duty to a female child she had never seen, who might replace in her heart the half-sister Sarah or the infant Ada Mary. Zintkala Nuni (Lost Bird) would be raised and educated as a white child, given every opportunity, with an expensive education provided by a wealthy father. She would be the daughter to follow Clara proudly into the suffrage movement to aid in the betterment of all womankind.

Although Clara would one day change her mind, she believed at that time, as did Richard H. Pratt, the reformer and founder of Carlisle Indian School in Pennsylvania, that Indians removed from their language and their learned cultural heritage could be "saved" from the poverty of reservation life by Christian civilization. They would meld quietly into the American mainstream; or better yet, like the Dakota physician, Dr. Charles Eastman, Lost Bird might rise to fame as an example to her people of the benefits of the white man's world, an "Indian princess" with no recollection of the tragic events of her babyhood, no memory of her Lakota parents who died amid crashing gunfire, writhing in the Dakota snow.[36]

Clara disapproved of the reason her husband took Lost Bird from South Dakota. She would never accept the child as a mascot. Not realizing her own patronization, she vowed to educate Zintkala Nuni to become a refined young woman. Clara made her position clear when she underlined a passage regarding the baby in the January 1891 issue of the *Woman's Tribune*:

> In answer to many inquiries the editor of the *Tribune* . . . will state that, for herself, she rejoices in this opportunity, by the care and education of this child, to join in expiating, so far at least, the wrongs of our race against hers.[37]

Letters poured into both the Washington and the Beatrice *Tribune* offices asking about the welfare of the little Lakota child. Some of the notes contained haunting poems that Clara saved for Lost Bird to read when she grew up. On December 5, 1891, Harriet N. Ralston of Washington, D.C., sent this offering:

> The blood of a people undaunted of spirit
> Enriches the soil that of right they inherit.
> But ours is the shame, and til ages grow hoary,
> The pale-face shall blush in recounting thy story.
> Zintka Lanuni. Lost Bird!
> Daughter of Destiny! Heaven defends thee.
> Waken to life and to love that it sends thee.
> Within thy dark eye the race-fires are relighted.
> To glow in a type of humanity righted!
> Zintka Lanuni. Lost Bird![38]

CHAPTER 6

The Lion of the Party

Colby named the baby Marguerite Elizabeth on official adoption forms, but his cronies in Beatrice had already dubbed the Indian child "Leonarda." When Clara found out, she wrote a strong protest. She said that the child had been given "the melancholy but musical and soft-sounding Indian name" of Zintkala Nuni by her own people—that was her name! It was a difficult spelling, and from then on the Lakota baby's name was misspelled and mispronounced by everyone. To avoid confusion, Clara called her "Zintka" or "Zintkala."

After Zintka was taken from her mother's body and placed in an alien environment, she began her precarious life, treated alternately as "heroic princess" and "pitiful waif" or "dirty squaw" and "savage heathen," depending on who was looking at her in the glass case of her existence, forever a curiosity on public view.

Dr. Mary White, Clara's sister, said to have been the first woman physician in Nebraska, took care of Zintka until Clara returned to Beatrice on May 1, 1891—a telling four-month lapse.[1] Widowed at an early age, Dr. White had been remarried to lawyer Charles E. White in 1881. With the addition of the little Indian guest and the stream of visitors to see her, Dr. White needed more help. She hired a good-natured, rosy-cheeked German girl, Marie Miller (originally Möeller), as governess. "Maud," as they called her, had been Clara's kitchen maid since she was a girl and now, at seventeen, she was trusted enough to be chosen as a nursemaid. Maud was a pretty young woman from an industrious immigrant family, but she was crude; she uncorked bottles with her teeth and often made indecent comments at inappropriate times.[2] Clara felt these were simply cultural and educational deficiencies that she could gently correct, if she ever had time. Always protective of young girls like Maud, Clara had encouraged Leonard when he was a senator in the 1880s to introduce a bill in the Nebraska State Legislature raising the age of sexual consent from ten to fifteen. She would have preferred the age of eighteen, but was pleased nonetheless when the bill passed.

Clara's outrage over prostitution, child molestation, and white slavery, which she called "the most degrading servitude that hellish passions can conceive," led her to write an expose in the *Woman's Tribune* about the anguished condition of young girls lured into prostitution:

> I have traveled all through the section where the most notorious of these dives are located, and by representing myself as a procurer (Madam) and afterward as the proprietor of a dive looking for girls, I was able to see for myself what the press has never dared to publish.[3]

Clara found poverty-stricken girls of ten and twelve being sold by their own fathers and brothers, with no recourse but suicide or sordid lives of disease and degradation. She warned her readers:

> No woman can say it is no concern of hers, for in one shape or another the demon of lust lies in wait at every door. Every woman should place her daughters and employees on their guard against confiding in strangers who . . . lead them . . . to their ruin.[4]

Determined to protect the young women who worked for her, Clara told them never to open the door to a male stranger unless she was at home to determine his intentions. A local newspaper described the unexpected reception given a man who visited Clara's home without an invitation:

> One night, a would-be thief attempted to go through the house. . . . [Clara] heard the noise and, hastening below stairs, she came upon the fellow in a closet, into which, through a window, he had just effected an entrance. . . . [She] grasped him by the collar . . . engaged in the delightful occupation of pounding his head against the books and calling for help . . . [5]

She beat his head against a bookcase, and when the police arrived Clara delivered the unconscious criminal into the hands of the law.[6] Clara stood five feet nine inches in her stocking feet, a woman of enormous vitality. She was a pacifist until her family faced personal danger—then it was altogether another story.

Maud's employment considerably eased the workload for Dr. White. Her little charge, the Lakota "princess," ran the White household from the moment she was placed in a sunlit private nursery—a well-meaning mistake. In Victorian times it was a privilege for a child to have a room of her own. Clara and Mary had shared a room as children, and thought themselves fortunate to have privacy from their numerous noisy, bothersome brothers. But a Lakota baby did not normally sleep alone at night. Up to the age of puberty or later, she snuggled close to an aunt, or perhaps her cousins and—if chosen the lucky one—with Grandmother. Held in her mother's arms or wrapped in blankets and buffalo robes with her sisters was the natural way to breathe the frosty winter air. To the Lakota of the Northern Plains in 1891, shutting a baby away by herself all night was unthinkable.

Remembering Zintka's weakness for upper respiratory ailments (Dr. White's vigilance had kept Zintka alive after her first bout with pneumonia), Aunt Mary provided her sister's adopted daughter with the very best of everything.

In Dr. White's house, trimmed with gingerbread fretwork, Maud would rock Zintka to sleep while everyone tiptoed past her nursery. This Anglo-Saxon custom was entirely different from Zintka's former life, when the sound of drumbeats near and far away relaxed Lakota babies instantly to sleep—the louder the drum and the singing, the more comforting, like a mother's rhythmic heartbeat.

Zintka was lifted from her swinging wicker crib and fed from a silver-ringed bottle, always on schedule, never on demand, since Victorians believed in a proper nursery timetable, a long-honored method of rearing healthy babies. In contrast, Lakota mothers gave their breasts naturally for gratification and nourishment. Ethnocentric ignorance, not intentional malice, produced an unnatural and unhealthy environment for the Indian child, but who among Clara's immediate family could know the damage being done? Despite Dr. White's professional handling, Zintka coughed and coughed.

Sarah (known as Sadie), Eva, Dorothy, and Charlotte, Mary's funny and frolicsome daughters, built their days completely around Zintka's every baby delight. They adored her. In the passageways and parlors, the nursery and the spacious yard, four creamy cherub faces followed the baby and her nurse everywhere. They brought dancing, jointed-limbed paper dolls with real velvet and satin slippers to visit her nursery, a room decorated in filigreed white wicker, softened with pink fabrics and lined with toys: calico dolls with yarn hair and button eyes, wooden sleighs, and carved birds.

Morning glories along the picket fence brought the lively sisters out of doors in spring and summer to their secret garden playhouse. When Zintka was awake, the girls pulled Maud and the baby to their "exquisite" miniature house furnished with small wooden chairs and a table set with little blue and white china dishes. They played croquet and practiced archery on the lawn under the cherry trees.[7] In their world of fantasy Zintka was a visiting "faerie" princess. They offered her nibbles of jam tarts while Maud, still a teenager, also enjoyed the fetes and little dramas staged on Zintka's behalf. Dressed in white sleeveless pinafores to protect their clothes, the girls sometimes persuaded "Uncle Leon" to take them to his Arabian stables to feed the free-roaming peacocks and to watch "Old Black John and the white horses."[8] Uncle was fond of reading to children, and on one occasion after a picnic lunch, he eloquently read Longfellow's poem "The Song of Hiawatha" to his enthralled audience.[9]

Mary's medical practice and her husband's considerable income provided a lovely home and office. Although prosperous, Mary was practical and never ostentatious. A woman physician making house calls in her own black buggy was a rarity, especially on the frontier, but Mary invited no undue attention. She worked quietly and with dignity, and the women of Beatrice were grateful to have her.

While Mary kept Zintka, Clara had remained in her Washington *Tribune* office performing the usual journalistic duties, proving to Miss Anthony that although she had accepted the responsibility of the Indian child, this change in her life would in no way interfere with her devotion to woman suffrage.

On February 5, 1891, Clara lectured at the Women's National Press Association in Washington. The speech was entitled "The Waif of Wounded Knee," an enthusiastic discourse on the daughter she had never laid eyes on.[10] As the distinguished guests listened, Clara related the exciting tale of Zintka's escape after the massacre and her husband's daring rescue (as he had told the story to her). Describing Zintka's recuperation from her ordeal, Clara read from one of Mary's letters: She is a "bright, happy . . . baby, whom no one could help loving."[11] It was evident to everyone present that Clara was looking forward to motherhood. She ended her speech by saying:

> "The little dusky maid, although a full-blood Indian of the most warlike and uncivilized race, seems to take kindly to all the favors of civilization. She is well formed, she has a pleasant face and winning smile, regular features, and withal, a dignified and queenly bearing."[12]

During Clara's long delay in returning to Beatrice, Dr. White instructed Maud to feed Zintka ample portions of pabulum mixed with cow's milk— plenty of milk, yet another well-meaning Anglo fallacy. Although there was no Indian wetnurse in Beatrice, a white woman's breast milk would have been better than cow's milk. Many Lakota babies could not digest cow's milk, and full-blood Lakota adults often found it even more difficult.[13]

Cow's milk caused intestinal distress and was a perfect breeding ground for bacteria. Moreover, Victorian dairies where unhygienic: utensils were not sterilized, nor were milk temperatures regulated during transportation.

Dr. White had no way of knowing that the mental and physical needs of Indian children were not the same as the needs of white children. As reformers, she and the Colbys believed that because theirs was the dominant culture, the culture of progress and of Christian wholesomeness, they had "saved" the child from a life of drudgery, poverty, heathenism, and barbarity. Given time, they were sure Zintka would become accustomed to her new "civilized" life, a life they felt would offer better nutrition, an excellent education, and a more comfortable way of life.[14]

Meanwhile, in Washington, Clara continued to throw herself into suffragist work. She was tireless in organizing the National Woman's Suffrage Convention to be held on February 26.[15] A frequent guest in her home during this period was Dr. Mary Edwards Walker, who years before had disregarded the prejudices against women entering the medical profession. At the age of sixteen, Mary exchanged skirts for trousers: After graduating from medical school, she wore a man's frock coat and top hat, carried a cane, and wore a large and conspicuous pocket watch and chain.[16] During the Civil War, she had traveled behind Confederate lines to tend wounded Union soldiers, and was captured and sent to prison at Richmond. The "Confederate Army didn't know what to do with a woman prisoner and was therefore eager for [her] exchange . . ."[17] She was treated well and released unharmed. Five months later she became the only woman ever to receive the Congressional Medal of Honor—the highest military honor of the United States.[18] Later, the government took the medal back because she was a woman, and it would be decades before the honor was rightfully restored to her.

Clara appreciated Dr. Walker's brilliance but, seeing her oddly dressed friend coming up the steps, she would quickly close the curtains covering her front windows for fear the neighbors would see the eccentric lady.[19] Although a feminist, Clara was also feminine and conservative.

About this time, Leonard left Zintka with his sister-in-law and her family in Beatrice and traveled south to oversee the sale of 15,000 acres of land. In 1889 phosphate rock had been found in Florida. It did not take land speculators like Colby long to float articles in leading newspapers about the great discovery. Within six months, ten thousand feverish prospectors had overrun the swamps, hacking down orange groves and destroying the habitat for plant and animal life. They dredged for pebbles with costly pumps as the excitement spread. Colby acquired enough land to make an enormous profit and dug until he found a few pieces of phosphate and a load of ancient bison bones, the proof he needed to show that there was phosphate on the property.[20] It was clear and legal profit.

Clara did not question her husband's business dealings, let alone his whereabouts. On February 12, 1891, Leonard arrived in Tavares, Florida, on the 6:30 morning train. After roaming the beach along the lake adjoining the village, he wrote tenderly to Clara:

> My Dear Wife.
> Have just taken a walk in the sand. . . . I found some of the wild, yellow, sweet-scented Jessamine . . . I send you Jessamine & other posies including a little blue orchid.
>
> Yours.
> L. W. Colby[21]

Clara pressed these flowers and kept them, as she had often done in the past. There had been ample evidence over the years that the childless couple remained devoted to each other, and their romantic attachment was often reflected in the pages of the *Woman's Tribune*. On one occasion Clara wrote:

> . . . A noble spiritual atmosphere lifts my daily life from a common routine into a loving pleasure. Taking my face in his hands he has lovingly said: "Would I had wealth that I could place you a queen among women." With such a king for a husband, am I not walking in a queen's garden?[22]

Earlier, Clara told Elizabeth Boynton Harbert: "The writer wishes that some of the authors . . . about Woman Suffragists' homes could peep into this one, sanctified by perfect love and trust, remembering at the same time that the unhappy home is the exception in our ranks, and not the rule."[23]

Clara's suffragist newspaper also reflected changing views on motherhood. She reviewed new books on child care while organizing Miss Anthony's seventieth birthday banquet, to be held on February 15 at the Rigg's House, calling on her suffragist sisters to enshrine the "holy day."[24] A *Washington Post* article mentioned Clara's eloquent testimonial at the reception for "Saint Susan."[25]

With Leonard's blessing, Clara had made Washington, D.C., her winter headquarters six months of every year since 1888. Along with her many journalistic and suffragist duties, Clara was now trying to figure out a way to keep her newspaper in Washington and also bring her family together under one roof year-round. Tirelessly, Clara and other suffragist leaders lobbied among the wives of state legislators, conservative Supreme Court justices, and every member of President Benjamin Harrison's cabinet. In addition to her efforts to obtain the vote for women, Clara wanted to find a job in government for Leonard.

For the first time in fourteen years, Republicans controlled both houses of Congress as well as the presidency. The United States Senate was called the "millionaire's club" and Congress the "billion-dollar congress."[26] With money flowing freely, Washington society women hosted an endless round of elegant parties and splendid receptions.

Money was important, but Washington wives knew as much, if not more, of the goings-on behind the scenes in government circles than their distinguished elected or appointed husbands; more political appointments were inveigled in front parlors, at the Friday Morning Music Club, than through the normal all-male channels. At the dinner table, wives of leading lawmakers learned who was on his way out and who was eagerly waiting to replace him. Through an underground system of trusted servants, messages were written on flowered calling cards and delivered discreetly through kitchen entrances. Of course, women were exempt from political rules, having never been allowed equality to play the game in the first place.

As in most political administrations throughout the world, powerfully subtle suggestions, given by wives and mistresses to their husbands and lovers at vulnerable moments, could work miracles of persuasion and change countless lives in the nation's capital.

Two of Clara's special friends included the motherly and domestic Caroline Scott Harrison, a talented painter, pianist, and horticulturist, cofounder and first president of the Society of the Daughters of the American Revolution and, incidentally, wife of the President of the United States, Benjamin Harrison; and Mrs. William H. H. Miller, the wife of the U.S. attorney general, who was "Mrs. Harrison's most intimate friend in Washington."[27] It was no secret that Mrs. Harrison bent the rules a bit and was, at the beginning of her husband's administration, a powerful influence.

In late February 1891, Clara saw both Mrs. Harrison and Mrs. Miller on various occasions. Mrs. Miller showed an avid interest in the story of Clara's newly adopted Indian daughter, as did Mrs. John W. Noble, the wife of the Secretary of the Interior. The latter was especially curious, since her husband was under direct fire in major newspapers across the nation for his controversial views. He contended that Indians on South Dakota reservations had not been defrauded and were not starving, despite numerous official reports to the contrary.[28]

Encouraged and advised by Miss Anthony, Clara judiciously let it be known at every opportunity that her husband, General Colby, savior of the Ghost Dance baby, hero of the Civil War, and a patriotic "straight up" Republican lawyer, was available for a Washington appointment.[29] By April 14, 1891, letters of endorsement for Leonard Colby flooded the office of William H. H. Miller, the U.S. attorney general.[30]

On March 19 a reception was given in Clara's honor at the exclusive Park

Avenue Hotel in New York City by the Woman's Suffrage League.[31] Solos by violinists, pianists, cellists, and concert numbers were followed by glowing comments by Miss Susan B. Anthony and Mrs. Lillie Devereux Blake (another of Mrs. Harrison's friends), who spoke of Mrs. Colby's outstanding educational background and her untiring public service achievements, not the least of which was her award-winning newspaper.[32] Something intriguing was astir, something was being whispered behind the perfumed swirl of fine Brussels *point-de-gaz* lace and hand-painted Chinese fans.

On May 1, 1891, after traveling by way of a woman suffrage convention at Englewood, Illinois, Clara—still slim, attractive, and vivacious, looking fifteen years younger than her forty-four years—arrived in Beatrice to rejoin her handsome husband and to meet her famous Lakota daughter for the first time.[33]

Knowing that Miss Anthony would read her homecoming report in the *Tribune*, Clara mentioned the child only after an offhand comment about the scenery:

> So many correspondents have expressed an interest in Zintka Lanuni, the waif of Wounded Knee, that we are sure they will all expect a little mention of her. . . . She has now but a slight cough and a fast fading scar on her cheek to show the result of her terrible four days' exposure on the field of battle. She gets around in her propeller in a very lively way, and if there is any tendency in her to the gravity [solemnity] of her race it has been held in abeyance by being a pet and a plaything of all in the sister's home. . . . She is quite as winning and lovable as babies of her age are apt to be and her awakening intelligence is watched with more than the usual interest.[34]

Clara's understated mention of her precious little bundle undoubtedly did not fool Miss Anthony, whose experienced views on motherhood (she baby-sat for Stanton's children) were well known:

> O this babydom, what a constant, never-ending, all-consuming strain! We should never ask anything else of a woman who has to endure it. I realize more and more that rearing children should be looked upon as a profession which, like any other, must be made the primary work of those engaged in it. It can not be properly done if other aims and duties are pressing upon the mother.[35]

In June 1891, less than a month after Clara returned to her midwestern summer home and office, Beatrice residents were surprised when President Benjamin Harrison unexpectedly appointed one of their own, Leonard Colby, to the illustrious position of Assistant Attorney General of the United States, as provided by act approved March 3, 1891.[36]

During the "gay nineties," an age of excitement and change in the country, portable typewriters came on the market, peanut butter appeared on grocery shelves along with book matches and Wrigley's chewing gum, Thomas Edison's motion picture machine became popular, telephone service was available between New York and Chicago, and the Coca-Cola Company was founded.[37] And General and Mrs. Leonard W. Colby were ready to enter the glitter and prestige of official Washington society.

Several days prior to the public announcement, General Colby opened an envelope addressed to the "Husband of Clara B. Colby."[38] In it was a unsigned barb: "We Kansans congratulate you Gen'l on your appointment & also of being the husband of Clara B. Colby. You are the boy to get there."[39] Washington was known as "a paradise of woman," and with the note, Colby must have realized that "what a man became often depended on his wife and daughters." Leonard may have scoffed, but Clara kept the letter for twenty-five years.

Over the summer, Clara fumbled at motherhood while attending the many social events in her husband's honor. Although distracted with research, writing, editing, printing, and mailing her eight-page newspaper, she occasionally described Zintka's progress: "She has grown rapidly, and is learning everything. . . . She is affectionate, observing, has a shy but fearless gravity with strangers, and with her own family is merry and playful. Her affecting story and winning ways gain the love of all who meet her."[40]

Zintka was over a year old and walking in September when the Grand Army of the Republic held their annual reunion at Grand Island, Nebraska. In a special ceremony General Colby and his men of the Nebraska National Guard were awarded commemorative medals "for their gallant service in protecting the border . . . on the frontier in the late Sioux War."[41] Clara wrote that Zintka was a sensation at the reunion:

> . . . her frequent presence on the review stand around which she ran in fearless play, and her being introduced to the assembled thousands in the amphitheatre, interest or curiosity impelled at least ten thousand persons to seek to see her at her tent, which splendid opportunity the writer made good use of by distributing suffrage literature to all who came. The little dusky maid was thus a missionary in more ways than one.[42]

Shortly after being touched, pinched, patted, and surrounded by thousands of strangers, Zintka was once again placed under Dr. White's care. Mary was the only physician allowed to touch the child because of Clara's distrust of the medical profession after their mother's death at the hands of an inebriated doctor.

Clara could not have managed without Maud, either, whose delicious German food and youthful companionship were pleasing. Although Maud was not refined in manners or speech, the young woman was intelligent, she took directions cheerfully, and she was eager to learn. More important, Zintka liked Maud. But Maud's small waist accentuating womanly curves, and her fresh complexion and sparkling exuberance, did not go unnoticed by others. Her beauty turned heads, but she was not allowed to have male callers. Clara felt responsible for the girl. She had watched her blossom and now hoped to mold her into a fine young woman, protected from the evils she imagined lurking outside the door.

Later that month Clara received an invitation to accompany a prestigious party of twenty-six newspaper reporters to Denver on the newly completed Chicago and Rock Island Railroad. Maud had family concerns and could not accompany Clara; sister Mary was away vacationing and Leonard was on a business trip. In the *Tribune* Clara wrote of her decision to make the trip anyway:

> The editor of the *Tribune* had regretfully declined to accept the invitation but it being very strongly urged that the *Tribune* should be represented on the trip, finally agreed to go on the condition that she might take along the rest of the *Tribune* staff, namely Clarence, and Zintka Lanuni.[43]

In 1891 over 9,000 Americans died in railroad-related accidents and 80,000 were seriously injured, but Clara loved traveling on "the cars" and could not pass up a free trip. The articles she wrote on her many travels were popular with housebound women who rarely had the opportunity to go anywhere except to church. The prosuffrage journalist wanted her readers to enjoy "something of the best that comes its way along all lines of thought and activity . . . to keep life from being monotonous."[44]

The trip to Denver was a symbolic journey Clara would not soon forget. Clarence was never a problem, but Clara now had to face cross-cultural motherhood for the first time alone with Zintka the toddler. Probably over a year and a half old, and always dressed in suffrage white ("A woman can never be too fine while she is dressed in white," wrote Jane Austen), Zintka could run. In fact, despite constant illnesses, she could climb with amazing agility compared to white children of the same age.

Clara settled the two children in a passenger seat, leaving Zintka in the care of Clarence while she prowled the train to get information for her story. At first, the train ride was uneventful, although the passengers stared and whispered while Zintka jumped up and down on her plush-covered seat, snatching feathers out of a woman's hat in the row behind with squeals of delight, her teasing dark eyes peeking over the back of the seat at the glaring matron. Clarence sat placidly with his hands folded in his lap, looking blankly out the window, while Zintka ran up and down the aisle waving her sticky, candied hands. The other passengers drew back and women pulled their skirts aside and guarded their belongings. Clara was so busy interviewing the conductor that she was oblivious to the excitement in the adjoining passenger car.

In Denver they "were received by the Governor of the State and the Mayor of the city where a little congratulatory speech-making was in order. A ride around the city and a visit to the principal buildings . . . proved very enjoyable but the writer was spending these precious hours with an old school friend, Adele Overton Brown, enjoying all those reminiscences of old friends that, like wine, improve with age."

While Clara visited with Mrs. Brown, she left Clarence holding his little sister's hand. A huge floral display "in which the words Chicago, Lincoln, Denver, were wrought in roses" was presented to the head of the party, and during the journey around Denver "under the guidance of enthusiastic Denverites," Zintka rearranged the arrangement.

Clara rejoined the group in Colorado Springs and discovered the floral disaster just as the party was heading up the cog-road to the top of Pikes Peak. She tried unsuccessfully to persuade the conductor to take them "by steam," which would have been much faster, but the slow, "wonderful ascent" on the dangerous cog-road won out: " . . . In about an hour we stood over 14,000 feet . . . and gazed into the infinite distance with awe and gratitude."

Everyone was indeed grateful they had reached the top alive. At 11,000 feet above sea level, Zintka had hung dangerously out of the window, proving herself "the lion of the party." Amused, Clara held on tightly to her legs. Papers and notebooks fell and slid everywhere, along with her hat, handbag, sack of toys, and cloth diapers—but she did not care; the child was seeing something she had never seen before. Clara wanted Zintka to experience the whole world, a world without sexual, racial, or physical repression against women of any kind—a world Zintka might see within her lifetime.

Clara was exhausted by the time they reached the top of Pikes Peak. While taking notes, she turned her back for a moment and Zintka crawled out on a precipice overlooking a drop of thousands of feet! The spectators were horrified, but not Clara. She used the opportunity to teach the child about heights. Clara did not believe in physically punishing children—she believed in educating them. Together they threw a coin over the side of the cliff and watched it fall until they could see it no more. During this experiment, Clara lost her train of thought, she forgot her newspaper, her deadlines, the research, and suffrage meetings ahead. On top of Pikes Peak with her Indian child, Clara had even forgotten Susan B. Anthony. She wrote that Zintka was "everywhere the object of much interest and admiration. . . . All too soon we had to return, and the most of us returned to Colorado Springs and took train for home." With her usual optimism, Clara dryly commented that Zintka was "already doing missionary work for her race, making people realize its possibilities and that there is a kinship in human nature deeper than race separation."[45]

When the exhausted travelers arrived in Beatrice, to celebrate their homecoming Leonard lifted Zintka up onto the saddle of her first Shetland and, holding her steady, walked the black-and-white pony named Cricket up and down the street.[46] At every turn the child inspired crowds of gaping onlookers. Clara received many letters requesting information about the Indian baby, and poetry continued to pour in from across the country. Seeing an opportunity to lure readers, Clara offered Zintka's picture as a premium for new subscribers to the *Tribune*.[47] This tribute came from Margaret E. Sangster and was published by *Harper's Round Table* in 1891:

> Child of the battle, infant waif,
> Zintka Lanuni, the sweet Lost Bird,
> Lives with her captors to-day and . . .
> She is growing up in the white man's tent,
> Daughter and princess, her childhood spent.
> In learning and knowing the dearest things,
> This little Lost Bird, whose feeble wings,
> Too weak to fly, one day were furled . . .
> Zintka Lanuni, all blessings be
> With the little Lost Bird of Wounded Knee

CHAPTER 7

Kicking Bear's Prayer

The large bright room at the corner of Eleventh and G streets in Washington, D.C., was Clara's home from November to May every year. From the large first-floor studio, a narrow wooden stairway led down to a basement office where Clara printed her bimonthly newspaper, the *Woman's Tribune*, on an old-fashioned Washington press. Printing was tedious and messy work, but she did it believing that the information recorded in her paper was "made in behalf of woman's emancipation . . . an immortal contribution to the history of the struggles of the race for freedom." Years earlier, when Leonard had owned the *Beatrice Express*, Clara learned the "journeyman" trade, and the experience had proved invaluable.

A friend visiting the *Tribune* described Clara's cramped but comfortable newspaper office:

> There were no tobacco stains on the floor, no fumes of smoke in the air, such as are common in masculine editorial rooms; but roses on the table, hyacinths on the mantel-piece over the open fire, and a cheerful little canary-bird hanging in its cage in the large, sunny window. . . . The lounge, covered by day with a spread, upon which Mrs. Colby, after working often till midnight, lies down to snatch a brief repose, rising again at six to resume her labor.[1]

Leonard took one look at the apartment and said it would never do for living quarters of the Assistant Attorney General of the United States! He had a wife, two children, and a nurse to house, besides needing ample room to entertain guests. They went house-hunting, found a more spacious home in a fashionable neighborhood, and by November 5, 1891, confusion reigned. Thousands of eight-page newspapers to be researched, written, edited, hand-set to type, printed, folded, and mailed consumed most of Clara's time. She also had to deal with a two-year-old child who was either sick in bed or busily plunging her little hands into black, sticky printing ink; a teenage nurse who suddenly cared more about the way she looked in the mirror than her duties; and a boy of severely limited intelligence who could only follow simple directions. There were lectures to give, stacks of correspondence from readers and writers to answer, social functions to attend, a husband to wait on, meals to plan, and a house to maintain—and above all, Miss Anthony to appease. Distracted, Clara began running in circles. She was finally persuaded to place Clarence in a boarding school a few hours from Washington by train. The boy needed special care and Clara, guilt-ridden, could no longer provide it.

Miss Anthony was still annoyed at Clara for adopting the Indian orphan against her warnings and advice. Eventually, her hard feelings came to the surface. From her home in Rochester, New York, Miss Anthony complained to suffrage leader Harriet Taylor Upton:

> I have written to Mrs. Colby to try and pull out some of the *irons* she now has in the fire—instead of putting more in—& letting the half of them spoil. I said it because she feels so conscience smitten to leave that big—boy at school—so longs to have him with her at home! She needs less there—rather than more—it does vex me to see our women tie themselves hand & foot with children . . .²

For fear of further provoking Anthony, Clara sacrificed family time for the relentlessly demanding and all-consuming work of obtaining from Congress a bill giving women the right to vote for members of the House of Representatives. As chairperson for NAWSA, the National American Woman Suffrage Association, Clara was responsible for the organization of state workers across the country to "secure memorials or petitions from all bodies and organizations of men and women."³ It was an arduous undertaking and required the coordination of "a great army of persons willing to make a sacrifice." Miss Anthony noticed Clara's loss of concentration, a loss she correctly attributed to the added workload of husband and children now with her in Washington. Again, Anthony grumbled to Mrs. Upton with underlined emphasis:

> Mrs. Colby writes me she did send out a copy of the *Tribune* with Senate Hearing speeches . . . and that she didn't mark the speeches with red or blue pencil as I asked her to do . . . so she <u>lost</u> me <u>my two</u> special <u>points</u>—by doing it her own way—since no one knew the <u>particular</u> point for which the paper came to them!! but so it goes—I wish I lived there in that Washington office—And I really ought to do so. . . . I wish the <u>right woman to run it the year round</u> . . . Truly yours, Susan B. Anthony.⁴

Had Miss Anthony moved to Washington as she threatened to do, Clara's life might have been better organized, but a showdown with Leonard would have been inevitable.

Anthony's disapproval of Zintka's adoption echoed throughout the suffrage movement, where a great deal of racial prejudice smoldered. Clara was ridiculed by other suffragists, who made snide, hurtful comments about the Indian child to Clara's face and behind her back.[5]

Elizabeth Cady Stanton was more sympathetic than most suffragist women, however, having raised numerous children while campaigning for the vote.[6] Her husband supported her, and thus encouraged, she put her family first and was a constant source of comfort to Clara. She wrote about expanding the *Woman's Tribune*: "It is too bad the Vanderbilts & Astors cannot give you some of their millions."[7] Mrs. Stanton also told Clara of Miss Anthony's general criticisms: "She does not like your articles on dress and labor, your poetry & Zintka."[8] Anthony and Stanton often disagreed with each other as well, but their friendship remained strong despite differences in opinion. Anthony was harshly critical when Stanton did not lecture more for the cause, to which Mrs. Stanton answered: "Your abuse is sweeter to me than anybody else's praise for, in spite of your severity, your faith and confidence shine through all."[9] Likewise, Anthony's brusque remarks did not bother Clara in the least, and Susan faithfully continued her financial support of the *Woman's Tribune*. Having once had her own newspaper, the *Revolution*, Anthony understood Clara's problems and her devotion to the paper as few others did.

Although General Colby tolerated his wife's work for woman suffrage, he did not take the cause seriously. Clara talked him into all sorts of schemes and he went along with them halfheartedly. Once, Clara planted this bit of promotion in the *New Dacatur* (Ala.) *Advertiser*:

> General L. W. Colby, Assistant Attorney General of the United States, and husband of the editor of the *Woman's Tribune*, an equal rights paper of the highest standard, has recently presented the Confederate flag taken at Mobile, April 12, 1865, to General Dabney Maury, the ex-Confederate commanding officer. General Maury, in his letter of acceptance, says that when he and General Colby "fight again it will be side by side." Now, stand by your promise, General Maury, as once you stood by your guns. When the tug of war is on for a constitutional amendment in favor of woman suffrage, remember that General Colby is on the woman's side, and by the memory of that Confederate flag and the Southern women who suffered for it, "stand thou with him!"[10]

Leonard could be manipulated only just so far, and then he found it necessary to remind Clara of her inferior status as a woman. She tolerated what she called "a homily upon the superiority of man, which was very docilly received, as befitted the situation," and teasingly called him her "liege lord."[11] Mrs. Stanton understood Clara's position and commented: "There may be a man here & there who would sacrifice himself as a mother does for his children. I have never seen one, but I have heard of such beings."[12]

As time passed, Clara confided more of her problems to the elderly Mrs. Stanton, and vice versa. Stanton was overweight and her health was poor. She was backing away from suffrage appearances, saying that she did not want to "parade my infirmities."[13] She had great difficulty climbing stairs and sitting for long periods of time, and although she spoke eloquently, she did not like her speaking voice: "Next to myself of all things I dislike to hear my beloved Susan."[14]

Clara's lecturing and newspaper schedules overlapped and interrupted her family responsibilities. Except for Maud, she had a hard time keeping staff, and never understood why. Always on the run, overextended in every direction, she was disorganized and her household suffered for it.

After much persuasion, Clara's seventeen-year-old niece Mary Bewick came from Wisconsin to live with the Colbys as assistant editor of the *Tribune*, while attending business college at night. Mary recalled her first impression of Zintka:

> This child was three years old when I arrived in Washington to make my home with Aunt Clara. She greeted me at the door, dressed in a very dainty white dress, and her first words to me were, "Is this my cousin Mary?" When I replied, she jumped into my arms and gave me a joyous welcome I shall never forget.[15]

Mary enjoyed Clara's cosmopolitan parties where congressmen, Hindu philosophers, military officers, visiting royalty, artists, musicians, and American Indians met and mingled. Mary was fond of her aunt and uncle:

> My memory of him [Leonard] is very dear. He never failed to bring in beautiful flowers for the Saturday evening "At Homes." He was a wonderful host and Aunt Clara's beautiful spirit always joined in with Uncle Len to make this a happy evening for the hundreds who dropped in.[16]

The Colby home reflected the general's passion for exotic antiquities, hieroglyphics that he collected and housed in reddish-brown ostrich-plumed mahogany cabinets with handles designed to resemble lotus blossoms. Clara decorated to suit his interest in Egypt, with bronze statuettes of the goddess Isis and her husband Osiris and their falcon-headed son Horus, god of the sky. Rich Oriental rugs and gilded wallpaper bathed rooms in a mysterious and flattering red glow. Guests sat at a polished mahogany dining-room table, warmed by the heat from black marbled fireplaces veined in red. Sandwiches, fresh fruit tarts, tea, and jam cookies were served with mother-of-pearl cutlery that was silver-monogrammed with a C; the only discernible touch of Clara's were the china plates etched with the slogan "Vote for Women."[17]

In early April 1892, a delegation of fourteen Chippewas came to visit, four of them in native dress, led by Red Bear, chief of the Leech Lake band. Clara described their clothing, which frightened Zintka:

> Across the Skies wore a head dress made of elk skin and the hair left on, and to this were attached scalps. He had the good taste to have only Indian scalps as if there had been any of white men, it is probable the people present might not have looked on it with as much good humor. At the best it was an eerie thing. The eagle feathers on it, however, made it look very stylish.[18]

Showing a well-meaning ignorance of the sanctity and purpose of the Sacred Pipe, Clara "made them a little speech of welcome and asked them to take a cup of tea . . . as a woman's way of smoking the pipe of peace. Tea and cake were then passed to them and they seemed to enjoy it. . . . Zintka allowed the "civilized Indians" dressed in suits to "carry her about," but of the others she "seemed to be afraid . . . [and] could not be persuaded to stay near them . . ."[19]

Clara was proud when White Cloud stepped forward and gave her "the name 'Charity's Queen.' . . . The young lady [Maud] he called 'Red Rose'. . . . [R]eaders will live to see the time when there will be no Indians such as we have read about in the story books, but will only find bright, capable men, of a color different from that of any other people. . . . It is stoutly affirmed that the proportion of bad men among the Indians is less than that among the whites."[20]

In the attorney general's office, Leonard was mainly involved in reviewing depredation claims against Indian tribes that had been piling up for nearly sixty years. He set aside older complaints and began at once to settle the most recent Pine Ridge "friendly Indian" claims against the Ghost Dancers, amounting to a hefty $100,000. After the judgment was paid, it was proven that the original claims were drafted by the notorious Pine Ridge trader James Asay.[21] This amazing fact supports the likelihood that Leonard Colby rewarded Asay with federal funds for the trader's help in obtaining Lost Bird. One of the largest amounts—over $5,000—was claimed by Philip Wells, which also leads to serious speculation about his activities regarding the Lost Bird.[22]

When Colby entertained Indians visiting Washington, he always reminded them that he was a mixed-blood Seneca, displaying his Indian daughter Zintka and presenting each guest with a special peace medal.[23]

He met chiefs of many tribes and gained their confidence, a maneuver that would prove of great benefit to him in the future.

Clara was a gracious and friendly hostess and did not interfere in her husband's business schemes—but she did know that Leonard was not an Indian. In 1884 she had written a confidential letter to his aged father, Rowell, asking if it were true that her husband had any Indian blood. He replied skeptically but added, "I have heard it intimated that at an early day, during some of the conquests of Indians, the British captured and brought over many fair captives whose blood became mixed with the colonists' . . . from which the dark complexion in the Webster and Colby families had its origin."[24]

Clara researched her husband's genealogy thoroughly to the earliest colonists and then back to England, yet she could never find an Indian in his bloodline. It was only a romantic notion that his grandmother had been a Seneca maiden, but Clara said nothing. If he wanted to be an Indian, whom could it possibly harm?

On one occasion, Santee Dakota interpreter Reverend James W. Garvie brought a Lakota delegation to a reception in the Colby home. He later told his family that when he first saw Lost Bird, she threw herself into his arms. Unlike cousin Mary, who thought it was a sweet show of affection, Garvie felt instinctively that there was something wrong with the clinging child, and he could barely free himself from her embarrassing grasp.[25]

Clara was especially touched by Garvie's visit; his group included former Ghost Dancers Little Wound and Kicking Bear. When Garvie tried to explain the Egyptian statues to the Indians, the Lakota raised their eyebrows and exchanged looks of amazement at the strange animal heads with bodies of humans and the bronzed figure of Osiris, who, Colby told them, was a fertility god who became chief god of the underworld. Christian missionaries had often told the Indians not to worship idols, yet here were important government officials, Christian men, displaying green-fleshed gods in their homes! *Witko.* Yes, crazy.

Seeing Zintka must have brought back the horror of Wounded Knee to the Ghost Dancers, but Clara scurried around to try to make them feel comfortable. Naïvely, but with some perception, she described the poignant visit:

> Zintka had been confined to the library for some days where she had been enjoying herself during a trifling illness, while the household all revolved around her. She had, therefore, to receive her visitors in that room, and they found her in the long white wool wrapper in which she always looks her very best. . . . [T]he . . . interest of the occasion centered on the three chiefs who were as friendly and talkative as they could be. . . . When Zintka had overcome

her first alarm at their strange appearance she was quite inclined to make up with them, especially with Kicking Bear. They all talked about her and to her a great deal, always saying Zintkala Nuni, which they said was the right way to speak her name . . . while most of the party were downstairs looking curiously at Indian relics, (the little bead bonnet with the United States flag worked on each side, which Zintka had on when she was found, seemed to interest them most), [Kicking Bear] stayed behind and went through a very interesting performance with Zintka. He had previously with some difficulty extricated from the beaded leather cape over his right shoulder the feathers which have an important significance in connection with his office as a medicine man, and had offered Zintka her choice of them. Of course she chose the red, and she kept it firmly in her hand during the rest of the visit. Now, Matowa Natake [Kicking Bear] put both his hands on Zintka's head and spoke in a low voice: then placed one hand on her chest and the other on her forehead, still continuing the invocation. Then he kissed his fingers, laid them on Zintka's mouth and back again on his own, after which he stood . . . with bowed head.[26]

Feeling overwhelmed with pity for the clinging child and remembering his slain relatives at Wounded Knee caused Kicking Bear grave anguish, and he could not raise his head. Tears of helpless grief fell down his face onto his fringed shirt and the Persian carpet under his feet. How was he to kidnap the Lakota girl and hope to escape alive from Washington, so far from his people? At least he knew where she was. All he could do was pray for her and hope that, despite her bizarre surroundings and constant illnesses, she might someday find her way back to her traditional life force, the heritage of her ancestors, before she suffered irreparable harm.

Clara had to be away from home for several weeks in 1892 while she traveled across the country with Miss Anthony. She left the child in Maud's care and arranged for a printer to publish her newspaper, which she wrote before she left.

Meanwhile, General Cobly brought in his brother-in-law Charles E. White to assist him in the attorney general's office, and hired numerous old friends in various states to take depositions on Indian claims. At one time as many as twelve of Colby's closest comrades were on the payroll.[27]

In reviewing the depredation claims, Colby found that many Indians accused of wrongdoing over the years had never been given due process. The courts proceeded with whatever evidence they had on file and usually rendered judgment against the tribes. Colby wrote:

These judgements without service of process . . . [are] void, whether against white persons or Indians. . . . There is no provision for service upon the Indians or their representatives . . . thus we have a law by which the Court of Claims can render judgement against the United States and the different tribes of Indians for upwards of $34,000,000 without service of process. . . . It seems to me that such action must be regarded as null and void as against those interested who have never had their day in court, and that any moneys so paid and charged up can be recovered back by the Indians some time in the future.[28]

During Harrison's crumbling administration, Colby's depredation claims began to irritate some congressmen. Watching from his tidy desk near Colby's office door was New Hampshire attorney Charles R. Corning, a meticulous Harvard-educated lawyer also working for the attorney general.[29] Corning was a nervous but astute individual who wrote detailed office journal notes and carefully recorded his daily activities in indexed diaries at home. Nothing got by him. Corning held the same prejudiced view of Indians as most of his co-workers, noting after the Wounded Knee Massacre, "The Sioux Indians are having a magnificent Ghost Dance with U.S. troopers for refreshments. There vermin might as well be cleaned out now as at any other time, the sooner the better."[30]

At first, General Colby was friendly to Corning. In his personal diary, Corning noted:

> In the evening we called on Gen. Colby. His wife is the embodiment of a self willed sensible woman who stamps out shams and false pretences. I like her. Zintka, the little two years old Sioux Indian baby played with her foster parents and put me to deep thinking. Among her toys is the quaint, uncouth doll which was found with her on the battle field of Wounded Knee, a sad and pathetic little thing—that makes the whole world kin.[31]

Within a month, Corning's snooping began to irritate Colby and the two drifted into opposite corners. Corning wrote of a "public affair" and frequent absences.[32] Corning noted: "Colby will surely entangle the office in . . . difficulties."[33] The attorney general's office was in sad shape according to Corning: "Colby's shiftless & unsystematic way of conducting . . . business is sickening. He has been gone three weeks yet but two communications have we had. . . . Colby has appointed Senator Morgan's son as Assist. Attorney and the fellow never studied law! Colby is getting ready for a change in Presidents. He is a tricky & deceitful cuss."[34]

When the general brought in his brother-in-law, Corning was furious: "C. E. White of Beatrice is now in charge of the office. He is a rusty, conceited . . . quasi-barrister but more a loan agent and Colby has put him in. Colby is a rascal yet a charmingly nice one, but his rope is bound to fetch him. He claims Indian blood & I can begin to see where it comes in."[35]

Corning met secretly with his old friend, the politically powerful New Hampshire senator William E. Chandler, and told all. Corning believed there was evidence that Attorney General Miller and Colby were involved in depredation fraud, being paid to speed up specific claims before others, a most serious allegation. Senator Chandler had "gained his earliest reputation for persistency, coolness, and moral courage" during Abraham Lincoln's administration, and was appointed by President Lincoln as first solicitor and judge-advocate of the Navy Department.[36] He had years of investigative experience and was known for "criticising freely the action of men who forgot their moral obligations or were shirking their official duties to the detriment of the public good."[37] Corning had tattled to the right man.

Chandler informed South Dakota senator James H. Kyle, an ex-Congregational minister, who in turn called for an investigation by the Committee on Indian Depredations of the United States Senate. The already weakened Harrison administration was appalled. On April 13, 1893, the committee met in a special hearing with Senator Kyle as acting chairman. W. H. H. Miller, the attorney general, General Colby, and Charles Corning were called to testify. Corning wrote: "He [Colby] will strive his utmost to retain his place for there is a goodly revenue besides the high jinks."[38] Corning may have had a more sinister motive for attacking Miller and Colby. Embittered when he was passed over for a salary increase, he wrote: "I am wholly bereft of ambition & even common place fidelity after eighteen months of contemptible & undeserved treatment. Nay, down in my soul I have so strong a contempt for Miller that I hope he will by political necessity, be relegated to his Indianapolis home, never again to emerge."[39]

A crucial record book was mysteriously missing, and Colby's testimony that his signature may have been forged left the committee with little evidence to form a case. At one point in the proceedings, a senator asked Colby about another new set of depredation claims, a long list signed by ranchers along the Cheyenne River off reservation land. Speaking of the so-called Ghost Dance Uprising, Senator Charles J. Faulkner (West Virginia) asked: "You say there was no war unless the troops commenced it!" Colby: " . . . The Indians did not fight, except in self defence."[40] The senator questioned: "They did not go on a marauding expedition?" Colby responded: "No, sir . . . although there are over $500,000 claims put in. . . . I believe most of these depredations of white men; that they took advantage of those troubles to steal cattle and take them off and charge it up to the Indians."[41]

The senators did not like the fact that Colby had secured the half-breed depredation claims but had spoken against the ranchers' claims. The committee hearings came to nothing, and both the ranchers' false claims and the inflated mixed-blood claims were both paid.[42] But Colby's reputation was tarnished. He confided to a lawyer in Beatrice: "Senator Chandler is out to get me."[43]

Running scared, Colby sent President Harrison a personal gift and received a reply on January 11, 1892:

> Your letter of the 8th Ins. has been received, and also the bridle and whip made from the hair of the Arabian Stallion, Linden-Tree, presented by the Sultan to General Grant. The work is the most beautiful I have ever seen and the gift very highly prized for its own sake, but much more as an evidence of your respect and good will. . . . I beg to assure you that you have given me very much pleasure by this gift. Very Truly Yours, Benj. Harrison [44]

Harrison was having troubles of his own in the press and at home. Unusual tragedy plagued his administration, including the deaths of a number of close friends and associates. Harrison was a politically beaten man by 1892, and he took no active part in his campaign for a second term. His wife Caroline died quietly "like the snuffing of a candle" on October 24, 1892, two weeks before her husband was defeated for reelection by Grover Cleveland.[45]

With Mrs. Harrison's death, Clara lost an ally and a friend. Meanwhile, Leonard tried to improve his damaged image. He presented Attorney General Miller with an Arabian colt, a flattering gesture that did no good.[46] With the change of administrations, Colby lost his job and was replaced by attorney Charles B. Howry, whose first order of political business was to hire Charles Corning as special investigator for the Justice Department. Corning was to go to the Pine Ridge and Rosebud reservations and find solid evidence against Colby.[47] Corning insisted he could prove Colby had committed fraud. He took his wife and spent nearly a year on the reservations, making approximately $10 a day, a princely sum in 1892.[48] But Rosebud interpreter Thomas Flood was assigned to assist the official, and he knew why Corning was there.[49] No amount of intimidation (Corning threatened to cut off government rations) had any affect.[50]

Corning saw before him a difficult but not impossible task—to find Indians who would betray their own people. He needed written proof or sworn statements that Colby had padded the Asay depredation claims, but the trader's influence was still a factor and his slithering tracks had been erased by prairie winds and time.[51] In his annual reports as assistant attorney general, Colby had always made sure every penny was accounted for, including the cost of laundered towels ("55 dozen") by laundress Fannie Jackson.[52]

When Corning finally lost his job as special investigator, he had to face yet another crisis: His wife had been a teacher at Pine Ridge, and the

Lakota children became her life's calling. She refused to accompany her husband home. Corning's professional and private life crashed down around him and he eventually suffered a nervous breakdown.[53] Thousands of tax dollars had been wasted on yet another dead-end, politically inspired federal investigation.

The Colbys rallied after Grover Cleveland took over the presidency and the general lost his job. Leonard Colby's numerous Indian contacts now paid off when he traveled to the Five Civilized Tribes in Oklahoma. Citing his Seneca grandmother and assuring them that he could protect them from the many depredation claims still pending against the tribes, he talked the Creek, Otoe, Missouri, Cherokee, and Muskogee nations each into giving him a contract for $4,000 per year to serve as tribal attorney for three years.[54] He succeeded despite a published warning from the Commissioner of Indian Affairs:

> Doubtless many Indian tribes will be solicited by attorneys to enter into contracts with them for their employment as counsel to defend them in Indian depredation claims. . . . [F]acts have been so distorted and misrepresented as to give rise to the suspicion that their purpose was to create undue alarm in the minds of the Indians, or mistrust respecting the safety of their trust funds or other money held by the government, hoping thereby to strengthen their chances for employment by the Indians at a good annual salary to defend them in depredation suits. . . . [T]here seems to be no necessity for the employment of such counsel.[55]

Leonard Colby walked away with nearly $50,000 in tribal funds for doing nothing.

By now, he also had his fingers in the Cherokee Strip sale, a tract of land 200 miles long and 57 miles wide bordering the south line of Kansas, with 9,400 square miles and six million acres.[56] The government had bought the land from the Cherokees in 1891 for $8.5 million dollars. In 1893 President Cleveland issued a proclamation declaring that the strip would be opened for settlement on September 16. At noon on that day cavalrymen patrolling the borders fired their guns in the air as a signal that settlers could enter the coveted lands. Thousands rode in buggies and buckboards across the lines, searching for the only chance they might have in their lives for a piece of earth to call their own.[57]

The Cherokees watched while their land was taken, but their purchase price had been delayed and by now they were afraid they might never get the money. Lawyers hired by the Cherokees lobbied for payment in what was called "a gigantic steal." Attorneys received a fee of 10 percent to promote the sale. An article in The Outlook, a popular magazine, noted: "The unscrupulous lawyer, . . . recognizing that all that could be legitimately done could be amply compensated . . . could well influence the Indians to believe that he could really bring about the disposal of the land for their benefit, so that when Congress . . . finally should settle the question, he could go to the Indians, point to the settlement as his achievement, and demand his percentage according to a previously made contract."[58] Leonard Colby was among the lawyers who made a killing on the Cherokee Strip, but he may have celebrated too hard on at least one occasion when he was caught off guard in Eufala, Oklahoma, after attending an all-night party with Creek leader Captain Grayson. The two apparently had imbibed too much and woke up the next morning in their hotel room to find that unnamed companions had stolen their cash and personal belongings.[59] Soon afterward, Colby got into trouble with the Cherokees when it became clear he was playing each side against the other, saying "the future of the five nations depends on their adopting my scheme."[60] The Cherokees responded:

> The General advises our people to petition Congress to make a State out of this Territory. We do not wish to take issue with the General, but we still believe that the honor which heretofore has so distinguished the American people has not deserted them. Then again, the Cherokee people gave General Colby a handsome fee to look after their interests and to keep back the very thing he advises his clients to do. . . . Our people have been treated worse than slaves. Nothing can remove the stain the white man once placed upon our people. . . . Let us all stand together and fight off statehood and win the approval of all liberty loving people. Just as soon as statehood comes, the Cherokees will be exterminated as a race of people. May that day never come.[61]

From Oklahoma, Leonard wrote to Clara: "I enclose you a 'posey' picked on the road for you yesterday. I hope you are well. Don't work too hard. You are a nice good wifie & are dearly loved by your affectionate husband, L. W. Colby."[62]

Whenever Clara was away from home lecturing and the general was also out of town, little Zintka was left with Maud or cousin Mary. "Please bring my dear mother back to me soon," she prayed at night before bed, and then "she tucked her Mama's photograph under her pillow and fell asleep."[63] Every morning she climbed up on the front window seat to look for Clara, hoping she would return. Pressing her face against the window, she said the morning prayer her mother had taught her:

> Now I wake to see the light
> Yes, God who kept me through the night,

To Him I lift my thoughts in prayer
And thank Him for His watchful care.
Oh keep me Lord throughout this day
And drive all naughty thoughts away.[64]

Plagued by guilt for having left Zintka, Clara came home from suffrage campaigns loaded down with gifts. For a few days she spent every possible moment with the child, and then she was off again with Miss Anthony, promising to return soon. It was the same nationwide campaign schedule she had maintained for years, only now there was a small lonely person left behind, standing in the doorway with one arm raised, waving in slow motion until Clara's carriage disappeared from sight.

CHAPTER 8

The Heart Wound

American voters, believing Benjamin Harrison's associates were "perverting the government to the benefit of special privilege," elected Grover Cleveland president in 1892. It was said that "the magnitude of Cleveland's victory astonished everyone, for it was the most decisive since the reelection of Lincoln in 1864." Allen Nevins, Cleveland's Pulitzer Prize–winning biographer, considered that the country needed "a leader of unyielding courage and rocklike principle . . . in the fearful crisis that was coming."[1] A triumphant Cleveland took over an administration that was troubled from the start. After a decade of Gilded Age prosperity, progress, and expansion, the middle and working classes began to imitate the wealthy, paying extravagant amounts for land, houses, race horses, carriages, fine furnishings, and fancy clothes. Although a hint of danger was in the air, the New York World and the Tribune held a competition to see which newspaper could find the most American millionaires. The Tribune won, listing more than 4,000 names, among them John D. Rockefeller in oil, Andrew Carnegie in steel, and John P. Morgan in finance and railroads. Ironically, before the year ended, men who had represented the American Dream during years of prosperity, entrepreneurs who had driven themselves and others to the top, came under the scrutiny of disgruntled laborers. Railroad rates rose so high that "it cost a bushel of wheat to ship a bushel of wheat to market. At those prices, who could afford to sell?"[2] The labels "robber barons, bloated bond-holders, and money sharks" began to appear in the press.

The Colbys spent part of the summer of 1892 in Beatrice. Zintka stayed with Mary's girls (Sadie especially doted on her) while Maud visited her parents. Clara traveled the campaign trail as chair of the Federal Suffrage Committee, having been elected to that position at the annual NAWSA meeting the previous February. Clara and Miss Anthony adopted a suffrage plan advocated by Francis Minor, a St. Louis lawyer and the husband of Virginia L. Minor, who argued "that women, as 'people,' were entitled under the Constitution to vote for members of the House of Representatives and that right could be activated by a simple majority vote of Congress. It became Clara's monumental duty to organize representatives in every state to hold petition drives and publish memorials for woman suffrage—a thrust Miss Anthony hoped would lead to a congressional amendment.

A childhood friend, Ellen Sabin, director of the Milwaukee Downer College in Wisconsin, invited Clara to speak, giving her an opportunity to visit brother William and the rest of the Bewicks. During family dinners, Clara's conservative brothers sat quietly, tolerating her suffragist claim of "equality before the law."[3] Even though the others rolled their eyes and thought she was much too liberal, William sat enthralled and enthusiastically supported Clara, especially her endeavors for the *Woman's Tribune.*

After leaving Wisconsin, Clara canvassed a number of states to spearhead petition rallies. She was leading the life of a corporate executive, with its attendant conflicts between work and home, loath to let family obligations interfere with business for fear Miss Anthony would disapprove. She finally returned to Beatrice toward the end of the summer, to a home that was refreshingly peaceful compared to the noise and congestion of Washington and the nights of sleeping upright in her seat on trains between lecture stops. August was hot, but even so the month passed quickly and joyously, as everyone seemed in particularly good spirits.

Clara never really had a chance to relax. She had held leading positions in the Nebraska Women Suffrage Association for sixteen years. Mrs. Gertrude M. McDowell recalled that it was Mrs. Colby "whom we considered our general."[4] Albert Watkins, in his book *History of Nebraska,* noted Mrs. Colby's hard work: "Whether her causes were worth the sacrifice or not, she has, of a surety, been a martyr."[5] Clara did not consider herself a martyr even after Mrs. Stanton started calling her "Beloved Saint Clara."[6]

August and September of 1892 would prove the last happy season Clara spent in the state of Nebraska. A chill wind blew on the day she and her family boarded the train in October for the return trip to Washington, D.C. The last good-byes brought tears from Sadie, who ran alongside the train, waving to Zintka as Maud held her up to the window.

Maud's family was there, too, to see their daughter off. When Maud first returned from the East, Henrietta and John Miller had been amazed at the girl's transformation. Her beauty had become more refined, her English diction much improved, and newly-acquired manners made her appear to be a real lady. John Miller held General and Mrs. Colby in the highest regard and was proud that his daughter was receiving an excellent education in the Colby household. All summer Maud had regaled her family with amusing stories about the famous people she had met in Washington:

Miss Anthony and Mrs. Stanton were frequent visitors, as were congress-men, famous artists, and writers. Nothing could have pleased the Millers more than to see their lovely daughter gain a social standing they could not provide for her. And she had also learned to set type for Mrs. Colby's news-paper, a practical achievement.[7]

The Colbys returned to a glorious autumn, when the magnificent white Capitol building took on a golden hue against a flame-red evening sky. Intellectuals and government officials also came streaming back to Wash-ington.

With the change of administrations, General Colby lost his position and his successor Charles B. Howry began an investigation into Colby's tenure in the attorney general's office. Leonard was allowed to finish a few cases still pending, but when he tried to take on more, the new assistant attor-ney general bluntly told him, "Your employment here would not be accept-able."[8] But Leonard had made shrewd land investments and had already been hired as attorney for the Five Civilized Tribes.

In Washington, Zintka started having nightmares. Her general health was poor and at night she saw giant eyes peering in at her through the win-dows.[9] When Clara was at home, she sang and prayed with Zintka, rock-ing away her childhood fears. There were no child psychologists to consult, although Clara read and reviewed the latest guides on motherhood. But even if there had been professional help, Clara's suspicions of the medical profession were so strong she probably would not have taken their advice. Her prejudice against childhood vaccinations also kept Zintka from receiv-ing the added protection against contagion she so desperately needed. Clara would not chance an inoculation that might kill her Indian child. She now understood that Zintka's intolerance of city water and cow's milk was serious and that Zintka required fresh air and exercise. The child had seemed healthier in Nebraska than in Washington, where her lungs filled with industrial pollution and strangers coughed in her face. In a large city she seemed to lose all immunity to upper respiratory infections.

The *Tribune* was besieged with requests for information about Zintka—her likes (the zoo, hiking, and band music), her favorite pets (a Maltese cat and Senator, a "Siberian stag hound"), and her general fear of death mentioned from time to time in the *Tribune*. Clara was pleased with her readers' inter-est in the child. She wanted Zintka to follow in her footsteps, to be as stead-fast and courageous as Elizabeth Cady Stanton and Lucy Stone's daughters, perhaps even more so since she represented a race disenfranchised.

In early December 1892, Clara returned home from a particularly try-ing day lobbying on Capitol Hill. When she walked in the door, Zintka rushed into her arms. Something was terribly wrong. Clara learned that minutes after she had gone out that morning, Maud had packed her belongings, left the child with the washwoman, and vanished without saying a word. Greatly alarmed, Clara took a hackney and searched the streets, giving the nineteen-year-old girl's description, questioning cabbies and street vendors. Maud's unexplained disappearance frightened Clara to the core. The girl had given no hint of unhappiness in Clara's busy household. Her duties were the same as they had always been and she never seemed disgruntled. Clara felt Maud was a friend after having given her a home for so many years.[10] As her carriage clattered down street after street, a terrible guilt swept over her. Clara had not watched the young woman closely enough or given her the motherly attention she should have received. Perhaps Maud needed new dresses or a higher wage. Clara could not rest until she found her. Late that night, acting on a carriage driver's tip, Clara went to a dingy boarding house near the Capitol. Inside, the cold, dark hallway was lit by a single dim kerosene lamp. She found the young woman's room and knocked on the door, but Maud refused to answer. Clara's words are not recorded, but she must have spoken firmly to the girl, telling her that she was devoted to her welfare, that nothing could stand between them after the many years of friendship they had shared; just for heaven's sake, open the door!

Finally Maud relented, much distraught, and Clara comforted the wretched girl. Whatever had made her run away from the only home she knew in Washington, from those who cared for her as a member of the family? Maud then confessed that she had become pregnant in Beatrice in July and could not bear to face anyone. She had hidden her bulging belly behind aprons and printing smocks, or with Zintka in her arms, afraid Clara or the general might notice and question her. She feared they would send her home in disgrace. Clara assured Maud she had no such intentions and she now offered to adopt Maud's child as her own.[11] She was willing to make that sacrifice, putting aside her own time, effort, and finances for the good of the child. Clara's philosophy of sacrifice was exemplified during her college years when she wrote:

> Sacrifice has to do with the highest part of our nature. Thus it is evident that the highest and noblest gift is that of one's self. . . . [S]acrifice should be to us a pleasure rather than a duty. . . . It is only what we give that we really retain, and he who wished to save his life, must consecrate it to some great purpose. We can never fulfill these claims, unless we have within us the spirit of sacrifice, and upon this depends the success of our lives.[12]

Inspired with this conviction, Clara came immediately to Maud's assistance with discreet plans. The baby was due in late March or early April, and Maud needed a safe place to stay. Clara took her to Philadelphia to a rooming house owned by a kind acquaintance. Secluded, Maud could spend her confinement in security and peace, and give birth with Clara beside her. After the baby came, Maud could find work at the World's Columbian Exposition in Chicago, where Clara planned to spend the summer months of 1893.[13] Clara kept Maud's secret from her niece Mary and from Leonard, who was in Nebraska clearing up old debts now that he had lost his prestigious government position.

During this troubling time, the *Woman's Tribune* reflected Clara's anger. She quoted Elizabeth Cady Stanton on the plight of fallen women: " . . . they have no protection in church or state under the canon or civil law. Though the victims of men, they are hounded like wild beasts by men from one shelter to another, dragged into the courts, taxed by the state, robbed of their property, shunned by society at large, and left to perish on the highway.[14]

Clara continued her active routine. In February came a crushing blow. Proud of the ceaseless work she had completed in 1892 to secure a suffrage amendment, she prepared a paper to be given at the February 1893 NAWSA convention: ". . . I was able to report that a representative woman had been secured from each of thirty-nine states, in most cases the committee member being president of the State Association. Although the work of securing a committee required much time, yet before the year was out I had secured petitions and memorials from twenty states . . ."[15] Clara's biographer, the Reverend Olympia Brown, noted that "notwithstanding this magnificent report the National American Association decided at once to discontinue this line of work, and of course discontinue Mrs. Colby as a chairman of the committee. By this action . . . Mrs. Colby was thrown out of an opportunity to advocate this measure for some ten years. This was a great disappointment to her, as she had worked most zealously and effectively. She hoped she had laid a foundation for a line of work, which would soon be successful, and thus open the way to the Anthony amendment."[16] All of her work—the hundreds of hours of travel, the neglect of family—had seemingly been for nothing.

Undaunted, she continued to work. While Mary looked after Zintka, Clara went to Chicago to make final arrangements for the booth she would have at the Women's Congress of the Chicago Exposition from June until October. It was not until late February that Clara realized she had not received her usual weekly letter from Maud. She then wrote to Maud, but her letters were returned. The girl had again disappeared without a trace.

Distraught and confused, Clara tried to go on as usual, but her mind wandered. To help make ends meet, she took in a special boarder:

We had a long visit from a Japanese (Buddhist) priest whose gentleness won the heart of the little girl. To no other visitor has she ever responded with so much warmth, and at the same time such quiet tenderness. She would also bow to him quite to the floor, with a grace that matched his own, every morning when she entered the room and would then lead him to the breakfast table. It was a beautiful instance of the responsiveness of childhood. Zintka never bows in that way to anybody else and if instructed to make a Japanese bow, [it is] comparatively forced and ungraceful.[17]

The boarder stayed through the month of March and may have been in the garden with Zintka the day she found the first flower of spring. Among Clara's belongings she kept a pressed memento to remind her of that special day. A note with faded petals reads: "Flower found by baby Zintka Mar. 3, 1893 & passed up through the window with much glee."[18]

Clara continued her popular Saturday evening "at homes," which so delighted her niece when famous people came to call. The Hawaiian queen Liliuokalani, "a poet, and composer," was a guest of the Colbys not long after she had abdicated under duress. Her reign was overthrown by annexationists supported by U.S. diplomat John Leavitt Stevens, who wrote: "The Hawaiian pear is now fully ripe, and this is the golden hour for the United State to pluck it." United States Marines had landed to "protect" 2,000 Americans with huge property interests, men who economically dominated Hawaii and soon jubilantly hoisted the American flag over the government buildings.[19]

The queen came to Washington, Allan Nevins wrote, to throw "herself upon our sense of justice, and declared that a great wrong had been done her." President Cleveland decided he did not want the Hawaiians despoiled as the Native Americans had been, and he ordered Old Glory pulled down. The press was furious, saying: "Native rule, ignorant, naked, heathen, is reestablished . . ."[20] But Hawaii was safe for at least a few more years.

On May 5, 1893, Wall Street stock prices plunged and on June 27, the market collapsed. Seventy-four railroads went into receivership, 15,000 businesses failed, and 600 banks closed in a financial crisis that would continue for four more years. The market was still fluctuating during the first week of June as Clara prepared for a return trip to Chicago, where the exposition had yet to feel the effects of the Panic of 1893. Clara attended the World's Congress of Representative Women, the largest and most brilliant of any of the series of events at the exposition; twenty-seven countries and 126 organizations represented by 528 delegates brought women leaders together for eighty-one meetings. Ten thousand people attended, and Clara's lectures were packed.[21]

Susan B. Anthony was by far "the central figure of this historic gathering." Audiences broke into applause at her presence, policemen held back
mobs of people trying to touch the hem of her dress. Mary H. Krout, writing for the *Chicago Inter-Ocean,* saw Miss Anthony mobbed by adoring
crowds at the Fair and wrote: "Men no longer regard her as the arch-
enemy to domestic peace, disseminating doctrines that mean the destruction of home and the disorganization of society."[22]

At the end of the women's Congress, Clara was more inspired to help
women than at any other time in her life. She had sold or given away all
copies of the most recent editions of her newspaper and had met wonderful women from all parts of the world who congratulated her on the importance of her paper in uplifting women's role in the family and in society. She
also met Captain Richard H. Pratt, founder and superintendent of the
U.S. government's Indian training school at Carlisle, Pennsylvania. George
E. Hyde, in *Spotted Tail's Folk,* described Pratt as "an enthusiast. He imagined that he was bringing the greatest of all boons to the Sioux by offering
to take their children far, far away into an unknown land and keep them for
from four to six years, bringing them home again, if they lived, changed and
completely alienated . . ."[23] Captain Pratt advised Clara to educate Zintka
in the East, completely away from her own kind, and to raise her a strict
Christian. Clara believed Pratt was an "authority" on the Indian with many
years of experience, and she took to heart all that he said.[24]

She returned to Washington and arranged for Mary to take Zintka to
Madison while she covered the events at the Fair for the *Woman's Tribune.*
There had been no word from Maud since February, but Clara had
received an enthusiastic letter from Miss Anthony: "we must buckle on
our armor for a triple fight, and we must shout more loudly than ever to
our friends all over the country . . ."[25] Uplifted by Anthony's resounding
courage, Clara could not wait to get back to Chicago.

On June 1, Zintka brought in the mail and sat down beside Clara while
she opened each parcel. One letter caught Clara's eye. The postmark was
Baltimore, May 28, 1893:

Mrs. Colby,
    Will you kindly tell me what you know of the young woman who
formerly lived in your family calling herself M. C. Miller? She came to
my house in the winter in a delicate condition [and] has since been
confined—she says she was taken by you when quite a child & lived
with you until her marriage to a John Miller half brother of your
Husband, who is acting a sailsman [*sic*] for a Chicago house. My suspicions have been aroused as to her being married at all. The man

treats her in the most unkind way as far as attention and giving her money goes. I have wanted her to apply to Gen. Colby for help but she says he dose [*sic*] not care for her any more as they parted in anger— for her sake & my own I would like to know the truth. Please address

Mrs. Skinner
#5 E. Biddle St.
Baltimore. Ma.[26]

On the envelope, in Clara's handwriting, is a note written in her purple ink: "The letter which broke the dreadful fact to me."[27]

Clara soon heard from Leonard, who was supposedly in Beatrice on business. He had been away from home a great deal since Christmas:

> My Dear Wife.
>
> I have been busy here and at Fairbury trying to pay up the judge-ments obtained against me last term, some debts, etc. Times are very hard, money unobtainable, no prospect for crops, horses not worth the feed, the banks are all frightened & everything at lowest ebb. I don't know what I shall be able to do. 4 mortgages foreclosed & a judgement against me.[28]

In the same letter he told Clara:

> . . . am trying to arrange to take Leopold & Linden Tree [his prize Arabians] to Chicago if I can get the right place. I don't know how things will come out. . . . everything is in bad shape. . . . Kiss the babe for me and do not fret. I can not tell how much money I can bor-row to pay any one. . . . Don't know when I will return in a week or so I hope. Yours, L. W. Colby[29]

Clara's beloved husband of twenty-two years never seemed to have any money, yet he wanted to exhibit Arabian stallions at the World's Fair Horse Competition at the Chicago Exposition?

On the front page of her newspaper the next day, she published a melan-choly poem entitled "A Broken Wing":

> I walked through the woodland meadows,
> Where sweet the thrushes sing,
> And found a bed of mosses,
> A bird with a broken wing.
> I healed its wound, and each morning

It sang its old sweet strain;
But the bird with the broken pinion
Never soared as high again.
I found a young life broken
By sin's seductive art,
And touched with a Christ-like pity,
I took him to my heart.
He lived with a noble purpose,
And struggled not in vain.
But the life that sin had striken
Never soared as high again . . .

As she retraced the last year in her mind, the ugly pieces fell perfectly into place. Protected between the pages of her diaries were her late grandmother's Victorian warnings—adages that may have haunted Clara in the days of agony ahead:

> . . . if young women would but love their husbands (and there is a great deal more in that . . .) be keepers at home and make that attractive by smiles, economy and pleasant ways, 9 out of 10 husbands would stay at home, for it is the forsakeing [sic] the society of the Wife for more congenial which leads to the evil . . . but [when] a poor stray one goes wrong it only proves, that man left to himself will go farther and farther to ruin.[30]

With Grandmother gone, Clara had no one to advise her, yet no hint of scandal would betray what she called a "heart-wound."[31] Janet Lecompte wrote that Victorian "women diarists and letter writers valued success, achievement, and optimism, the ingredients of the era's much-prized progress. As a consequence, women consistently denied any stress or failure, maintaining a facade of assurance and serenity in their writings, even in the face of personal disaster."[32] For a leader in the woman suffrage movement to admit that her husband was keeping a mistress and child was to disgrace the entire philosophy of the women's movement—that if women held equal status with their husbands, they would create better family relations and gain newfound respect. After Miss Anthony's huge success in Chicago, Clara could ill afford the dishonor, which might reflect upon her mentor. In 1893, fresh from joining women applauding their freedom from homebound drudgery, she could not trust her "heart-wound," the "dreadful" confidence to even her closest relatives and friends.

Clara wrote of her sorrow and then destroyed the pages, making a note that she had done so.[33] A kind of madness came over her, she did things without thinking, with her head full, her heart beating. She went over and over the things Leonard and Maud had said, the way they had looked at one another over the years, and Maud's disappearances, first when she found that she was pregnant, and again just before giving birth. Clara analyzed her husband's past, as far back as the Nebraska Senate race when "Mrs. Colby's husband" had been openly accused of consorting with a prostitute. Clara was barely able to function, but she could not let Mrs. Skinner, the woman who had innocently informed her about Leonard's affair, to find out the truth.

Clara wrote thanking Mrs. Skinner for her concern, and asked that she send a telegram if the man came to visit Maud again. During that same week, Clara received a note from Mrs. Skinner saying the man had returned: " . . . though stating that she [Maud] was going to Annapolis, she is I am sure still in Baltimore. I have just seen the man who got the carriage for her & he will send the driver to me & I can find out where he took her. She dose [sic] need a friend some one to turn her from the pain of sin she has entered. Yours Truly, Annie Skinner."[34]

It was a short train ride from Washington to Baltimore on the Pennsylvania, Northern Central, and Western Maryland lines. Clara rushed to Union Station. After talking to Annie Skinner, she found her husband that evening with his mistress and their baby son. She did not burst into their cozy hotel room and create a scene. Instead, she rapped gently on the door. When Leonard answered the knock, Clara stared past her surprised husband to the voluptuous young woman, the friend she had taught to read, write, and behave like a lady. There were no tears, just a quiet request that Leonard return to his home. Devastated, Clara turned and left. She did not find out until later that the baby, as yet unnamed, looked exactly like his father.

On April 1, 1893, Maud Miller had given birth to a handsome boy with glistening black hair and olive skin. She did not want to go on record as having had an "April's fool," so she changed her son's birthdate to April 2.[35]

Baltimore was much closer to Washington than Philadelphia, and the move there was surely Leonard's idea. It was a picturesque city for lovers. The docks on Light Street were lined with banana steamers, and the United Fruit Company's white fleet tied up on Pratt Street to unload their succulent cargoes. Romantic steamboat excursions sailed to Bay Ridge, Annapolis, Tolchester, and Claiborne, and there were misty mountain drives and picnics at Gwynn Oak with hurdy-gurdies playing "Just Tell Them That You Saw Me" and other popular songs of the day. Baltimore had a large German population who spoke Maud's first language, and they owned restaurants, dance halls, and banquet rooms that provided the gaiety and excitement she loved.[36] Penniless, she would wait for Leonard Colby to visit her, knitting, caring for his child, painting seascapes, and cooking his favorite foods. And then, when he arrived, the clandestine, passionate lovemaking was exciting enough to keep Maud waiting again for a very long time.

When Leonard returned home to Clara's private tears and anguish, he comforted her and assured her that Maud was simply the passing fancy of a middle-aged man but with a terrible consequence—an unwanted child. He swore never to see them again, and Clara desperately wanted to believe him. She had been away so often, she blamed herself and forgave him. The girl Clara had turned from a coarse parlor maid into an articulate friend now seemed like a wicked seductress, yet Clara's strict Christian upbringing left her without a stone to cast, and she forgave Maud as well.

She wrote to her suggesting she give up the child and look for work. On June 8, 1893, Maud wrote back to Clara in the perfect penmanship she had been taught to use by her benefactress.

My Dear Mrs. Colby,

[W]hatever you think best I am ready to do. I rec'd $10 this morning and so paid for my board till next Wednesday . . . but I am ready to leave any time. . . . You are a true and noble friend, and God only knows how I regret that I did not tell you how matters stood when I was still in Washington. . . . I have prayed for help and strength as I have never prayed before, and my future will prove that I am sorry for my past . . . but I am not the only one that sinned, nor I the greater sinner of the two. My youth and ignorance were taken advantage of. I was a pure minded a girl as ever lived till that man got me in his power. . . . I am . . . thankful to do anything else to redeem myself and make amends for the past as far as can be done. By earnestly praying for strength daily, I will yet with God's help lead a useful life, and my aim shall be to help those who are as weak as I have been . . . for I knew only too well that I was sinking deeper in sin every day. I needed a true friend if ever a person did, and since you, above all other women, came to me to be that friend, I feel that God sent you. It must have been awful for you to find this out, and yet, it was the best thing that could have happened, and dear Mrs. Colby, God will help you too. Write to me whenever you can . . . Yours, Maud [37]

Leonard wrote from Lincoln, Nebraska, on June 12, 1893:

My Dear Wife:

I have been very much worried on these financial & other matters for some time, but I can't always do as I wish or would. Circumstances and our own infirmities control us, & involve one when perhaps wisdom would have made things easy. I am going to try & straighten everything out & then when the pressure is relieved sell everything or give it away, & get relieved of the financial past any way. You may take your time & sell off all the lands or lots I have if you can. I am oppressed & discouraged greatly. Yours, L. W. Colby.[38]

On the envelope Clara later wrote: "Last Letters addressed to Wife."[39] The word *wife* is smeared downward, as though the pen had fallen from her hand.

Leonard wrote from Beatrice on June 15:

Dear Wife:

Rec'd your letter with the sealed package "to be opened on the train" also the Washington papers & *Tribune* sent—thanks for the thoughts. . . . This whole country is on the edge of bankruptcy. Two banks went up in Omaha yesterday [in all, twenty-one banks failed in Nebraska] & everything is gloomy & at a standstill. Not a dollar of money can be collected, or got at any bank. . . . I could not sell the best horse for $25 cash. . . . Financial ruin is upon the nation. . . . I shall try to unload everything, horses & lots & all. I do not see any way out. . . . I had no idea of the condition of things. . . . You should collect every dollar, make the paper a monthly or take an interim of some months, get that place in Chicago at a salary, put Clarence on the farm, Zintka with Mary etc. etc. I write you this so you can have an idea of things, they are the worst I ever saw. Yours, L. W. Colby.[40]

On June 15th he wrote again, supposedly from Nebraska:

Dear Wife:

Have been now taking depositions & meeting with the military board yesterday & today. Will return to Beatrice tonight. Expect to start back sometime next week. Will be in Chicago a day or two to arrange for showing Leopold & Linden Tree if I can. Everything is in the worst financial shape imaginable, all business stagnated. . . . I don't know how I shall come out, whether I can stem the tide or not. If you write me after receipt of this address me at Chicago, "care Grand Pacific Hotel." I will go there for mail. You have no idea of the financial situation out in this country. I believe half the business men in Beatrice will break up. No money can be got—no man can borrow of the banks on any security. No one pays any debts. Yours, L. W. Colby.[41]

Clara was still planning to return to Chicago to cover the fair for the *Tri-bune*. She wanted Maud to join her there. A letter from Maud on June 20 sounded grateful.

My Dear Mrs. Colby:
—The work you spoke of in your last letter for Mrs. Ralston at the Fair would be a splendid thing for me, I think, for it would be so much easier than setting type, for my eyes have been weaker than ever since my illness. That would give me a good standing again, and is work at which I could see any of my friends, and could also let my parents know just where I was and what I was doing. If Mrs. Ralston is willing to give me that work, I would be very thankful, and I would do my best for her. . . . But I suppose room rent & board is higher in Chicago now than ever before, and it would depend entirely on that whether I could make both ends meet or not. I shall insist upon a certain sum for baby's support, as you suggested in a letter, and that together with what I would make would cover expenses, I think. I hope you can soon find out whether I can depend on this work or not. I am so anxious to do something, so that I can feel free once more. I have paid for board another week; it may be some time before we can go, so I paid this while I still had the money. I am so sorry to hear that Zintka is not well, & sincerely hope that she is getting better by this time. . . . Very Truly Yours, Maud.[42]

Throughout her marriage, Clara's constant belief in Leonard always brought out the better part of his nature. But Maud's seductive passion had ignited a spark that Clara knew she must extinguish before the flames burned to ashes what was left of a family foundation. With a husband who had forsaken his wedding vows, a retarded boy, a three-year-old child who needed continuous attention, a newspaper foundering during a depression, and not a friend in the world to confide in, Clara took her sorrows to God. Had William been right about Leonard after all? Miss Anthony, too, had warned Clara: "You can not have your cake and eat it too."[43]

Maud could not make up her mind whether or not to join Clara in Chicago, but by the end of the summer she had decided not to give up her child. Clara feared that if Maud told her parents or friends what had happened, Leonard's reputation and law practice in Beatrice would be ruined. She had failed "to protect him" once—she felt it her duty to protect him now. With repressed anger, Clara wrote to Maud from her booth at the Chicago Exposition on September 19:

It may be that you can better expiate the wrong you have done by openly bearing your shame and leaving it as a legacy to the child, but I want to spare you this. You have no right to think first of your own selfish mother pain or pleasure only of what is best for the child. You have sinned against the sweet confidence of trusting friendship: Used your maidenly grace and beauty to drag man down instead of lifting him to nobler thoughts: Your sin is one that strikes back at every home in the land and you have no right to consider yourself in the matter, only what is best for the baby. If you were going to reinstate yourself with your friends . . . give up the baby. I can give you a scholarship to Lincoln Business College . . . but I do not see any immediate outlook for you if you retain the child. But in either case count on me for friendship, for sisterly sympathy, for what ever help one struggling suffering soul may be to another. . . . May our Father guide you to the right course. . . . Some day when your spiritual eyes are opened you may come to a realization of how great a wrong to man, woman, wife & friend, is such an invasion of the highest & holiest relations of the human family & will then be willing to have suffered if in any way it may have tended towards righting the wrong. . . . I can yet extend my hand to you in sisterly help & bid you take courage for the future. But I cannot see how I can be of any present material aid if you do not give up the baby nor will I consent to any deception on my part.[44]

Clara took the podium to address a suffrage rally with Miss Anthony at the World's Fair. Her address, "Women in Marriage," had been decided upon because it was Miss Anthony's particular favorite. Clara stood before her large audience with head bowed, knowing that her words were hollow, given the state of her own marriage:

". . . Love, it is commonly said, is an incident in a man's life, but makes or mars a woman's whole existence. However this is one of the many popular delusions. . . . To one who believes in the divinely intended equality of the sexes it is impossible to consider that any mutual relation is an incident for the one and the sum total of existence for the other. . . . Whatever mistake one has made has acted upon the other and reacted equally upon the first. . . . The ratio of divorce for the whole United States is about one for every fifteen marriages. In a far larger portion pride holds the parties together, or insensibility makes them indifferent to wrongs, or principle leads to silent endurance . . ."[45]

CHAPTER 9

Back Alleys

Clara was now feeling guilty about her family, and she returned to Washington from Chicago three times to see Zintka and Leonard. Still, the fear of losing her husband weighed heavily upon her. He was rarely at home anyway, claiming that he had to settle debts in various states. Clara wrote of her anxiety in the *Tribune:*

> This has been a particularly hard year for the editor of the Tribune, who has performed fourfold duties so as to eke out the receipts of the paper so much decreased by the hard times and by the demands of the World's Fair upon subscribers. While spending fifteen weeks in Chicago, attending the Congresses, sending back all matter for the Tribune and having all correspondence forwarded for attention, studying exhibits and exhibitors, and keeping headquarters for the distribution of suffrage literature . . . did not lay up a store of strength and nervous energy to meet the manifold postponed cares and perplexities that greeted the editor's return.[1]

Clara wanted to believe Leonard when he told her that he was no longer seeing Maud, but his long absences must have caused suspicion. She continued to counsel Maud and back her financially in Baltimore. In September 1893 Clara began to notice a new strength in Maud's letters. On September 11, Maud wrote of her child:

> Dear Mrs. Colby . . . There are plenty of homes where I could put him, and perhaps in this city, but as I cannot wean him this winter there is no need of thinking any more about it for the present. No matter what my poor baby is, I have too much mother feeling for him to run any risks with him that are not absolutely necessary. . . . Baby's name has been decided on. His first name is Paul . . . [2]

Maud's taunting implication was that Paul's last name might yet be Colby. Clara found out later that Maud had named her son Paul Livingston,

Leonard's mother's maiden name. However, his last name was yet to come.

In September, more than six months after Paul was born, Clara was still paying all of Maud's expenses. On September 28, Maud made firm statements about the child, intimating that there was something better in store for him:

> . . . I could never think of leaving him behind. . . . You must be mistaken in saying that a child can be weaned before a year; I could not think of such a thing, for I feel that it is running a great risk, and I will take no chances on losing him. My plans for the future are still undecided; and I don't think there is any immediate hurry, and I make no promises one way or the other about giving him up . . . but that can be decided later on. . . . A child's place is with its mother; she has a duty toward it that no one can perform for her, . . . I shall keep mine with me,—but then that is an afterthought and can be decided any time. At present all my time is spent in caring for him, and by the time he can be weaned some plan or thought may suggest itself that has not been spoken of.[3]

Clara cut back to one meal a day—fruit and bread. Every cent went to Zintka's care, to the *Tribune*, and to Maud. Leonard also borrowed money from his wife, saying he was completely without funds.[4] Clara returned to the capitol using free railroad passes given to correspondents covering the fair. She wrote often to Zintka, who spent the rest of the summer in Madison, being shuttled from one relative to another.

Zintka missed Leonard, whom she called "Papa," the only father she had known, but Leonard had forgotten all about his Indian "curio." She had been his mascot when he wanted to impress Nebraskans and Indian delegations, but now she was a burden. He had other, more important persons on his mind. Meanwhile, Clara hovered about in a daze. Sometimes Zintka was pampered with her mother's guilty affection or by inquisitive newspaper reporters, and was shielded and overprotected; but just as often, she was ignored and neglected. Yet Clara tried as best she could to care for her during the greatest turmoil of her life. Zintka's doings and travels were still a regular feature of the *Tribune,* and the façade of family solidarity continued. On the rare occasions when her husband was at home, Clara made sure they were seen together as husband and wife. She invited Harriett L. Coolidge, from the magazine *Trained Motherhood,* to interview them, and Coolidge saw that it was Clara who took special interest in her child:

> The mothering of little Zintka, the . . . Indian baby . . . shows how one mother's heart went out in its warm, true mother love to this poor little orphan.

Even now this adopted mother, busy woman as she is, being editor of a woman's paper, lecturer, housekeeper and mother, still finds time to guide this little life in the way it should go, and hopes with much care and loving patience to make of her a good American citizen. All mothers will watch with interest the mothering and education of this . . . child of the prairie. It is one of the most interesting cases of child study to be found in America.

Indian mothers are very poetical, and although they usually educate their . . . children without the aid of books or schools of any kind, these little ones have *Heart* culture and *Physical* culture, which is so often lacking in the children of civilized mothers.

. . . Zintka has her doll. She is very fond of this doll, although it is so unlike the lovely ones with which our . . . daughters play. . . . [S]he has a bracelet on her arm. It is the same one which she wore when she was a tiny baby; in fact she had it on when she was found. [S]he is fast becoming a civilized . . . girl, and has attended a kindergarten for a long time in Washington, D.C., where her adopted parents now reside. She is very fond of music, and I wish all mothers could hear her sing the pretty . . . kindergarten song about the pigeons, making the nest with her fat little brown hands . . .

The specimen of Zintka's writing . . . was given me by the little girl herself. . . . Persons who are making a study of the pencillings of . . . children will, no doubt, find much of interest in the crude work. . . . [H]er adopted parents . . . are so patient and loving towards her that we may expect to see her develop into a strong, lovable woman, although at times the roving nature of a little Indian girl leads her . . . feet and hands into mischief.[5]

Mischief was an understatement. Zintka grew willful and disobedient. She played in her yard only until her mother was distracted—then she was gone. In a few moments she would be in her favorite place: the back alley. Outside the Colbys' high garden gate, Zintka entered another world, an accepting world where black servant women treated her gently while joking, laughing, and singing uplifting songs as they washed and hung out heavy loads of bed linen and towels. She found a special friend about her age, and the two played tag between the clotheslines, freshly laundered sheets slapping them as they ran by. The two girls may have learned to skip rope together, jumping side by side to a popular skipping song, a bigoted tune of the times:

> By the holy and religerally law
> I marry this Indian to this squaw
> By the point of my jack-knife
> I pronounce you man and wife

Sober live and sober proceed
And bring up your Indian breed.[6]

Zintka had no idea what she was singing. She only knew there was something infinitely comforting about the women gossiping on their stoops and singing religious hymns, big wooden washtubs overflowing with steaming laundry, the aroma of lye blended with an exotic smell of flowers, the bustling aprons and white turbans of the younger women, and the handsome black men passing by with a tip of their hats to the ladies. Zintka loved the people in the alley and spent every moment she could in their company.

The back door of the speakeasy often enticed a crowd of children. Zintka loved to stand outside listening to the music. Piano and banjo strains filled the alley, and Zintka danced with her friends to their own cakewalk promenade, singing "Come on eph! Come on eph!" or:

My coal-black la-dy
She is my ba-by
You cannot blame me no, no . . . [7]

Although children were not encouraged to go in, the music pulled Zintka until she stood next to the pianist, watching the dexterity of his left hand, with its quick octave jumps, while his right hand swept the keyboard in strong syncopated chords, vigorous robust notes, music that roused senses—"Rastus on Parade" and "Happy Days in Dixie"— some of the first original ragtime tunes that captivated the Lakota girl from Wounded Knee. Within five years they would take the country by storm.[8]

The girls laughed and imitated the older ladies who clapped their hands "pattin' juba" beside their tubs—women just thirty years removed from slavery, whose love of song had upheld them spiritually.[9] How they enjoyed life! In the alley there was poverty comparable to the teeming, congested immigrant ghettos of New York's Lower East Side, with its mixture of Irish, Germans, Jews, and Italians. But in Zintka's ragtime alley, she saw only fun, warmth, and compassion. No one told her not to soil her white dress, no one scolded her to hush, to keep still; just outside her back fence she was happy and free from tension and sorrow.

The day finally came when Zintka brought her friend home to meet Mama. Earlier, they had played in the backyard hammock. Then, when Zintka got up her nerve, the girls, covered with dust, walked into the front parlor holding hands, just as Clara was pouring tea for a small group of suffragist leaders. There were long seconds of shocked silence as several delicate china teacups paused in midair.[10]

Although suffragists claimed they represented all women, they did not regard black women as equals. Stanton and Anthony wanted the vote for white women before black men were enfranchised, and they made that emphatically clear—regardless of their abolitionist backgrounds.[11]

Clara had applauded Booker T. Washington in the *Tribune* and called Sojourner Truth the "most remarkable woman that the colored race has ever produced."[12] She had hugged Frederick Douglass on the speakers' platform and had defended the board of the Wimodaughis Club when they admitted a mulatto woman to their meetings, despite the indignant resignation of the secretary and several members. She had protested when white women refused to walk in prosuffragist parades alongside a "Negress," and Clara had "preached to more than a thousand people at the Bethel (colored) church" in Washington.[13] Yet there in her own parlor, among her suffragist sisters looking on disapprovingly, the newspaper rhetoric instantly dissolved into a hard, socially unacceptable reality—the face of an innocent dark-skinned child.

Clara hurried Zintka and her friend to the kitchen, and the Negro girl was quickly ushered out the back door despite Zintka's loud protests. Enraged, Zintka yelled and stamped her feet. Finally, she went upstairs to her room and stood at her window looking down at the children in the alley, a world now seemed closed to her. It must be dreadful to be a Negro! She was not to play with Negro children, and yet her own skin was nearly as brown as theirs. She was white because Mama had told her she was raised white. What was she? Was it dreadful to be an Indian, too?

Clara wrote a *Tribune* article describing her view of the racial incident:

> Zintka has not failed to learn that there is a prejudice against color. . . . Washington is intersected with alleys, inhabited by negroes of the poorer class. The rule is that back of houses, tall, spacious and fair to see, there are small, crowded tenements, whose tiny yards are usually filled with the washing by which the women support their families. It does not need any color prejudice to necessitate very stringent rules that the child of the house shall not frequent the tenement of the alley. It was for one of these . . . that Zintka sought permission to play with her. . . . To head off any remonstrance, Zintka carefully stated her name and where she lived, adding: "She is not very colored, only brown, about as dark as I am!" A little later, she put her arm beside that of the little black girl and having made the discovery that there was not much difference in color, our little maid forthwith brought her friend to her mamma to show that she had stated the fact correctly.
>
> Ex Consul Waller, of Madagascar . . . called one evening with his wife at Zintka's home. This interesting and intelligent couple were quite the heroes

of the occasion but Zintka seemed to fear lest they might not feel quite at home. Laying her hand on Mrs. Waller's arm, she stood looking very sympathetically and earnestly into her face for some time, and then quietly said: "I am not white, neither!"[14]

Between 1890 and 1899, black lynchings averaged more than 180 per year and the life expectancy for nonwhite Americans in general was less than thirty-three years.[15] Nonwhites did not have easy access to medical facilities, and they died of illnesses such as tuberculosis at an alarming rate. Besides the social unacceptability, which suffragists did not perceive as prejudice, Clara feared that Zintka would be dangerously vulnerable if exposed to sicknesses in the alley.

Prejudice of many kinds and from unlikely corners ate at Zintka's self-esteem at an early age, even when she was among her adopted parents' extended families. When she visited her Grandmother Colby in Freeport, Illinois, a local reporter followed her around asking questions. "A Dark Little Stranger" had come to town, and she noted that Zintka was "a little rougher and stronger than the others. . . . She has a tawny skin, jet black, straight hair, and dark, closely set eyes, the unmistakable traces of her race, but they are not of marked prominence. . . . Although the neighborhood children find Zintka an agreeable playmate they occasionally cannot refrain from reminding her that she is an Indian . . ."[16] It was a polite way of saying that they taunted her, yelling "squaw" and other hurtful remarks.

Zintka stood up against her assailants, however, remembering the poem of courage her mother had taught her:

> Listen, little maid, I've a word for you!
> And this is the word; be true, be true.
> For truth is the sun & error the night,
> Be brave little maid & stand for the right![17]

Zintka turned on the bullies with a strength beyond her years, scaring her cousins and the neighbor children until they finally left her alone—completely alone. The Indian girl raised as a white child had no model to look up to, no Indian face to look into except a wooden carving scowling in front of the cigar store.

Back in Washington, Zintka was forbidden to go to the alley, but she went anyway. Clara had too much on her mind, and she could not watch the child every moment. She tried to keep the girl inside by paying her a small wage for helping around the house: "In the desk where I write she has a drawer. Of the book shelves some are hers, and she has special cor-

South Dakota Home Guard sniper Riley Miller in 1893. Miller joined ranchers in the sanctioned murder of Ghost Dancers prior to and after the massacre at Wounded Knee. For years Miller made his living exhibiting scalps and artifacts taken from his Lakota victims.   (Photograph courtesy of Jim Ross Collection.)

Pine Ridge trader and whiskey runner James Asay with an unidentified child and his wife Margaret (Buffalo Bill's mistress). James Asay brought a ten-gallon keg of whiskey to Seventh Cavalry officers the night before the Wounded Knee Massacre. The Asays were evicted from the Pine Ridge Reservation for the illegal sale of liquor.
(Photograph courtesy of J. Kadlecek.)

Wedding photograph of Clara Bewick
Colby, suffragist, newspaper editor,
and educator, 1871.
(Photograph courtesy of Thomas Bewick.)

Wedding photograph of Leonard W.
Colby, Civil War hero, lawyer, judge,
assistant attorney general of the United
States, and brigadier general of the
Nebraska National Guard.
(Photograph courtesy of Thomas Bewick.)

Zintkala Nuni, the Lost Bird, in 1891,
Beatrice, Nebraska.
(Photograph courtesy of Helen Bewick.)

Lost Bird playing in window curtains,
Washington, D.C., 1893.
(Photograph courtesy of Helen Bewick.)

Lost Bird at the age of three
in Washington, D.C.
(Photograph courtesy of Brown
University Archives.)

Suffragists (*left to right*): Bessie Potter, Susan B. Anthony, and Clara Colby in 1890. Miss Anthony called Clara "my pen artist" and asked her to write her biography. Clara reluctantly declined and later regretted that decision. (Photograph courtesy of Sophia Smith Collection, Smith College Archives.)

Assistant Attorney General of the United States Leonard W. Colby with his adopted daughter Lost Bird, 1898. (Photograph courtesy of Helen Colby Collection.)

Leonard W. Colby's longtime mistress Marie "Maud" Miller Colby in middle age. Colby finally married her in 1906 after she had inherited a quarter of a million dollars. (Photograph courtesy of Nebraska State Historical Society.)

Paul Livingston Colby, aged three years, Leonard W. Colby's son by Marie Miller. (Photograph courtesy of Helen Colby Collection.)

Clarence Colby, the child Leonard
and Clara Colby adopted from an
orphan train, pictured here in 1906.
(Photograph courtesy of Helen Colby.)

A tall teenager, Lost Bird (far right) stands with unidentified group
in Beatrice, Nebraska in 1907.   (Photograph courtesy of Helen Colby Collection.)

Standing (*left to right*): Marie Colby in her knickers next to her husband, Leonard W. Colby, in 1924. Others unidentified. (Photograph courtesy of Helen Colby Collection.)

A copy of this photograph of Clara B. Colby was placed under the coffin quilt and was buried with Lost Bird on July 11, 1991 at Wounded Knee, South Dakota.

(Photograph courtesy of Joan Indermark.)

The reburial of Lost Bird at the Wounded Knee Memorial Gravesite, July 11, 1991. Walking around Zintkala Nuni's grave is Arvol Looking Horse (second from left), 19th-generation Keeper of the Sacred Calf Pipe of the Lakota Nation.
(Photograph courtesy of Nathan Blindman.)

Zintkala Nuni, the Lost Bird, at the 1915 Panama Pacific Exhibition in San Francisco.
(Photograph courtesy of the New York Public Library.)

ners in the den and library. Her greatest diversion is to arrange her papers, shorthand notes, etc., classifying them in the leaves of a magazine. She takes dictation, folds Bulletins and directs papers, imitating in a wonderful way all the usual features of each performance."[18]

Clara's Saturday-evening teas continued and the Gandhi family were frequent guests. She also corresponded with Leo Tolstoy about the conditions of starvation in his country.[19] She was just regaining her equilibrium, when to her horror she discovered that Maud Miller was secretly writing to Leonard and that he had been sending her money.[20] No wonder Maud had seemed self-assured and indifferent to Clara's prayers, friendship, and job offers.

An ugly scene with Leonard followed and he again swore his complete innocence, but this time Clara would have none of it. She wrote bitterly to Maud, who responded:

> You ask me why I wrote to Mr. C.—and how it was that I received money from him. My reason for writing was that baby was sick, and that I feel it my duty to tell him of it, for baby is his as well as mine, and I cannot see that it was a breach of confidence toward you for me to write to him under the circumstances. If baby had not recovered when he did I would have written again. When I wrote I told him how much money I had. . . . [H]e gave me some the day I left Washington, and naturally, he would want to know if I had any of it left, and how it was spent. So he sent me enough to pay my expenses for another week, and my board is now paid up. . . . I did not ask him to send it, but when he did, I thought it was very thoughtful of him to do it. He does not ask me to write and I do not ask him, but if ever the same thing should happen to baby again, I would not hesitate a moment to write to Mr. C.—To write to him as your husband may not be right, but to write to him as my child's father informing him of the child's illness is not an unpardonable wrong.—It does not seem so to me. I am trying to do what is right in this matter, but to make a promise that I will not write to him again is something I cannot do. I would rather not accept money from him, but I do not think it wrong for me to do so, as long as the baby is in my care. . . . His letter was a short one, but very kind, and to know that he thinks of his helpless baby when it is sick, is a help to me and not a hinderance.
>
> You know I want your help and that I appreciate what you do for me. Don't have hard feelings toward me, but be my true friend as you have been always. My lot is so hard to bear and I need all the help I can. Write to me soon. Yours Sincerely, M.[21]

Clara's accounts show that the "short note" Leonard sent to Maud was a telegram costing $37, money he had borrowed from her while pretending he was broke.[22] Clara again moved the sly young woman further away from Baltimore to a Philadelphia boarding house owned by Mary Watson. Clara was afraid Mrs. Watson might find out the truth, yet she wanted to know if Leonard was sleeping with Maud. Her fears were realized when Mrs. Watson wrote:

> My Dear Madam—As I suppose you are interested in the welfare of Mrs. Miller I will tell you a few things which may be of interest to you. She was here only a short time before it was evident something was amiss. We thought she was the victim of misfortunes and she had our deepest sympathy. We have sinse [sic] had reasons to believe that she was not blameless. We could not have allowed her to remain here so long except from consideration of her youth and interest in her dear little child. . . . She went from here I believe . . . saying she expected to stay there (?) a few days waiting for some letter or letters, then go to Washington before going to her parents in the west. If she has a home and pass and you have any influence over her I trust she may be persuaded to go to them as soon as possible. . . . I must also add, in my own behalf—that you placed me in a very trying and questionable situation which even your interest in Mrs. Miller could not justify. Believe me, Very Truly yours—Mary H. Watson.[23]

Clara must have asked for details to get this reply:

> Dear Mrs. Colby: If you have known Mrs. Miller in Nebraska and in Washington you must know her well enough. . . . I think my first letter to you was plain enough to make dissembling unnecessary. In your letters you have kept entirely clear of the matter which we both understand [the child], and have not committed yourself to one word. And yet you ask me to lay before you the facts in which I founded my unfavorable opinion. I do not think we shall reach any further conclusion, and regret that I cannot be of assistance to you. Very Truly yours, Mary H. Watson.[24]

On February 28, 1894, Clara wrote to Maud:

> There is no money in our firm for family or other expenses save as I furnish it, and has not been for nearly two months: and this condition must exist yet a while longer. I mention this that you may understand

pto the amount you need to have. . . . Now

why I must figure down just the amount you need to have. . . . Now while I am willing to stand by you financially, and give you my back-ing . . . I can give you no sympathy or friendship while you persist in writing to that party. I forgave the past and would stand by you as if you were my sister in any effort to make reparation or to live an honorable life in the future, but I have no tolerance or charity for such continu-ance in wrong-doing as is implied in your writing to him. As long as your financial claims are recognized you have no need as you have certainly no right to seek to continue correspondence. You can take your choice. If you want my friendship, countenance or assistance you have to merit it, by showing a desire to break off all dishonorable rela-tions and communications. Whatever is needful for that party to know shall be conveyed honestly and in a friendly spirit by myself, and you may count on me to the death if you are true and honorable. There cannot be so much satisfaction in such correspondence that you should wish to lose the help and sympathy of one who at such cost has acted the part of a sister to you, but who will never aid and abet any-thing further in the line of that conduct which has brought so much ruin. . . . Hoping that you will receive this in a right spirit and respond to it as you were now standing before the bar of God where you must some day answer for all the sins not repented of here . . . [25]

Maud wrote complaining that she could not be expected to wash diapers:

. . . Little things I wash myself, but it's impossible for me to do the larger things and for them I must pay seventy-five cents per dozen. . . . I am living here with Mrs. Spencer, the woman that will see to Paul when I go west. Did I tell you the arrangements I made with her? She will charge like everything but I know he will be safe and have the very best of care. She will take him for one or two or three months but she expects $20 a month. . . . This $20 she wants in advance. . . . A weakness has come on me the last couple of months for which I am under treatment now. I don't think I will ever be really well again. . . . Now don't be angry with me . . . Very Sin-cerely Yours, M. [26]

No letters from Leonard Colby to his mistress have been found, but it can be inferred that Maud wrote with the strength and self-assurance of her lover:

Dear Mrs. Colby: I cannot give you any answer different from the one already given you. I do not think I would be doing right in making a promise that I will never, under any circumstances whatever, write to Mr. C.—again. I am sure I would be doing my child a great wrong if I made such a promise. Your feeling in the matter is only natural, for he is your husband, but my feeling is natural too, for he is my child's father. I write to him very seldom, but I will never promise to stop writing to him altogether.

You do not tell me if I am to expect a [free] pass to Nebraska or not. If you will get me one, let me know how soon I can get it, and if you do not expect to get one for me let me know that. I expect to go west in a few days, and I want to know whether I can count on a pass or not. I am ready to go—have Paul provided for, etc. and I am now waiting on an answer from you . . . Very Sincerely, Maud.[27]

Blackmailed, Clara could not allow the scandal to hurt her husband's position or her work for woman suffrage, and Maud knew it. Clara was reduced to begging:

> . . . You still do not make me the little promise for which I have plead so earnestly. You say you know what I say is true, but you entirely evade the point as to whether you have chosen the friendship . . . or illegitimate clandestine correspondence with one who has hurt you. . . . This is a question you have got to meet fairly and squarely before you go West. If you do not make me the promise I ask I shall make no statement that will protect you—nor countenance you in any way, shape, or manner. I am firm now in order to protect both of you if it may be possible from open scandal in the future. I am not prepared to help you to make such expensive arrangements as you have contemplated for the baby, especially when you offer me no hope for the future. . . . There cannot be two of us sending money. . . . You must promise to refrain from corresponding with my husband. . . . Is this too much of an injured wife to ask of a woman who professes to wish to live honorably in the future?[28]

Leonard's whereabouts were unknown when Clara went to Philadelphia and begged Maud to give her husband up for good. Clara broke down and Maud promised never to see Leonard again, but she refused to stop writing to him. Maud planned to leave her child with one of Clara's friends while she visited her family in Nebraska. Clara also arranged to pay Maud's tuition to a Chicago business college. A series of letters followed, in which Maud appeared to be mending her ways, although she was still accepting money from both Clara and Leonard:

My Dear Mrs. Colby: Your kind and encouraging letters show me that you have faith in me and that you think me sincere when I say I want to give up this life and be honorable hereafter, and since you believe in me still, that helps me to believe in myself, and gives me hope for the future. In a recent letter from Mr. C—he says it may be two or three weeks before he returns, as his business detains him longer than he thought it would. He says he will send me money soon as he knows I must be out. . . . I must take what he sends as long as I am here, or until he has seen you for he does not know that a new declaration of independence has been made by me . . . [29]

In another letter Maud demands money and a train ticket home, and hints what will happen if she doesn't get it: "I rec'd a letter from home yesterday and the folks are looking for me now, and unless they see me very soon I know there will be trouble. My sister's letter says so."[30]

Leaving Paul behind, but not with the woman Clara arranged for, Maud took Clara's money and left for Nebraska. On her way home she stopped in Chicago, where Leonard may have been on business:

I am this far on my way home, and expect to arrive there tomorrow at about three. I did not leave Paul at that home, as I told you I would, but with a nice kind woman, who I know will be good to him. . . . You must not be hard and cold toward me. . . . Please write to me, and write just Beatrice, do not give the house number—I will call for the letters myself. . . . [D]on't make things harder by turning against me now . . . Sincerely, Maud.[31]

Whether Maud actually attended college is a matter of speculation, although she received money from Clara for tuition, room, board, and books. The school she ultimately chose was not the one in Chicago, as planned, but Western Normal College in Lincoln, Nebraska. Not two hours away, Leonard Colby was practicing law in Beatrice. He took whichever cases the court gave him, as his scheme with the Five Civilized Tribes had not as yet given him the lucrative contracts that would make him financially secure. One notorious murder trial was long remembered by the citizens of Beatrice. They packed the courtroom to see Leonard Colby, a court-appointed attorney, defend a man alleged to have brutally murdered a friend.

"Just say 'spoons' every time they ask you something," he told the killer, "or you'll hang." They agreed that if Colby got the killer off, the man would sign over one of three farms to him.

On the witness stand the demented man muttered, "Spoons." He stared blankly at the prosecutor.

"Spoons? What does that mean?" The state's attorney stood directly in front of the accused slayer. He held up a pearl-handled knife.

"This is the murder weapon, isn't it? The one you killed James with?"

"Spoons." The man was glassy-eyed.

The jury snickered and whispered to one another.

Leonard Colby was pleased. His plan to plead insanity for his client was working.

The trial went on all day and the defendant took the witness stand twice. The jury's verdict was not guilty by reason of insanity, and Colby solemnly led the man back to his office. Once the door was closed and bolted, Colby got down to business. He leaned back in a chair and put his feet up on the desk, his arms behind his head.

"Well then," he said. "You're as free as a bird now. Let's have that deed."

The murderer stared at his lawyer, his mouth open, his chin disappearing into his collar.

"Spoons," he mumbled.[32]

CHAPTER 10

Scandal

Alike amid the greatest triumphs and darkest tragedies
of life we walk alone.

ELIZABETH CADY STANTON

The *Nebraska State Journal* ran a headline in December 1894 that read:
"COMPLETE VINDICATION OF GENERAL COLBY OF NEBRASKA. CAN FIND NO
FRAUD":

> . . . The persistent fight made by Senator Chandler upon the office of the assis-
> tant Attorney-General in charge of Indian depredation claims . . . was caused
> by a clerk named Corning. . . . Senator Kyle of North Dakota . . . claimed that
> a large number of frauds had been perpetrated against the government in the
> matter of Indian depredation claims allowed on the South Dakota and
> northern Nebraska border. Mr. Corning not only utterly failed . . . [to prove
> allegations] . . . but showed himself so absolutely incompetent that he was dis-
> missed from the service . . .[1]

The general often traveled to Oklahoma and was never idle when it came
to Indian money. Oklahoma historian Angie Debo, who exposed wrongdoing against the Creek Nation in her classic work, *The Road to Disappearance,* wrote of Colby's schemes. She said that after the Creeks
requested distribution of $1 million dollars of Oklahoma land money in
1893, "other persons had laid their plans to secure it."[2]

On November 6, one month before newspapers announced the dismissed charges, General Colby spoke before the Creek Nation at Okmulgee, Oklahoma. Principal Chief Legus Perryman introduced Dew M.
Wisdom, the U.S. agent, who in turn presented General Colby. The Creeks
assembled in joint session, listening attentively to every word. Colby captivated them with his sincerity and conviction, his words punctuated with
eloquent references to their courageous battles against the formidable

Andrew Jackson during the Creek Wars. They heard the experienced lawyer fresh from Washington, a former Assistant Attorney General of the United States, remind them that his own grandmother was a full-blood Seneca. Then he told the tale he had described so many times that he must have believed it himself, the moving story of his beloved daughter, Zintkala Nuni, the Lost Bird, whom he said he had found under the body of her dead mother after the massacre at Wounded Knee. After he had touched their hearts and transfixed them with dramatic gestures, he got down to his real mission.

A reporter for the *Muskogee Phoenix* wrote that Colby "said the Indians have between 9,000 and 10,000 claims against them aggregating about $37,000,000. . . . Gen. Colby had studied the question thoroughly and advised the Creeks to employ a competent attorney at once to defend them . . ."[3]

Agent Wisdom recommended Colby for the job and then, despite the fact that he was a Progressive, he spoke against statehood and allotment, calling settlers "scallawags." He got everyone in a good mood, joking that Oklahoma Territory . . . "was now as poor as Job's turkey and Lazarus would be a banker in comparison (*laughter*)."[4] Wisdom's humor, combined with Colby's ringing speech, brought down the house and the Creeks hired Colby on the spot, his salary set at $4,000 annually.[5]

On November 9, the National Council of the Muskogee Nation hired him for three years at the same salary "to defend the interests of the Muskogee Nation in all suits pending or that may hereafter be brought in the court of claims or the Supreme Court of the United States."[6] After the Creeks and Muskogees fell for the scheme, the Otoe and Missouri Indians employed Colby on November 20. Finally, the cautious Cherokees, led by Principal Chief I. C. J. Harris, were persuaded on December 19.[7] Colby's emotional story of Zintka's rescue and his devotion to her worked every time—there was never a dry eye. Ironically, lawyers like John Beck, a Cherokee, could find no employment with his own tribe.[8]

During Colby's lifetime, several history books listed the general's achievements, but his work with Indian tribes was rarely mentioned, although he admitted he was attorney for the Cherokee, Osage, Choctaw, Creek, Chickasaw, Otoe, Muskogee, Missouri, and Seminole Nations. Vowing to protect tribes against (groundless) depredation claims, he earned an enormous amount of money during a time of national economic woes.

Less than a year after Colby "alarmed" the Creeks into falling for his scheme, tribal officials discovered the intrigue and blamed each other. Angie Debo described the result:

In 1894 after the first year's salary had been paid they repealed the law creating the contract. The Chief [Perryman] at Colby's request referred this act to the [Creek] Supreme Court, which declared that the Council had no power to revoke this obligation. Perryman then issued the warrant to pay Colby's salary under the original agreement. He explained his action . . . but the Council threatened to impeach him and passed a resolution again repudiating the contract, forbidding the payment of Colby's salary, and notifying the Department officials that Colby's employment was not recognized.[9]

Ignoring the council, Treasurer Samuel Grayson (Colby's old drinking crony) "made a payment on the warrant . . ."[10] When the full-bloods found out about it, "smoldering financial dissatisfaction burst into flame."[11] Many other alleged frauds were discovered in the investigation and the Creek people realized

> . . . that . . . $200,000 had been lost through embezzlement. Armed bands from different parts of the nation began to collect at Okmulgee, and . . . a delegation of the malcontents seized Chief Perryman and Treasurer Grayson, seated them in a drugstore on the square, and addressed accusing speeches to them.[12]

Caught swindling their own people, and fearing for their lives, Perryman and Grayson promised to return Colby's wages to the treasury "and entreated their accusers to present their grievances to the council, but a crowd quickly assembled and began to abuse them."[13] They were mauled until a brave, unnamed stranger jumped up on a fence and began an eloquent speech. The furious mob "gradually turned to listen and the imperiled officers went to their hotel. . . . Perryman then went to his home near Tulsa and remained there during the rest of the session."[14] Perryman and Grayson were eventually found guilty and impeached for embezzlement, but Colby got his money, paid to him on a warrant issued on paper elaborately illustrated with a buffalo bull.[15]

Debo wrote that the Creek government then went into a decline from which it did not recover: "as the white people rushed in to build the towns and develop the oil pools and purchase the farms, the full-blood Creeks were wholly unable to adjust themselves to the new order."[16] They tried one last time, "under a great native statesman named Chitto (Snake) Harjo," to form a tribal government based on their treaties, using the system of light horsemen to carry out their orders against the intruding white men.[17] Outnumbered, their leaders were arrested by the federal government.

Despite the harmful consequences of his pilfering, Colby maintained strong connections with the Cherokees. It was during his tenure as their attorney that the Cherokee Strip land sale passed Congress. The general might just as well have fallen headfirst into an unguarded treasure chest.

Over 6,000 acres of Cherokee land opened in 1893. Newspaper reports stated that the land would be made available "in the old-fashioned race-horse way, and the swiftest riders will get the best claims." Tribal lawyers, including the general, supposedly representing their clients, cashed in on the claims using various legal and illegal maneuvers. One astonished member of the House of Representatives called the sale a "fraudulent, disreputable, and dishonest" transaction. During the extraordinary session of the Fifty-third Congress, T. J. Hudson asked for a resolution in the House calling for an "investigation of the allotments and settlement of the so-called Cherokee Strip," but found that "so far as the Government officials were concerned there was no corruption justly chargeable to them. . . . The wrong-doers ought to be exposed and punished."[18] But Hudson found the "wrong-doers" were too slippery and occupied high offices.

A lawyer could easily defraud Indians by taking power of attorney over orphans and dispersing their money as he saw fit. Between 1907 and 1913, Kate Barnard, a courageous commissioner of charities and corrections in Oklahoma, investigated and found full-blood Indian children living in the open fields "like beasts," without clothes, while the guardians collected their royalties from oil land. When she found that guardians had placed normal Indian children in insane asylums, she pushed a bill through the Oklahoma Legislature making orphan Indian minors wards of the state.[19]

Fake guardianships and under-the-table payoffs were not unusual. Huge sums of oil lease money disappeared without a trace.

Claiming near-poverty in his own state, General Colby kept bank accounts outside Nebraska. In Painesville, Ohio, records show that his investments were looked after by the firm of Tuttle and Hubbard.[20] Years later, when the time was right, a mysterious half-million dollars suddenly appeared in Colby's possession.

While Zintka's adopted father was busy exploiting her story to steal from Indians, he was rarely at his Washington home. Zintka often sat on the stairs in front of the house hoping for his return. In early May 1894 she was playing there with her dog when a man came up to the door and Zintka looked up at him and grinned. "You look like a little Indian girl," Zintka said. Clara watched from the window at what happened next and reported in the *Tribune*:

> Notwithstanding the silk hat, and elegant morning suit worn by the caller, the little Indian maiden recognized the kinship and greeted with pretty prattle and trusting handclasp the French Indian, Honoré J. Jaxson; who had come . . . to express his appreciation of the attitude of the editor of the Tribune towards the

Indians and . . . to see the little girl whose pathetic story he had known. Nothing ever pleased him so much, he said, as her spontaneous friendly recognition of him. Mr. Jaxson has acquired some newspaper notoriety as the man that walked ahead of Coxey's Army (a large group of unemployed men walking across the country protesting government policies) . . .[21]

Zintka loved being outdoors and she loved animals. Harmony with nature created for the Lakota an inner balance of body, mind, and spirit. Living in a non-Indian world, however, Zintka could not develop that full understanding.[22] Clara somehow knew this concept, but her musings on Zintka's love of animals was seen from a non-Indian perspective—for example, when Zintka lost her dog, Senator:

> [Every day] Zintka went out to play with her in her nice back yard. . . . [Senator] would jump on her and tear her aprons all to pieces. At last the rule was made that Zintka could only play with the dog in the morning. Whether this hurt . . . Senator's feelings so that she grieved herself sick we do not know, but certain it is that the little dog lost her appetite, became very thin and a few days ago died. As she wasted away her long slender face became very beautiful in its gentle, pathetic expression, and we learned to love the dog so much that we would have given a great deal to save its life. A few mornings ago Zintka was told that the little doggie was dead. She went right down to the yard and looked at the dog and said nothing. But when the breakfast bell rang Zintka did not appear. At last she was found still gazing sadly at her dead playmate and was overheard saying, "Senator dearie, I did love you." With great reluctance Zintka at last went in . . .[23]

Zintka brought a cat in from the street even after Clara said, "Why Zintka, that is somebody's pet cat."

"Oh, no," she replied, "it is nobody's kitty."

When Clara refused to let her keep the cat, she "was solaced" by a poem that she always wanted to hear:

> Nobody's kitty was out in the snow
> Nobody's kitty had nowhere to go
> Nobody's kitty cried: Miew, miew, miew!
> Somebody pity me. Do Do Do! . . .[24]

Zintka seemed to crave a closer knowledge of nature. One day while out walking with Clara, the girl witnessed a midair fight between a chicken hawk, grasping a snake in its beak, and a number of smaller birds. Zintka began reciting a poem of which Clara said "she is very fond." In her own culture, it would have been a personal song or prayer, but Zintka repeated the verse her mother had taught her:

> Then stay at home my heart, and rest,
> The bird is safest in its nest,
> O'er all that flutter their wings and fly,
> A hawk is hovering in the sky.[25]

Zintka often asked her mother to repeat a story about a canary. Reading between the lines it is easy to see why:

> It is about a little girl who had a lovely canary. Its name was Jack. Jack had one fault, he sang too much; he sang very sweetly and would sing for hours together. The little girl would say, "Dear Jack, do be quiet for a little while." Still he would sing in spite of all. Then the little girl would put him in a dark closet. It did not matter; still he would sing. His cage door was always opened every morning after breakfast and he would hop out and keep on singing. But one morning Jack flew away and the little girl felt very sorry. She called and cried in vain. At last she put on her hood and took the empty cage and wandered all over the farm. Just as she was returning, sad and weary, she heard her dear bird's voice. He was in the middle of the road, and seemed quite delighted to see his mistress. The little girl put down the cage, opened the door and called to her little feathered pet, "Jack, dearie, come home and you may sing as loud and as long as you wish," . . . The bird flew into the cage and has never flown away since. He sings to his heart's content. Zintka never tires of the story and says again and again, "Tell me the story about the lost bird that was always singing," and then she adds, "She was a good little girl to let her bird sing and make all the noise he wanted to."[26]

Clara reported many of Zintka's experiences in the *Tribune*, perhaps hoping the general might read them. The newspaper also included this poem submitted by Isabel Darling of Fruit Vale, California:

> "Lanuni! Lanuni!" the south wind is calling,
> "Zintka Lanuni, come out here and play!
> We'll sing in the chimneys,
> And swing on the grapevine,
> We'll fly to the mountains and whistle all day.
> We'll dry up the water that stands in the hollows
> We'll cuddle the birds in the trees
> And call for the flowers and the bees,
> So come, for 'tis summer, we know by the swallows,

And the frost cannot find us,
And the ice cannot bind us.
We'll hunt the wild goslings—we, you and I.
Come, baby, and try
Zintka, Zintka Lanuni!"[27]

Occasionally, Clara wrote that Zintka "wished she could see her papa" more often, but in truth the general was no longer a vital part of Zintka's life and it was Clara who wished to see him.

Clara barely managed to keep her newspaper going because she was still lending money to her husband, thinking he was penniless. Maud was cashing in on both of them—but not for long. In June 1894 Clara dropped Zintka off with her mother-in-law in Freeport, Illinois, and returned to Beatrice unexpectedly, reaching the darkened town unnoticed on a late-night train. It was not difficult to slip quietly through the kitchen door of her own house, past her summer office, up the stairs near the nursery and across the hall to the bedroom she had so lovingly decorated. This time, however, Clara burst in upon her husband's passion. She demanded that the surprised lovers leave the house, but Leonard lashed back, saying he would no sooner abandon his mistress than Clara would give up her newspaper and suffrage, a devastating option. It was her choice!

This was not the first indication that Leonard resented her suffragist activities. Although she loved him, why should she give up her life's work, betraying hundreds of women who awaited her newspaper, and why give up Miss Anthony and Mrs. Stanton for a lying, unfaithful husband? The agony of rejection, of knowing in her heart that her husband no longer loved her, of seeing his arms encircling the body of another woman, stung like no other physical or mental pain she had ever experienced. Full of anger, guilt, and worry for her future and that of a small child twice left fatherless, Clara turned to her faith for the decision:

> On my knees before God in prayer have I sought to be delivered from this duty, but He has laid it upon me and now I am ready to accept it and to consecrate myself to its success.[28]

Clara decided to keep her newspaper and continue to work for woman suffrage. As a final cruelty, Leonard wanted to take Lost Bird away from her, but Clara refused. She knew he would continue to exploit the child and there would be no end to it.

During the train ride back to Washington, memories of the past twenty-two years of marriage, of laughter and of love, must have filled her heart. Alone in her grief, she realized how much more Maud and Leonard had in common than mere greed and lust. Maud had given him what she could not—a son. They had taken the money she needed to care for two young children, one of them mentally handicapped, and they refused to discontinue their illicit relationship. Somehow, she must find a way to survive the anguish of infidelity without becoming bitter and hardened to life. She could not allow them to destroy her sense of self.

Clara said nothing to Leonard's mother when she picked up Zintka. The child was coughing again. By the time they reached Washington, Zintka could barely breathe. Frightened, Clara called in a doctor, something she had never done before. Dr. Shute diagnosed a severe case of whooping cough, administered medicine, and stayed all night with Zintka, saving her life. He noticed that Clara was exhausted and suffering mental anguish that seemed to reach beyond the illness of her child. After she confided in him, the gentle doctor prescribed a vacation for Zintka and Clara—just the two of them—to rest at the seashore until they had both recuperated. For the first time in her life, Clara took a male physician's advice. As soon as Zintka was able to travel, she took her to the Atlantic seaboard.[29] About this time, Zintka displayed what her mother termed "her roguishness" when a train conductor kindly remarked, "I wonder when I will see you again?"

"You won't know me when you see me again," she snapped. "I will be an old woman."[30]

In return for free advertising in the *Tribune*, a friend allowed them two weeks at Asbury Park, New Jersey, in "a comfortable and well furnished cabin . . . 3 blocks from the beach with roomy and shady yard."[31] The doctor had been right—sea air relieved Zintka's cough and the rest was good for both of them. If nothing else, her husband's rejection brought her closer to Zintka, and her motherly affection deepened. Holding hands, they walked along the beach and out on a jetty, dangerously wet and slippery; high waves curled up and over the sides, spraying seawater into holes between the rocks. Clara could not afford to buy candy at the stalls lining the boardwalk, but they ambled down the steps to the shore carrying fruit and bread in a basket. Together, mother and daughter built tall towers in the sand and collected bluish smoky shells and moon snails.

When Clara returned to her work a new sadness swept the *Tribune*. On the front page of the next issue appeared a poem by William Ernest Henley, a poet of the day:

WHAT IS TO COME?

What is to come we know not. But we know
That what has been was good, was good to show,

. . . We are the masters of the days that were.
We have lived, we have loved, we have suffered,
even so . . .
Let the great winds their worst and wildest blow,
Or the cold weather round us mellow slow;
We have fulfilled ourselves, and we can dare
And we can conquer, though we may not share
In the rich quiet of the afterglow.
What Is to Come?[32]

Clara had no idea what to do next. She could not tell Miss Anthony of her husband's affair. When she asked to take Zintka along on suffrage lectures, Anthony wrote:

As to your proposition to take the Indian baby to meetings with you—I say "No" most emphatically—for you to do so would be an imposition upon every household in which you should be inter-tained—and upon every audience as well—And beside that nui-sance—you would distract the thought from the one point of woman's enfranchisement—and turn to adoption of Indian babies—the amalgamation of the races & all sorts of side thoughts. . . . No, no, if you go anywhere . . . for the purpose of helping our work along—go by yourself. . . . My dear—it is a crazy thought . . . and would be a crime if carried out—you had vastly better not go into another state campaign than to exhibit that untutored Indian girl of yours—so don't think of it—Lovingly yours, Susan B. Anthony.[33]

Leaving Clarence in boarding school, Clara took Zintka to her sister's home in Beatrice. Mary took one look at Clara and knew something was wrong. After swearing Mary to secrecy, Clara confided her sorrow, know-ing full well what Mary's reaction would be: No Bewick had ever been divorced! Leonard would surely come to his senses. Time would pull him away from scandalous relations with a low-bred woman.

Clara joined the suffrage campaign in Kansas, but the trip was a fiasco. She was so distracted she could not even follow a train schedule, let alone a dozen lectures across the state, getting to a place two hours late, drenched, only to find it was the wrong town on the wrong day.[34] Virginia L. Minor, a longtime friend from St. Louis, died, adding to her grief. She came back to Beatrice—past her former home where Leonard slept with his voluptuous mistress, past the fragrant rose garden she had planted—a wounded soul. Clara was not the first or the last public figure to live a bittersweet lie—an outward façade of family harmony and happiness darkened by the clouds of reality, the American family divided. But Leonard would come back, there was no doubt about that. He thoroughly enjoyed hosting parties where he stood like a knight, one foot on a chair, enthralling his guests with Civil War and Indian battle exploits. He savored the atmosphere, the intellectual stimulation of celebrities who came to his comfortable home, made hospitable by the social graces of a brilliant wife. It would take time, but Clara was sure he would eventually come back to her.

Not realizing Clara's predicament and disapproving of her purpose to write a "first-class home paper in every way," including issues other than suffrage, Miss Anthony wrote to Mrs. Stanton:

> . . . I see Mrs. Colby announces she is going to omit her paper this summer. . . . [T]hat will just finish it.—The friends everywhere seem to have lost heart over the Tribune—her Coxeyism, her Indian religionists sufferings—and now her dress page—there doesn't seem to be any consecutiveness about her paper—If she hadn't such piles of encumbrances—her house, boy, Indian & etc.—If she were free-footed—she would be just the person to come straighten & help me dig through the mountain piles in our back garret—alas I know of no one to look to . . .[35]

The women in Beatrice read Clara's newspaper and Mary heard the thoughts of her patients regarding Colby's affair. She watched in disgust as her brother-in-law reestablished his law practice, hiring as his private stenographer the lovely Miss Maud Miller, who had left her young son to be raised in a private home in another town. Some townspeople were appalled by Colby's brazen adultery, and he was taken off the guest lists of some wealthier families. Because of his shameless behavior, he was temporarily shunned by peers. According to Fordyce Graff, city clerk and a friend of Colby's, the reaction did not seem to bother the general:

> He didn't care what people said about him. He was a good talker, I'll tell you that. He made 'em big promises. He was so polite, you'd never think he was a crook. He'd strut. The better class wouldn't have much to do with him but most of the men liked the rascal, anyway. You have to remember, the General was a patriot—a Civil War hero—and a man couldn't forget that! Every fourth of July he'd be on that white Arabian, leading the parade down Court Street. The men cheered 'im and the women couldn't keep their eyes off 'im.[36]

Only once, in June 1895, Colby's private life caught up with him. He was passed over for the position of adjutant general, and the newspapers made note: "In selecting his new staff officers, Governor Holcomb has omitted Gen. Colby, the old-time warrior who has been identified with Nebraska military affairs for many years."[37] Historian Norma Kidd Green, whose family knew the general, wrote: "L. W. Colby was a brilliant man of great egotism and a rather uncertain code of ethics—and, I assure you, I am stating it mildly in comparison with the words used by Beatrice people."[38] The wealthy families of Beatrice, the Kilpatricks, Westons, Cooks, and Elliots had as little to do with Colby as possible, although his brash appeal continued to amuse and delight the male citizens of Beatrice. Clara's women friends of many years simply ignored Maud Miller as though she did not exist.

In Washington, Zintka had crying fits, awakening in the night from terrifying dreams. In them, she ran screaming from someone who was shooting at her. Clara tried to soothe her, but the nightmares continued.

In April 1895, with public demand for more detailed information about Zintka and wishing to increase circulation during a time when they were in distressing need for money (and perhaps in an effort to appeal to Leonard), Clara began an interesting column in her paper called "Zintka's Corner." Here she wrote regularly of Zintka's doings, sayings, and problems:

> . . . in any case of violent and continued crying [mothers] should make a vigorous application of cold water to the head. . . . [I]t is always an effectual way to stop crying because it diverts the attention and quiets the nerves.
>
> A child can be . . . accustomed to . . . darkness although allowance must be made for inherited nervousness. But in the beautiful evening hours which precedes tucking the child in bed the mother should sometimes rock and sing to it in a dark room, taking it to the window to see the life still active in the streets and the gleaming lights which show where other little people are going to bed. Everything should be done to teach the child that the room is absolutely the same when the light is out. Call attention to some object, put the light out and ask the child to bring the object. The lesson can be conveyed under the guise of pleasant games. Even the shadows which make the terror of the dark can be turned into objects of delight. "I so paid (afraid)" said a little one not long since as she glanced around the room and then buried her face in her mother's arms to hide the pictures made on the wall by lights from the street . . .[39]

Zintka's remarkable clairvoyance fascinated Clara. She often made reference to this ability: "One peculiarity . . . is her ability to read the thoughts of those about her. She has on several occasions interpreted looks from strangers and impetuously answered their unspoken inquiry in her own baby fashion . . ."[40]

Clara believed Zintka had inherited a spiritual acumen as well as a love of music, which became more pronounced. By the time Zintka was five years old, she was restless. She paced, wandered, and frequented the alley to hear her favorite tunes. She learned the musical variations of ragtime to play at home on her mother's piano. Clara's relatives and friends misunderstood ragtime, and thought the child was simply banging out tunes without regard for classical grace.[41] Zintka could play every rag she heard by ear. Realizing her natural talent, Clara begged Leonard to send a little money for piano lessons but, although he could now well afford the request, he continued to ignore his Indian daughter.

By September 14, 1895, Zintka was confused about her identity. Clara wrote that "she is always trying to figure out her exact status in the human family, being bewildered by all the remarks she hears . . ."[42]

Zintka was not alone in her confusion. After Clara asked her sister Mary to talk to the general, she received this letter:

My Dear Sister—

I must write you. . . . I went to see Mr. Colby because you wished it, & I had promised it, I gave your desire (for him to come & make a home) as best I could. He ridiculed the idea, said "When he wanted to become a nun or enter a convent he would as soon live with you as not" & talked at length along that line. . . . [H]e read me two letters where he had generously sent Zintka 10.00 & 5.00 dollars respectively, & I call that generous for three years support. I told him you had given him all your young days & that as a man he couldn't cast you off in your old age without any support. Well as I came through the hall I discovered that low creature had left the doors open just far enough to hear every thing. I was so angry to think I had not noticed it before so that I might have banged them shut. Well the next day after that I heard a story that makes your sufferings seem light, but also shows you can never move that man to mercy to say nothing of decency. He had a mistress long years ago by whom he had three children, he took a little child to this woman to care for and bring up. The son of another woman. He then deserted her, left her to take in washing or anything else she could find to do, & never provided her with so much as one dollar, the 4 children are living now— I know their names and address—there is no mistake about it—you know their mother. I did slightly—but a gentle refined educated beautiful girl—she soon lost her beauty by that life—neglect—& poverty. She died about a year ago, & the children do not know who their father is, but her brother & her people do. It was while she was toiling to support her family & this boy, that he had his children by

Miss Frazier & then got her property—the old Col. Sabin house away from her—then she had to go the same way Mary Davis did. I do not know how old Miss Miller's child is, but the youngest girl of the family I am telling you about, is about 13 years. This with Miss Frazier's in between or about that time does not proclaim him very amstemrous? [sic] neither does it argue much for your ever winning him back to a decent life.

I was used up . . . I was still mad at the thought of that door being open—so I phoned down—"was he in?" No! Was this his stenographer? Yes. Well, you give him this message for me. This is Dr. White, tell him that I know where his three children by one woman & the one by another one & can tell him about them. He has lost track of them for several years & I can give him any information about them he wishes, if he will phone or write." She said with great impudence "I think you'd better write." I said, "You give him my message and he'll decide which to do."

In the P.M. I was asked for—was not in & a message left to call up the office which I did three times, but could get no response, & I left the next morning. Now if you believe this—which is not likely, as you have never believed anything against him—if you wish to know the names, & where they are you must in your letter promise not to use the information to make the relatives any trouble, especially the brother who has devoted his life since old enough to earn a living for them & who takes care of them now that the mother is dead. The boy he took to her never knew he was not her son, & is now a worker in cut glass, is a fine looking fellow they say.

Darling sister I would not have written all this but I think you ought to know, & perhaps you will at last cease to try to get him back. Tho I am less in favor of a divorce now than ever, as they say Miss M [Miller] will move heaven and earth to give her boy a name, even tells he is going to get a divorce & marry her. God bless & help you. Write soon to your loving sister. Mary.[43]

CHAPTER 11

Whites Only

Harriet Beecher Stowe's novel *Uncle Tom's Cabin* was first published in 1852, eight years before the Civil War. The book had jolted the American conscience with an appeal to look upon slavery as a crime. Stowe died in 1896, and ironically, that was the year in which the Supreme Court upheld racial segregation by sustaining the "Jim Crow car law," giving individual states the right to provide blacks with separate facilities for education, transportation, and public accommodations. The wave of segregationist measures designated drinking fountains, public benches, rest rooms, railroad cars, hospitals, and theater sections as "whites only" or "colored."

Since Zintka could not avoid public transportation, she became the target of humiliating racial slurs. She was called "chinee," "tar baby," "squaw," or "nigger" so often that by the age of seven, the child had become uncomfortable and guarded around white people.[1] A Washington reporter interviewed Zintka and her mother about this time:

> . . . her restless Indian spirit has not yet entirely settled down to eastern methods and eastern manners. She plays with the children of the neighborhood . . . but despite the warnings and admonitions of Mrs. Colby, is not always choice in the selection of her companions—Zintka being of a dark complexion naturally, perhaps, sees no crime in the dusky skins of the darkey children, . . . It is Mrs. Colby's constant care to guard her from association with children with whom she should not associate and to aid her and instruct her in the rules of propriety.[2]

Shuttled from one caregiver to the next, Lost Bird never seemed to fit in, although her teachers in Washington were said to "marvel at her deftness of hand, her ingenuity, her close observation and her readiness at imitation."[3] When the child first went to school she was carefully observed:

> [She] was more studied and more interesting to the pupils than any book that ever was written. Her nationality bothered the scholars somewhat and

their curiosity on this point earned them the scorn of Zintka. She is very proud of her ancestry, a Sioux always is, so when they asked her if she was a negress she wilted the inquirer with one scornful flash of her eye. During the balance of the afternoon she would have nothing to do with that particular set of children and will probably remember the insult . . .[4]

After having been told she should not play with black children, she was thought to be one. It was all very confusing. Zintka disliked school because the children stared, made fun of her, or asked rude questions. She was too exotic to be accepted as human. They could not get past the fact that she was an Indian—and to them a museum piece rather than a person.

The questions Zintka was asked, she asked her mother in turn. Did her family live in a tipi? Did they really scalp women and eat babies as the children at school told her? Clara had studied Indian history more than most. She read about them in books written by white historians and anthropologists and entertained Christian English-speaking interpreters and mixed-blood Indians in her home. Since Clara could not speak to a full-blood Indian except through an interpreter and had never visited a reservation, her information came from reformers such as anthropologist Alice Fletcher and educator Elaine Goodale Eastman.[5] So Clara answered Zintka's questions from the white perspective, as best she could, and added the story of the Lakota mother who had loved her baby so much that she died using her body as a shield to protect her on the bloody field at Wounded Knee.

Although living in an alien society and confused about her place in the world, Zintka always cherished this loving image of her real mother. Clara had an unwavering faith in Zintka, and Mrs. Colby's greatest gift to her adopted daughter was that mental picture of maternal love. Clara bonded with Zintka after having raised her from a baby, but Zintka's bonds had been formed before she was born.

Clara's problems, especially the lack of money, had become so severe that even Elizabeth Cady Stanton heard about her difficulties. The possibility that "the best suffrage paper ever published" might fold brought Mrs. Stanton to the rescue.[6] From 1895 until a year before her death in 1902, Stanton played a major role as contributing editor of the *Woman's Tribune*. The interdependence between Clara and Stanton kept the newspaper afloat and Stanton's opinions continuously in print.

Clara prodded Mrs. Stanton to write her memoirs for the *Tribune*: ". . . I began my reminiscences at Mrs. Colby's suggestion, and at the point of the bayonet she has kept me at them ever since. . . . For whatever weariness or pleasure the readers of the *Tribune* have experienced in perusing these chapters, they may blame or praise Mrs. Colby."[7]

The hectic nature of Clara's life kept her continually on the move, which meant that little Zintka, too, lived a hurried life. Clara was driven, and she would not slow down. Work meant not remembering the hurts of the past, not feeling the lingering sorrows. Mrs. Stanton told her that she was doing "Herculean work," and the two cooperated so closely together that some chapters of memoirs and untold prosuffrage leaflets and articles were the work of both women. After Stanton had written a paragraph or two, she told Clara: ". . . add something of your own and put your name on it."[8]

Although Stanton contributed constant editorial advice and articles, she was unable to help Clara financially. From 1894 on, Clara made a living for her family by lecturing and by writing magazine articles. After one lecture, Zintka dictated her first letter for the *Tribune* readers, which clearly contained a message for Leonard to come home:

> My mamma says I must write a letter to the little children who read my corner and I think I ought to, because I am now seven years old. . . . I have been to Onset Bay with mamma and I had four baths in the ocean water, that is very salt: and I had a very good time splashing about. I wish you could have been with me. One night when it was dark, mamma and I went in our bathing suits from Miss Hatch's to the beach and had a bath all alone, and it wasn't moonlight.
>
> Mamma gave a lecture there, with some stereopticon slides and Indian pictures, and one of them was I . . . The other day I saw two carrier doves and if we owned one, and put a letter on its neck it would go straight to papa: and if papa took one with him to Nebraska and then tied a letter on its neck and let it go, it would come straight back to us. These doves were brownish red with white on their necks all frizzled up, and on the face. The bird man called them homing pigeons. I think it is very wonderful that they can fly so many miles over woods and waters to find their home and not lose their way. Well, I must say good-by for this time,—Zintka Lanuni Colby[9]

Besides lecturing on Indians, Clara spoke on varied topics as "New Light on Ancient Egypt," "Using the Horizontal Heat Ray to Dry Food," "Dual Personality," "The Esoteric Teachings of the Gnostics," "Irish Stories," and "The Mystery of Sleep." She also gave talks on famous writers of the day— Bergson, Whitman (her favorite), Churchill, Shaw, Bjerregaard, Browning, Margaret Fuller, Thomas Carlyle, and Ibsen.[10] Lecturing brought in just enough money for her to eke out a meager existence.

Meanwhile, Mrs. Stanton had been writing major portions of a book entitled *The Woman's Bible.* A radical, feminist criticism of the Bible, excerpts of it appeared in the *Tribune.* The controversial subject brought furious disapproval from Miss Anthony: "It seems to me—that your

espousal of the Woman's Bible—and the publication of it in your paper—
has cut off all possibility of your gathering around you the majority of the
suffrage women. . . . [*The Woman's Bible*] . . . is so flippant & superficial."[11]
Clara defended her right to publish Stanton's views: ". . . the *Tribune*
would not hesitate to give Mrs. Stanton's word on any subject relating to
the status of women . . . and there are many who consider that the discussion is not harmful to the cause of woman's equality; but rather vital to true
progress."[12] With these words, Clara took her stand, knowing she was in
the middle of an ugly situation. Angered at her suffrage colleagues, Mrs.
Stanton snapped that *The Woman's Bible* would have been a success if not
for ". . . Susan and her cohorts," meaning Anthony as well as Reverend
Anna Shaw and Carrie Chapman Catt, the women who had taken over
the heavy scheduling and travel burdens for the aging Miss Anthony.[13]

The *Woman's Bible* controversy came to a climax in Washington, D.C.,
during the NAWSA convention in early January 1896. After a heated
debate, the association voted to denounce Stanton's book. Clara was
shocked, and although Miss Anthony had seen it coming, she called the
renunciation: ". . . a piece of the rankest blasphemy . . ."[14] Miss Anthony's
view of the Scriptures was less militant:

> [The Bible] was written by men, and therefore its reference to women
> reflects the light in which they were regarded in those days. In the same way
> the history of our Revolutionary War was written, in which very little is said
> of the noble deeds of women, though we know how they stood by and
> helped the great work; and it is the same with history all through . . .[15]

The convention was already in turmoil when Clara decided on the spur of
the moment to allow Zintka to attend an evening session to hear her
mother speak. Susan B. Anthony presided over the session, dressed in her
dignified black silk dress and red shawl. She introduced Mrs. Colby, who
then stepped to the podium. Meanwhile, Zintka had slipped away from the
person entrusted to watch her, and when Clara began to lecture, a sudden,
terrified hush fell over the audience. Overlooking the podium was a
draped choir balcony, and there, balanced on the railing, her arms outstretched and a look of triumph on her face, walked the Lost Bird. Clara
looked up and saw Zintka, but no one dared move or shout in case the
child might lose her balance and fall. Placing her confidence in Zintka's
remarkable agility, Clara regained her composure and finished her speech,
little of which anyone heard. Then she left the stage, pulled up her dress
and petticoats, and rushed up the stairs to the balcony, where Zintka
jumped happily into her arms. Relieved, Clara took Zintka down to center
stage. She later made light of the incident in the *Tribune:*

Usually she goes to bed at 7 o'clock, but on Saturday evening, when her mamma was going to talk for a few minutes she was allowed to go, and very much enjoyed the experience. . . . She made herself quite at home in various parts of the church but was best pleased when cuddling up to Miss Anthony—she was placed by her on a chair.[16]

Describing Miss Anthony's reaction, Eleanor Claire Jerry wrote: "One can only speculate as to how gently Anthony placed [Zintka] there."[17] Thereafter, Clara was not permitted to bring Zintka to suffrage meetings. Anthony made it clear what she thought of Clara's household: "In my humble opinion . . . [y]ou owe it to yourself to disentangle yourself & fix upon the one thing & give yourself head & heart & soul to it! Young as you are—talented as you are—it is a crime for you to fritter yourself away on the scores of things—& in the scores of directions!!!"[18] In January 1896 Miss Anthony wrote to "the pen artist" of the woman suffrage movement:

My! how I wish you could be lifted out . . . into the broad and open freedom of surroundings that would give you your whole time, brain & body to writing and studying—I feel the world—our cause especially—robbed because of the enslavement of poverty with its appalling burdens—that holds you away from the grand work you long to do—.[19]

Publication of *The Woman's Bible,* combined with Zintka's antics, left Miss Anthony's associates (especially Carrie Chapman Catt) furious with Clara. Miss Anthony continued to send occasional gifts of cash, which also annoyed Catt.[20] But Clara had made formidable enemies within the suffrage movement—women who would conspire against her in the years to come. Standing firmly behind Zintka and making light of anything unpleasant connected with her, Clara was ridiculed behind her back by the women she most wanted to please.

Stared at, petted, and doted upon, Zintka had to fight racial prejudice. But no less hurtful was the zealous grasp of devout Christians such as Clara's wealthy distant relative Edwin Mauger, who sometimes took care of Zintka in his Brooklyn home. Letters reveal that on at least one occasion, Zintka ran away from Mauger's home so suddenly that she left her belongings behind.[21] How forcefully he had urged Zintka to submit to the will of God, or to him, can only be speculated upon. In a righteous protest reminiscent of Clara's father, Mauger had written to Clara after she published portions of *The Woman's Bible:*

My Dear Mrs. Colby:

It is with sorrow that I feel compelled in loyalty to my Lord—after looking over your paper rec'd today—to request you to discontinue sending it any longer to our address. . . . I dare not refrain from doing so, without the loss of a good conscience before God. The occasion of my thus writing . . . is . . . the paper's endorsement of Spiritualism, & your personal participation in the publication of the "Woman's Bible." . . . Dear friend Clara, . . . our prayers will not cease to ascend for your deliverance from Satan's snare.[22]

Mauger's alarm about Clara's "endorsement of Spiritualism" referred to her growing interest in psychic auras, spiritual healing, Spiritualism, and New Thought, a religious movement of the time that helped make her life more manageable in a world of change. She described it as:

. . . the philosophy which recognizes man's inherent divinity, . . . All the great scientists of the day agree that, about and through everything,—there is a play of Eternal Mind. . . . It matters not by what name we know it but it does matter that we know it as the (Radiant) Center from which we have come forth and to which we are still attached as a ray to its sun . . . from which all physical manifestations, all sense of beauty, all intellectual activity, and all spiritual aspirations have come forth . . . the cosmic consciousness.[23]

Clara's strict Baptist father, Thomas Bewick, was appalled. He died in April 1897 while still estranged from her, and it broke her heart that he could not bring himself to understand that she had a right to believe the way she wanted to believe.[24]

For years Clara had been interested in spiritual séances, even attending a few with Miss Anthony, and she frequently held palm and aura readings in her home.[25] Zintka's own clairvoyance only added to her interest: One night, Zintka sat beside her mother when the lamps were extinguished and the medium went into a trance. Zintka knew immediately that the woman was a fraud, but she sat through part of the séance quietly. When the medium called up the "Indian spirit guide," Zintka threw a tantrum and overturned the table.

Miss Anthony generally disapproved of Clara's mystical side, but she remained a close mentor, regardless of the criticism she heard from younger women in the movement. Anthony's Quaker belief in freedom of expression extended to everyone. By late summer 1897 *The Woman's Bible* rift within the suffrage movement had subsided as far as the outside world was concerned. Clara was delighted when she was invited along with Miss Anthony's closest friends to the Anthony family reunion in the Berkshire

Mountains near Adams, Massachusetts: "There is no one I would person-ally love to have present more than your own dear self," Anthony wrote.[26]

A reporter at the reunion noted that Miss Anthony was accompanied by "some of the most distinguished representatives of progressive women in the United States, whose fame is second only to that of their General, as they call Miss Anthony."[27] The friends included Carrie Chapman Catt, Reverend Anna Shaw, Clara B. Colby, Rachael Foster Avery, Harriet Taylor Upton, Lucy Stone, Ida H. Harper, and May Wright Sewell. It was a glorious occa-sion, and photographers captured the happy guests surrounding their hero-ine at her birthplace in the bright July sun. The reunion photo in Miss Anthony's famous biography shows a young Indian girl dressed in immac-ulate white standing alone and off to one side of the crowd. Her unhappy face peers out from beneath a heavy white hat festooned with flowers.[28]

CHAPTER 12

Cuba Libre!

Cuba consists of one large island surrounded by 1,600 smaller ones. It includes some 2,100 miles of magnificent coastal shores fringed with coral reefs, cooled by ocean breezes in summer and warm winds from the southeast in winter. In 1898 the capital city of Havana was home to Spanish despots who had ruled the country for 400 years. Virtually none of these corrupt government officials was Cuban, from the governor-general and his regional governors, treasurers, magistrates, and administrators, down to the parish priests; all were Spaniards who ruled like czars.

Even before the Civil War, American industrialists had been urging the annexation of Cuba, hoping to divide the Spanish colony into four slave states. At least five major Cuban insurrections (most of them plotted in the United States) against the Spanish colonists failed during the nineteenth century. The U.S. slave trade officially ended in 1865, but wealthy Americans continued to hold slaves in Cuba until 1886, when slavery was finally abolished by the Spaniards. Under the burden of high Spanish taxes, American-owned sugar and tobacco plantations began losing money at an alarming rate, thus germinating the seeds of the Spanish-American War.

A Cuban junta made its headquarters in New York City. Backed by rich U.S. entrepreneurs and adventurous mercenaries, it planned an organized rebellion that began in February 1895 under the auspices of an organization whose motto was "*Cuba libre!*" ("Free Cuba!")[1]

President Grover Cleveland had taken a firm stand against imperialism, but when William McKinley took office in 1897, debates intensified in the U.S. House of Representatives. Numerous Spanish atrocities caused some congressmen to call for formal sanction of the Cuba Libre movement. Through "pure love of liberty," American mercenaries joined the insurgents and in many cases led them in covert terrorist operations. American investments were exposed, causing a furious protest that McKinley could not ignore. He told "the Spanish Government that the barbarities . . . must be stopped and the war conducted more humanely, or the United States would intervene."

Despite an outward show of impartial neutrality and an outcry from anti-imperialists, who claimed he was about to break international law, McKinley asked Congress for money to bring all U.S. citizens home. The justification was that American lives were threatened. "Sure of the right, keeping free from all offence ourselves, actuated only by upright and patriotic considerations, moved neither by passion nor selfishness, the Government will continue its watchful care over the rights and property of American citizens . . ."[2]

Theodore Roosevelt, Assistant Secretary of the Navy, resigned his post in order to raise and lead a regiment of "Rough Riders" recruited from cowboys (and Indians) in the West. He also selected members among his athletic friends in fashionable eastern society. They became known as "Teddy's Terrors," and "Roosevelt's Rustlers," apt names for men who relished a fight. But Roosevelt was not the only eager buccaneer. Real estate tycoon John Jacob Astor, great-grandson of the family's founder, equipped an entire battery of men.

The best-known mercenary in Nebraska was fifty-year-old Leonard Colby, looking thirty-five, with not a gray hair on his head. In 1896 he joined Cuba Libre, calling his loose organization the American-Cuban Volunteer Legion. He claimed to have raised over $1.2 million and to have armed 25,000 volunteers at a fort near Matamoros, Mexico.[3]

When the U.S. Naval vessel *Maine* exploded in Havana harbor on February 15, 1898, killing 250 officers and men, the disaster aroused the indignation of the American people. An outcry from congressmen, urged on by the newspapers of William Randolph Hearst, pulled the United States into the Spanish-American War and out of the devastating economic depression of 1893–96.

In 1896 Leonard Colby began a series of visits to rekindle his marriage to his faithful wife. Flowers arrived at Clara's Washington home, he had his picture taken with Zintka, and he lavished gifts upon both of them.[4] The general promised to leave his young mistress and start a new life with Clara. He would find another location for his business, perhaps in Chicago, and reunite the family. Exhilarated, intoxicated, and seduced with romance like a young girl, Clara vowed to do everything possible to help him. And there was one thing he did want: an appointment as brigadier general for a volunteer legion. Clara began at once to visit congressmen and their wives in an effort to gain support for the husband who had been redeemed. Her work quickly paid off with letters of endorsement:

My Dear Friend:
  I have been to see the President for Mr. Colby, and urged his appointment. It gave me great pleasure to do so, both on your

account and on his, and also in the interest of the service, because I believe he would make a most excellent officer . . .

I also saw the Secretary of War and told him about Mr. Colby's qualifications, and that South Dakota joined with Nebraska in urging the appointment. I very much hope he will secure it. I shall be glad to do anything more I can if it will accomplish the desired result.—Believe me, Very truly yours, R. F. Pettigrew (U.S. Senator)[5]

Swayed by her love for Leonard, and horrified by his stories of an estimated 500,000 Cubans slain by the Spaniards, she expounded the familiar American outrage, despite her usual pacifist views, calling for a "Holy War. . . . All history shows that civilization has progressed only by stamping out the barbarous, the cruel, the degenerate."[6]

Clara's college classmate Martha Poland Thurston, wife of Senator John M. Thurston, died unexpectedly in March aboard a ship off the coast of Cuba.[7] She had refused to allow her husband to go without her. Martha's death influenced Clara to such a degree that she determined to accompany General Colby when the call to arms came. She wrote to Miss Anthony saying that she owed $1,500 to creditors and that she wanted the suffragist organization to pay this amount in the event that some of the "monsters of the pearl of the sea" should swallow her up.[8]

Miss Anthony replied on April 20: "Your letter about going to war received, but I think when you come to your senses you will decide not to be food either for malaria, yellow fever, starvation or bullets of Cuba and Spain, but if you go my best wishes go with you."[9] On May 10, Anthony wrote again: ". . . it is rough enough for our men and boys to rush into the melee! Pray! Our women and girls had better hold themselves aloof until they have a country that recognizes them as responsible members thereof. . . . Give my best wishes to Mr. Colby."[10] Elizabeth Cady Stanton also urged Clara to wait: "I hope you will not go to Cuba. . . . I wish I could see you for a long talk . . ."[11]

On June 3, 1898, Colby was commissioned brigadier general by President McKinley. Clara and Zintka could not accompany him back to Nebraska because Clara was anxiously awaiting her war correspondent's credentials, the "only pass issued to a woman's newspaper during the war."[12] Katherine "Kit" Blake Coleman of the *Toronto Mail and Empire* had been the first woman war correspondent and Clara followed suit, making clear her reasons: "It was the object of the writer in securing this pass to be able to accompany her husband with a recognized status, and in a capacity which would give her opportunities and protection to which she would not otherwise be entitled."[13]

Clara wired Beatrice newspapers of the general's arrival, and the patri-

otic citizens of Beatrice went wild. Clara published a letter to Zintka written by her niece Mary, describing his reception. (She also wanted Maud to
know there had been a reconciliation):

> My Dear Little Zintka: I want to send you a letter to tell you about the great
> time we had when your papa came back from Washington, and you must put
> it in your Corner so all the cousins can read about it. Beatrice was very
> proud that Uncle Leonard was made Brigadier General, because they feel he
> belongs to them. Well, we all knew when he was coming home, . . . and the
> people all turned out to meet him, and cannons were fired when the train
> got here. They took a carriage for him all covered with roses, and it was
> drawn by four white horses. There was a parade. Everybody turned out, and
> the big, beautiful white horse, Don, was in it, too. There were two
> bands . . . who marched along as proudly as if they were going to war, too.
> Then we all went to the opera house and had some fine speeches, and I was
> very proud of Uncle and what he said. Then there was a big reception . . .[14]

In the meantime Colby had engineered a coup of his own. His adopted son
Clarence had been in Beatrice working in the Colbys' stables. Leonard
somehow secured a position for Clarence as a bugler in the army. If the boy
lived through a battle, which was unlikely, he would be eligible for a pension,
letting the general off the financial hook in future years. Clara wrote a glowing account of her son: "[M]any of the editor's friends will remember the curly
headed little fellow who used to accompany her on her lecture trips. And now,
sixteen years old and nearly five-feet ten, and a splendid horseman, he is a
Bugler in the Third Regiment U.S. Vol. Cavalry."[15]

Although the army was unprepared for war, troops were shipped to the
south to train for tropical warfare. Clarence was sent by rail to a national
camp at Chickamauga, Georgia, site of a famous Civil War battle. Much to
Leonard Colby's dismay, instead of shipping out to Cuba from Tampa,
Florida, as had Colonel Roosevelt, the general also received unceremoni-
ous orders to join the troops at Chickamauga.

On June 21, Clara got her war correspondent's pass, which stated that
"military commanders are requested to permit her to pass freely, so far as
in their judgement it is proper and expedient to do so, and to extend to her
such aid and protection, not incompatible with the interests of the service,
as she requires."[16] After "a continuous stream of questions when Zintka is
in the house," Clara took the child to Beatrice to stay with Mary's daughters. Zintka wanted to go with Clarence and her parents to Chickamauga,
and she protested so much that the general bribed her with "a wheel"
[bicycle] if she would stay at home and behave.[17]

Shortly after the general left with his command (with over $1 million),

Clara took a train for Georgia, accompanied by her sister, Dr. Mary White. Clara's niece took over the *Tribune* and she soon received a nervous letter from Miss Anthony: "I hear that Mrs. Colby has gone to the front. . . . She did not send me a good by—I hope no ill may befall her! It is a risky thing for her to go into that climate—to say nothing of the enemy's country, but she is equal to whatever she undertakes."[18] Despite Miss Anthony's warnings, Clara's dream of reuniting her family was about to come true.

Several letters from Clarence to Zintka appeared in the newspaper, this despite the fact that Clarence could barely read and write. Clara also published letters supposedly written by Leonard to Zintka. The following is one of the only remaining examples, for no other letters from Leonard Colby to his daughter have ever been found.

> My Dear Little Zintka: And how is my little girl! Well, I hope. The boys in camp have been having a very wet time and it has been too muddy to drill. Two brigades have started for Porto Rico, but I am still here and expect to be until September when we will all go to Cuba.
>
> My little wrens are still happy in their nest in my desk in the surgeon's tent. The two birds take turns sitting on the four little eggs and I expect soon to hear the "peep, peep," of the little ones hatching out.
>
> Your brother Clarence came over from the "rough riders" Sunday and took supper with me. I gave him a box of ginger snaps to take back to his camp. Clarence looks very fine with his sword and revolver. Here's a kiss. Good-bye, sweetheart. Papa[19]

On August 15, Clara and Mary reached Chattanooga, Tennessee: ". . . My husband met us and brought us to the beautiful Inn . . ."[20] No sooner had she reunited with Leonard than word came that the war was over, after only 113 days: "The policy is now to encourage sports and reviews, and whatever may break the monotony of camp duties, so as to alleviate the disappointment felt by the soldiers when peace was declared . . ."[21] Although frustrated "without having performed heroic deeds of valor," Colby's letters to law partners reveal a man in a good mood. His expensive stationery bore two crossed flags—on the left the American flag waving in the breeze, and on the right a white five-pointed star on the red triangle of the Cuban flag and the words "Viva Cuba Libre!"[22]

On September 3, 1898, Clara wrote Zintka and her readers:

> Dear Little Girl: I have not been able to find out the things that would interest little people, because I have been for more than ten days constantly by the bedside of our dear Clarence [ill with typhoid

fever]. . . . I was at papa's headquarters when he rode up with Clarence. You would have thought it was fine to see the General wash that poor tired boy and dust off his clothes, and fix him up. We stayed at headquarters that night, and the next morning I took him up to Lookout Mountain to take care of him. Here your Auntie Mollie has been detailed for service by the Sternberg Hospital. . . . Papa and I went yesterday to see the natural bridge on the mountain . . .

We have some friends tenting about a quarter of a mile above the cottage where we stay . . .[23]

Despite Clarence's illness, Clara and Leonard were together again: "My first night in camp was on the fifteenth, the day before the grand review. The quiet sunset sent its long rays of color to fight the shadows among the tall trees; the white tents looked cool and comfortable in the twilight, and the sound and stir of camp grew more romantic as the darkness deepened. . . . I noticed that the passion flower here grows wild by the roadside . . ."[24]

Alarmed by large numbers of sick men at Chickamauga, Colby asked and received permission to transfer his brigade to more healthful surroundings. Clara's brief resumption of conjugal bliss—less than a month after five years of separation—ended when the general hurried his men from the squalid camp at Chickamauga to Anniston, Alabama. Clara could not go with him. She wrote to her daughter:

Dear Zintka—

I am still watching by Clarence's bedside and have no news to make a bright little letter for your Corner this time. . . . Papa went to Anniston . . . and he likes the camp very much. The air is fine and the water pure. It is called Camp Shipp, after Lieutenant Shipp who was killed at Santiago.

I am glad you have learned to ride your wheel so nicely, and now you must go to school and learn other things as well, Your Loving Mamma.[25]

By October 8 Clarence was feeling better and Clara wrote that "Papa is coming up here in a few days to take us down to Anniston, Alabama."[26] She included a portion of a letter Leonard had written her: "I have heard nothing about going to Cuba with my brigade. The troops are in good health and anxious to start for Cuba or at least to know what is to be done."[27] Her next letter to Zintka told of the general's care in bringing his wife and son to his side: "The camp at Anniston is the prettiest I have seen. Every regiment has a hill slope to itself, and the white tents on the clearings and among the green trees look very picturesque . . ."[28]

Clara took Clarence to Beatrice and, intending to surprise her gallant husband, turned around and returned to Camp Shipp like an excited schoolgirl about to rendezvous with a first beau. But it was Clara who got the surprise. In her absence Maud had moved into her husband's tent and was shamelessly determined to stay there. The young woman threw her arms around the general and begged not to be sent away, comparing her supple twenty-three-year-old figure to that of the older wife. Clara stood by in shock while Maud caressed Leonard. When she reminded her husband of his promise to start anew, Maud grew bolder, kissing his lips, opening her bodice to expose large, firm breasts, rubbing and pinching his fingers over her nipples, detailing his sexual cravings that only she could satisfy. The erotic display nauseated Clara, who later wrote to her lawyer of Maud's "brazen conduct in connection with my husband in my presence . . ."[29]

No longer the victim of her own illusions, Clara faced the reality that after twenty-one years of marriage, she had lost her husband. But she had progressed from victim to survivor, and had no intention of divorcing her husband to accommodate Maud Miller. Yet she may have thought betrayal at her age was the price she must pay for the autonomous life she had been allowed to live. She dealt with the separations in her marriage because she found creative fulfillment in her work.

Clara refused to blame her husband for his misbehavior.

Maud's vulgar exhibitionism only proved to Clara how the girl had manipulated Leonard from the beginning. Clara remained at Camp Shipp for four days, enduring open displays of adultery that became increasingly flagrant whenever she tried to talk to her husband. But she refused to leave until the general gave her a generous amount of money for Zintka and promised to send more regularly. It was a hollow promise, but at least she made sure she did not leave empty-handed when she returned to Washington with Zintka.

On New Year's Day 1899 General Colby and his mistress, with the $1 million raised for Cuban relief, were in Matanzas, Cuba, on what he called "a confidential mission" for President McKinley.[30] They had found the beautiful city, about ninety miles east of Havana, ripe for the picking. The citizens who had once bragged "*Robamos todos*" ("We are all thieves") had been devastated by the war, and prices were low.[31]

Using an alias (or rather, marrying Maud to a Cuban, Tomás H. Martínez, who afterward mysteriously disappeared), Colby purchased 17,000 acres of sugar and coffee plantations, deeded under Maud's new name, Maria C. Soler Martínez.[32]

Surrounded by sugar, coffee, and tobacco plantations, the city was second only to Havana. In 1898 writer Henry Houghton Beck described Matanzas:

The Yumuri Valley was dotted with country seats, where rich planters entertained their guests with prodigal hospitality. Their massive town houses
were miniature palaces built with showy colonnades and stone verandas,
and furnished with lavish expense. On the coast were their summer cottages, where their families could enjoy the refreshing northern sea-breeze in
the inclement heat. . . . [E]venings were filled with gayety and sumptuous
entertainment. All is now changed. Emancipation and insurrection impov-
erished the rich planters. Many of the finest estates passed into the hands of
Spanish immigrants and adventurers . . .[33]

For a month Colby and Maud played "amid the pathos of faded grandeur."
They visited the natural subterranean passages known as the Caves of Bel-
lamar, traveling down rocky hillsides in an old-fashioned two-wheeled
volante to the recesses of the high-vaulted chambers. Here they saw crys-
tals of stalactites and stalagmites of "bewildering beauty and lustre."[34]

Sending Maud ahead, the general returned to Anniston in February
1899, and then home to Beatrice, where he received a hero's welcome:
"More than 12,000 citizens gathered in Chautauqua Park to welcome the
boys home, and witness the big parade." Leading on Linden Tree, his white
Arabian, Colby basked in the praise of "one of the greatest demonstrations
ever given in the city."[35]

One of Colby's first duties upon returning to legal practice was on behalf
of his client, Mrs. Maria C. Soler Martínez. She filed a million-dollar
depredation claim against the United States government, which she held
responsible for ruining her husband's sugar and tobacco plantations during
the Cuban insurrection. Litigation was held up for years, but eventually
the long wait proved to be worth it.[36]

CHAPTER 13

The Trip Abroad

Zintka had been bribed to stay in Beatrice and so avoided the typhoid and malaria epidemics in Chickamauga. But shut indoors in Washington during the following winter of 1899, she suffered the first of many recurring eye infections. "Sore eyes," now known as trachoma, was a highly contagious malady to which all schoolchildren were susceptible, but Indians particularly so; their immune systems offered little resistance to European diseases.[1] Hugged, patted, and kissed by guests in Clara's home, Zintka fought alien viruses with her life. The winter bout with sore eyes left her blind in one eye for several months, and she could not attend school. That winter, Clara again consulted the man she now referred to as "the kind physician, Dr. Shute," although he always advised the same cure—sea air and saltwater baths.

During Zintka's recuperation, Clara made plans to attend the International Council of Women scheduled for the summer months in London. She was anxious to go for several reasons—the curing effect of sea air on Zintka, the opportunity to see her grandparents' old home and the historical sights of Great Britain, and to have the *Tribune* represented at the grand Council.

In May Clara visited Miss Anthony in Rochester for two days and reported that it had been "a lovely visit," but upon her return she found a letter Miss Anthony had written the day she left:

My dear friend:
 . . . The more I think of your taking your little eight year old with you, the greater the unwisdom seems to me. What you need is an absolute rest from home, children and newspaper, and to take any one of them along with you will defeat the desired end. With your optimistic head, it looks easy for you to find a home for her after you get in London, but you see you are to arrive just in time to be at the opening of the Council, which will make it the easiest thing for you

to take the child to the meeting with you, and among strangers she will be even more trouble than in the Washington meetings. If you were going over for the health or pleasure of the child or yourself, the case would be quite different, but you are going over to improve yourself, get new food to give to your audiences, whether listeners or readers, and you want to be free to go and come, to accept invitations to public entertainments and private hospitality, which you cannot do, if it means taking a child along with you, so I beg you to abandon the idea of doing so altogether, and beg your sister once more to take care of her during your absence. I know I am right in giving you this advice, but if you insist on taking her, you must not feel grieved after getting over there, if I do not press your name upon the different parties for invitations to the various social connections. I know the child will be just like a ball and chain to you from your time of sailing until you get back home, and you have no right to burden [me] or your friends, who want to do for you, with the added entanglement. Affectionately yours, Susan B. Anthony.[2]

Clara understood Miss Anthony's fears, but she had no intention of leaving Zintka behind, despite threats to prevent her from staying in influential homes and attending important receptions. She did not feel that her child was "a ball and chain," but a little companion on her many adventures. The little girl had missed school that winter and, considering her delicate health, this might be her only opportunity for world travel. Clara would use the journey to teach Zintka more about history, science, architecture, world cultures, art, and literature than she could possibly learn from books. Furthermore, Clara was not going to England simply to "improve" herself. Besides the council sessions and sightseeing, this would be an educational and sentimental journey home.

Using the last of the money Colby had given her, Clara and Zintka boarded the red-and-black steamship *Anchoria* carrying wicker suitcases filled with warm woolen underwear, gloves, and earmuffs. They set sail June 10, 1899, from Pier no. 54 in New York.[3] (Miss Anthony had sailed June 3 on another line.)

Clara was never more at home than at sea: "The ocean has fulfilled all my expectations and satisfied the longings I have felt for it for a quarter of a century."[4] The voyage took ten days and was not monotonous. Zintka loved to watch the ever-varying waves as much as Clara did. When Clara thought Zintka should rest in the cabin, she beguiled the restless child by reading poetry—"Evangeline" and "The Song of Hiawatha." But they stayed on deck as much as possible:

One day there were few who could venture to the table, but we came in from our mad dance on the waves in our chairs lashed to the boat, with appetites sharper for each meal than for the previous one. After a royal day, never to be forgotten by the few who ventured to stay out, we were kept awake by a hubbub in the lower part of the cabin. A Swede assured all within the sound of his voice that the ship would go down within two hours, and then he fell on his knees and began praying. Others prayed, cried, and swore, according to sex and temperament. Many, however, laughed immoderately, and all this, with the breaking of glasses and the rolling from side to side of everything movable, made a din that banished sleep.[5]

Zintka heard her mother's description of the horrid Bewick sea voyage to America, and Clara took her below to see how the people in steerage were getting on:

> . . . there was no hilarity or expressions of friendliness. It was the silence of despairing endurance or an open outcry at their discomforts. The . . . accommodations were abominable, considering that they paid within a few dollars of as much as the second cabin which had a fairly good table, comfortable berths and excellent attendance from the cheerful and obliging stewards.

Zintka never tired of watching the huge waves and was thrilled one day when the ship passed close to an iceberg. Another day they saw huge black whales blow blasts of steam and then disappear into the deep. It seemed as if the porpoises were following her as she ran squealing with glee along the deck, while graceful seagulls wheeled and dived at their wake.[6]

Mother and daughter stood on deck in the rain as the ship followed the rocky coast of northern Ireland. Every so often, Clara pointed out a castle overgrown with ivy under a leaden sky. At last they landed at Glasgow, Scotland, and Zintka set foot "on the soil of Great Britain." They spent three days at the cozy North British Hotel in St. George's Square, looking down at the statues of Queen Victoria and the Prince Consort below, with a center monument of Sir Walter Scott. Everywhere they went, Clara taught Zintka about the buildings, museums, and towns they visited and the people who had lived there, saying: " . . . every mile has the historic background of . . . human interests covering two thousand years."[7]

By rail they traveled through the heart of England, reaching London in ten hours, after passing through the Norman fortress town of Durham, then past Newcastle, York, and Peterborough, catching glimpses of noted cathedrals and crumbling Roman walls. In London Clara soon made the acquaintance of a celebrated singer, Madame Antoinette Sterling, who was pleased to take some Americans with her to St. John's Wood, where she entertained them at tea in the shaded garden of her quaint and "charming" house.

Clara then found an apartment in London "that would delight any novelist or poet if he could bear to be next neighbor to the Westminster slums."[8] In the evening, Zintka leaned far out the window to see Big Ben, the Parliament clock, "whose illuminated face told the time better by night than by day. . . . The bell is heard all over London and even out at Windsor Castle. The House of Commons always sits until midnight, when Parliament is in session, and sometimes much longer, but when the Members are ready to go home the Speaker touches an electric button and out goes the light."[9]

Clara wanted to show her daughter the sights. They visited the Zoological Gardens, saw the "Lord Mayors' show," when the "incoming Lord Mayors of the City of London ride in the procession in their gorgeous coaches," drawn by eight prancing horses. Clara took Zintka to Madame Tussaud's waxworks where she saw Red Riding Hood and "was impressed by the little princes in the Tower of London, whose pitiful story of their being blinded by their cruel uncle and then being killed by being thrown headlong down the Tower stairs was told in action by the wax figures." Zintka was horrified but fascinated by the story and begged Clara to take her to the Tower to see where the boys had fallen. Zintka also saw where the notorious King Henry VIII ordered his wife Anne Boleyn beheaded in 1536.

Zintka looked up at the famous gate at the Tower of London where the heads of executed men and women had once been displayed above the entrance, and she had many questions to ask about the English monarchy.

After learning the history of murder and intrigue surrounding the British throne, it must have seemed strange to Zintka when she got the chance to see the current heir to the throne in person. On July 8, at the Horse Guard's Parade in St. James's Park, Clara reported the seats were filled "with the fairest ladies of the land in dazzling costumes and holding up dainty hued parasols with here and there an officer in uniform."[10]

Joining in the throng of 200,000 people, Clara and Zintka

were suddenly transported out of the hustling crowd and led by a private path through the shrubbery out to a shady hill slope overlooking the road by which the reviewing and the reviewed had to pass and near enough to the stand to watch the Princess of Wales, with her daughter and grandson, the heir to the throne, and to see the Prince of Wales lift his hand in salute as each regiment passed by. We could hardly believe our senses that this good fortune had come to us, and almost felt that some fairy godmother must have mistaken us for her best beloved princesses in disguise.[11]

Actually, they accomplished the feat when the wife of a ranking military officer saw Zintka and became interested in her history: "With the intimation of a fee coupled with the mention of 'the Americans,' which was the passport to everything," the woman bribed a gatekeeper for the "coveted privilege." The slightly illegal entry became more interesting when "at a given signal we were to slip nonchalantly through the crowd, pass the row of policemen guarding the path to the keeper's house, up a step ladder over a wall at the back, through the shrubs and there we were in Paradise." Zintka watched the spectacle and her mother's intense fascination with the royal family from behind the shrubbery enclosure.

Zintka found her favorite attraction in London at the Greater Britain Exhibition, where she was allowed to take a ride on a Canadian swan boat, which went around a lake "brilliant with its myriads of colored lights." The ride itself was of no special interest, but the little boat suddenly glided through a replica of the Cave of the Winds, where "weird, fantastic shapes were made to seem alive." Zintka was told that the monsters she had seen represented "beings which the Indians supposed to inhabit the Cave of the Winds in the great Northwest." Ironically, the Indians referred to were Zintka's own people, the Lakota. Young as she was, she was confused, thrilled, and horrified at the exhibit, and Clara did not have the knowledge or background to explain that this crude display was only an ignorant exploitation of Wind Cave, a Lakota holy place in the sacred Black Hills of South Dakota.[12]

Clara had no money to pay someone to look after Zintka, so while she attended council meetings, she left her daughter alone to play in St. James's Park. She explained to her readers that "it was quite safe to leave Zintka for hours in the Park as there were places near the water's edge where the ducks used to come and take the bread from the children's hands not at all disturbed by the near-by wading of little urchins in the shallow water. There were plenty of keepers to maintain order, of which, however, I never witnessed a violation." The possibility of accidental drowning or child molestation did not cross her mind, even though there was danger nearby:

> There was one enclosure that interested me greatly. . . . [M]en lay basking in the sunshine which was mild and genial. Perhaps they were night workmen taking their day sleep in the open in preference to some stifling lodging; perhaps they were men out of employment with no home to go to. At any rate, there they were peaceable and unmolested, and nobody telling them to "move along," or "keep off the grass."[13]

The travelers did have the opportunity to visit the homes of influential people after all, when they spent six days in Cheltenham in the Cotswold

Hills, northwest of London. Clara gave drawing-room lectures at country manors and enjoyed garden parties every afternoon, one "on a beautiful farm of 400 acres, where the elegance of the home had a setting of roses and borders of lavender and a wealth of flowers, old fashioned and rare . . ." Meanwhile, Zintka "was in clover here, for there was a dear little girl not too old to be her playmate and a large garden with walks and drives, and cycling, and everything else that could make a child happy."[14]

Clara chose a steamship with the Indian name *Menominee* for the "delightful" return voyage, in accommodations with "theatrical people, students, teachers and ministers, who like the slow voyage for its rest and health-giving." Zintka's eye problem was no longer a source of concern:

> Zintka and I bade good-bye to England. . . . The sea air and baths accomplished for Zintka what Dr. Shute . . . thought it would, and after a week's treatment in London her eye, which she had not been able to use for months, was entirely cured and she enjoyed the sightseeing as much as anybody . . .[15]

But Zintka experienced discrimination on the return voyage: "In a gathering of people there will always be some whose intellectual possibilities limit them to grumbling about their own surroundings or a curious prying into other people's affairs. We had both these classes and they served to give points of avoidance." With Zintka by her side, Clara also became the victim of bigotry, something she had grown used to:

> I may relate that my habit of early rising, not only to greet the sun, but to watch the changeful beauties of the dawn, and, perhaps, also the early gymnastic exercises which I engaged in when I thought I could do so without observation, gave rise to the rumor that I was a sun worshipper. I was approached with the remark that it was said there was a sun worshipper on board, to which I answered, "Yes, I should think there would be many."

Relieved that the discrimination would soon end, they entered the inner harbor of New York "fat and hearty . . . and thus with gratitude. . . . [W]ho could help feeling a thrill on returning to the land where are those we love best, and where work and its blessings await us."[16]

The trip to England was a turning point in their lives. Clara had spent every penny she possessed to take Zintka abroad, and when they returned home she could not pay the rent and they were evicted. Undaunted, Clara lectured in earnest, bringing in just enough to pay for food and lodging in a dilapidated old house in one of the poorer neighborhoods of Washington. As soon as the rent was due, they moved again.

Miss Anthony was upset that Clara had ignored her advice to leave Zintka at home.

On November 20, 1899, Anthony fumed:

From your recent postal card and letters, it looks to me as if you were getting deeper and deeper into the mire. It does seem such a waste of your marvelous powers of expression for you to be forever trying to raise money to pay the current expenses of running a house, a newspaper office, and about a thousand other things . . . and it is simply because you are perpetually trying to do half a dozen things at the same time. . . . Old Ben Franklin said "three moves were equal to a fire," so one more move will finish up your goods and chattels if not your spirit also. . . . Then at the close of your hopeless complications you say, you "expect to give some lectures to help along." In such a state of perfect physical and intellectual collapse as you must be in, it is worse than idle for you to think of doing yourself or your audiences justice. You cannot go before audiences with intellectual and magnetic power, nor can you put on paper the magnetic power of which you are capable, unless you religiously keep your mind and body in proper conditions, and *that* you *cannot* do while you have to walk the streets trying to collect old bills for the *Tribune*, nor in moving from house to house to save rent paying . . .[17]

Miss Anthony often contradicted herself. First she criticized Clara for doing too much and then she gave her added burdens, errands to run, or meetings to attend. After the forceful letter of November 20, she wrote just the opposite on December 22: "My how I wish I could be in two places—& see to a hundred things at a time—instead of just one poor small place or thing."[18]

There was indeed another move, but Clara did not lose her belongings and the *Tribune* went out on schedule because brother William sent his sister enough money to pull her through. Clara wrote often to the general, gently reminding him of Zintka's needs, but he rarely replied; when he did, it was to claim that he could barely make ends meet. Clara's marriage to Leonard Colby was over, but like Elizabeth Cady Stanton, who had maintained a civilized separation from her husband, Clara refused the scandal of divorce. On New Year's Eve 1899, she wrote:

My Dear Husband:

Although you have not answered my last letter, . . . yet I cannot let the old year and the old century pass into the eternity behind us without sending a word from my heart to yours.

I do not need to tell you of my doings because I continue to send you my paper; and I must not write of my thoughts or feelings which indeed you know full well. But lest you may have misconstrued my silence—or, I might better say my acceptance of your silence—I take occasion at this season of good will to give you this assurance of my continued love and loyalty. If the time ever comes when you free yourself from the associations which have brought only disgrace and misery to all, and you again want a home with all that it implies of honor, influence and companionship you may count on me to go with you even to the uttermost ends of the earth if you desired, and help you to build up our life again. All this I have said before to you but say it now lest you might imagine that time or circumstances could make my love & loyalty change or falter. All I ask in return is that you regulate your relations to your wife and to others according to your own highest ideals and to that standard to which you would hold your fellow man before you would respect or trust him. When the time comes that you can offer me thus I shall be glad to hear from you and you need not fear that, wherever I am or in what new environ-ment I may be placed, your appeal would be in vain.

When your heart is tender towards God; or thrilled with thoughts of duty and service; or there comes a memory of earlier ideals and aspirations & of my sympathy with you in these, or there flits over your mind a gleam of hope that the afternoon of life may yet reflect the glory of its morning, then think of me for I am praying for you. Faithfully yours, Clara.[19]

CHAPTER 14

The Missing Bond

"You are a woman;
Give a future to my women!"
SITTING BULL
to Anthropologist
Alice Fletcher

By the turn of the century, the world had changed for women, and more than 1 million of them were working at manual trades in America. Half a million people entered the United States every year, and thousands of poor immigrant women and their families crammed into eastern city tenements, often a dozen people to a room. The streets were filled with peddlers and carts, throngs of children, elderly people, and men who were out of work. In congested buildings where mattresses cluttered the floors; often cockroaches and other vermin roomed with the tenants, and so did sickness.

Of the 8 million cars registered in 1900, many were being driven by women. Telephones were common in city offices, and electricity the norm. New inventions caused people to yearn for what they could not yet afford, and the newly arrived immigrants competed for jobs traditionally held by Americans of African descent. Race riots broke out, creating an unpleasant atmosphere for Zintka, whose dark skin and impoverishment made her vulnerable to racial slurs every time she left her home. Instead of ignoring bigoted slights, as Indian women at that time were taught to do, Zintka responded boldly to insults—much like a white woman. She did not turn the other cheek.

Ironically, in February 1900 Clara was elected to chair the suffrage movement's Committee on Industrial Problems Affecting Women and Children. Miss Anthony, now eighty years old, wanted Clara to write a chapter for the fourth volume of the *History of Woman's Suffrage*, a critical analysis of the enormous congressional work that women had accomplished for the vote. Only Clara could write about the lobbying she had consistently spearheaded, month after month, year after year. With these new responsibilities given to her by the woman who always told her not to add more "irons to the fire," she forged ahead, leaving little time to think of herself or of Zintka.[1]

Clara had recovered from Leonard's rejection but continued to believe that her errant husband still had the moral fortitude to recover his honor. Occasionally, he wrote her a few lines and enclosed five dollars or stopped in for a brief yet romantic visit when he was in Washington. These small attentions kept her hopes nourished. Back in Beatrice, Maud waited anxiously for his every return. He often came home with a souvenir, usually a book to improve her vocabulary and mold her character to fit his own. On May 18, 1901, he brought her *The Helmet of Navarre*, a swashbuckling fantasy set in sixteenth-century France, in which women swooned into the strong arms of gallant, impassioned lovers. The frivolous tale was just the sort of literature Maud could understand. On the inside cover of the novel next to the date, Leonard wrote "Marie C. Martinez," with the middle initial shaped exactly the way he wrote the first letter in "Colby."[2]

In the meantime Clara decided not to let the world pass by. The average life expectancy for a white woman in 1900 was only 51.08 years and Clara was fifty-four, although everyone said she looked fifteen years younger. Always working to improve herself, she read *The Prevention and Cure of Old Age* by Eleanor Kirk, *In Search of Soul* by Horatio Dresser, and *Healing Thoughts* by Josephine Barton.[3] She was growing and evolving spiritually, and thus becoming more sure of herself. The New Thought religion she studied taught a higher level of consciousness, which meant more love and more joy in her life. She suffered, to be sure, but she accepted the suffering, which lessened her anger. During the dark days, Mrs. Stanton sustained her, although, true to herself, Clara did not always agree with Stanton or take her advice. On March 6, 1900, Mrs. Stanton suggested in a letter that Clara "put the little Indian girl in Hampton school, throw the paper to the winds and devote yourself to Literature and oratory."[4] But Clara felt that boarding school for Zintka was entirely out of the question. Even though she could not give the child enough time (or rather she chose not to for the sake of suffrage), sending her away to school would have been yet another form of abandonment and might cause more grief than Zintka could bear.

Clara had kept Zintka's Indian belongings—her beaded cap, moccasins, and bracelet—treasured mementos the child loved to look at and handle. But at the age of ten, Zintka began to touch them more often and to question Clara in detail about Indians, about their religion and customs. Clara noticed the increased interest and it made her vaguely uneasy.

At the Pan American Exposition in Buffalo, New York, Clara and Zint-ka were walking along the midway when the girl stopped suddenly, as if mesmerized. She dropped Clara's hand abruptly and ran through crowds of milling people toward the sound of drumbeats. The Indian Congress, rep-resenting various tribes, had set up camp and were giving a public dance exhibition. The *Tribune* reported that "Old Geronimo, the celebrated Apache prisoner of war, is here and is the hero of the camp . . . with his kindly intelligent features, and his evident satisfaction in writing his auto-graph for the young girls who gather around him."[5]

Zintka got his autograph and a pat on the head, but she was only inter-ested in finding members of her own tribe. To Clara, all Indians seemed "Indian," but Zintka went to look for the Lakota. Clara wrote: "There was a very large delegation from the Sioux Nation and when one of them learned who Zintka was the word went quickly around and she became the centre of animated and friendly curiosity."[6]

As she visited with one Indian after another, her hat came off and her silken black hair fell loosely down her shoulders and back. Hours passed, and toward evening Zintka refused to leave. As Clara pulled her away, many Lakota eyes followed hers, and Zintka looked back at them and held their gaze until the hurrying crowds closed in around her.

Clara had always insisted that it was wrong to kill and stuff birds to wear on hats, the preservation of wildlife being one of her important causes. But the Lakota were covered with beautiful bird feathers, and their rhythmic dancing was like the beating of Zintka's heart. With her own eyes, Clara had seen the intensity of the instantaneous bonding between Zintka and her people, a spiritual magnetism beyond anything she had experienced with the child. Given the circumstances, Clara had laid emotional claim on her as strongly as most loving mothers could have, but Zintka was unable to return the intimacy; she could not feel with her white adopted mother what Dakota scholar Joseph Iron Eye Dudley calls a silent "one-ness of soul and spirit and mind . . . and the strength that came with this oneness."[7] In many ways this lack of familial communion was as painful to Clara as Leonard's rejection. In an indignant and self-righteous tone, she ended her description of the Lakota dancers: "Let us hope that the next Indian Congress will exhibit their development and education and not parade their discarded savagery as a show."[8]

Zintka reached early adolescence at approximately the age of ten. Clara was unprepared as she watched the girl come into her native spiritual inheritance. Unlike the non-Indian, who learns religion and then teaches it to others, Zintka's spirituality was as inherent as her breath, and flowed outward. Her cultural imprint was never more strongly felt than now; Zintka's forced acculturation had changed her outward behavior but not her soul. The beginning of a lifelong struggle to repair the severed bonds of her heritage had begun.[9]

Nothing Clara said or taught her of non-Indian ways kept Zintka from the irresistible pull of her Lakota heritage. The grief and bitterness of racial discrimination only compounded an already desperate situation. The girl became frustrated, morose, and often physically and emotionally out of control. She yearned for her Lakota mother and again suffered terrifying nightmares. Her restlessness could not be contained, and it became almost impossible to keep her at home. At first Clara felt betrayed and hurt that Zintka ignored her love. She had expected her daughter to resemble her in intellectual and emotional development, but instead Zintka disliked school, was immature and spoiled. If Clara left the girl to have a cup of tea or a quick nap, Zintka would disappear. Then followed frantic visits to the police and agonizing searches. When spring arrived, Zintka's behavior only worsened. Suffering from confinement during the day, she looked fitfully for ways to escape the stuffy house. Clara felt the child needed firm discipline and a sense of safety that she could not give Zintka in Washington while she lectured for their living and fulfilled her responsibilities to woman suffrage. She wrote to her cousin Thomas Pope and his wife, Anna, who owned a dairy farm near Madison, Wisconsin. Would they please take Zintka for the summer? Lush green pastures and rolling hills covered with white cedar and spruce trees seemed just the place for a child who loved the out-of-doors. After some time and with much hesitation, Anna wrote back: "Dear Clara— . . . How I wish that I could give you a satisfactory answer. I would love to do anything for you that was right and I would willingly do Zintka's washing & ironing, cook her food etc. etc. and could do so with pleasure but to take the responsibility upon myself of caring properly for her I know I can not . . ."[10]

Disappointed, Clara wrote again, pleading with Anna to change her mind. Finally, she relented.

Anna's friends and family knew her as "an angel." Self-sacrificing and devoutly religious, she had raised four children, working long hours. She nursed sick neighbors, was generous to the poor, and gently prepared the dead for burial. Rude manners and bad smells upset her. Anna had been a teacher before marriage, and she possessed that certain refinement and sensitivity so often recompensed by an early death from a hard life on the farm.

She followed her husband's every command.[11] Thomas was a strict Baptist Sunday-school teacher, a no-nonsense man who had earned his farm with honest sweat. A good provider, the tall, dark-haired man believed strongly against tobacco in any form and refused to grow it as a crop. He ruled with religious vigor over tall, eighteen-year-old Henry and the other children: Ruth, aged sixteen, Leon thirteen, and Roy, the twelve-year-old.

On Sunday, Thomas did not permit his family to work, play music, or even read unless it was a Sunday-school lesson he had provided for them. Once the boys were caught "jumping on cows' backs" in the barn and severely punished.[12] The children grew to hate Sundays. After church they would sit and stare at one another in restrained silence. Into this austere environment came the troubled Zintkala Nuni, the well-traveled Lakota girl who loved ragtime.

Exhilarated by the fresh air and beautiful countryside, Zintka wasted no time in rushing to the barn to jump in the hayloft, despite her white dress. Clara, relieved to see her happy, let her go. Mrs. Colby was on her way to the International Woman's Press Union in Detroit, afterward returning to Washington to rest:

> [It is]. . . a perpetual picnic in July and August for stay-at-homes in Washington. . . . [T]he electric cars furnish cooling breezes as they carry you swiftly to . . . the Library where it is always pleasant. . . . The editor of the *Tribune* has invented an individual pleasure in putting poetry in type out in the backyard in the early morning. Low-hanging peach trees laden with fruit, and trumpet vines with their brilliant blossoms, make a fit environment for such work. A near neighbor sings hymns in a rich baritone voice and off in the distance a young lady practices concert airs, while near and far are the pleasant sounds of the world waking up to its ever recurring duties.[13]

While Clara relaxed, Zintka's behavior on the farm was getting on everyone's nerves, especially Henry's. He chafed under his father's strict supervision and broke every rule he could. The anger he felt toward his zealous parent he took out on small animals and younger children. When he found that Ruth was terrified of cats, he delighted in chasing her around with a low-growling, clawing tomcat.[14] In the wintertime, his keenest pleasure had been taunting the few Indian children who lived near the ice pond. He owned a pair of shiny ice skates, which the Indian boys could not afford. Henry teased them until they chased after him, fell, and hurt themselves on the burning ice.[15]

Henry had a grudge against Zintka from the moment she arrived. The children were embarrassed to have a dark-skinned Indian sitting with them in church. And she did not act like the white girls at all. Zintka ran and climbed as fast as the boys and often successfully challenged their games. She wanted to go wherever the boys went, even into the pigpen. And although she started each day with a clean dress, by noon her clothes and stockings were covered with dirt, and burrs tangled her hair. The fields seemed like paradise to her.

At first, Zintka's letters were full of the adventures she was having, but something must have upset her. Clara dedicated a poem to Zintka in the *Tribune*, one which ended on a worried note:

A DAY ON THE FARM

Zintka Lanuni's up early and bright,
And hastens into her clothes,
(for the boys milk the cows almost ere it is light).
Then with Henry to the cream'ry she goes . . .

Quickly back with the sweet, new milk they come,
(Though they leave the cream behind),
Each little bossie must now have some
And each piggie that she can find.
"For Aunt Anna's box I've piled the wood in,
So full that the lid will not down.
Now I can tell momma how good I have been,
In the letter I'm sending to town."

Now tis time for good night and a kiss all around,
Then Zintka remembers her prayer,
"God bless my own momma and all the dear friends,
Who gave me such loving care.

Make me a better girl every day!
More faithful, and kind and true.
Care for dear brother and guard his way,
Bless and keep my dear Papa too."

So the little hands rest and the feet are still,
That have done loving errands all day.
O! Father in heaven keep my child from all ill,
Since from me she is now far away.[16]

Apparently Zintka was not safe "from all ill." For whatever reason, she became desperately frightened at night and insisted on sleeping on a cot in Anna's room or in bed with Ruth.[17] She seemed to feel protected by the company of women.

On July 30 Zintka wrote Clara, and the edited letter appeared in the *Tribune*:

My Dear Mama,

I have not written to you since last week. I hope you are well. You must come to my birthday. Aunt Anna is going to make me two kinds of birthday cake.

Just last week I had some chokecherries; they were black. And our apples are almost ripe.

. . . Uncle Thomas is now getting up his oats. Roy is watching his cows; Ruth is ironing now. Aunt Anna is making apple pie for dinner and I am going to make one too.

We have got such a great high swing in the barn, and we can swing so high in it. Ruthie and I jump up high. We stand up in it.

I was glad to get your card and Ruth and I got the mail. Aunt Anna says the poem was very nice. Ruth said it must have taken you a long time to write it, but I said it took you but ten minutes.

Grandmamma is over at Uncle Charley's and I have not been over since you went away, but Uncle says he will take me soon.

We have two pet lambs, and we keep them in the front yard, and Roy and I have lots of fun.

I have learned the tables clear up to the tens. I must close. Good-by. I love you. Zintka.[18]

There was no mention of Henry in this letter.

Storms had been frequent, and Zintka could not bear the sudden flashes of light and the roar of thunder. When they came, she screamed and hid under a bed, covering her head and ears. Zintka's violent reactions betrayed her weakness to the sadistic Henry, who resolved to teach her a brutal lesson.

One day, when it was evident that a storm was approaching, Henry and his brothers asked Zintka if she wanted to play in the cornfield. Never wanting to be left behind, Zintka willingly climbed aboard the wagon for the trip to a faraway field, filled with row upon row of ripening corn. The boys played games until dark clouds gathered in the west and the wind picked up. Then, at a prearranged signal, each ran off in a different direction just as the storm broke. Strong and fast as she was, Zintka would have had no trouble following one of them had she not been so restrained. It must have taken all three boys, with the eighteen-year-old Henry the strongest, to keep her down. Precisely what they did to her is unknown, but they left her as flashing bolts of lightning lit up the sky and splinters of thunder cracked around her and a strong gust of hail hit the cornstalks. As they raced away, the boys could hear Zintka's panic-stricken screams: "Leon gone! Roy gone! Henry gone! Everyone gone! Mother! Mother!

Help me!"[19] She shrieked and writhed in the muddy cornfield until her terror waged its mental and physical toll.

This oral remembrance, handed down to grandchildren, was said to have been a hilarious boyhood prank. There is no written record of how long Zintka remained in the field before someone found her, or whether she finally came wandering home, disoriented. The only recollection was that when she came into the farmhouse, she was filthy; Anna and Ruth were disgusted by her appearance and thought she had been playing in the pigpen again.

As the summer days wore on, Clara had not managed to make enough money to return for Zintka. Week after week and especially on Sundays, she silently faced her tormentors. Depressed and alone, she refused to bathe, her hair became matted, and her ears flamed with infection. The ears drained and the foul odor caused Anna many hours of extra work airing out the mattress and bedding on a small second-floor balcony. Anna tried to make Zintka's birthday on August 5 a happy one, hopeful that Clara would be there, too. But Clara did not come. Finally, on October 6, 1900, Clara returned to Wisconsin, sure that the strict fatherly discipline had been good for Zintka. She expected to find her daughter changed, and indeed she was. The vigorous girl she had left to bask in the cleansing sunshine was now a sullen wounded animal. Clara cleaned up her daughter as best she could and took her back to Washington. Shortly after they left, Anna found Ruth's curly hair crawling with lice. Ruth's locks were cut off, and when her hair grew back in straight, she blamed Zintka.[20]

Henry remained the black sheep of his family. He was the only one of the three boys who did not attend college. He openly defied his father by marrying a girl of another faith, and later moved to a distant state where he worked for years on the railroads. One day Henry's train ran over and killed a little girl playing on the railroad tracks, and later he would be wrecked by alcoholism.[21]

"Zintka's Corner" in the *Tribune* ended abruptly as the child's severe depression signaled a nervous breakdown. She soon came down with a scrofulous infection, and sores spread over her face. Clara tried every remedy and accidentally used medicine that was too strong for Zintka's constitution.[22] The girl was in anguish. The cost of being taken from the Lakota was more than the loss of her language, her music, her food, her family kinship; it was the loss of her identity as a human being, the loss of her mind.

Zintka continued to mourn for her real mother. She threw herself against walls and prayed for death. Clara was struck as if beaten, but she still did not understand. She sat by Zintka's bedside for hours, blaming herself for the girl's torment. Perhaps during those long days and nights of mental turmoil, Clara sang a lullaby for her daughter that reminded her of her own gentle English mother:

ROCK ME TO SLEEP

Backward, turn backward, on time in your flight,
Make me a child again, just for tonight!
Mother, come back from the echoless shore,
Take me again to your heart as of yore—
Kiss from my forehead the furrows of care,
Smooth the few silver threads out of my hair,
Over my slumbers your loving watch keep—
Rock me to sleep, mother, rock me to sleep!

Backward, flow backward, oh, tide of the years!
I am so weary of toil and of tears—
Toil without recompense—tears all in vain—
Take them, and give me my childhood again!
I have grown weary of dust and decay,
Weary of flinging my soul-wealth away—
Weary of sowing for others to reap;
Rock me to sleep, mother, rock me to sleep![23]

CHAPTER 15

"My Heart's Blood"

While Clara struggled to understand what had happened to Zintka, news-papers reported that the Northern Cheyenne in Montana were Ghost Dancing, eleven years after the massacre at Wounded Knee. The Cheyenne's government agent found out and ordered the ceremonial leaders to be beaten and imprisoned at hard labor, and the Ghost Dance went underground once again.[1]

By April 1901 Zintka had recovered enough so that Clara could leave her for short periods of time. Early one morning, she walked to a post office nearby and returned less than twenty minutes later to find Zintka entertaining a vis-itor. She was sitting in the parlor on the lap of a traveling salesman.[2]

This incident (still remembered with horror in the Bewick family some ninety years later) illuminated for Clara the extent of Zintka's problems. The once-reserved child now showed careless personal hygiene as well as difficulties with social relationships. She appeared to be sexually preco-cious and at the same time displayed a newly learned sense of helplessness, including an inability to recognize potentially dangerous situations. These are the classic symptoms of a sexually abused child.[3] She had begun to turn herself into a victim.

Yearning for her own people, Zintka felt the pull of spring as instinc-tively as the blue heron is drawn toward its northward flight. She paced at the windows as if caged, longing to be outdoors to breathe fresh air. From Clara's attitude and unspoken words, Zintka knew that she was a burden, and the effort to live up to Clara's lofty vision was far more debilitating than any threats of punishment. The young woman's only source of relief and consolation came in the frenzied search for her heritage.

Zintka begged to visit Wounded Knee, but Clara had neither the time nor the money, much less the inclination, to allow her daughter to return to her homeland.[4] Bearing the weight of her parents' defeated hopes, Zint-ka's inevitable sense of inferiority was increased by a psychological and spiritual incompatibility with her surroundings. From the moment Zintka had become her adopted mother's "duty," Clara had believed she could improve upon nature by providing a more "civilized" life for the girl than the one into which she had been born.[5] But as time went on, Clara found that no amount of sympathy or love or pity or education could change the initial circumstances of the child's strong Lakota heritage.

After many inquiries, Clara and Zintka went to visit A. C. Towner, the Acting Commissioner of Indian Affairs, on March 18, 1901, and made formal application to enroll Zintka as a Minneconju.[6] The commissioner explained that in order to obtain an allotment of land on the reservation, it would be necessary to find relatives among the Wounded Knee survivors who would claim her. On April 6, 1901, the matter was referred to Ira A. Hatch, the U.S. agent on the Cheyenne River Sioux reservation, "with instructions to fully investigate . . . and if possible, establish the identity of the said Indian girl."[7]

The agent responded on July 29, saying that in his opinion Zintka was the daughter of Rock Woman and Crane Pretty Voice, both belonging to his agency. He included a joint affidavit "from the alleged parents" and a "statement from [John] Yellow Bird to substantiate the same."[8] Towner was suspicious of the reports and wrote to the agent at Pine Ridge, John R. Brennan (the same Brennan who had "secured" the scalp of Dead Arm during the Home Guard atrocities). "It will be noticed that the accounts given by . . . Mrs. Colby and the statements of its claimed parents differ decidedly. Further, the statements of Yellow Bird are very meagre and unsatisfactory."[9]

Towner instructed Agent Brennan to push the matter "to the end that the identity of the said claimant may be fully established."[10] Brennan searched for Yellow Bird and his half-brother, Chester White Butterfly, for eight months but could not find them, despite the fact that Yellow Bird ran a successful trading store at Pine Ridge. Brennan reported to Towner on August 29 that he would "endever [sic] to secure the information asked for in your letter."[11]

But John Yellow Bird wanted no part of it. To avoid scandal, he simply dropped out of sight. By November 1901, it did not matter to Clara who came forward to claim her daughter—any tribal member was acceptable. Commissioner Towner obliged by taking Agent Hatch's testimony, which said in part: "They [Crane Pretty Voice and wife] had seen a child at Yellow Bird's store and recognized it as the one they had left on the ground for dead."[12] They described the man who had adopted the child as "an army officer, . . . about thirty-five years of age, of medium height, had a thin mustache [Colby was clean shaven], and wore a grey suit of citizen's clothes [Major John Burke wore a gray suit and had a mustache]. . . . The mother at first objected to letting her child go, but after reflecting on their poor condition, agreed to it . . .[13]

George Bartlett, who originally claimed to have taken Lost Bird from her mother's frozen grasp, was still concerned about Zintka's welfare and corresponded with Clara for fourteen years regarding her health.[14] At the time of the massacre, he had been a U.S. marshal and owned a trading store at Wounded Knee, eventually selling out to Louis Mousseau. In 1902 Bartlett was a sharpshooter and ammunition salesman for both the King Powder Company and Peter's Cartridge Company based at Cincinnati.[15]

At Clara's urging, Towner twice instructed Brennan to interview Bartlett, but the agent refused, with a vague claim that Bartlett was "not thoroughly reliable" and had been thrown off the reservation "for some offence against the law."[16] Having gotten rid of the man, Brennan had no intention of looking him up again. Likewise, Brennan summarily dismissed Bartlett's witnesses, saying: "Long Woman, wife of Feather On Head, has been dead for several years. Feather On Head we cannot locate."[17]

Despite the questionable evidence, Clara insisted that Zintka had waited long enough for an allotment. After delaying the matter with the Indian office for nearly one year Towner demanded an answer from Agent Brennan. Brennan explained his delay, admitting: "[T]he more I investigate the matter the more difficult I find it to definitely establish the identity of Lost Bird."[18]

Commissioner Towner was tired of the confusion and probably tired of Clara's constant visits to his office. On July 15, 1902, the Secretary of the Interior authorized the Office of Indian Affairs to enroll Zintkala Nuni, or Marguerite Elizabeth Colby, "as an Indian belonging to her agency with full tribal rights as such."[19]

Years later in 1925, the chief of police at Cheyenne River Agency asked for information regarding Lost Bird for a journalist who wanted to write a "sketch" of her life.[20] The officer located Felix Crane Pretty Voice and his wife and interviewed them, and then placed a copy of his findings in Lost Bird's official enrollment file at the agency. This time Felix changed his story. He admitted that he had never even seen Lost Bird before the massacre:

> Felix Crane Pretty Voice says at the time of the Wounded Knee battle and previous for some time that he and his wife had been living apart, that he [had] first seen Lost Bird . . . after the battle in the custody of officer who adopted her . . .[21]

The policeman also took testimony from James Ax or Brown Sinew:

> That he was in the battle of Wounded Knee in 1890, . . . and that she [Lost Bird] was found and picked up by an officer of the United States Army

shortly after the battle and taken to the Pine Ridge Agency. . . . That he had heard from other Indians who were in the battle of Wounded Knee, that the father of Lost Bird was not sure whether he was her father or not and for that reason was willing to give her away . . .[22]

While waiting news of the allotment during the summer of 1901, Clara and Zintka spent a week in Beatrice visiting Dr. Mary White. Every day, Zintka went to the fairgrounds to ride the carousel and stayed for hours. Mesmerized, she rode around, around, and around on the painted wooden horses, and Clara needed help to pull her off at the end of each day. News spread of the child's strange behavior, and a small crowd gathered to witness the struggles.[23]

Leonard Colby, listed in *Who's Who in America*, was now adjutant general of Nebraska and living openly with his mistress—a scandalous situation. Maud, now Marie C. Martínez, had become a model housewife and posed as the general's private secretary.[24] He tutored her, using the literature of his choosing, and gave her expensive gifts, including jewelry and one particularly exquisite vase decorated with the molded form of a naked woman, with arms and long flowing hair thrown back over the rim, a smile on her lips.[25]

Zintka was visiting her father one day when the general's brother, veterinarian David Colby, brought his family to dinner. After the meal, the children played outside on the lawn. Zintka pulled herself up onto the black leather seat of Dr. Colby's spring wagon and bounced up and down. The doctor's two sons watched, one stretched out on the grass beside the wagon, his arm behind his head, and the other leaned against a tree. When Zintka stood up on the seat and started to jump, the boy lying on the grass told her to get down. She did not obey and he began to taunt her: "Ha-ha! Yer ma's a dirty squaw! Ha-ha! Yer ma's a dirty squaw!"

Zintka jumped harder and higher on the wagon seat.

"*Ha-ha! Yer ma's a dirty squaw!*"

With her back to him, she jumped as high as she could.

"*Ha-ha! Yer ma's a—*"[26]

Zintka swung in midair and landed feet first on his stomach. The younger boy's screams brought Dr. Colby and his wife out of the house, and they rushed their son to the hospital to be treated for serious internal injuries.[27]

General Colby dragged Zintka out to the stable and beat her with a riding whip while her younger cousins watched. Then he threw the whip at her fallen body and stomped off in disgust, leaving Lost Bird huddled in the hay, her legs blistered. The cousins crowded around to see if she was cry-

ing. Zintka sprang to her feet, grabbed the horse whip, and chased the terrified children into the house.[28] From then on, her Colby cousins said that
Zintka had "reverted to a savage."[29] Eighty-four years later, a family member recalled that Zintka was "meaner 'an cat shit."[30]

There is no record of Clara's response to the beating, but she was
strongly opposed to physical discipline, and the welts on Zintka's legs must
have brought a furious reaction. Directly afterward, Leonard gave Clara
enough money to take Zintka on a trip across country, ostensibly for the
child's health.[31]

Clara took Zintka to the Pacific Coast by the southern route. They
stopped at Yuma, Arizona, where Zintka bought a doll from "a medicine
man, in paint and feathers, . . . for a quarter."[32] They visited Charles F.
Lummis, the famous author, journalist, and ethnologist, where Clara
wrote: "Zintka seemed to fit naturally into the general atmosphere of this
family so free from critical curiosity and she thoroughly enjoyed her visits. . . . From the first she had been chummy with Mr. Lummis."[33]

They continued up the California coast to visit author Jessie Benton
Frémont, daughter of Missouri senator Thomas Hart Benton and widow of
explorer John Charles Frémont, the first Republican candidate for President of the United States. Clara took Zintka for daily baths in the ocean
and for long walks along the seashore. On the return trip to Washington,
Clara had Zintka read Dr. Mary Allen Wood's book on female sexuality,
What a Girl Ought to Know.[34]

The trip seemed to relax Zintka and to improve her state of mind, and
she entered public school that fall. Problems did not arise again until they
spent Christmas in Madison, Wisconsin. There Zintka may have seen
Henry, the cousin who had terrorized her the summer before. Clara and
Zintka were the guests of Clara's brother William and his wife, Jennie, the
embodiment of wifely obedience, a sweet, kind woman who adored her
husband, as did all of their children and grandchildren. But something
went wrong. For reasons unknown, Zintka chased Jennie around the
house, intent upon stabbing her with a hatpin.[35]

When they returned to Washington, the New Year did not seem promising. Clara had accepted the position of corresponding secretary for Reverend Olympia Brown's Federal Suffrage Association, an organization
founded to seek a congressional resolution that would recognize women's
right to vote under the Constitution. The job involved lobbying in Congress, and the pay was hardly enough to provide proper care for Zintka.

The Lakota child had grown into a tall, strong young woman with muscular shoulders. When angry she became vulgar, irritable, and rude, and
more and more resistant to all of Clara's efforts and plans. Her uncontrol-

lable outbursts were more frequent, and Clara wore herself down with the physical responsibilities of the newspaper and her deepening anxiety about Zintka's future.

In early October 1902, Clara's mentor, Elizabeth Cady Stanton, died after a lingering illness. Clara wrote of her death to Susan B. Anthony on October 9:

> My beloved friend,
>
> My heart turns lovingly and tenderly to you in these early days of our loss. . . . I trust you are well—[you] will be thinking that because our dear friend slipped away you are to do so too when you get to be her age [but] because you are spare, take exercise & eat frugally—have a much better chance for longevity . . .
>
> The romance—the pictures, the delights of the dear old days of individualism, centered around you & Mrs. Stanton. May you live long to be for us the embodiment of these. Ever yours in the bonds of personal love, united grief and the notion to the Holy War. Clara.[36]

Attempting to keep Zintka indoors, Clara bought a better upright piano with money she took in from boarders. Zintka's anxiety was soothed through Scott Joplin's ragtime tunes, and she played out her hurt. But the moment Clara turned away, the keyboard fell silent and Zintka was gone.

In October 1902, Clara corresponded with Captain Richard H. Pratt, founder of Carlisle Indian Industrial School in Pennsylvania. Pratt was a strict Christian reformer of the old school, and at that time considered an expert on Indian children. He had once said: "In Indian affairs I am a Baptist . . . because I believe in immersing the Indians in our civilization and when we get them under holding them there until they are thoroughly soaked."[37]

On October 14, Clara wrote to Pratt:

> Dear Sir: You probably know all about my adopted Indian daughter found on the battle field of Wounded Knee when about four months old. She is now a little over twelve with health thoroughly established after eye trouble & other indications of scrofulous tendency which seem to have been all overcome by special care so that now she is a superb specimen physically. She is bright in her school, the fourth grade and the teacher says is doing remarkably well. She is mechanical and artistic in her gifts & should have special instruction along these lines. She has quite a talent for the piano & years ago learned to manage the sewing machine & the type-writer. So much for her possibilities.

At this time there seems to be a rebellion in her blood, a surging & irresistible desire for the open air; . . . Because I love her so dearly I have hesitated to make plans for her going away to school; but now I have come to the conclusion if I am to keep her love I must send her away . . . [S]he resents the espionage which I am forced to keep over her to keep her out of danger and to keep her from running wild with the colored children for which just now she seems to have a great liking. The more I do for her the worse the situation becomes. Can you take her at Carlisle? An early reply will greatly oblige. If there is any Red Tape with the Government in such cases I can probably make that right here as I have secured her tribal rights. Yours very truly. Clara Bewick Colby.[38]

Captain Pratt responded:

Dear Mrs. Colby: I have your letter about your adopted daughter. . . . I should be glad to take her at Carlisle . . . but I am very sure it would not be the best thing for the child. My experience warrants me in saying that it was a mistake to have her origin made known so widely, to have so much of that terrible affair centered in her so that wherever she goes the picture of Wounded Knee is on exhibition. I will go still further and say that for her sake I am very very sorry you had her "tribal rights" established, and for her sake also I am sorry you call her your adopted Indian daughter. It was such a splendid chance to pay no attention whatever to her past or her origin, and to treat her as you have done, as your own child with a modest and quiet explanation only where such explanation became imperative. To send her here would be to abandon very largely your twelve years of noble motherhood and relegate her to tribal rights and Indianism. I believe . . . a little maturity and she will have passed beyond the conditions that so influence her now and distress you.

If you are fixed in your purpose to change her surroundings for a time I would put her as far as possible away from contact with Indians of any sort. Keep her isolated from them . . . Very faithfully yours, R. H. Pratt[39]

Clara took Captain Pratt's advice to heart. She wrote to him again on October 17:

My Dear Sir: I am very grateful for your candid letter, and I am sure your advice is good. It falls in with the thought that I have held all these years and with my instinct as to what is best to do now. Yet I have been sorely tried and most of all by the complications that others make in judging her harshly and not holding her in the thought of love.

I have never shirked the duties of the situation, have kept her as close to me as was the burden to Christian's back. I have made everything subservient to the care of her. I have given her more personal care than I ever knew a mother to give to her own children. She has every advantage of school, of travel, of being loved and well received by my friends; and every moral aid that I could devise both in the directing and shielding. Yet the apparent result at this moment is a child that I cannot leave with any one else and that minds me only when I am around. Verily she is of the redoubtable and indomitable Sioux.

However I do not want to make what I have done of no avail by flinching now and I feel sure it would be in the end at least as much a violation of her nature in one way to put her with Indians as it is in another to keep her with the white race, and subject her to the constant espionage that is necessary amid the dangers of a city, especially where we are surrounded by colored people who are very attractive to one side of her being. I don't know but I shall have to take to the woods with her.

I too am very sorry that I could not give her the public neglect to which a child is entitled; but at every moment of her life she has been a marked character. Everything from the "chin, chin Chinaman, eat dead rats," which she has had flung at her from babyhood . . . to the rude stare in the street car and the importunity of the determined interviewer, has contributed to make her conscious and assertive of her race. Doubtless I have aided by fostering race pride with the intent to offset the other, but I have tried to do it judiciously. For instance the Sunday School study of Moses came at a time when she seemed to think it would be delightful to go and live among the Indians and "be out of-doors all the time." I took occasion to draw the parallel between the babies, both found, adopted and educated by people of another race, and both as they grew older feeling the drawings to their own people. Then I showed the trouble Moses got into by being in too much of a hurry and that God would not let Moses go to his own people until he was prepared to do the work for them. . . . So I try to have her feel that if she is ever to go to the Indians it must only be when she can do them good and give them the benefit of what her peculiar lot has given to her. The pitiful story of her dead mother . . . seems to appeal to her just now, and this mother stands to her for freedom while I represent the power that compels and constrains her. It is pitiful for us both.

By securing her tribal rights I mean that I have had her placed on the roll to receive an allotment of land and I am sure this was right that she may never have to blame [me] for not looking after her material welfare in the future. Clara Bewick Colby.[40]

Boarding school seemed a bleak solution, but Clara could no longer cope. She enrolled Zintka in a finishing school for girls, the Salem Academy and College at Winston-Salem, North Carolina.[41] The yearly cost—$112.50 for board, household expenses, and tuition—was high and Leonard refused to cover it. Clara wrote several letters in December begging her husband to pay for his daughter's education, but to no avail. Finally, she arranged with the school to pay the tuition in installments, and on January 1, 1903, Zintka entered classes.

She did not last a week. On January 8, 1903, Clara was shocked to receive a telegram telling her that Zintka had been expelled from school and was on her way home. The principal followed up with a letter the next day:

> My dear Mrs. Colby: . . . [I]t is impossible to have your little girl become a regular member of our school family. . . . [W]e found out at once that Zintka could not remain. . . . [S]he has been thrown in contact with young people in the city schools from whom she has learned things which she should not have learned. Hence we felt that there was no other course left for us but to return her to your care. . . . I think you have a problem before you in the care of this child. . . . Very truly yours, J. H. Clewell, Principal.[42]

Clara wrote to Mr. Clewell implying that he was prejudiced against Zintka because of her race, and the principal wrote back without explaining the true nature of his concern:

> I now desire to state that one or two impressions which you received are not strictly correct. . . . [W]e declined to receive her not because of trivial matters, but because there were clear cut indications of influences which we knew would bring serious evil to the school . . .[43]

Zintka was expelled from other schools in 1903, including St. Mary's Academy at Alexandria, Virginia, a Catholic school.[44] The principal wrote:

"Dear Mrs. Colby, I regret very much we cannot take Zintka back. It is out of the question. She was too troublesome, and many of our children object to her. . . . I am Sincerely, Sister M.—"[45]

Clara's continued requests for tuition funds angered General Colby, who realized that his curio was going to cost him more than he had imagined. On March 7, 1903, he threatened Clara:

> I am not made of money and have been struggling to pay my debts. . . . I may come to the point when I shall stop paying anything. . . . I am poor [and] you have as much as I do. . . . [Y]ou cannot depend on my being able to send money, pay rent or anything and you should arrange to govern yourself accordingly. Times are dull & business very slack out here. Lawyers are the worst off of any of the professions. Yours, L. W. C.[46]

During the summer of 1903, Leonard Colby was brought before the Nebraska Grand Jury and charged with embezzlement of Nebraska National Guard funds.[47] The charge was never proven, but it was a close call. Soon afterward, Clara asked for tuition and clothing money for Zintka's fall term, and that was the last straw.

In early August the general demanded a divorce. In a daze Clara wrote a letter to herself on August 11, 1903:

> The second fateful day in my life. I want to think and yet I dare not think. I must have time to get accustomed to the idea presented, so that when I think I may be just to all. Just now I seemed absolutely stunned into a strange unnatural calm. Why is it that I can laugh and talk and plan when I am actually dead. Only on August 5, my birthday, I was trying to think what I had to be thankful for, being determined to find something. And this seemed the greatest boon that life had to give that my love had lost the power to grieve me. That out of ten years of suffering had come peace—not the loss of love. I have not thought to call it that. . . . I can see that one should depend only on God for happiness. . . . I must express myself and am putting down my thoughts the better to analyze them. Can I for love's sake tear love out of my heart? What do I owe to myself in the matter? I ought to have stood for my dignity as a wife ten years ago, but I was so much in the bondage of my love and of conventionality that I could not. I made myself believe and have up the illusion, that by my forbearance I should win him back. God help me to do the right thing now. . . . Other women, alas how many women have gone through

with this and held their heads high, lived it down and been happy. My heart is torn with conflict. Sometimes I accede; sometimes I fight, sometimes I run away.[48]

Clara wrote to her sister, and Mary's advice strengthened her:

My Darling . . . I feel strongly to have you fight the divorce, till you have driven that creature off. If you should go there & she did not leave, & you knew of any guilt—prosecute her.

I do not think God will hold you responsible for his soul, half as much as He will hold him for destroying all your earthly happiness as he has done. My precious sister it is a memory an ideal you hold to & love is not that man. Your pure nature never could love him & if you were obliged to lie with him as he is—it would be hell to you. He died for you years ago & now in justice to your self & for all the blame . . . that people have seen fit to bestow upon you, & they have, for not living with him. I beseech you don't let him get a divorce. . . . Your loving sister Mary.[49]

Clara wrote to her husband to inform him that she would not give him a divorce, and he replied with a bribe on August 16:

Dear Clara: I received your acknowledgement with the passage of scripture.

Under the circumstances which have existed for many years, and the conditions and incidents which are a part of our lives, it seems for the best interests of both that our marital relations which remain only in name, should be legally dissolved. It will be far better for you as well as me, and the misery and unfortunate publicity of such proceedings will not be as great or as lasting as we might at first imagine. I wish you to institute legal proceedings for such purpose.

I will bear all of the expenses, and furnish the required proofs. I will also agree on the amount of alimony to be paid you, and sell everything I have to pay it. You should have enough to purchase a home, if you wish, and two or three thousand dollars beside,—say six or seven thousand dollars in the aggregate. If you wish I will take and provide for Zintka in addition.

Now all this is not pleasant, but may be regarded in charity as one of the misfortunes or punishments which too often come to persons who have not the wisdom, judgements, character, or something to prevent the same. I want to be as just and honorable as my nature will allow. I am willing to assume all the blame in such proceedings. The many excellent qualities and virtues, which you possess, and which perhaps are an aggravation or reproach to me now, would add to my respect and esteem for you if our enforced ties which only legally exist, were severed. . . . Yours Respectfully, L. W. Colby.[50]

Clara remained adamant in her next letter:

> My beloved Husband: . . . I think you have been so blinded with the transient and evanescent emotions of purely physical conditions that you have lost sight of the deeper relations between mind and soul. It was not without significance that we were born on the same day and brought together from far over land and sea: that we chose each other . . . that we had the same intellectual ambitions, aesthetic tastes, and ethical ideals. For more than twenty years we slept in each other's arms, with a restful stimulating exchange of magnetism. . . . Our interests were identical and in all important matters we, to use your own expression, "stood by each other." We were a solid front to the world; our home the centre of the best social life of the city, and often the best of the state and nation were welcomed there. . . . When you left Washington, you expressed the purpose of removing to Denver or Salt Lake, and making a home for us there. There was not and never has been, a hint that you did not contemplate a future home together, and when I put the question to you the last time I saw you, you said you could not leave Beatrice until you had straightened out your property matters: giving me to understand that you still had it in mind . . .
>
> You once wrote me that if I failed you—for you, God, and Truth, and Beauty would die. I have not failed you . . .
>
> I have this offer in place of your dissolution of our difficulties: Settle with the other once and for all on a money basis: and make a home with me in Beatrice or elsewhere—preferably the latter. United we could live everything down and dispel all clouds. . . . How many times I have signed myself to you . . . "Semper eadem." I sign them now with my heart's blood. Clara Bewick Colby.[51]

Annoyed, the general sent a draft for $35 and offered to pay $420 per year to support his wife and daughter if she would agree to a divorce, to which Clara replied:

> My Beloved Husband: Why should you not sacrifice a guilty creature who has doubly betrayed the home that sheltered her and the

woman who befriended her rather than the wife of your youth who has been faithful to her trust . . . ? I endured the hardships . . . working beyond my strength . . . when you were in the Senate and at all times I lent my aid and counsel to the lines of action which made you a man of promise and influence. Remember that in your hour of greatest need I proved my love for you . . . C.B.C.[52]

On September 30, 1903, Leonard answered:

. . . The marital relation should have something more than friendship as a basis, in fact it seems not necessarily to require or include such friendship. . . . But my mind is made up and I shall have to do what is necessary, however unpleasant it may be to attain the desired object. L. W. Colby[53]

Clara wrote asking for money saying: "My over thirty years of married life; my self-respect as a woman; demand that I shall not be cast aside so unceremoniously."

Realizing that Clara was stalling, Leonard wrote on December 1, 1903: ". . . You really seem to be coming to correct conclusions as to my irreformable character. . . . My reform cannot be along your lines. You look at matters from an entirely different point of view."[54]

In November Zintka again came down with trachoma and Leonard obliged with $35 to cover treatment, rent, clothing, and school tuition fees—hardly enough, but better than nothing. Clara wrote on November 11:

. . . I should think you would like to see her. I am corresponding with the principal of Bishop Hare's school at Sioux Falls, S.D. . . . I am determined to get her out of all this Washington influence which has been wholly bad from the beginning. . . . There she will come in contact with a few Indian girls, daughters of native clergy, & with girls of very good families, ministers and missionaries largely, who will be very good for her to know, and will perhaps shape a very useful and honorable career for her. The school is Bishop Hare's pet project. He lives in it and talks to the pupils every morning. . . . As ever, faithfully yours.[55]

Leonard did not want Zintka placed nearby. On November 20 he wrote:

I do not see that a conference would tend to change my mind in the least, and you must not meet me with such an idea. My mind is made up & it is only a question of details. . . . I have no money to pay your expenses for such trip. I am hard up. . . . Yours etc. L. W. Colby.[56]

In early January 1904, Clara sold many of her personal belongings to pay half a year's tuition and took Zintka to Bishop Hare's All Saints School, one of the nation's finest boarding schools for young women. A local newspaper noted Zintka's arrival in South Dakota, the first time she had seen the state in which she was born:

> . . . For the past few years the General and wife have resided in Washington and Zintka has attended the public schools there. She is now thirteen years of age and old enough to hear many strange things about her parentage and was much talked about, her peculiar history making her an object of curiosity. To prevent the unpleasant consequences of this it was decided to place the little Zintka in some more select and secluded school where she would be under the watchful care of instructors interested in her welfare . . .
>
> The greatest care is exercised at the All Saints School to prevent anything of a nature to wound her sensitiveness from coming to the ears of the child. She has shown remarkable talent for music and is unusually bright for one of her race. It is the intention of Mrs. Colby to give her a good education and to advance her in music as far as her talents will permit. Mrs. Colby returned to Washington yesterday. Little Zintka clung to her with sobs and declared that she could not stay more than a week among strangers . . .[57]

A few days later, Leonard Colby was interviewed in Norton, Kansas, where he had gone to represent a client in a murder trial. The reporter noted his youthfulness:

> [He does] . . . not appear more than 40, not a tinge of gray in his raven locks. In explanation of his wonderful physical preservation he offers two apologies: one, that his moral rectitude is responsible in great part; another—the reason for his black hair, his great grandmother was a full-blooded Seneca squaw.[58]

General Colby gave a complete history of the Wounded Knee Massacre and of the Lakota infant he had saved. He ended his heroic tale saying that he was "now educating her in all the culture deemed elegant and civilizing."[59]

CHAPTER 16

Boarding School

"If a child goes wrong the mother is always blamed, and always blames herself."

CLARA COLBY
1904

Clara returned to the jammed streets of Washington, but the old elegance seemed to have vanished from the capital city. The avenues were congested with clangorous, vibrating Mitchell runabouts, Fords, Locomobile steam cars, Cadillacs, and Oldsmobiles that scared the horses. Passing slower horse-drawn carriages, the vehicles rode up on curbs and over sidewalks with little concern for the safety of pedestrians, who tried to steer their children out of harm's way.

In the few months that Clara was away, her neighborhood had become surrounded by slums populated by new immigrants. The original homeowners had sold out to low-rent landlords and moved away to the suburbs. The poor newcomers hung out their wet laundry indiscriminately, threw garbage in the gutters, and sat on the front steps of overcrowded tenements day and night to escape the stifling summer heat. Everything they did seemed loud, and many families wore ragged clothing and lived in misery.

No sooner had Clara arrived at the *Tribune* home office than she received a hysterical eight-page letter from Zintka:

ALL SAINTS SCHOOL

January 10, 1904

My precious mother:

... I must come home, for if I don't I shall die of grief. I am just able to write for I feel quite weak and I have a back ache a headache and

I am unwell. . . . I must come home for you know precious I can not bear to have any one take care of me when I am sick but you for when I am sick you know I always come and sit on your lap for you to hug. I have cried now for two whole nights, and very nearly 2 whole days for you precious mother you know I have slept but very little and have not eaten since you left me but one piece of dry white bread and before I could get that eaten up . . . I began to cry and I felt like screaming, but dared not. . . . Mother dear I pray for you both day and night, and every time I begin to cry I kneel down and ask God to move your little heart and tell you to let me come home. . . . Last night . . . I began to call you. I went downstairs and called and called in a low tone but received no answer from you . . . then Miss Coleman came in and stamped her foot, snapped her fingers and told me I should have to stop crying or she would shute [sic] me up and feed me for one day on bread and water. . . . Mother dear please for God sack [sic] don't keep me here. . . . [T]he whole thing smells just like an old hospital. . . . Mother if you really loved me you would not keep me in the pain and agony I am in. . . . [I]f you see any mistakes you will know and remember that I am trying to see through gallons of tears. . . . I hate every teacher in the whole building . . . [W]hen you are away from me I have no one to love or to love me. . . . At night I hug and kiss the pillow you laid your head on and even kissed the floor in the room we occupied together. Mother dear . . . you won't keep me in this . . . suffering. God bless my precious precious mother. I am your loving daughter, Zintka L. Colby.[1]

The next letter came from the matron at All Saints School:

> Dear Mrs. Colby: . . . [W]hether we are really able to do anything with Zintka will depend a good deal upon you. . . . [I]t is quite evident that she intends to have her own way. . . . Most truly yours, Helen L. Peabody.[2]

When Zintka realized that her mother was not going to come back for her, she threatened to kill anyone who came near, and she screamed that if they touched her, she would kill herself. By the end of January the situation seemed hopeless and the principal wrote:

> Dear Mrs. Colby,
> With this I am sending you an official request to remove Zintka without delay. . . . [S]ome times she seems gentle and teachable; at others

she is absolutely hard, and talks freely of murder and suicide. She told me she would run away. . . . [She] asserts that she has from the first intended to be so naughty that we would send her away. Of course in being sent she is again getting her way, which for her own sake she ought not to have; [She said] . . . that she is accustomed to living with people, not animals, and that we are all animals. . . . [T]here seems no way for her to learn except by very bitter experience. Most truly yours, Helen L. Peabody.[3]

In response to an appeal from Clara to visit his adopted daughter and to pay the school tuition, Leonard Colby wrote on January 31, 1904:

Dear Clara:
 . . . The child evidently is too smart for them at the All Saints School, and they are lacking in patience, determination and tact. Miss Peabody writes like a sick saint. . . . Zintka has . . . accomplished her object and won. . . . [The Bishop] . . . has been obliged to place it in the hands of incompetent persons who are capable only of dealing with stupid goodness or milk-and-water characters. . . . I leave for Norton, Kansas, this afternoon and cannot make any arrangements until my return. . . . Yours etc. L. W. Colby[4]

The general did not visit Zintka or pay for tuition, but Clara held firm, and by February 15, there was a change: "Dear Mrs. Colby: . . . Zintka does seem to be doing better . . . she is respectful and tries to be on time.[5]

The staff at All Saints felt "encouraged on the whole," and Zintka's repeated suicide threats subsided after gentle but firm attention from Miss Peabody. But the girl's troubles leaked to the press, and George Bartlett read of Zintka's difficulties in a newspaper article and wrote a concerned letter to Clara from Little Rock, Arkansas, where he had gone on business: ". . . I am wondering if you have had the trouble with 'Zintkala' that this paper states. Will you kindly inform me on this. . . . I am very anxious to get a recent photo of 'Zintkala.' Will you send me one? I will thank you ever so much if you will. . . . I am Yours very truly, Geo. E. Bartlett."[6] The man who had found Zintka and pried her from her dead mother's arms at Wounded Knee had not forgotten the Lost Bird.[7]

Clara was able to breathe a little easier until the middle of March, when she received an irrational thirty-page letter from Zintka containing the words *come home* forty-three times. Two more letters followed, one seventeen pages long and another twenty-one pages, the latter containing thirty requests to "come home." Zintka alternated between hysteria, scolding, cajoling, begging, threatening, and manipulating, hoping to break her mother down, the same mother she had stubbornly refused to obey in the past.

March 17, 04

My dearling mother,

. . . I myself think you have taken a very large burden upon your hands, keeping me here in this school that's not doing me one bit of good. . . . I really have come to the conclusion that you don't realize what you are doing. You add one year to your looks every time you do it. Now mother dear don't tell me to quiet down because I'm not stirred up. Don't tell me to have controle of myself, for that won't help you nor will it help me. Don't tell me not to worry . . . and please don't tell me to brace up for that won't do good either. I've borne it so long and I think I might be allowed to come home. . . . Just think the Marine Band will be there soon and the warm weather and my pleasant home, books and pictures and mother and everything that's nice instead of being here. . . . I'm so tired of snow and cold damp weather. . . . I do want to come home, my bicycle my skates my home my mother my good times, are all in that one little home. I want you to devote this summer to the home to the paper and your work and to me. O O O O O . . . my dear sweet little room with all my pictures on the wall and my window allways open and the pretty peach blossoms to look out on. . . .

I would like a new dress in my Easter box and make it real pretty won't you? . . . Please send me the [New York] Times. I nearly go crazy. . . . I have a question to ask you, and that is what is the reason of my eye bleeding. Last night it bled for three or four minutes and frightened me a little, and this morning when I tried to read . . . it was all blurred before my eyes. Its my right eye I'm speaking of. . . . My eyes feel like they had sticks in them. . . . I nearly go frantic when I think of comming home. . . . I think it would be nice if you send me the list of words I mispell. I'd give $25,96,00,00,00 dollars if I could come home. . . . Write soon, precious, with bushels of love, and kisses. I am your own loving daughter, Zintka Colby. P.S. I wish I could come home while May was there, can't I?[8]

The winter of 1904 was one of the coldest on record in South Dakota. The bleak miles of hard-packed snow, the white, barren lifelessness, without a tree or living thing in sight, can hardly be imagined to one unaccustomed to harsh winters on the Northern Plains. Zintka's tribe had endured, even relished the frigid winters when deer were easier to track. They broke holes in the ice-covered streams and rivers, washing and then drying themselves in the wind.[9] Nothing was more fulfilling to body and soul than to come out of a hot sweatlodge into the cold night air.

But Zintka had not been raised in her native climate, and her first winter there seemed like living in Siberia. Furthermore, at All Saints (an all-white boarding school except for a rare Indian missionary's daughter) the eleven-year-old girls in her sixth grade class shunned the tall, thirteen-year-old Lakota girl. Zintka became more depressed and ill. She wrote again on March 24:

My precious mother,
    . . . I am so lonesome here without any mother or father. I am dreadfully afraid that I'm going to have consumption. It's awfully tight and its hard to breth. I can't take long breths without half strangling to death. I feel like I did when I had congestion of the lungs, and when I do cough my head just nearly splits open, and so do my sides. . . . Dear me . . . the wind howls in at the windows and makes such a dreadful noise, it makes me nervous. I really and truly feel as if I'd rather die than live. . . . It sounds like a regular hospital here with all the moans and groans and crying. . . . Boom Boom Boom Boom hear the thunder. . . . I send you a piece of my lunch wrapped in paper. . . . I'm sick in bed in the inf. so really I'm just as well off home as I am here. If I was home then you wouldn't have to work yourself to death to get the money to keep me here, don't you see. I——know————what————I'm————going————to ware on the train when I get ready to come home. . . . I coughed so hard this morning I thought I'd cough up a lung. I have not heard one word from Papa and I have written him three letters. . . . [Y]ou think you have got me away from you now so you are going to keep me away. . . . I am your loving daughter Zintka Colby.[10]

Sat. March 26, 1904

My darling mother.
    How I wish I could come home and hear the noon bells ringing telling me to get your lunch for you. . . . I had to laugh again this morning when I read where you said just buckle down and learn double. PRECIOUS MA, don't you really think you'd ought to take me home. . . . I can just see myself now standing in my front door, some cool evening with my thin summer dress on maybe going on an errand for you or perhaps taking the mail, sitting at the window playing away at the piano. . . . [T]here's a train whistle. . . . O O O I do want to come home

so bad. . . . [Mother] I juss gave one scream. I don't know what to say to you to get you to let me come home. . . . Now honestly mother this really is the truth I scream or make some dreadfull noise because I am so happy about comming home. Of course you have not said anything about comming home yet, but I certainly take for granted that you are going to let me come. . . . I am your loving daughter. Z. Colby. . . . I'd like the [New York] Times.[11]

Zintka's desperate letters to her mother did not reflect the matron's reports showing improvement in school. Miss Peabody wrote on April 14: " Dear Mrs. Colby, . . . The change in Zintka is remarkable. . . . She gives no trouble whatsoever. . . . She seems to have no trouble with her eyes now, and it has been some time since she complained of them. . . . With best wishes to you I am Cordially yours, Helen L. Peabody.[12]

Clara had decided to move her newspaper to Portland, Oregon, to make sure Zintka did not return to the old Washington neighborhood. Also, a major campaign for a suffrage amendment had been launched in Oregon. The national suffrage organizations were focused on the vote in Oregon, and Clara felt her newspaper would help the cause.

She wanted to move the first of May, but with no help from Colby for Zintka's expenses, she could not earn even rent money and her landlord finally sued. Angry that Leonard had not responded to his daughter's needs, Clara attacked him (but not by name) on the front page of the *Tribune* while he was still facing charges for embezzling National Guard funds:

> The renown of the successful general is almost invariably achieved by accident or by the reckless sacrifice of his soldiers. It is at best a very doubtful honor to have mastered an enemy by superior force and equipment. The warrior class serve a purpose in the barbarous stage of the world's development, but they will soon be outgrown. The destructive elements of life can not hold rank with the constructive. Military glory is even now fading in the brilliant light of the achievements in the arts and sciences which are heralding the era of peace, prosperity and fraternity.[13]

The attack was not well timed. Leonard Colby despised scholars and intellectuals and all they stood for. She wrote to him on May 6, 1904:

My Dear Husband:
     . . . It is certainly your duty and should be your privilege to do something for my support, and certainly for Zintka's. Do not add to the perplexities of my present position by making it impossible for her

to be educated where they have been so good to her, and throwing her back into the public schools of Washington, and into irregularity. I am now owing them [All Saints] $100 for her . . . then I shall have her expenses back and the fitting her out with something to wear as she has outgrown all her things. . . . Do not say you cannot afford to contribute towards the support of your . . . daughter. [It] is too manifestly absurd. I have too high an appreciation of your abilities as a lawyer to believe any such nonsense. . . . I hope you will answer this at once, and come to the rescue. As ever yours, Clara.[14]

While Zintka sat "on the steps looking off as if longing to be up and away," Leonard Colby did not come to her aid. On the contrary, he wrote Clara on June 1, 1904: ". . . I have exhausted my present resources, and as I wrote you some months ago, cannot be depended on financially. . . . As indicated, my circumstances are financially very embarrassing. Yours, etc., L. W. Colby"[15]

A few days later, Zintka was bitten on the arm by a dog and she wrote a graphic description of the attack to her mother. This time Clara weakened. She wrote to Miss Peabody, who answered:

> . . . I am sorry you do not realize that I would always notify you in case of serious trouble. The fact that Zintka wrote with the bitten arm ought to indicate that the trouble was not acute. The arm is doing well. The nurse has watched it carefully and has not allowed her to use it. We had the Dr. to see it twice, and of course his bill ought to be paid at once. Very truly yours, Helen Peabody[16]

Still alarmed by the attack and the wound, which Clara did not trust to any doctor, she appealed to her brother William. Zintka was sent to Madison to recuperate at her Aunt Mary's home. William noted after her arrival:

> My Dear Sister:
> . . . I was at Mary's this morning, but did not see Zintka as she was in bed. Mary went to the depot to get her at 4 A.M. Mary said she looked remarkably well and she could not find the terrible sore on her arm that she expected to from her letters, so we have to conclude that this has been another instance where she has worked you . . . to accomplish a desired end. With lots of love and best wishes, I am as ever your loving Bro. Wm. Bewick.[17]

Zintka came home to Washington to play her piano and to stand, as she had dreamed, in the front door of her home "in a thin summer dress."

Calmer and more obedient, she helped her mother pack for the move to Portland. Then Zintka accompanied cousin Edwin Mauger's family to their island home in Maine for the summer. By August Clara had found a two-room apartment in Portland and published her first *Tribune* issue on the West Coast.

In Maine the Maugers caught Zintka sneaking off to meet a boy, and they sent her to Clara in Oregon.[18] Before she left, Zintka could not find the ring or sheet music Mrs. Mauger had lent her. Clara sent Mauger's letters to her husband with a plea that he pay the tuition debt at All Saints School so that Zintka could enroll for the fall semester:

> . . . I want very much to have Zintka go back . . . because they have known how to deal with her with kindness and firmness. . . . This attraction for the boys is the all dominating influence of her life at this time. When she is older and her judgment developed let us hope she will be different. But safety is now the thing to be thought of. I cannot give it to her. . . . I could not keep her off the streets save as I locked up her clothes and you know that sort of thing cannot last with a girl stronger than I am by a good deal. . . . It is an awful problem we have to deal with. As Ever Yours, Clara.[19]

The years 1904 and 1905 were marked by a series of misfortunes for Leonard Colby. After his indictment for alleged embezzlement, his brother, Dr. David Colby, got drunk and his team of horses ran away with him. His buggy overturned on the railroad tracks and dragged the doctor to his death.[20] Then a second brother, Edward, died, leaving Leonard's grieving elderly mother, Abigail Livingston Colby, in the care of an unmarried daughter, Abby, in Freeport, Illinois. This arrangement ended in tragedy after the police investigated reports that Abby was sadistically abusing her mother.[21] The allegations were proven when authorities found Mrs. Colby covered with bruises. They took her to a hospital but she refused to press charges against her own daughter—or, as Clara put it, "she hugged her chains"—and died not long afterward.[22] Leonard's mother had been a gifted artist, but a cruel streak ran through the Colby family, and the elder Mrs. Colby was one of its victims. Daughter Abby was never prosecuted for her crime.

Again the general refused to pay Zintka's tuition debt. She was therefore not allowed to return to All Saints School for a second year. When Clara threatened to send the girl to live with her father, the general told his wife that if she sent Zintka, he would put her in the state reform school. Clara had only one other choice—the one she most dreaded: a government Indian industrial boarding school at Chamberlain, South Dakota. Zintka wanted very much to go. On October 11, 1904, Clara wrote:

> My Dear Husband:
> . . . [W]ithout some aid from you I was obliged to place her in the government school. . . . [W]hile Zintka has to eat and sleep with the Indian girls and do her stint of work, . . . she can wear her own clothes and I fitted her out well for the year. . . . If she could have gone to All Saints she would have been graded up instead of down, socially, educationally, and morally. I fear this will build a barrier between her and the place she ought to occupy as our daughter. There is, I am sorry to say, no instruction in music unless it is paid for extra. . . . I am living with the greatest economy . . . .25 [cents] a day, including fuel. . . . Think of your wife living like this when things are flush with you.[23]

But Leonard Colby was not as blissful as Clara believed. After eleven years of waiting for him to divorce Clara, Maud Miller Martinez got fed up and left the general, with the ultimatum that if he did not divorce his wife, he would lose his twenty-nine-year-old mistress. Maud moved to Lincoln, Nebraska, and began seeing other men.[24]

The tables had turned on the fifty-five-year-old lothario, and Colby began sending Maud expensive gifts and flowers, promising to divorce Clara at the earliest opportunity. Maud knew a great deal about Leonard's financial activities—perhaps too much for him to let her go.

Meanwhile, one mile north of Chamberlain, in the Missouri River valley, Zintka was living among her people and she was happy:

> November 4, 1904
>
> My Dear Mother,
> . . . I must write you a nice letter and tell you what I am doing. Mrs. Flinn is a matron now and so of course I help her. She has put me in charge of the little girl's dormatory, for inspection to see that they do it well. I am also detailed to the sewing room, and have charge of 12 big girls, and I am also office girl.
> I have been setting the table . . . for some time. . . . Ruth Tracy is just dead gone on Moses and she just loves the ground he walks on. . . . Sorry to say she's a white girl but she seems to suit Moses. I am very foolish but never mind . . .[25]

Shocked at Zintka's candid remark about a "white girl," Clara blasted her husband:

. . . This is a burning disgrace. . . . You ought to want her to be well educated and be an honor to us. I cannot understand your indifference to the welfare of the child you yourself took. For good or evil we have separated her from her own race and now we must give her the advantages of a white child and what is due to her as our adopted daughter. . . . It was a mistake ever to have sent her to an Indian School, although I did it by the advice of the Commissioner and other people who know much about Indians. . . . Do put heart and brain into the consideration of this problem, and do what will best fit the girl to become a respectable member of society . . .[26]

As harsh winter weather kept the schoolchildren from playing outdoors, they spent much of their time in crowded, stuffy rooms. Zintka and many others fell ill:

January 16, 05

My Precious mother,

I have been sick and I am still in bed the Dr. comes to see me everyday. We have a very bad case of Diptheria and the school is quarenteened, so we cannot go down town . . . I wish you could spare 2.00 to send me, as I would like to get something very much with it, and not one cent of it will go for foolishness. It is something that will last forever, providing someone does not steal it. I must tell you my temperature was 105 Sunday and Sat. night it was 100 . . .

We had a party here Tuesday night Jan. 10, 1905 and every boy put his own money in, and took a girl and only the girls that we[re] chosen could come. . . . [T]hey danced until 11:30 P.M., then they went over to the dining room and had supper. We had chocolate cake vanilla cake candy, bananas, fruit cake and jelly cake and vanilla ice cream. I enclose the invitation I got, and I felt so funny going over there with this great big tall boy. I would not [be] a pin to him. He is the tallest boy in school next to Edward Red Hail. . . . Write soon precious . . . losts of love and kisses. [The letter was signed with a mispelled word in Lakota that meant "much woman."][27]

The Indian Training School at Chamberlain was overcrowded and it became the object of two federal investigations into conditions there during 1904.[28] The authorities found the industrial work on the farm to be "not satisfactory." Moreover, there was a constant turnover of employees and a lack of basic school materials. The cook had recently quit, there was not enough light in the classrooms, and the buildings had no running water.[29] Although the superintendent, John Flinn, reported "good health of the pupils," he wrote in 1905 that a new hospital was under construction and "when it is completed we will be in better shape than ever before to care for our pupils."[30]

Despite conditions at the school, Zintka was described as "happy and full of life."[31] But during the winter, an epidemic of trachoma plagued the school and Zintka again caught the dreaded eye disease. A white "speck" grew over the cornea of her right eye, and a specialist was called.[32] He advised that she wear dark glasses at all times. The superintendent wrote General Colby for financial assistance to pay the doctor bills, and this time the general sent $10.[33]

Zintka's illness frightened her mother, and Clara borrowed money to have the girl sent to Portland by train. Zintka did not want to leave Chamberlain, but once in Portland she recuperated. It did not take her long to discover a nearby "pleasure resort" called The Oaks.[34] The exciting sounds of barrelhouse banjos, a hot piano, and hands clapping to honky-tonk syn-co-pa-tion brought Zintka out at night to hear the catchiest "Maple Leaf Rag" in Portland.

CHAPTER 17

"Chi"

Portland, a major river port and the largest city in Oregon, extended up the banks of the Willamette River near the point where it flowed into the great Columbia. A garden paradise in 1905, with a comfortable population of 125,000, "Rose City" flourished below the majestic snow-capped glacier slopes of Mount Hood. The city was preparing for the June opening of the Lewis and Clark Centennial and Oriental Fair, an exposition to commemorate the exploration of the great Pacific Northwest territory by Captains Meriwether Lewis and William Clark.

In the early days of her recovery from trachoma, Zintka never tired of hearing Clara's noble and enduring story of Sacagawea (Bird Woman), a Shoshone Indian who had been the two explorers' favorite interpreter and guide. She had led them to the Pacific coast carrying a child on her back. This brave woman had been captured by enemy warriors and then married to a French-Canadian trader and interpreter, Toussaint Charbonneau.[1]

Clara described Sacagawea as a romantic feminist figure, but at the same time she criticized "uncivilized" Indians for dressing in their native clothing. It was a confusing message for Zintka.[2]

During Zintka's recovery, Clara wrote to her longtime friend, the dentist Clara McNaughton: "I have not a penny in sight."[3] Dr. McNaughton loaned her money, and in February Clara and Zintka moved into an old house and rented out three rooms to boarders. The Victorian house had wide porches with a view of the Willamette hills, with easy access to a nearby trolley. Clara hoped the rooms would be rented throughout the fair, although she found many a homeless person whom she could not turn away.

The Oregon suffrage movement, dominated by the suffragist Abigail Scott Duniway (sister of Harvey Scott, powerful publisher of the *Oregonian*) annoyed Miss Anthony and her comrades to such a degree that for years they had tried to force her to step down. Carrie Chapman Catt wrote Clara: "Now the one question is how to get at it without her. I am sure the state could be organized if she were only out of the way . . ."[4] Clara went about trying to do just that. At the yearly Oregon suffragists' meeting, Clara nominated another woman for state president and she herself was nominated for vice president. Mrs. Duniway flew into an embarrassing tirade, exclaiming, "I positively cannot work with Mrs. Colby. . . . She has never succeeded in any cause which she has championed!"[5] An indignant outcry followed and a woman in the audience interrupted Duniway, saying: "It's an outrage. The idea of that woman speaking of a lady like Mrs. Colby in such terms!"[6]

But the damage was done. Mrs. Duniway won another term as state president, and she turned on Clara like a lioness, spending much of her energy during the election year attacking Clara as a "freak, parasite and . . . old tramp."[7] Duniway called anyone who did not do exactly as she demanded "a parasite," so the charge had little effect on Clara. She still planned three books, gave twenty-two lectures sponsored by temperance leaders, and traveled over 800 miles by rail and 250 miles by stagecoach throughout Oregon.[8] She also published articles in national magazines such as The Arena.

Meanwhile, the woman then caring for Zintka could not control her, and the teenage girl easily sneaked away to The Oaks to learn the latest song, "Weeping Willow: Ragtime Two-Step," by her favorite composer, Scott Joplin. When Clara returned from her travels, she found a job for Zintka at a friend's café, the Ralston Lunch Room—which, she noted, was "frequented by the best people" at the fairgrounds. This would be a lucky break for Zintka, as Portland store owners were "prejudiced against having an Indian" work for them.[9]

On June 1, 1905, 40,000 people attended the opening exposition ceremonies and saw varied exhibits such as the Trip to Mars, the Haunted Castle, the Palace of Mirth, and a pair of trained elk that were driven off a forty-foot tower into an immense tank of water every day.[10]

Clara desperately wanted Zintka to keep her job. She wrote to Dr. McNaughton:

> I have to get her off with a clean white waist & apron . . . every day and then I go at eight and take her around a bit before I bring her home. She likes it very much and is getting satisfaction. She will . . . keep out of mischief and learn a great deal . . .[11]

The lunchroom was located near the center of the fairgrounds, where a large bronze statue of Sacagawea stood "surrounded by beautiful sunken gardens of exotic plants and flanked by splashing fountains."[12] Customers could not help but compare the statue and Zintka, who was having so much fun that she became nervous and overstimulated by the questioning crowds. She broke out with eczema around one ear and down her neck. The skin irritation itched and spread over her face, and Zintka eventually lost her job. Clara wrote to McNaughton that "Zintka has a sweet disposition but of the butterfly variety."[13] She was not, after all, Sacagawea.

On July 22, 1905, Carl Montgomery, Clara's lawyer and an old friend of the Colbys', wrote from Nebraska:

> . . . Mr. Colby called at my office . . . [T]he situation has reached a climax [and] he will leave Beatrice and go elsewhere . . . and then get a divorce . . . without your knowledge. He is willing that everything shall be done to protect your name and reputation . . . *provided,* that the divorce will follow. He also states that he will . . . consent to a judgment for at least $6,000.00 alimony. . . . He states further that you ought to know that he would be honest with you in the ultimate payment of any alimony awarded. . . . Yours Very truly, C. S. Montgomery.[14]

In August Clara took Zintka to Chemawa, a well-known Indian boarding school a short train ride from Portland, although she begged to return to Chamberlain and her own people. The girl despised Chemawa and wrote, "My Dear Mama, Why have you not written to me long before this, when this is my second letter to you . . . ? I am . . . lonesome . . ."[15] Zintka asked her father for clothes and she was surprised when he sent $100. Meanwhile, Clara lectured to raise rent money. On August 16, after hearing Clara was having a hard time, suffrage leader Isabella Beecher Hooker wrote: "Pardon me for asking if the child has not a father as well as a mother & was it not he who brought her to you as a precious burden who needed a mother's care as well as a father's? I must know why it is that you are helpless & almost poverty stricken."[16]

General Colby visited Montgomery again and again, and Clara knew she was powerless to stop the divorce. She penned her anguish to her lawyer:

> . . . Perhaps it is best for him . . . and . . . self-respecting for myself to be honest in this matter as I see now I ought to have been 12 years ago when I covered it all up so as to shield him. . . . These have been very expensive years as regards Zintka. [I put] her in Bishop Hare's school of which Mr. Colby approved but [he] did not aid me to pay the bills. . . . I felt the importance of having her there. Would I have kept her there the whole trend of her life would have been different & I think she would have moved to be a teacher to help her race. But

with past . . . dues still unpaid they would not take her. . . . I had to send her last year to the Government school which I consider had been a great detriment to her. . . . In charity I have had to accept his statements that he could not do any more. . . . So I leave the matter of alimony to you as a lawyer and as a friend . . . Clara[17]

Trusting everything to Montgomery, she wrote: "Of all the pangs I am enduring . . . the one I cannot bear is to add to the disgrace and unhappiness of my husband. If this is to be my last relationship with him let it reflect the love and tenderness I bear him."[18]

The government school at Chemawa was no match for Zintka. She hated the matron, who had intercepted a letter she had written to a boy:

Dear Friend

I received your letter about two evenings ago, and as I didn't have time to answer right away I shall take the time now. I got home last night, and really I didn't know that I was going until the same afternoon. I didn't expect to leave until after hoppicking time anyway but my people sent for me to come right away so I had to go.

You must come up after the fair, and then I shall be sure to see you.

Answer soon and don't let anyone see this you have been letting the boys read them but you need not trouble yourself to do so anymore.

And I want you not to use the word "Gee" because it does not sound nice: and you don't want to be counted in as common persons that use slang and by-words. I know I haven't anything to say of much interest.

Send the letter to below address,

>   And believe me as ever
>   Yours truly
>   Zintka Colby
>   335-19th Street & Market
>   Portland, Ore.

P.S. Be sure and tell me when you are coming up.[19]

The matron sent the letter to Clara, but it seemed innocent enough and Zintka defended her right to correspond with whomever she pleased:

I suppose Mrs. Theize sent you the letter I wrote to A. Tyler, and I suppose she thinks you will almost take my head off but I told her I was perfectly willing you should see it. As there was nothing in it I was ashamed of. . . . And as long as he is the only friend I have in

Chemawa I'll stick up for him every time through thick and thin. I never even talk very much to the other boys, only to say Hello, and pass on, and I don't bother my mind about them, for I am busy thinking of other things usefull, and it makes me tired. I only write to him as a friend and nothing else, just the same as I would write to my brother. I'd just like to marry him just to spite Mrs. Theize. I would she thinks you will scold me for writing to him. You know I haven't kept anything away from you, and I let you read his letters of course they were only funnie ones, and they didn't mean a thing. I'm not like some girls here, write one day to one boy, and the next day to another. If I have a friend in school among the boys I want just one friend and I don't care to talk to anyone else, or act like a crazy girl when I see one or even speak to one. Really it makes me mad, when I think of it. If I want to write to him I'll do it, but not if you don't want me to. . . . [Mrs. Theize] said to me, You didn't come here to fall in love and I had a good mind to say, Who do you see that has fallen in love, bah. It shows what she thinks of all the time. I no more think of love for Arthur than I do for a piece of burned rotten stump. I like him because he is kind to me and he has very go[od] manners, and is an artist, and a very smart boy.[20]

Zintka did not describe the punishments she received for wrongdoing, but because of her defiant behavior, she must have come in for her share. As the spoiled child of prestigious parents, Zintka probably intimidated school authorities, and they had to be careful how they treated her. The superintendent, E. Chalecraft, wrote, ". . . [U]nder the personal direction and control . . . Mrs. Theisz was diplomatic, careful and faithful in her duty toward Zintka and used her utmost endeavors to lead her into the right way of living . . ."[21]

Other Indian children at boarding schools did not fare as well. In one survey, writer Robert Gessner described corporal punishment at such schools: "I have seen them whipped with a hemp rope, also a water hose. . . . Indian boys chained to their beds at night . . . underfed, roughly treated—hard work—child labor—lonely, frightened, flogged, exhausted children—ever hungry children . . . walking with heavy cordwood on their shoulders around and around the school. . . . [A teacher] seized a club . . . [and] beat the girl until she fell, and beat her on the ground."[22] Gessner reported that some children had been whipped to death.[23]

Severe punishment at Indian boarding schools continued until well into the 1960s. A child who wet the bed might have stood all day with the wet sheet over his head. Another who disobeyed would be forced to climb up a pole, and whenever he got tired and slipped down, a teacher lit a match under his feet. Catholic boarding schools for Indian children bear harsh criticism from a man who remembered bitterly the sound of "the belts" when he was made to crawl between the legs of several nuns standing in a row. Another woman recalls stealing a pickle because she was hungry; for punishment, she was locked and then forgotten for a day and a night in a small cellar where spiders and rats crawled over her legs. Many Indian children were sexually abused in boarding schools by pedophiles who looked for jobs where they could satisfy their predatory urges.[24]

On September 22, 1905, Zintka wrote a long letter to her mother that marked a turning point. Besides the spelling errors, which she knew Clara would notice, there was an unmistakable Indian tone to the letter, which must have upset Clara:

> ...I shall come marching home in my uniform of blue sure enough. chi ... I think I shall be a better girl next time. ... I'll pay for having it [a trunk] brought to the house if you will let me have it. chi ... I suppose you will have another paper out ready waiting for me to do up. chi ...[25]

Chi was a slang word, much like saying "Gee." Young Indians in every tribe have changing slang terms, just as others do.

Another letter came from Zintka on September 30, 1905, describing health and cleanliness at the school:

Precious mother,
    ... Mrs. Theize told me yesterday that I couldn't go home until I got rid of the itch as she calls it [lice] ... and I am trying hard to get them well fast. Lots of girls have it not only me. ... You know the rats chewed my rope you put on the valese so it is not useable. ... Love and Kisses As ever your loving child Zintka L. Colby[26]

In December Clara wrote to Leonard asking him to send Zintka a Christmas present:

> ... Zintka has many good traits and I trust that the moral conscience will develop in time. I will not speak of her faults but I think it my duty to put you on your guard about what she says in her letters, if anything should seem improbable to you. ... [W]hen she sits down to write she seems to be impressed with all kinds of fancies which she writes about as truth. ... I do not want her to feel cast off ...[27]

But Leonard was in no mood to buy Zintka presents. His mistress was nearly beyond his reach, and he responded harshly: ". . . prayers & tears . . . will accomplish nothing. . . . [W]hat I ask of you is to obtain the divorce."[28]

It was a sad Christmas holiday for Clara and Zintka. Clara had been evicted for not paying the rent, and she had only a few days to pack for yet another move. Clara told Zintka about the divorce, which did not seem to mean much to the girl, but when she told her that she would have to return to Chemawa, Zintka stormed out of the house and the police were called to bring her back. After a troublesome row with harsh words on both sides, Clara escorted Zintka back to boarding school. On January 9, 1906, Zintka wrote:

My Precious Mama,

I hate it here. And I'm not learning one thing. I don't know as much now as I did when I was going to public schools. All I learn now is badness. And you always say "If you be kind and nice to the girls they'll be kind and nice to you" but they are not, I've tried that plan, the nicer I am to them the meaner they are to me because they think, Well, she is not mean and she won't do this, she won't do that, we can just run over her all we want and treat her as mean as we please. . . . I wish you wouldn't make me stay here. . . . I think you might keep me home anyway until you can make arrangements for me to go to S. Dakota. I want to go there very very much. I wrote to Mr. Flinn . . . and told him I wanted to come back there. . . . I don't belong here anyway and these are not my tribe of indians and I hate it here. S. D. was the only place I was ever really and truly happy and why can't I go back there. . . . This comes from my heart and not from my lips only, believe what I say mother. I'm telling the truth . . .[29]

Leonard Colby's demands for a divorce continued. He told Montgomery that if Clara gave him a divorce, he would promise with "his sense of duty and honor to meet such an obligation" of generous alimony and child support.[30] Clara responded on February 6:

. . . Thank Heaven that for these many years my life has been full of pressing duties that if I would keep up at all, [I had] to ignore personal feelings. . . . I have given up my principles about obtaining a divorce. . . . As far as the money is concerned, make sure of . . . $2,000. I have been practically without support from him for 13 years. . . . The opportunities are scant for a woman of my years. . . . I do not know what Mr. Colby has saved, but for many years he has been putting his real estate in the name of another. I think this is the secret of his wanting the divorce. . . . Mr. Colby has been selling off his stock and trading for land in Oklahoma and Missouri . . .

As far as Zintka is concerned, let there be nothing said about her in the decree, and then she will have a claim upon us both. I have had all the trouble, and nearly all the expense, and I am hoping to guide her past the difficult and willful age and fit her to earn her living in music or nursing, her two aptitudes. She is in her sixteenth year and is now at Chemawa . . . but she makes a terrible protest against going there and I am never sure when she is going to rebel. She is Mr. Colby's legally adopted daughter, and I want nothing done to prejudice her right to inherit from him . . .[31]

In February 1906, as a last resort, Clara sent Leonard a copy of their wedding vows, the text they had written for their marriage thirty-five years before:

L.W.C.—Choosing you alone from all the world, I take you, Clara to be my wedded wife. I will love and trust you as my nearest and dearest earthly friend. I will cherish and protect you in sickness and in health; in prosperity and in adversity, and seek your comfort and happiness always. With you and for you will strive for the noblest and most beautiful life; and may God grant that between our hearts there may be such a holy union, that when the angel of death shall end this earthly tie that binds us, we may come into even a closer and more beautiful spiritual relation.

C.D.B.—Leonard, I take you, choosing you alone from all the world to be my wedded husband. My heart's best love I give you as my best and most intimate earthly friend. I will trust you, honor you, assist you, and always seek your welfare. With you and for you, I will seek all womanly graces, all sweetness and strength. I will be your loving wife through all the varied fortune that life may bring us; and if God wills I shall but love you better after death . . .

Clara ended her letter saying: "I have copied this as my last protest against the separation. I have kept my vows, and will keep them."[32]

On March 30, 1906, Leonard brought a divorce suit against Clara in Beatrice. Through her lawyer, Clara countersued and won the divorce on grounds of abandonment and nonsupport.[33] On April 3, Montgomery wrote to inform Clara that she had won the divorce but that Leonard had only given him $1,000, several land notes payable upon his own discretion, and he did not pay all of Clara's legal fees. "Mr. Colby seemed anxious to keep entirely secret the transactions as regards the amount and method of settling your alimony. . . . He said from time to time he will remit you funds for use on [Zintka's] account."[34]

The divorce scandal made the newspapers and caused a backlash among suffragists. The powerful Reverend Anna Shaw wrote to Ida Husted Harper: "I wish she had waited until the [Oregon] campaign was over."[35] Ironically, during the same month, Clara's mentor and faithful supporter for over twenty-six years, Susan B. Anthony, perhaps the greatest woman suffrage leader the world had ever known, died after saying her last words: "Failure is impossible."[36]

CHAPTER 18

"No One Need Ever Know"

Zintka was miserable at Chemawa. A nonwhite physically but a non-Indian socially, she was typical of many Indian children who suffered the same lonely void when taken from their tribes.

Restless and yearning to be free, Zintka's ancestral roots pulled loose in April 1906, when San Francisco was rocked with the worst earthquake in its history. The disaster left nearly 500 people dead. The entire Pacific Coast reacted with horror, the teachers of Chemawa were distracted, and class schedules were temporarily interrupted. Zintka saw her chance to make a run for it, but she did not get far; the police brought her back promptly. The superintendent of the school wrote to Clara:

> . . . From the time Zintka came to Chemawa we saw that there was something wrong in her way of looking at life. . . . She has been reasonably obedient to her teachers but has . . . all the time seemed to avoid the better class of pupils and associated with the less desirable ones. . . . In talking with the matron at the Police Court, I found that [Zintka] had been there once before, which was a surprise to me.
>
> . . . If you desire us to keep her, . . . place her in our hands permanently without giving her any hope of leaving the school until such time as we are satisfied there is a radical change in her. If you do this I will take steps to impress upon her the necessity for a thorough reformation.
>
> . . . The first step . . . would be the necessity of having her change her manner of dress. She said to me . . . that it seemed to her that the Police and everybody watched her when she was on the streets. I informed her that the reason was . . . her flashy way of dressing . . .[1]

One evening a younger classmate let two boys into the girl's dormitory, and Zintka was with the group when they were discovered. But this time Zinkta defied her matron, jumped from a window, and disappeared into the night.[2]

The Lost Bird had flown. Clara waited anxiously for her daughter to return to Portland, but the weeks and months passed by without a word.

Determined to find out if she was really Sitting Bull's daughter, Zintka headed for South Dakota. A destitute sixteen-year-old girl without clothes or money, Zintka had placed herself in serious danger. But she was a clever and articulate young woman. She had traveled extensively and knew from her mother's financial problems that ministerial associations, churches, and travelers' aid societies assisted stranded and homeless people. Using all of her resources, Zintka made it as far as the tent city of Lemmon, South Dakota, about ten miles from the boundary of the Standing Rock Reservation.

Lemmon did not officially become a town until the railroad reached there in 1907, but it already had a general store, a lumber yard, a livery stable, three gambling houses, and four saloons where whiskey sold for five cents a shot.[3]

Looking for work, Zintka met "Indian Pete" Culbertson, owner of a newly organized Wild West show. He was a handsome man with a "genial smile and explosive laugh." According to local tradition, he was stolen from his parents when a mere child, by Indians. He lived with this tribe until he had grown up, making many trips with them to various other tribes while a boy. In this way he "became conversant with the languages and habits of several tribes of the Lakota Nation."[4]

The truth was that Pete Culbertson was an ex-convict from pure Norwegian stock. His family had experienced at least one "Indian scare" when he was a boy, but he was not stolen by Indians. Like Buffalo Bill, Culbertson exploited his association with Indians to publicize his Wild West show, wore his hair long "using coffee for a dye," and had "the bluest eyes you ever saw."[5] He twirled a "pearl-handled colt sixshooter" and he was an expert horse thief. Pete rode up to Montana alone to the Crow Reservation and came back herding fifty to sixty horses at one time. He was tough, wiry, and "full of life," and was a devil-may-care with women.[6] The showman owned extensive property at Lemmon and operated a large ranch on Pine Creek about forty miles north of the Standing Rock Reservation. His wife usually rode in his show as a cowgirl, but in 1906 she was pregnant. (She later gave birth to a son she named Martie, billed as "the smallest cowboy in the world.")[7]

Zintka was hired to take Mrs. Culbertson's place as a cowgirl. Indian Pete's Wild West toured for several months, and Zintka learned "top work"—standing on top of the saddle of a galloping horse. She tried "vaults," hitting the ground with her feet and then vaulting back to the saddle, and "drags," holding on to the saddle and hanging close to the ground off the side of the horse.[8]

Cowgirls had to display a dashing, daring, happy western spirit in the shows—and they looked the part, dressed in what they called "loudrags": broad-brimmed cowboy hats, brilliant shirts with heavily fringed leather skirts, beaded bolero jackets, colorful silk scarves, high boots with jingling spurs, and long white fringed gloves. Fancy western attire suited Zintka, and she enjoyed the loud stomping and thunderous applause from the crowd. Outrageous behavior for a woman, such as chewing tobacco and popping a whip, were common and ranch people outside the show grounds often looked down on rodeo and Wild West showgirls unless they were married and touring with their husbands.[9]

Culbertson's main tent held 10,000 people, with other tents for sideshows, stables, mess rooms, and living quarters. There were "bronco busters," trick riders, sharpshooters, and a band of Indians that was instructed to surround and attack "a prairie schooner." Yelling Indians in war bonnets were the favorite acts of the two-hour show, and the more noise they made the better the customers liked it.[10]

When Zintka had earned enough money to take care of herself for a while, she visited the Standing Rock Agency at Fort Yates, North Dakota, to look for Sitting Bull's relatives. But Sitting Bull's people lived far from the agency, and going there required the prior permission of the agent. The inexperienced new man, William L. Belden, had taken office on May 1, 1906, and he knew virtually nothing about the 3,461 Hunkpapa, Yanktonai, and Blackfeet under his charge. That year deaths exceeded births, with tuberculosis and mumps the leading cause of infant mortality. The Hunkpapa were grieving.[11]

Indian women on the reservation were accompanied everywhere they went and turned their eyes away from men, especially strangers. They were taught to sit with legs to one side, and to work industriously and quietly.[12] In contrast to the modesty and gentleness of other young Lakota women, Zintka, by Clara's example, looked men straight in the eyes, laughed heartily, and stated her business in no uncertain terms. When Zintka appeared at Fort Yates, the gaudily dressed cowgirl must have seemed offensive to tribal members. Her dream of living with her own tribe, of being accepted, loved, and taken in, had brought her thousands of miles. There was a big buildup, a feeling of wanting desperately to belong—and here she was, finally among her people. But she had no one to give her backing, no extended family of well-wishers to offer help. Instead, Zintka brought attention to herself, pretentiously claiming she might be Sitting Bull's daughter. Many of the Indian police who had participated in the medicine man's death still lived and worked at Fort Yates. Zintka was not only viewed with suspicion, she was seen as a person out of balance with her people, with nature, and with her own life. The imbalance created a cultural barrier over which she could not climb. She could not even speak the Lakota language. Eager to find relatives, Zintka appeared pushy and nosy, and asked too many personal questions—all traits considered ill-mannered in Indian culture.[13]

The Lakota at Standing Rock left Zintka alone to the realization that no one wanted anything to do with her. If she had stayed there longer and showed a willingness to listen, the outcome might have been different. The Lakota shunned her just as they often rejected students who returned from eastern schools thinking they knew how to change everything overnight.[14]

Agency records have not been found noting Zintka's arrival at Fort Yates, although oral-traditional stories relate that she came during an unusually rainy spring and summer. Zintka ended up standing in a downpour in the middle of a muddy road screaming: "It's me, Lost Bird! Zintkala Nuni! Please help me!" Ironically, she mispronounced her own name because she could not speak her native language.[15]

Rancher Ed Lemmon recalled that Zintka's job with Pete Culbertson "didn't work out" after she returned from Fort Yates.[16] Enough clues remain to form a plausible interpretation of her break with "Indian Pete." The whole town knew Pete had been arrested for the brutal murder of an elderly Indian named Few Tails on January 10, 1890, just days after the Wounded Knee Massacre. He and his two brothers had ambushed Few Tails, but the man's widow and relatives escaped. The military investigated and identified Pete Culbertson among the killers. When questioned, he boasted, "I have shot one of those damned government pets, and if any more of them want to be fixed, let them come this way." The Culbertson brothers were acquitted in a jury trial after their lawyer claimed the U.S. government had been at war with the Lakota.[17] Pete returned to the Lemmon area a hero bearing a collection of Indian scalps, peace pipes, and Ghost Dance shirts.[18] If Zintka found out about the murder, she would not have remained with his Wild West show.

Ed Lemmon also remembered that Zintka was seen in the company of "August Back's son."[19] Mr. Back had a lumber freighting business, and his wife, Caroline, a Norwegian immigrant, was beloved for her kindness and sweet hospitality to strangers. Zintka had a way with children, and it is possible she was working as mother's helper for the Back's seven children until she earned enough money to move on.

Ed wrote in his autobiography that Zintka "drifted back to the reservation, the G-string, and the blanket."[20] That was the white perception of the flashy cowgirl's sudden disappearance from Lemmon. In reality, Zintka had gone to the Pine Ridge Reservation, still searching for relatives. By then, she had taken off her "loud rags."

At Pine Ridge, she found Neglicu, or Comes Out Alive, whose English name was Mary Thomas. Mary was the baby who had been taken to the Holy Rosary Mission after the Wounded Knee massacre, then washed up, wet-nursed, and quickly given to a Lakota woman. Raised among her own people, Mary had heard the story of the Lost Bird, and now the two young women saw that they resembled each other. Mary could speak English and the meeting was a happy one. Mary taught Zintka to say Ina ("Mother"), Ate ("Father"), and gave Zintka a kinship role by calling her "my twin." Zintka referred to Mary as "my twin sister" for the rest of her life.[21]

Zintka had always wanted to see the grave of her relatives at Wounded Knee, and Mary arranged for the trip. As they approached the site, the monument erected by Joseph Horn Cloud and others in May 1903 stood tall on the hill overlooking the valley where the slaughter had taken place. The two young women rode up to the memorial and Zintka walked over to the cemetery where she saw for the first time the long, lonely mass grave where the bloody corpses of her relatives had been stripped and packed down together, one man reportedly buried alive.[22] Oral tradition relates that Zintka lay down on top of the grave, with arms outstretched, and cried.

On June 14, 1906, while Zintka was still with Mary at Pine Ridge, Leonard Colby married his longtime mistress Maud Miller Martínez, in the parsonage of the Methodist Church in Beatrice.[23] The marriage took place a few weeks after Maud had suddenly received a large sum of money.

HALF A MILLION DOLLARS

A special dispatch from Havana announces . . . the claims of Mrs. Marie C. Martinez for . . . property injured and destroyed during the Cuban insurrection, and the establishment by final judgment of the highest court of her title to the real and personal estate of her husband, Tomas Hernando Martinez, who went to Mexico and thence to South America at the close of the Spanish-American war, leaving valuable properties undisposed of in several of the provinces of Cuba.

The claims allowed . . . $216,666, while the real and personal estate of Mr. Martinez settled by the decree, consisting of 17,000 acres of land, sugar and tobacco plantations and other interests near Matanzas, is appraised at over $400,000.

Mrs. Martinez is certainly to be congratulated upon her good fortune, as are also her attorneys, whose fees will doubtless be commensurate with the amount obtained for the client . . .[24]

On their wedding day (which Maud entered into her Bible as June 14, "1892"), Leonard and Maud left for a honeymoon trip to Switzerland. In a bizarre coincidence, the next day John Robinson's Circus pulled into Beatrice. Out of the cars jumped a band of Indians led by "Chief Little Cloud." They demanded to know where General Colby lived because the chief declared he had come to take his daughter Lost Bird back to South Dakota! A newspaper reported that the Indians

> . . . entered residence after residence and inquired for Colby. They finally located his home place . . . and when they entered the occupants were frightened out of their wits. The Indians warwhooped and pounded their flesh. They carried tomahawks and bows and arrows. Chief Little Cloud was informed that General Colby was married only yesterday and with his bride had gone away on a wedding trip. . . . [P]eople wonder what the Indians would have done had they met General Colby . . .[25]

"Chief" Little Cloud was not a chief, but he was indeed a survivor of the Wounded Knee Massacre. Records dated 1890 and a deposition taken in 1921 show that his father, mother, and three of his brothers aged eight, ten, and twelve years of age were killed in the massacre. He stated that he and his wife escaped injury but that he lost three horses, a harness, a farm wagon, bedding, and cooking utensils. He did not say that he had lost a baby daughter.[26]

John Robinson probably heard about Zintka in Wild West circles and had angered Little Cloud enough to increase ticket sales in Beatrice. He made sure that Little Cloud's picture appeared in a war bonnet on the front page of the *Beatrice Daily Express* the day the big top went up. After the circus left town, however, Little Cloud never contacted Colby again.[27]

By January 1, 1907, Zintka had worked her way back to Portland and was living with Clara. After hearing about Maud's inheritance of half a million dollars, Clara sent Zintka to her father. A note from Clara said:

> I love and pity her . . . but having tried all my resources . . . and also feeling that as your adopted daughter you ought to know her and plan for her,—I sent her to you. . . . Do not let her be idle. . . . You must assume the responsibility for her future. . . . [T]here is much prejudice against the Indian here and I could never get her in a store even in the holiday rush.
> While she is unemployed and uncontrolled she will not be

happy. . . . [S]he was never happy with my quiet ways . . . [S]he wanted to be on the go all the time, and would resort to any expedient to get money to go to the theatres, the dime vaudeville, the most demoralizing thing on earth. . . . [T]hen there is the Oaks . . . where it is most dangerous for girls to go. Without her being willing to mind me I simply could not protect her; and was in terror for fear she would get into serious trouble.[28]

Maud was mortified. With her new wealth and her dream of respectability and social position, she now had to mother an Indian. The situation got worse when Maud discovered that Leonard was paying quite a bit of attention to Zintka, giving her money and expensive jewelry.

The Colbys were rich and could have easily afforded music lessons or perhaps a private tutor for Zintka to catch up on her schoolwork. But they did nothing for the girl, even though their house was fitted with fine crystal, silver, and china, and boasted an indoor bathroom, an Edison phonograph, and an electric-motor washing machine. The living room was decorated with Indian blankets thrown over chairs, peace pipes, and other Indian artifacts. A large painting above the fireplace provoked comment. It showed a mounted military officer chasing Indians with sword raised above his head.[29]

Zintka was placed in the ninth grade in public school although she was now seventeen years old. The white girls in Beatrice "wouldn't have anything to do with her."[30] She was "quiet in class," said Tom Damrow, a fellow student, but he had another reason for remembering her. She sat directly across from him and one day he happened to glance over at her and nearly fell off his chair. She had cut her arm with a hat pin so deeply that it drew blood. He watched her expressionless face as the blood trickled down her arm.[31]

At night Zintka often slept in a park or on the front porch swing of a house belonging to a family down the street. The mother of the house had several children, and Zintka played with them and was good to them. The woman always offered breakfast to Zintka, whom she said was "afraid to be home at night."[32] Another Beatrice woman remembered that her mother told her never to speak to Leonard Colby on the street, even in passing. She was to cross over to the other side because "he could not be trusted with young girls." Conversely, the men in Beatrice thought Colby was a patriotic hero, a man living exactly as he pleased—with whomever he pleased—a man's man.[33]

General Colby's side of the story was somewhat different. He told his clerk that he locked Zintka out of the house at night when she did not obey him.[34] Whichever story is true, Maud "was jealous of Zintka" and wanted her shipped back to Portland.[35] Zintka wrote to her mother that she would soon be coming home. Clara responded with a letter to Leonard:

> . . . Zintka tells me you say you are going to send her back to me. . . . [F]rom what I can gather from her letters you have not set her about anything or made any attempt to control her . . .[36]

On December 22, 1907, Clara became alarmed at something Zintka had written about her father, and she wrote Leonard again:

> . . . Now comes this letter that leaves me more in the dark than ever. How is it that she has money like this? and what are you trying to do for her and with her . . . ?[37]

Colby hastily replied:

> She had been attending the City schools here . . . and was doing fairly well, but she insisted on going to an Indian school. . . . I then succeeded in getting her in at Haskell, but they know nothing of her record at Chemawa or elsewhere, and it is not wise to enlighten them. . . . She is not allowed to leave Haskell without a chaperone . . .[38]

Colby had indeed entered Zintka at Haskell, but only by lying to the superintendent to gain her admission:

> I write you for information in regard to admission to your school of Zintka L. Colby, the Indian babe which I found on the field of Wounded Knee on her dead mother's back the fourth day after the battle. She seems desirous of attending an Indian school and mingling with her own race . . .[39]

When Clara found out that Zintka was attending Haskell, she relaxed for the first time in years. She wrote to her friend Belva Lockwood:

> I had always been under great bondage to my love for my husband. . . . [H]e married and . . . I was freed from that. All the long agony was over, and I found that there were whole worlds in my being that he had never touched at all, beautiful, and rapturous as had been my young love for him . . .
> I have been planning . . . to go to the International Suffrage

Alliance in Holland in June, and stop two or three months helping the suffragists in England.[40]

She also informed her sister Mary about joining the more militant protests: ". . . Would it not be glorious if I could get into prison for the cause . . . ?"[41] On January 2, 1908, she wrote Zintka at Haskell:

My Dear Zintka,

Happy New Year to you. Now that I know you are in the Haskell Institute, it is a Happy New Year for me. I have ordered the Youth's Companion to come to you direct, and have mailed you the late numbers from here. I also mailed your pretty calendar and a card to hang up in your room. I am so glad to know you like the school and are doing well. Be sure and be a good girl and plan all the time to stay there until you graduate. You say you want to be preparing to earn your living; well, dear there is no preparation you need so much as to settle right down to hard work and get your mind settled. When you develop the power to stick earnestly at any one thing, determined to succeed in that you will be able to do anything . . .

I expect you have had a great old holiday time. . . . We had a . . . Fellowship Circle Watch Night. . . . We had readings from Shakespeare, singing of old songs, and as the old year was dying we sang "Nearer My God to Thee" and stood in perfect silence holding the thought of higher and more perfect life for the coming year. When the horns and bells announced that the New Year had come we sang the Doxology, "Praise God from Whom All Blessings Flow" . . .

. . . I only have one large room; the piano slants out and with the screen makes a place behind which I can boil a kettle or dress.

I have taken all my New Year's money . . . to make a payment on the piano . . . because I think you are going to be a good girl. . . . [T]hen I shall be so proud of you and glad I saved the piano for you . . .

Dear Girlie, if there is one more thing I want to especially urge upon you it is that you take each day as it comes and settle that day's duties. . . . I hope you have a church there. Do you wear a uniform(?). . . . Be sure to keep yourself clean and take care of your skin. . . . I shall expect a letter from you once a week. . . . Good-by Sweetheart, . . . Your loving mother[42]

Clara had no way of knowing that Zintka had not enjoyed "a great old holiday time." She was pregnant when she had enrolled at Haskell. And the general did not invite her to spend Christmas in Beatrice.

Although Zintka tried to study, it was evident to school officials that she was with child, and they sent her home in late March 1908. Zintka had gotten pregnant in Beatrice, and although Colby was not identified as the baby's father, his subsequent letter to the superintendent on April 7, 1908, exposed his plan to get rid of the evidence:

Dear Sir:
. . . I had learned the facts from her on her arrival, . . . which was the first intimation I had of such condition of things. I am having her taken care of the best possible away from here. . . . Yours Very Truly, L. W. Colby[43]

On April 1, 1908, the general placed Zintka at the Milford Industrial Home, about twenty-two miles west of Lincoln, Nebraska, under the name Marguerite E. Fox. (Colby had notarized census records showing Black Fox as her father.) She was listed as an "Indian" from Beatrice.[44]

Inmates at Milford were sentenced by court order to one year in the institution, regardless of when their babies were born. If a young girl had no money to care for her child during that year, the infant was taken by the state and placed in an orphanage to await adoption.[45]

A search of Beatrice court documents shows no evidence of Zintka's placement at Milford. Of course, Colby had full access to Beatrice court records.

The original name of the Milford reformatory was the Nebraska Maternity Home, founded in 1887 on thirty-seven acres of land overlooking Milford. Two four-story dormitories, a hospital, a dairy, water tower, and laundry building made up the grounds. According to an undated pamphlet, the regime was strict: "The rising bell sounded at 5 am, and all inmates were at their work stations by 6:30. Chapel was nightly at 8, with lights out at 9." The rules were that no visitors were allowed except in the presence of the superintendent, and all letters were read by the same.[46]

If a girl came to the home in need of "discipline," her arms were forced into a "reddish brown leather straitjacket that buckled tightly across the back."[47] A dark attic room in one of the dormitories—not big enough for a bed—was used for solitary confinement. (The building is still standing, and the room is testimony to its onetime horrors.) The plastered ceiling of the small, unventilated cell sloped inward on both sides. A tall girl could only stand up straight in the middle of the room; otherwise she hit her head or had to hunch over. Milford residents remember that some women were tied for hours with their hands up, sometimes scratching the ceiling plaster with their fingernails. There was a small window that was nailed shut, and the room was intolerably hot in summer and freezing in winter. Graffiti found on the walls still remains: "Sylvia—another heart-broken girl," and "twenty-four more weeks in this hellhole." The superintendent (always a woman) lived in quarters directly below the discipline room, so that screams brought immediate and unpleasant attention—a gag, especially if the matron was mean-spirited.[48]

April 1908 was unseasonably warm. On April 21 the temperature rose unexpectedly to between 81 and 85 degrees Fahrenheit, and the dark "hellhole" on the fifth floor could have reached a stifling 100 degrees. It could have been a death trap for a pregnant, claustrophobic, dehydrated Indian woman in a straitjacket.[49] The next day, April 22, 1908, Zintka lost her child, a stillborn baby boy.[50]

Infant corpses from the Milford Industrial Home were taken about two miles southwest and interred in the Blue Mound Cemetery. The home was a state-operated facility, and there were special plots designated to contain an undetermined number of bodies. The remains were lowered into the ground—often without services of any kind.[51]

For evident reasons, Colby did not inform Clara of Zintka's pregnancy and kept her forced confinement at Milford a secret for as long as possible.

Believing her daughter to be settled and happy at Haskell, Clara sailed to Europe in early May 1908 aboard the U.S.S. *Celtic.*She was abroad five months and gave forty speeches in halls, at garden parties, in drawing rooms, in parks, and on street corners. She was also the special guest of the Countess of Aberdeen at her castle in Dublin, Ireland.[52]

In London, Clara participated in the dangerous suffrage demonstrations of June 13 and 21 when 10,000 people filled Parliament Square. While waiting to speak, Clara was surrounded by an angry mob of "hundreds of boys and young men . . . determined not to let the speaking proceed. They surged forward as if to push [her] wagon over, which seemed many times in imminent danger. . . . They broke down the back of the wagon . . ."[53] Beating back the men with umbrellas and yelling "Votes for Women," twenty-seven suffragists were arrested and spent three months in Holloway Prison. Clara was present when the women were released, and she attended the "ex-prisoner's breakfast" where Mrs. Emmeline G. Pankhurst spoke. Clara reported that not one of the militant suffragists "has ever seemed to regret her incarceration but all are consecrated with the conviction that they [were] . . . doing the service for the cause of woman's freedom . . ."[54]

In her travels—one week in Paris, one week in Holland, ten days in Ireland, and months in England—Clara had sent letters and postal cards to Zintka at Haskell from various points of interest, but got no reply. When she returned to Portland in October, she found a confusing letter from Zintka, postmarked Milford, Nebraska, on August 8, 1908:

Dearest mother,

Your letter dated July 18 has been received and I was so glad to hear from you. . . . No, I am not at Haskell any more. I don't know where I'm at. I'm in the United States some-where. . . . Zintka L. Colby.[55]

It was evident that Zintka was disoriented and did not know where she was or how she got there. Given her love of the outdoors and freedom, and her physical strength, it is possible that she was brought to Milford against her will, perhaps drugged with chloroform.

Alarmed, Clara left Portland on the first train east and went directly to Milford. The austere stucco dormitories seemed forbidding despite the green-ferned wallpaper in the waiting room. Clara's reaction to her daughter's misfortune is missing from her diary, but it is known that she was not allowed to take Zintka out of the institution.[56]

After learning that Leonard and Maud had purchased the huge Paddock Block Hotel and Opera House in Beatrice for $150,000, Clara wrote to Leonard on November 18, 1908:

> . . . Zintka . . . must be encouraged to feel that she can make something of herself and helped to do it. . . . To be a nurse has always been her desire. I talked with Miss Ward about this [and she] suggested a special training school at Lincoln where the course is only one year. At this they pay $50 a year for tuition and books and clothes have to be provided. . . . I believe the term begins in January. . . . Miss Ward thought she could arrange to have Zintka leave as early as that . . .
>
> Zintka needs very much some glasses. She cannot get on well in her studies without them. . . . [I]t would cost much less than ten dollars. . . . I shall be glad to . . . co-operate as far as I can in whatever is for Zintka's benefit.[57]

But the Colbys had no intention of paying for tuition or glasses for Zintka. It was evident who now held the purse strings; Maud's pretentious stationery displayed a photograph of the "Paddock Block—Hotel and Opera House," and in larger letters below the picture were the words "Mrs. Marie M. Colby—owner."[58] Some Beatrice residents remember that Maud flaunted her wealth, tipping male employees and car mechanics extravagantly.[59]

Knowing that the father of Zintka's baby did not reside at Haskell, Leonard tried to have her readmitted there, saying: "Nothing whatever became public in regard to her difficulty and results were such that no one need ever know a thing about it."[60] But the superintendent at Haskell disagreed. Zintka was too far along in her pregnancy when she was expelled from the school: "The circumstances under which she left here are known by too many of the pupils and therefore I do not believe it would be pleasant for her here."[61]

Unwilling to pay for nursing school as Clara suggested, Colby left Zintka at Milford for the full year. At Christmas she was surprised to receive presents from him, but he did not come to see her even though he was less than two hours away. Zintka's Christmas letter to her mother had to be written in the presence of the matron, and its style and tone appear artificial and her handwriting tight compared to her usual correspondence.

> Milford, Neb.
> Dec. 28, 1908
>
> My dear mama,
>   I am going to write you to-day telling you what a nice Christmas I had. The presents you sent me were very nice. . . . Now I must tell you what papa sent me. He sent a half dozen fine handkerchiefs, a perfumed bag, a roman gold bar pin and a nineteen hundred nine calendar. This is the first time I have heard from him since August . . .
>   Your lovely letter of Dec. 20th has just come. . . . I have just eight weeks and three days until my eleven months are up, then I have four more weeks until my year, and it really doesn't seem possible I have been here as long as I have. . . . Your loving daughter, Zintka L. Colby.[62]

Clara could not understand why the general did not visit his daughter, and she pleaded with him: "I should be glad if you would take the trouble to reply to the letter I wrote you some weeks ago about Zintka. . . . It would be a great satisfaction to Zintka . . . if you would go there and see her. It is such a little time and distance from Lincoln, will you not do it very soon . . . ?"[63]

Zintka had been at Milford for nearly a year in the company of women whose past lives had been less than exemplary. As one inmate incarcerated in a home for women put it:

> I was no bad girl when I got put away in the Home. Now I know everything bad. I lived with the vilest women, the down-and-out kind, who have taught me and lots of other girls more innocent than I, how to solicit on the streets.[64]

CHAPTER 19

The Bride's Gift

A cold east wind dropped more than a foot of snow on Portland in early January 1909. Despite the hard chill, Clara awoke refreshed on New Year's day, although she had hosted a "splendid Fellowship watch night" until 3 A.M. As the winter days wore on, exuberance danced across the pages of her journal. She noted a meeting or class every night and a social calendar that filled her busy days with visitors, writing, afternoon teas, and special dinners with dear friends.[1] Clara had never seemed more vivacious and full of life with new ideas for the coming year.

Drawing on her experiences in England, she lectured almost daily on English suffrage. With her earnings she hosted the Press Club and was reelected president of the Fellowship group. At one of her "at homes," talk turned to fasting and its benefits. She decided to find out for herself and went four days without food and felt fine afterwards.[2] She had her "aura" read by a psychic who foretold " . . . that my life within the next three years would arrange itself along much simpler lines—spiritual rather than intellectual."[3] At one of her Saturday night parties, sixty people came "to hear a Yogi," whom she said in her journal was "nothing special."[4] About militant suffrage Clara wrote to a friend: "I am bursting to go back [to England] and help to the finish."[5]

For the first time in thirty-eight years, Clara had several male admirers, including a lawyer and a professor. The third was a platonic friendship with twenty-five-year-old Albert Chalivat, whom she described as "my French boy."[6] She had first met him when he came to see her about "his art-business which interested me. Then we became friends, and I wished him to have a feeling that he was dropping into home life when he came in, and over a cup of tea we have had many a good chat."[7] On January 12, 1909, she noted in her journal that Chalivat "came in for afternoon tea & presented me with a beautiful hand mirror."[8] She accepted the personal gift. Having a younger man's attention must have been flattering for a sixty-three-year-old woman.

On January 21 Clara gave a small dinner for her special professor friend, whom she always referred to only by his initials, H. V. M. She also invited Dr. Chapman, an editor of the *Oregonian,* and his friend, Mrs. Baldwin. Clara served a five-course meal for them, prepared on a one-burner stove. The menu consisted of "clam chowder, boiled salmon garnished with hard boiled eggs and carrots, mashed potatoes, pickled lamb's tongues, Waldorf salad, steamed apple pudding, coffee, apples, etc."[9]

Clara's resolution for the New Year had been "to do just what I wanted to do all the time." She had a large intellectual following and she basked in her many friendships. On January 26, for example, she noted that she had breakfast with "Mrs. Perdue . . . Mrs. June McMillan Ordway to Lunch . . . Mrs. Richards on to tea. Mr. Chalivat came in the evening full of his Omar Khayam [sic]. I read Whitman to him."[10] Chalivat had become a regular in her inner circle, and he assisted by running errands, folding papers for mailing, making coffee, and "help[ing] me get ready for press club."[11]

The *Woman's Tribune* was mailed on March 4, with help from Chalivat.

On March 5, 1909, Clara sailed alone by steamer to San Francisco, and then took a train to Palo Alto, where she had "a glad reunion" with her sister Mary.[12] Women in San Jose gave a reception in her honor on March 12. She spoke at the State Normal College to 500 students and faculty on March 17, on the 25th she lectured at Stanford, and then at "the Polytechnic."[13] One day she walked eight miles and met with a wise old friend who had gone blind. The happy woman told her the philosophy she lived by: " . . . three stores of happiness; the memory of the joys and pleasures she has had, the love of her dear friends, and the anticipation of the future." Clara wrote to Ida Husted Harper that during the month, "I did the best work of my life."[14]

On April 18 she returned to Portland, but the rest of April 1909 is mysteriously missing from Clara's journal. The pages were scissored away because they contained words either Clara (or sister Mary, who later took possession of the diary) decided were too horrible to preserve.

Letters reveal that by mid-April Chalivat had decided to leave Portland for a two-year canoe trip to Hudson Bay with a Dutchman and a fellow Frenchman. Clara gave "a little reception for him where he could explain his plans."

One week before his intended departure, on April 29, 1909, Zintka arrived "quite unexpectedly" from Nebraska after being released from the worst year of her life. Leonard had bought her clothes and complained that he had to pay her train fare of $36 to Portland. That night she must have told her mother what she had endured at the Milford Home.

Clara wrote that on the following evening "Albert came in . . . and I invited him to dinner as before. He was full of talk about his proposed trip and this greatly interested Zintka." She expressed the wish that she might "make such a trip." It occurred "at once to Albert what a good companion she would be, her manners, and . . . he would never have to be ashamed of her."[15]

> After dinner [Zintka] played the piano for which she has a wonderful gift. A friend came in and made a call. I wished to see her home and attend to some matters so I said Zintka could entertain Mr. Chalivat with her playing while I was gone. I do not think I was away more than an hour, and when I returned they had arranged to make the trip together. I would not consent at the time.[16]

The two young people were immediately and passionately attracted to one another. Clara knew what Zintka had been through, and she wanted her to "be a loved wife and a virtuous woman," as any mother would hope for a daughter. Chalivat had been Clara's friend for six months, but he knew only Zintka's romantic story—not the whole truth. Suddenly there were new plans:

> Albert told me they had made up their minds to marry. He said my consent was desirable but not necessary, and they would marry anyway. He appealed to Zintkala if this were not so, and she agreed. He did all the talking and planning, but she seemed prettily acquiescent. . . . Albert insisted they must be married the next day, as he would have to make an entire change in his outfit, and he could not do anything till this was off his mind. I was bewildered, and had not yet thought what the girl was to do now that she had come back to me unexpectedly. I did not want to stand in the way of what seemed to promise well for both, so I made as good a wedding as I could in the brief time and a number of our friends were present. By Albert's request, Zintkala was married in . . . buckskin . . .[17]

A guest wrote that Zintka "was nervous as any American girl before the ceremony and clapped her hands in excitement every few minutes."[18] But shortly after the wedding, someone brought to Clara's attention the fact that in the state of Oregon a white person could not legally marry an Indian. After spending the night together, they went to Vancouver, Washington, the next day and were married there by a justice of the peace.

That evening Clara "gave a reception for them at which Zintkala wore a pongee silk which I had got for her as being of light weight for the trip."[19] A witness noted that Zintka recalled the words of a favorite book when she said "I feel the call of the wild . . ."[20] Ironically, in Jack London's book by the same title, the hero, a dog named Buck was taken from his home to a foreign place and learned to be brutal in order to survive. He was befriended by a kind man, but after his death the faithful animal returned to a wild, free life. At the party Zintka also told her friends, "I want to get into the open. I will care for him always. We are in for a hard time but we care for each other, and we shall be very happy indeed."[21]

The two were madly in love but penniless, so the trip had to be postponed. Clara wrote to Leonard for wedding money but, of course, Colby refused and did not send anything to "Zintka or on her behalf."[22] The newlyweds spent the next blissful days with Clara, and Clara made herself scarce to give them privacy.

But less than two weeks after the marriage, Zintka was taken to a doctor after which Clara wrote to Leonard, "[I]t has been discovered that Zintka has a serious ailment for which she . . . will be for some time, under the doctor's care . . ."[23]

After enduring a year of terror and pain and after losing a baby boy, Zintka's dream for a happy married life was destroyed when she found that her husband's wedding gift had been syphilis. When the physician told her the dreadful diagnosis, Zintka flew into a rage and Clara's apartment then became "a battleground."[24] Under constant verbal and physical attacks from Zintka, Albert drowned his misery in wine. In a violent scene on May 22, Zintka threw him out of the house. The police must have been called, because the national newspapers picked up the story, reporting that she "had forsaken her husband."[25] A few stories told that Chalivat had fallen from grace because of "his love of liquor." No one knew the real reason.

There was no cure for syphilis in 1909. Physicians prescribed various remedies, but it was not until 1910 that Dr. Paul Ehrlich perfected a medicine he called "606, or Salvarson," which proved an effective treatment but sometimes required as many as fifty injections.

Chalivat continued to pronounce his love for Zintka, but she was disgusted and would have nothing more to do with him. Clara wrote to Albert's parents in Paris: "He is a cross between a hobo and a philosopher and in neither capacity was he suited to the girl. . . . Whatever there was of unpleasantness need not be recalled . . ."[26]

Clara tried to find a legal technicality so the marriage could be annulled, but to no avail. The expenses of the wedding, the reception, food and clothes, doctor bills, and lawyer's fees left her completely broke. Her newspaper, dedicated to the emancipation of women for twenty-five long years, folded unceremoniously, leaving her "saddened" and on a "downward spiral."[27] Zintka broke down utterly and the shamed son-in-law left Portland after having borrowed money from a friend "to work in the woods in Washington."[28]

On May 16 Clara wrote to one of her friends: "The case is far more than a personal conflict and is really a great moral drama where souls are at stake. . . . It is far different from what you . . . may see in the papers. . . . I expect somewhere there is a hill with a water view waiting for me but just now I am walking among the thorns and stones."[29] Many of Clara's friends wrote to her. The Reverend Olympia Brown commented, "I am sorry for you. . . . Too bad, too bad."[30] Later, she was more uplifting: "Shocked to hear of your seemingly overwhelming difficulties but inspired by the tremendous courage and wonderful versatility & resources you manifest . . ."[31]

Depressed and disillusioned with life, Zintka remained under a doctor's care in her mother's home for nearly a year. Clara suggested she attend nursing school to help others as she had been helped, but Zintka was totally apathetic and could not be enthusiastic about anything. To make matters worse during her convalescence, Clara's old friend, author and reformer Elaine Goodale Eastman, sent excerpts of her forthcoming novel for young girls entitled *Yellow Star*.[32] It was actually a fictionalized account of Zintka's life. Zintka sat up in bed, the victim of a disease that had swept away all her cherished hopes and aspirations of life, and possibly her capacity to have children. Powerless to prevent the future publication of *Yellow Star*, Zintka read her own idealized biography. She must have wondered how Mrs. Eastman, whom she had met several times as a child, could have known the details of her life. But the well-intentioned author meant no malice with her "heroine, an unknown waif, found alive in the arms of her dead mother after . . . Wounded Knee, [and] brought to a New England village by her adopted mother, trained in the graces of mind and heart until she becomes the leader of the young people and an academy graduate. As the book closes she is dedicating her life to her people as a field matron for the Government."[33] In one of the closing passages, Yellow Star tries to decide whether to stay with her Indian people or go back to white society:

> . . . I seem to be two people. . . . I'm pulled two ways at once; I so want to really belong, and I can't tell where I belong! I know, now, that I can't do for my people what I once thought I could, here on the reservation; and yet, isn't it my place?[34]

On December 23, 1909, Zintka suffered a relapse of symptoms with stupor and convulsions, which Clara would say was brought on by "ptomaine poisoning, hysteria, and tight lacing."[35] Two doctors were called in. The girl whom her uncle, Charles D. Bewick, described as a "very beautiful young woman, her skin so soft and smooth, her hair coal black, and her mind so alert," had degenerated into a syphilitic invalid.

When Clara pleaded to General Colby for medical funds for Zintka, he did not reply. The Colbys had joined the First Christian Church of Beatrice, and Leonard taught the largest Sunday-school class in the state of

Nebraska.[36] One of his pupils remembered attending with his father "just to see the hypocrite."[37] Another said Colby "knew his Bible as well as his law books."[38] For the occasion, Maud contributed a prayer (which she had copyrighted):

Grant, dear Father, Thy forgiveness, if our thoughts have gone astray,
If by careless word or action we have caused one pain this day;
May our hearts retain no malice as this day comes to a close,
And we pray Thy benediction to abide in our repose.

MARIE MILLER COLBY[39]

CHAPTER 20

The Nation of the Lakotah

Father's Day was first celebrated in Spokane, Washington, in 1910, but there was to be no celebration of that day in Zintka's sickroom. Aunt Mary paid Zintka's numerous medical bills, and by February the young woman was much improved. As soon as she could get out of bed, Zintka wanted to be on the go and looking for a job. By the last week in February, she had answered an ad for a position in Seattle, and Clara let her go.

On March 9 Clara received an embarrassing letter from Dr. Cora Smith Eaton, the treasurer of the Washington Equal Suffrage Association:

> . . . Zintka came here tonight at nearly 10 p.m., ostensibly to make a call on me, . . . She said she came with only two dollars on hand, two days ago and that she has exhausted her two dollars. She expected to go to work at once,—a big expectation, seems to me, in a big city,—and says she got a position in a doctor's office, "to sterilize his instruments" . . . but she has a very sore eye, and he told her to wait till the eye is better.
>
> The eye looks quite serious to me. I am not an eye specialist, but I have seen several cases like it that went on to ulceration, with a long siege of several weeks' disability. I gave her eye a treatment and presented her with an eye salve and some medicine . . .
>
> Then when I was seeing her to the door, she asked me for money. She asked for Five Dollars, but that looked like a big sum for her to pay back . . .
>
> My dear, you have my sympathy for all you have put up with all these years. It makes my blood boil when I realize it was not of your own choosing and that you have had to spend your life carrying out the whim of some one who does not even pay the cost in money, let alone in work and worrying. . . . Yours faithfully, Cora Smith Eaton[1]

Clara replied to Mrs. Eaton's letter the next day:

My dear friend: Your letter filled me with great regret. Zintka went to Seattle with my full consent. She said it would be easier for her to work, . . . I fitted her up with a very good wardrobe; . . . I was sorry to give her so little but it was all I had. . . . Zintka does not feel any obligation to tell the truth, and no shame when her untruth is discovered. She is not immoral, but *unmoral*. . . . I have tried to make her live and learn and do according to my ideas.. . . . Even if I devoted myself wholly with regard to her it would not satisfy her or develop her as I would want to. Yet I do not blame her at all. She has been sinned against in being taken from her proper surroundings. . . . I am sincerely yours, Clara B. Colby[2]

Clara went to Seattle and brought Zintka back to recuperate. Meanwhile, Clara was eager to start up her newspaper again. On March 26 she wrote to Ida Husted Harper: "I should hate to think of my ending up my long life of consecration to the most noble work that every engaged the attention of humanity with mere money-making projects. All I want is just enough to give me the opportunity to do the work for which . . . I am fitted."[3] Zintka answered another ad and went back to Seattle.

In April Clara heard from a friend in Washington and she replied:

> . . . I hope [Zintka] is earning her way and living in a decent place. She is a child of romance; I am sure you must agree that there must have been something very strange in her previous incarnation, or her psychic condition for so many adventures to happen to her and for her to fall always on her feet. I hope she will pay you what she has borrowed; it was very kind of you to help her.
>
> I am pegging away at real estate and think if I am to be overworked and nothing to show for it I might as well be undergoing this for the TRIBUNE . . . trying to please people seems to be the most deadening thing I have ever undertaken. I was born to speak, to teach, or to write, not to make money. Will you kindly . . . keep me posted as to Zintka.[4]

With her newspaper gone, her daughter's future uncertain and her ex-husband basking in his wealth and newfound religion, Clara began begging everywhere for money. Her family turned her down, her old school friends refused, and she was desperate enough to write to Joseph Els, a wealthy gentleman in Bickley, England: " . . . The reason I am writing to you at this time is to see if you would not like to give the WOMAN'S TRIBUNE a boost. To put it very forcibly it got stuck in the mud last year and it needs a helpful shoulder applied to the wheel."[5] None of her many efforts brought favorable results, and she was far too truthful to have any success in the real estate business. If a house was old, she told her client exactly how old and what needed to be done to it.

In mid-March Zintka sent her mother a postcard. She had been hired by a "sportsman's club" calling themselves Nation of the Lakotah. She wrote that she had "a good job" and "a great salary . . . don't worry."[6] The card itself, designed to promote the club, was enough to alarm Clara:

OMNICIYE TONKA LAKOTAH

The new lodge, Nation of the Lakotah, of which you are a member, will hold its first charter installation meetings . . . Saturday evening March 26, at 8 p.m. Every member is requested to be there on time, so the work of the meeting will not be delayed. It will be necessary for *EVERY MEMBER* to take the obligations of the order so you will be expected to be present. Bring a new member with you so he can join that evening. We have 250 members already signed up for the Charter installation—Let's make it 500 and start out the *Seattle Way.*—We can do it if you bring a friend who *ought* to belong.

N.B.—We have arranged with the chef to serve a little dog soup, grasshopper salad, horned toad a la Lakotah, and other good things to eat, drink and smoke, so don't eat too big a dinner—and COME SURE.

NATION OF THE LAKOTAH

W. S. PHILLIPS,
Itancan Tokahan

Zintka was made "a mascot" at the installation, and she soon wrote to Clara on the organization letterhead that listed Mr. Phillips as "El Camancho" of "a National Secret Society composed of American Sportsmen."[7]

My dear mother,

I have been so busy . . . making . . . a full buckskin dress, heavily beaded, which must be done by June first, and I have yet chaps & moccasins to make and bead. I got Dr's bill and it is 27$ which I shall be able to pay in a couple of months. I can pay no bills before July 10th, after that time I can pay all kinds of bills as I shall be getting one hundred dollars a month, combined with this Lakotah lodge. Mr. Phillips and I have signed . . . a contract with the Lyceum circuit, and play at every large city and town, putting on an original Indian play. When we play by the night it will be fifty dollars . . . twenty-five a piece, if by the month its one hundred dollars. After June first we will start and go through the state of Washington and Oregon . . . in the winter I think we shall take in California and down South coming back by way of New York, that is what he is talking about now, but it is not certain. You know every city and town that they intend making installations I shall have to be present, its nice to be the official mascot, as well as assistant sec. I certainly have my hands full. . . . Will soon be divorced. Thank the Lord. . . . Lovingly your daughter, Zintka L. Colby[8]

On May 24 Zintka was ready for the initiation ceremonies:

My dear Mother,
. . . I wish you could see me. . . . [Y]ou certainly would laugh. I am going to wear a buckskin dress . . . and moccasins, and a great big war bonet [sic] . . .
The first of June . . . the great doings is going to be pulled off, in other words I have seven hundred adopted fathers, doesn't that sound big. . . . A great big kiss for you. Zintkalla Nuni Colby.
P.S. Send the folks my best regards. Tell them I may make a great big mark in the world yet. Hope they have some hopes for me.[9]

Clara's investigation brought her the information that the Nation of the Lakotah was indeed a "sportsman's club," but that their exploitation of Zintka in secret ceremonies was not against the law. Clara wrote to Zintka:

. . . I do not understand what it is you are up to. I cannot believe that you and Mr. Phillips are going playacting together. If you are doing anything of that kind in Seattle send me the papers about it. I do very much wish I could come up and see you. . . . [T]he only money I have taken in in a long time is for some writing I did. I spared $5 of that to pay on the bill for your music with Mr. Wheeler, although I am still owing at the stores for all the things I bought you. . . . [T]hen you ought to have your divorce before you have much to do with anybody. Have you saved up money for that, or have you given up all idea of getting it. I do not suppose Chalivat will let you get it if he finds that you are in a good thing. He may be wanting to hold on to you to get a living out of you. Poor child, it makes my heart ache to think of these ne'er-do-wells that you allow yourself to associate, and get tied up with.[10]

Without telling "El Camancho" about Zintka's contagious disease, Clara addressed a carefully worded letter to Mr. Phillips:

I should be very glad to have a word from you as to Zintka. I get the nicest letters from her, but it would be a satisfaction to hear also from you what she is doing. Are you and she going off on a trip in some capacity for the Order. I cannot quite make out what is the plan. . . . She writes me to send her all the papers about her allotment in South Dakota, . . . I do not consider she is capable of looking after them for herself. . . .[11]

On June 1, 1910, on letterhead from "Phillips Practical Advertising Service," El Camancho answered Clara's letter.

My Dear Mrs. Colby:

Am glad you wrote about Zintkalla. Of course I have learned already that she is absolutely irresponsible and not fitted for anything in the world as far as I can see—that is if left to look out for herself. We pay her $7.00 per week, which will feed her and take care of room rent etc. She has made considerable more taking subscriptions for Mr. Bank's "Peace Pipe," a little magazine. . . . She was very sick with ptomaine poisoning but we pulled her through it. . . . I don't know how long she will "last"—but hope I can make her "stick" so far as the lodge is concerned. . . . [S]he has to be treated as you would treat a ten year-old child. Don't see how you managed to stand for her all these years! She certainly is a shining example of the old saying that you "can't civilize an indian" for she is absolutely worthless around the office or anywhere except as a spectacular "ballyho"—and that's where I can make her make good with the lodge. . . . I am going to take her on the road to "ballyho" in organizing other lodges over the state and as long as she is with the lodge will look out for her as best I can. . . . She will lie to me faster than a horse can run. . . . If she were thrown on her own resources in the position she occupies here she wouldn't last a minute. . . . I think perhaps when I get her out on the road she will be better off as she has too much time evenings to herself as it is.

. . . [T]he Lodge adopted her as the "daughter of the Order"—a mascot in fact—so if she had the wisdom to live up to the part she would be fixed for life—but I'm afraid all the time she will do some fool thing to everlastingly "queer" herself—and if she does they would drop her like a hot cake—It's up to me to keep her in line . . . so you probably realize something of my job![12]

Zintka knew how contagious she was, and one wonders how much pleasure she took from infecting the white membership of the Nation of the Lakotah.

Disappointed in her daughter's behavior, Clara told her friend Lilla Hill:

> I took care of Zintka the past year and she is dead weight for any-
> body that tries to do anything for her. I tried hard to have her culti-
> vate her musical talent, but she has spoiled her taste by rag time
> music, and will not buckle down to work. . . . She has many good
> traits, but seems . . . like a frisking lamb basking in the sunshine. The
> only tenet in her code of morals is to do what she wants to do. I real-
> ize that this is the governing principle of a good many white people,
> perhaps the majority, but they have the conventionality enough to
> pretend it is not so.[13]

By July 1, 1910, Zintka was so thin and ill she was back with Clara. The
"sportsman's club" must have gotten a rude though possibly well-deserved
surprise. To pay Zintka's doctor's bills, Clara had to sell the piano. She also
began divorce proceedings for Zintka. In late August the girl disappeared
again, and Clara informed Dr. Clara McNaughton: "Zintka is taking care
of herself . . . so I feel I need have no more responsibility for her . . ."[14]

Mrs. Eastman's book for girls, *Yellow Star,* influenced Zintka's life.
Although the author had not seen Zintka for years, Eastman's description
of her and the events then happening in her life were hauntingly accurate:

> Those who saw her . . . will remember the tall, swaying figure, the gliding
> step, the vivid, dark face with its touch of foreign distinction. . . . For Yellow
> Star had made her difficult decision—to go back to her own people and do
> for them what she could. . . . She wanted to live right in the camp . . . close
> to the people, to help the poor . . . women and children.[15]

Zintka returned to South Dakota and spent from August 1910 until the fall
of 1911 in search of relatives. This time she went to the Cheyenne River
Agency, about twenty miles west of present-day Gettysburg, South
Dakota. The original site is now covered by the floodwaters of Oahe Dam,
but in 1911 the thriving town operated a ferry that crossed the river to Forest City. Indian children ran down to the dock to see the boat leave, and
when it returned, they watched the visitors disembark and saw the supplies
being unloaded.[16]

The agency ran a large government boarding school and warehouses, but
the people lived in dirt-roofed and dirt-floored log cabins, tents, and tipis.

After the 1889 Agreement (which was no agreement at all as far as the
Lakota were concerned), the Cheyenne River Reservation had been
divided into four districts. According to historian Frederick E. Hoxie,
"Minneconjous lived on Cherry Creek. . . . Sans Arc communities could

be found along the Moreau River at places such as White Horse and On the Trees, . . . [and]the Blackfeet and Two Kettle bands hugged the Missouri . . ."[17] Secretary of the Interior John Noble had declared: "The breaking up of this great Nation of Indians into smaller parts and segregating . . . separate reservations for each of said parts marks a long step toward the disintegration of their tribal life . . ." but Hoxie described Lakota on the Cheyenne River Reservation as traditional and their "ways of life had not changed fundamentally for generations."[18]

In 1901 Zintka's enrollment in the tribe and allotment of land had been permitted only after Felix Crane Pretty Voice allowed her to be listed as his child. Now, for help in finding the Pretty Voice family, Zintka befriended an interpreter named Olney Runs After at the Cheyenne River Agency. Whites and Indians alike thought Olney was a "magnetic" young man. He took her along the old wagon road to Cherry Creek, past canvas-covered tipis standing next to log cabins. Between Cherry Creek and Bridger, Olney located Felix Crane Pretty Voice's house. Felix welcomed Zintka at once and treated her as if she were his own, but Mrs. Pretty Voice took an immediate dislike to the young woman she had once claimed was her child. Zintka stayed with the family for nearly a year.[19]

Zintka set her sights on Olney. He had attended school in Rapid City and spoke English, but he was unprepared for the likes of Zintka. She was worldly and attractive, and in the months to come the more she wanted to be with him, the more he held back. He cared a great deal for her, but he was cautious and remained aloof, which made her want him all the more.

During 1911, ration days brought relatives in to the subagency. Women carrying cloth sacks stood in long lines to receive their food, while the men chopped long slabs of salt pork and scooped northern white beans from great gunny sacks.[20] The beans were weighed on a large scale, and each woman opened her sack to receive equal amounts. The coffee beans were green. The women toasted them in a skillet over an open fire at home, and when the beans were browned and cooled, they borrowed a coffee grinder. There were never enough coffee grinders to go around, so women often pounded beans on a large rock with a smaller stone.[21]

Brown sugar was a popular ration, and the children got small chunks of it to eat like candy. The rest was taken home and melted down for syrup. Dried hominy was also a favorite. Boiled with salt pork, it made a delicious soup.

Ration day was a busy one for the men, who also attended business meetings or went to wačipis, or dances, while the older women cooked. The young people had foot and horse races, and the boys courted the girls, who were generally chaperoned.

Zintka's wardrobe was soon replenished with calico dresses that she made herself, just like the young woman in *Yellow Star* who "went to a grass dance . . . and lingered near an open window of the large, circular dance-house . . . gazing fascinated on the gorgeous . . . spectacle of painted, half-clad men executing their wonderful steps . . ."[22] No doubt Zintka witnessed many dances where the men displayed their masculinity in the beauty of dance.

Zintka probably went with the Pretty Voice family to the Fourth of July celebration, where Olney was allowed to see her. As the months passed, she experienced poverty and watched many little children and the elderly die from pneumonia—a death akin to drowning, when lips and fingernails turned blue.

The winter months brought swirling wind and snow and hours of chopping wood and hauling water. When snow thawed on the dirt roof of a log cabin, water leaked in and was absorbed into the dirt floor. Everything was damp. When an entire family lived in an unventilated one-room cabin, people got sick and irritable.

Zintka never felt like she belonged with Mrs. Pretty Voice, who did not approve of her habits and let her know by either ignoring her or making fun of her, which hurt Zintka's feelings. That was the Indian way of discipline.[23] Mr. Pretty Voice however, was always kind and tolerant toward Zintka, and she did not forget that due to his great kindness in accepting her as a daughter, she was allowed to have her name listed on tribal rolls.

But Zintka could not keep still. She was careless and pleasure-loving, stared at people, and she talked incessantly, especially during meals, when everyone else was silent. The Pretty Voice family realized that Zintka had been ruined for a normal quiet life in "going by white ways." Furthermore, she broke complex kinship rules, and the language barrier prevented her from learning what she was doing to displease others.[24]

Finally, the day came when Zintka missed the sound of the "Maple Leaf Rag." Clara had trained her to be assertive, which was contrary to the behavior of well-mannered Lakota women. She had no problem sharing, but she spoke out of turn, and too loudly, and she addressed people by their given first names.[25] More important, she lacked dignity. When she was a small child, Clara often remarked about Zintka's "queenly bearing." Through her difficult recent years, she had lost that quality. Formally, she could "read a person's mind," but as an adult she could no longer understand the silent language, the subtle, unspoken communication of facial expressions, gestures, and body movement.

In contrast to Zintka's imbalance, Olney gave a strong impression of spiritual strength and self-mastery at a young age. He was patient and respectful; he listened and observed carefully, and was in harmony with his peaceful surroundings, secure within his tribe. When Zintka made up her mind to leave Cherry Creek, she begged, "Olney, please come with me to California. We'll be in movies and Wild West shows and make a lot of money!"[26]

She was a temptation, but Olney refused the exciting offer.[27] Years later, he would say at a tribal meeting what he probably told Zintka: "We Indians will be Indians all our lives. We never will be white men. We can talk and work and go to school like the white people, but we're still Indians."[28]

After Zintka left for California, Olney Runs After did not marry for some time. He became a well-respected member of his tribe and of the Episcopal church, holding important positions. For his many unselfish deeds, his people presented him with an eagle-feather war bonnet when he was an elderly man, the highest honor they bestow.[29]

Before Olney died on June 14, 1983, he sometimes spoke of Lost Bird. Perhaps he wondered if he had made the right decision by letting her go. In quiet moments, he would sigh and ask, "I wonder how she is?"[30]

CHAPTER 21

Movies and Militants

"Kill me or give me my freedom."
EMMELINE G. PANKHURST

California was a boom state in 1912, a warm playground and a cheap place to live. It was a mecca for gilded youth and excitement. Sarah Bernhardt starred for Adolph Zukor (later the head of Paramount Pictures), while Mary Pickford, "America's sweetheart," earned $40,000 a film.[1] In 1913 Charlie Chaplin earned $150 per week, but two years later he got $10,000 a week and a $150,000 bonus.[2] Citizens of Los Angeles were so concerned about the decadence of movie actors, they tried to prohibit movies as "subversive of morals."

Zintka was hired by Pathé, one of the most successful producers of the era, and she appeared in *The Round-up* as well as in films for Essanay Pictures, Ammex Moving Picture Company, and Thomas Ince: *War on the Plains, Battle of the Red Men,* and *The Lieutenant's Last Fight.*[3] Cowboy-and-Indian movies were popular all over the world, but although "real Indians might . . . dash through a show at a Broadway theatre with great effectiveness, they would fail on a film where professional actors would make themselves vivid red men." Zintka watched beautiful white women paint their bodies brown and get the leading roles, while she, a full-blood Indian, played bit parts, usually as an extra. It was not glamorous to be an extra. They "were treated like cattle, herded around, given cheap bad box lunches, and they froze during night scenes."[4] As time went on, Zintka found it harder to find work.

By October 1, 1912, she was destitute. Zintka walked into the San Diego police station and got the attention of the sheriff by saying she was Sitting Bull's twin daughter and that her adopted father, Leonard Colby, could not be counted on for help. Sheriff Wilson disagreed. He immediately wired Colby and informed newspaper reporters. The next day, only after the story had made embarrassing national news ("Indian Maid in Poverty"), General Colby wired the sheriff his answer: "I cannot imagine how my little girl ever came to want. . . . I adopted her to give her an education. She is not related to Sitting Bull at all. Her father was Black Fox and her mother was Brown Hare [Hair]."[5] Colby did not want anyone to think he might have adopted a member of Sitting Bull's family. He told the sheriff that Zintka could buy whatever she needed, and he sent money to pay her bills.[6]

Zintka had gone to the police after suffering brutality at the hands of her boyfriend, Robert J. Keith, a Texas cowboy who had drifted to California after hearing that studios were paying a man $5 per day plus a free lunch for roping and riding. Cowpunchers like Keith

> . . . looked upon Hollywood as a kind of last trail town. . . . [T]hey created a closed society of their own in which a man was judged by the way he rode a horse, used his fists and held his liquor; they drank and played poker at a cafe called The Waterhole, where tequila and mescal were served in coffee cups. . . . [They] creased their Stetsons according to strict convention to show . . . what part of cattle country they hailed from, and . . . did what they could to make themselves at home off the range as they grew used to the . . . bone-shattering tasks demanded by . . . bosses who bawled at them through megaphones . . .[7]

But the pay was much better than punching cattle back in Texas, where they did not get paid for falling off bucking broncs. A good man on a horse, or one who could plunge a six-horse stagecoach over a cliff, knew he had a job in early western silent films. For a few extra dollars, cowboys were asked to do the evil "Running W":

> A pair of wires attached to hobbles on a horse's front fetlocks and connected to a ring that the rider held in one hand after mounting—Men destined to bite the dust while tearing along at a gallop simply kicked their feet free of their stirrups, aimed one shoulder at the ground, tripped the horse by yanking the wires and hoped they would not break any bones as the unfortunate beast went down.[8]

Robert ("Bob") Keith acted with Hoot Gibson, who became famous in movies after "a director offered five dollars . . . to let himself be dragged by a galloping horse. "'Make it ten,' said Hoot, 'and I'll let him kick me to death!'"[9] Along with Hoot, Broncho Billy, Tom Mix, and William S. Hart became popular screen cowboys.

Zintka had fallen in love with Keith on location when both were working for the Pathé Film Company near Orange, California. On May 26, 1913, Clara wrote to her daughter as if she were a child:

My dearie Girlie,

I was glad to hear from you after so long a time. You have not told me whether you got the Testament & Psalms I sent you for your birthday . . . or the Christmas book. When I do not hear from you for some time I do not know . . . what has happened. . . . My dear, I wish you would tell me more about yourself and your husband—Is he kind to you—Who does the housework he or you; . . . Have you the same cottage you wrote me about? . . . [W]hat salary do each of you get & what do you save? . . . With love & best wishes I am always your affectionate mother, Clara Bewick Colby.[10]

Zintka and Bob Keith were married on May 31, 1913, in Santa Ana. On the marriage license, Zintka signed with her stage name, "Princeton Davis," and under the line "Parents," she wrote "unknown."[11] The marriage may have preceded the birth of their son, Clyde. Nevertheless, Zintka had victimized herself again, marrying a man who beat her when he got drunk.[12]

A zealous reporter bent on sensationalism hounded Zintka about her Sitting Bull story, publishing articles such as one entitled: "Indian Girl's Story Has Strange Features," in which he called her "an imposter."[13] Zintka finally escaped from her brutal husband in October 1913, taking little Clyde with her. Because of her frequent name changes in show business, it is not known if she ever divorced Keith.

During her pregnancy, she may have sought medical aid. There was a 50 percent chance that the child was born without the deadly scourge of syphilis, which had already permeated Zintka's eyes and attacked the weakest organs of her body.

While Zintka spent 1911 at Cherry Creek and 1912–13 in California making movies as an extra for $7 a week, General Colby stopped sending Clara the promised alimony.

Suffragist leader Reverend Anna Shaw had called the militant English suffrage movement "undignified, unworthy—in other words un-American," but Clara borrowed money and went to London, where she worked diligently for the cause.[14] Reverend Olympia Brown said Clara went with the view of

. . . helping the English suffragists in their struggle for justice and in making acquaintance with many prominent English reformers. . . . Of her experiences in England she published, from time to time, most interesting accounts in the *Washington Herald* [and in the magazines *Arena, Harper's*

Bazaar, Overland Monthly, and *Englishwoman*]. . . . She threw herself into the work with utmost enthusiasm; she spared neither time, work nor money. Day and night, in season and out of season . . . everywhere and always . . . [15]

After 1911 Clara's outlook on suffrage became decidedly militant. Perhaps throwing bricks through windows in England vented some of her repressed anger, but she returned to America for New Year's, 1913. On January 31 Clara made the front page of most national newspapers:

> Four hundred women from every section of the nation and led by Mrs. Clara Colby . . . appeared before the House Committee on Elections today to appeal for the passage of the French Bill [named for Burton French] to give women the right to vote for Representatives in Congress. Mrs. Colby pleaded for a Constitutional Amendment prohibiting states from disenfranchising citizens on account of their sex.[16]

When teased about her newspaper exposure, Clara remarked, "He that hath a horn and tooteth it not, verily it shall not be tooted."[17]

Clara must have felt great pride in the early spring of 1913 when the House of Representatives passed a resolution to form a suffrage committee. The committee later reported affirmatively to the full Senate, the first favorable majority report on woman suffrage in twenty-three years.[18]

In May, after suing Leonard Colby for back alimony, Clara returned to England, ironically sponsored in part by a grant from the American Peace Society.[19] She dropped court proceedings against the general after he promised her lawyer he would send money, but he never did.

Militant English suffragists—led by Clara's friend, the indomitable Mrs. Emmeline G. Pankhurst, and others—had been arrested and taken to Holliway Prison in February and March. There they went on a hunger and thirst strike. Fearing that the women might die in prison, authorities inhumanely tied them down and force-fed them, thrusting tubes down their throats.[20] After hearing of their suffering, nothing could have stopped Clara from joining the militants in the land of her birth.

Clara wrote of the violence that broke out as a result of the harsh treatment of imprisoned women. After the force-feeding caused an uproar, the British Parliament passed what came to be known as the "Cat and Mouse Act," an equally tortuous but much more dangerous law that allowed women prisoners to fast from all food and water for up to nine days or until they were near death. When the protesters collapsed, they were temporarily released for an average of one to seven days and then rearrested to finish their prison terms. The alternating hard fasts and the violence of the rearrests broke the health of many.[21]

Although now sixty-seven years old, Clara was right in the thick of it. She wrote of her experiences during bombings and the burning of homes, schools, and pavilions. She described the smashing of windows and riotous scenes (one ninety-five-year-old woman, four feet six inches tall, was tackled by three men). In an article Clara wrote: "I have been the spectator of some very stirring scenes." Of her suffragist friend Annie Kenny, whom Clara saw rearrested, she wrote: "Poor little ghost of her former self, ashen gray in color. I bent my head forward and wept . . ."[22] At a huge suffrage meeting Mrs. Pankhurst gave a speech and was arrested again by 150 stick-wielding policemen. Horrified, Clara joined the women present who rushed upon the police "with the hope that she might escape." Clara said that if she had been close enough, she would have "interposed my body between those burly men and this frail woman who was then almost at death's door from her repeated incarcerations . . ."[23]

On August 22, 1913, the newspaper *Suffragette* reported: "A woman was arrested in Whitehall and charged with breaking windows in the Colonial office. She refused to give her name or any information about herself, and . . . she was remanded for further inqueries."[24] This may or may not have been Clara, for no one heard from her until September 19, when she wrote her niece Eva, "I have prayed that God will open the way for me to get back."[25]

Desperate to find money for her return trip to America, Clara accepted an invitation to attend a reception at Mrs. Winston Churchill's home. While there, Clara asked a Mrs. Belmont if she would buy the "Manchu princess cloak" Clara was wearing![26] It was the last gift Leonard Colby had given his wife so many years before. Amused, Mrs. Belmont declined, saying, "she could not afford it."[27] Finally, someone bought Clara a third-class ticket to New York on the *Lusitania*. On the voyage home, sitting on her wicker suitcases, "in front of a porthole," she wrote twelve letters to friends and relatives. Penniless when she arrived, she told Dr. Clara McNaughton: "I am wrapped up in a borrowed fur cloak having nothing warm of my own. I cannot tell what my future is to be . . ."[28]

CHAPTER 22

The Barbary Coast

"I'll bet you the time ain't far off when a woman won't know any more than a man."

WILL ROGERS

The 1914–15 edition of *Who's Who in America* listed Clara Bewick Colby, and it included seventeen lines of biographical information.[1] On the opposite page, Leonard Wright Colby garnered twelve lines. There are no letters or diary entries describing how she felt to have her name and accomplishments so honored. On the contrary, she wrote in her diary, " . . . I have not one cent on hand after all my hard work. . . . My problems seem insolvable from any point of view. . . . [W]hat shall I do?"[2] Fame was helpful only if it meant Clara could make a living more easily.

The only topic of interest was the war with Germany. Clara was against that conflict, claiming that suffragists were "hypnotized" when war burst upon the world.[3] Britain's queen of the Cunard line, the *Lusitania*, exploded after being torpedoed by the Germans. One thousand one hundred ninety-eight lives were lost, including 128 Americans. Clara had "shivered all winter" throughout the growing crisis, and such barbarism against innocent passengers brought her condemnation of war. She asked her sister, "Did you ever know such a muddle as the men have got this round world in?"[4]

Fed up with silent films, where white men and women played painted "Indians," Zintka joined Buffalo Bill Cody's Wild West Show, which had just merged with the Sells-Floto Circus for the 1914–15 season.[5]

The Wild West part of the huge extravaganza featured a "prairie outfit of Indians, ranch girls, cowboys and rangers." The circus parade was two miles long, with 450 horses and 600 people of all nations. There were two performances daily featuring forty clowns, 120 "world champion riders, daring and fascinating, and a menagerie of untrained and untamed beasts of the jungle." The big top was 160 feet high, with six 50-foot center poles, and the seats were twenty-one rows high with a seating capacity of 14,000 people. All lighting came from eight round gas burners on each pole. There were three rings and two stages with steel arenas, and a hippodrome track about twenty-five feet wide. All of this made Sells-Floto one of the largest circuses in the nation after the two main groups, Ringling Bros. and Barnum & Bailey.[6]

On May 1, 1914, the show played Hanford, California, the hometown of a nineteen-year-old Sells-Floto calliope player and clown named Ernest Cornelius ("Dick") Allen. Dick was the eighth of nine children. When he was only three years old, his weary mother and newborn sister died soon after childbirth, leaving him the motherless child of the family. His father, William, was a strict, clean-living Seventh-Day Adventist, but Dick would be the only one of his children whose name did not appear on the membership rolls of the church.[7] Young Dick decided to strike out on his own, and he ran away to join the M. H. Welsh's Circus in 1909, at the age of fourteen.[8] His father was disappointed, but Dick was always welcomed when he came home.

The calliope player had much in common with Zintka. They were both full of fun—energetic characters who both loved show business. Dick was at his best as a clown on stilts, roller-skating or boxing with kangaroos. Sells-Floto was known as "the best clowned circus" in the business.[9]

Zintka was so taken with the young man that she forgot to send her mother a birthday card on August 5, 1914. Clara noted in her diary: "No birthday letter from any of my people. This made a lonesome feeling . . ."[10] The next day, August 6, President Wilson's wife died, enveloping Washington in gloom. It was reflected in the entry: "I seem unwilling to do anything worth while. And what is worth while, when you cannot earn your living by it. I pray God that having allowed me to lose everything else He will not let me lose the will to work & the pleasure I have found in it."[11] Clara did not mention Leonard or Zintka, both of whom celebrated their birthdays on the same day. Nor did Clara make note that she had given up trying to get alimony, for not a lawyer in Beatrice had the courage to take up the case against Leonard Colby.

Sells-Floto and Buffalo Bill's Wild West Show passed through Madison, Wisconsin, on August 23, 1914, en route to Milwaukee.[12] Zintka left the train alone and called her Uncle William's son, Thomas Bewick, on the telephone. Professor Bewick had heard about Zintka's earlier life and he did not want her to come to his university office, nor did Mrs. Bewick want Zintka to show up at their home. Dr. Bewick agreed to meet her at the state capitol building. Once he got there, the gentleman was shocked to find Zintka flamboyantly dressed in a feather boa, flashy jewelry, and a big hat—normal wear for a Wild West and circus performer, but considered indecent for more conservative folk.[13] Thomas listened while Zintka told him she had been in films and could not save enough money to make the dream of finding her heritage come true. She believed she was related to Sitting Bull, and to find out she needed money to return to the Standing Rock reservation in South Dakota to search for relatives. Her first trip had failed because she had no cash to back the effort.

Dr. Bewick did not believe a word she said. He took her to a charitable organization and saw to it that she got a one-way train ticket out of Madison.[14] Disappointed and saddened that her adopted family wanted nothing to do with her, Zintka opened with the show in Milwaukee the next day, August 24. After her chilly reception in Madison, the atmosphere of the big top was that of a family. People appreciated the varied talents of each performer, regardless of nationality. Gregarious and loyal, the circus stars took care of one another, knowing that the multitudes of people they entertained were enchanted by them under the lights. Outside the arena, however, those same customers often thought performers were loose and deceitful. The pay was poor, but many in the show loved animals and much of their time was spent training them, rehearsing, and making elaborate costumes. The life had its adventure, but the constant travel proved difficult. Loading and unloading huge animals and bustling performers from forty-three rail cars, erecting enormous tents, and trying to stay comfortable living in tents in rain and mud was grueling work. But everyone turned out for the morning circus parades to thrill the youngsters in each town.[15]

An arduous schedule for July and August 1914 indicates the frantic pace of Zintka's life:

> July 8—St. Paul, Minnesota
> 9—St. Cloud, Minnesota
> 10—Fargo, North Dakota
> 11—Grand Forks, North Dakota
> 12–18—Canada, varied towns
> August 3—Missoula, Montana
> 10—Sheridan, Wyoming
> 11—Edgemont, South Dakota
> 12—Nebraska, various towns
> 17—St. Joseph, Missouri
> 18—Dubuque, Iowa
> 24—Milwaukee, Wisconsin
> 25—Racine, Wisconsin
> 27—Illinois
> 28—Indiana
> 31—Michigan[16]

It was said that the greatest showman on earth, Buffalo Bill, never missed a parade or a performance.

While Zintka was on tour, Clara aligned herself with the militant American suffragist Alice Paul, leader of the Congressional Union for Woman Suffrage, later the National Woman's Party. This clearly intensified the distrust and alienation of the largest suffrage organization, led by Reverend Anna Shaw and Carrie Chapman Catt, and bickering between the two groups behind the scenes turned to unpleasant rivalry.

On January 12, 1915, the first debate on the woman suffrage amendment "for which society has been working 45 years has come to a vote in the house. Defeated 174 for, 206 against." Clara sat nine and a half hours on the hard wooden bench hoping to have the opportunity to speak. She had only just begun when "a senator from West Virginia came and bent low beside me while he begged me to keep still."[17] The vote was a disappointment, but it brought Clara out of her depression, and she lobbied even harder among senators and congressmen, seeing as many as six a day. People were giving her their old clothes, and she ate dinner with a different person every night, as she had no money for food.

Lectures on a wide variety of subjects brought in next to nothing now that war was on everybody's mind. If not for the generosity of friends—Dr. Clara McNaughton, a dentist; Reverend Olympia Brown, president of the Federal Suffrage Association, of which Clara was corresponding secretary; and Belva Lockwood, the eighty-five-year-old lawyer and first woman to present a case before the U.S. Supreme Court—Clara would have starved. She was living hand to mouth: "People always enjoy my speaking but don't want to pay anything for it."[18] In February she was again depressed: "The time is getting short now, and I see no light ahead."[19]

Another reason for Clara's bouts with depression were the book manuscripts she submitted to publishers. All were rejected. In March she heard from Zintka. She had married Dick Allen and they now had a baby boy, but she did not mention his name. The Allens were working to feed two children. On March 31 Clara wrote to a friend, "My little Indian girl is in California and married to a white man."[20] She wrote back to Zintka that she hoped to see her adopted daughter when she accompanied the Federal Suffrage Association to their convention at the Panama-Pacific Exhibition in San Francisco in July.

Perhaps not to worry her, Zintka was not telling Clara the whole story. Zintka and Dick had left the Wild West/Sells-Floto sometime in the spring of 1915. In February Zintka wrote to the Commissioner of Indian Affairs, and he in turn notified the agent at Cheyenne River Agency: "Mrs. E. C. Allen . . . is in destitute circumstances, needing physician and medicines.

Husband ill; unable to work. Extend prompt relief . . ."[21] Dick Allen had fallen ill, but no mention was made of the nature of the illness. On April 14 Zintka wrote Clara:

> My dear mother, I did not want to answer your last letter because I was just . . . moving to Frisco and I wanted to wait until I got up here and got settled so you could have an address to write to me at. . . . I went over to Berkley [sic] yesterday to see Dr. McGillycuddy who used to be Indian Agent at Pine Ridge. . . . Well I will be here when you come so I'll be sure and see you. . . . With lots of love . . ."[22]

Dr. Valentine McGillycuddy had been Chief Red Cloud's bitter enemy. After his forced termination as agent at Pine Ridge, he had accompanied John Brennan when he took Dead Arm's scalp in the violence that preceded the Wounded Knee Massacre. When Zintka went to see him, she knew none of this. She borrowed a book from him, the second volume of the *Fourteenth Annual Report of the Bureau of Ethnology*, which contained a 1,136-page account of the Wounded Knee Massacre, called "The Ghost-Dance Religion and the Sioux Outbreak of 1890," by James Mooney. It also contained photographs and drawings of Zintka and other members of her tribe, ghost shirts, massacre victims, and the haunting words to Ghost Dance songs. McGillycuddy undoubtedly told her, as he had bragged to others, that if he had still been agent at Pine Ridge in 1890, the tragedy would never have occurred. As he spoke of his many good deeds as agent, she glanced through the book, stopping to examine the lifeless forms lying in the snow. She could have been looking at a picture of her own mother.

Zintka told McGillycuddy that she was short of ready cash. She wrote out a check for $25, and he gave her the money. The check later bounced. McGillycuddy tried to trace Zintka, but she was nowhere to be found. The Allens had moved with their two young children to San Francisco to start a vaudeville troupe, and they were having a rough go of it. Instead of traveling on a vaudeville circuit across the country, they played the theaters, saloons, and dance halls of San Francisco's Barbary Coast. It was said of vaudeville during that time that you never knew just what you were going to see or hear. There were bicycle acts, singers, and contortionists. There was Princess Rajah, who danced as "Cleopatra" with a seven-foot python. The Athletic Girls fenced, wrestled, and boxed, and an added attraction was Thalero's Dog and Pony circus.[23]

Dick Allen had a lariat-throwing act on the order of another vaudeville comedian, Will Rogers. Allen's rope tricks demanded timing and skill to perform in a confined space. He practiced Will Rogers's feats: "the flat spin—in which he twirled the rope in front or to the side, parallel to the stage . . . into the merry-go-round, in which the rope, constantly spinning, is passed from the right hand, under one leg, to the other hand behind the body, where the right hand picks it up again."[24] Dick tried spinning two ropes at one time and jumping in and out. Then he did the "Texas skip," dancing back and forth while spinning a large loop. Sometimes Dick lassoed Zintka, dressed in her cowgirl's garb, or an Indian dress.[25]

The couple lived and worked in various saloons in the heart of the infamous red-light district of the Barbary Coast. Some of the other vaudevillians who traveled across country would become famous stars: Buster Keaton, Charlie Chaplin, Jimmy Durante, George Jessel, the Marx Brothers, Eddie Cantor, and George Burns and Gracie Allen. Burns said new vaudeville acts "worked for practically nothing."[26] The acts "had to be between fourteen and seventeen minutes long" and a "dissy" was an act "that filled in on short notice for scheduled acts." Burns recalled:

> As long as we stayed healthy, we worked. We worked bad theaters and worse theaters. We dressed in boiler rooms, bathrooms, and closets. . . . In small-time vaudeville, performers usually worked three or four shows a day. . . . Sometimes, at the five o'clock show, there would be fifteen people sitting in a 1200-seat house.[27] . . . Nothing was so much fun as small-time vaudeville. . . . If you could twirl a lariat and chew gum at the same time, all you had to do was say, "Well seems to me that the Washington Monument's the only thing they got in that town that has any point to it," and you were Will Rogers.[28]

But Dick Allen was no Will Rogers, and Zintka's eyesight was growing dimmer. On April 17, 1915, she wrote to Robert G. Valentine, the Indian commissioner: "Times in California are pretty hard now and money to me seems almost a thing of the past. The position I am holding now brings me in barely enough to exist on."[29] She again pushed for a patent in fee on her Cheyenne River allotment. With a patent, Zintka could mortgage the land or sell it.

Zintka visited every church and charitable organization she could find rather than resort to prostitution. The Barbary Coast of San Francisco was

> . . . occupied by women of all colors and nationalities. . . . [T]he lowest . . . were the most popular, partly because of the variety and extraordinary depravity of the women to be found there, and partly because the police seldom entered . . .
>
> Every night, and especially every Saturday night, this dismal bedlam of obscenity, lighted . . . by red lamps above the doors . . . was thronged by a

tumultuous mob of half-drunken men, who stumbled from crib to crib, greedily inspecting the women as if they had been so many wild animals in cages. From the . . . windows leaned the harlots, naked to the waist, . . . while their pimps haggled with passing men. . . . If business was dull, the pimps sold the privilege of touching the breasts of the prostitutes. . . . Prices ranged from twenty-five cents . . . to a dollar.[30]

It was estimated that twenty-five thousand persons made a livelihood from vice on the Barbary Coast.

The Panama-Pacific Exposition opened in San Francisco in the spring of 1915.[31] It was to be the site of many conventions for women, principally the International Conference of Women Workers under Mrs. May Wright Sewell, the National Council of Women Voters, the International Purity Congress, and of great importance to Clara Colby, the Federal Suffrage Association of the United States Congress on July 11–13. In order to earn enough money to attend, she had given thirty-six lectures across country.

Clara organized much of the Federal Suffrage program, and she invited Zintka to join her for the convention. She helped her make an Indian dress, as Zintka was to attend as the "only Indian Suffragette." On the last evening of the congress, a grand pageant was arranged. Ida Husted Harper described the event:

> This was the last time I ever saw Mrs. Colby and I shall never forget the scene. It was at night in the splendid Court of Abundance, lighted only by blazing torches, and she gave the recitative for a long series of tableaux. She stood on the pedestal of a towering column, the soft wind blowing her summer dress and long flowing cape into graceful folds, making her seem like a piece of statuary harmonizing with the beautiful architecture. The memory typifies her own lofty and noble character.[32]

Zintka stood on another pedestal and represented Pocahontas. The breeze that blew her mother's dress also blew the beads and long fringes of her imaginative Indian dress. At that moment they were really on stage together, although their relationship had been an unfolding drama for many years.

Clara thought her daughter was a housewife in Hanford, California, and Zintka did not tell her otherwise. They saw sister Mary and visited with family and friends. Zintka stayed with Clara for a week, and since she had no money, Clara paid for everything and gave her a loan of $10. It was the last time Zintka would see her adopted mother.

By August 3, Zintka was having a more difficult time. She wrote Clara: "My dear Mother, I received your letter this A.M. . . . Clyde my oldest boy has the malaria and the baby has the chicken pox so I have had my hands full . . ."[33] When Clara got the letter, she was thinking of other things. Her brother William passed away on August 4, 1915. He had been kicked in the head by a horse two years before, and the brain damage left him erratic and unable to talk. Clara remembered him: "Dear good brother—kind, unselfish, as near perfection as a human being can be and yet he has [had] this suffering."[34]

When Clara returned to Washington, D.C., she had no home. On October 23, Mrs. Belva Lockwood allowed her to move into the second floor front of her house while she went south for the winter. In the room next to Clara lived Dr. Mary Walker, the Civil War surgeon who wore male attire and had won a Congressional Medal of Honor for her bravery under fire. Dr. Walker was constantly on the go and nearly as poor as Clara, who on November 13 had nineteen cents "in the bank & one cent in pocket. I have dry bread & tea for breakfast & dry tea & bread for lunch."[35] Ida Husted Harper discussed Clara's dire circumstances and suggested several times to Carrie Chapman Catt, president of the NAWSA, to include Mrs. Colby among the suffrage speakers for the national organization, but Mrs. Catt detested Clara from the days when she had defended Mrs. Stanton with regard to the *Woman's Bible.* Catt had firmly denounced militancy, and Clara's audacious involvement in English brick-throwing angered her. According to Ida Husted Harper, Mrs. Catt remembered with repugnance Susan B. Anthony's disgust when Clara adopted "that unspeakable Indian child."[36] For all of these reasons, Clara Colby was shunned by the national suffrage leaders.

Toward the end of November, as the weather turned colder, she wrote: "I dare not buy a shoelace."[37] But just as she was about to run out of money, a New Jersey suffrage union needed a lecturer. She was hired for room and board for fourteen lectures on street corners. In the rain, and without an umbrella, she "was carted around . . . and was thoroughly chilled. This went to my bowels . . . so I was nauseate and sore? . . . Of course . . . I was always able to do my work."[38] She was heckled "by urchins yelling 'Votes for men' but she raised her voice above theirs."

After receiving a letter from a friend who said she had seen Zintka walking with a young man on Market Street in San Francisco, Clara went to the offices of the Commissioner of Indian Affairs to plead Zintka's case, but she found the matter of Zintka's patent in fee mired in red tape.

Harder times befell Zintka, and she wrote again to Robert G. Valentine, U.S. Indian commissioner:

> Dear Sir, Some time ago I put in an application to the Indian agent Mr. F. C. Campbell of the Cheyenne River Reservation . . . and was

refused. I have tried several times for a patent in fee each time with the same answer, I have proven beyond doubt that I am quite capable of looking after my own affairs.

I should like to become a citizen of the United States. . . . Would it be possible for you to find out to whom the property went belonging to my mother and father who were killed in the battle of Wounded Knee that was fought in 1890. . . . Hoping to hear from you the earliest date at your convenience . . .[39]

Court records show that, although desperate, neither Zintka nor her husband got into legal trouble in San Francisco other than sickness and poverty.[40] They lived at various locations until they settled at 459 Turk Street. This was a short walk from the new City Hall, fifteen feet taller than the dome in Washington, D.C., its walls finished in Indiana sandstone and rich Manchurian oak. The building cost four million dollars.[41] Two blocks away in a seedy hotel room, Zintkala Nuni found ways to feed her sick husband and two children.

CHAPTER 23

The Voice of the Spirit

"She would not allow her love . . . to be a tragedy . . . on her soul. . . . She would not let pain win its one permanent victory: to make her forget her conviction, that joy is the meaning of human existence."

AYN RAND, *We the Living*

In 1915 the Kiowas began Ghost-dancing in Oklahoma. When the ceremony was exposed in 1916, the leaders were beaten and imprisoned at hard labor.[1]

There may also have been Ghost Dances held on the Cheyenne River Sioux Reservation, where Agent F. C. Campbell prepared Zintka's formal application for citizenship on December 16, 1915, with the advice: "By securing citizenship all your land is turned over to you by Patent in Fee, and all government supervision over moneys that may be due you is removed. . . . [S]ign the blanks . . . and return to this office. The matter will then be turned over to Major McLaughlin who is better acquainted with you than I am."[2] Ironically, the man who had most despised Sitting Bull and whom Lakota historians blamed for his death was to pass judgment on whether the Lost Bird would be granted citizenship and a patent in fee for her land.[3] Zintka did not remember meeting McLaughlin when she was young, but on at least two occasions the agent had been a guest in General Colby's Washington home. Zintka filled out the forms and sent them in, notifying her mother that she had done so.

Clara noted in her diary on December 20 that Dr. Mary Walker had taken sick: ". . . I have just given her my hot-water bag to cure her cough . . ." She looked in on Mary several times a day, but went on lecturing with a tin cup on street corners. Clara spent Christmas with Reverend Olympia Brown and then came home to check on her patient. She wrote that Walker was "in bed most of the time. I have given her most of her meals."[4]

William Bewick's widow, Jennie, came for a two-week visit in January 1916, and since Jennie was paying, Clara took her all over the capital, showing her the beautiful Capitol rotunda, the White House, the diversity of Georgetown, the Library of Congress, and Mount Vernon. They attended a lecture given by William Jennings Bryan and climbed to the top of the Washington Monument. By the time Jennie left Washington, Clara was completely worn out.

On January 26, Clara managed a line in her diary: "Was quite bad with grippe." Although terribly ill, Clara had to lecture for food money. She had no appetite, but forced herself to take tea. In a February 2 letter to Dr. McNaughton, she mentioned having pain in her liver and "indigestion."[5] She stayed in bed until it was time to lecture and went straight back to bed afterward. By February 21 Dr. Walker had recovered and Clara noted that the eighty-four-year-old Civil War heroine, the most decorated woman of her time, was still wearing her frock coat, man's suit, and carrying her cane at a jaunty angle. Nonetheless, Clara told McNaughton: ". . . I think she is quite pretty and very lady-like."[6]

Clara urged the Assistant Commissioner of Indian Affairs to help Zintka after she received the letter her daughter had written: "My dear Mother, . . . The babies have been very sick, thought I would lose them both and just as they were getting better Mr. Allen took sick. . . . I pawned everything. . . . It has been one bad luck streak right after the other."[7]

By late February Clara admitted that "for two weeks my face was so blotched with cold sores that I could not go to the capital. At last Feb. 18 & 19 I went up—saw . . . Judge Raker . . . saw Senator Lee . . ."[8] From her rented room, the Capitol was a sixteen-block walk. Unable to afford trolley fare, Clara trudged home in the evening after lobbying all day. She was exhausted, malnourished, and ill, and her diary entries reflect a sense of preordained fate: ". . . It seems to be the voice of the Spirit that I go to Oregon this spring."[9] She tried to heal herself with New Thought techniques, memorizing the passage: "God is the only reality—therefore there is no reality in . . . sickness . . . poverty [and] sin. Anger, . . . fear, sorrow and anxiety have no place in me. They do not belong to my real self & they have no power over me."[10]

But fear, sorrow, and anxiety had infinite power. Clara found it difficult to concentrate on her own healing after an alarming letter from Zintka:

My dear Mother,

    . . . I have had so much care and worry I am all in just about. . . . I lost one baby since writing you. My husband took sick again . . .

    There is an organization in California known as The Indian Board of Co-operation who has taken a great interest in me and they are

doing all in their power . . . in securing my money and patent in fee.
The field Sec. name is F. C. Collett, one of the finest charactered men
I believe I have ever met . . .

I have sent the oldest boy [Clyde] to Los Angeles in care of an
Indian lady. . . . She offered to take him with no expense. . . . She has
a beautiful home, no children of her own. I cannot care for him while
I am in such a shape and Mr. Allen sick most of the time.[11]

Giving her son to an Indian woman was the best decision she could have
made under the circumstances. Zintka's dream of moving her family out of
the big city to farm her allotment in South Dakota was still possible. She
wanted to return to her people, but Mr. Collett encouraged her to give up
the idea and sell the land.

Suffering from what she called "intercostal rheumatism" in her
unheated room, Clara told Reverend Olympia Brown, "[I]t leaves one so
that you can find a pain in any part of the body when you look for it, and
sometimes it finds you when you don't . . ."[12]

Clara was further disheartened by a threatening letter from Dr. Valentine
McGillycuddy. He accused Zintka of borrowing $26.50 from him and not
repaying the debt. Zintka had borrowed his book on Wounded Knee as well.
He told Clara: "She made herself liable legally."[13]

In light of Dr. McGillycuddy's past reputation as "the most investigated
Indian agent," an "insufferably . . . pompous" personality, "an autocrat and
a tyrant . . . and utterly unfit for the position of Indian agent," his fury over
the loss of his money and a book on Wounded Knee (in which he is
quoted) is not surprising.[14]

Clara notified Zintka of McGillycuddy's threat and urged her to repay the
wealthy man at once: "Do not neglect this," she told her, "as he is liable to
make you trouble. . . . [N]ow brace up my good girl. . . . Pray with all your
might for your heavenly Father to help you in this time of need."[15] Ever loyal
to Zintka, Clara wrote to McGillycuddy from her sickbed:

I am extremely sorry . . . Zintkala has not been in a position to
repay the loan, or rather make good the check. . . . [T]he sickness of
the two children, the death of one, and the long sickness of Mr.
Allen . . . left them deeply in debt. . . . I am investigating . . . here to
see if in such cases any relief is afforded. . . . Since she has been in
such dire distress, she may possibly have pawned your book as well as
her clothes. . . . It is much to her credit that she is making a great
effort to care for her family under these conditions, and if she has gotten money under false pretenses, which is probably too harsh a term,

for she doubtless expected to make it good—she always has the most extravagant expectations—think of what a temptation it is to be out of funds, out of everything with sickness to prevent working . . .[16]

There is no record of Dr. McGillycuddy's reply.

In March Zintka notified the chief clerk at the Department of the Interior: "I note that you suggest selling my land under the supervision of the Dept. I do not wish to dispose of my property. . . . It is the only place now that I have that I can call my own . . ."[17] In another letter she again refused to sell, saying: "I am getting ready to leave for South Dakota shortly and I would rather buy more property if I had the money than to sell what I have and I am very anxious to go there and settle down on the place."[18]

In April Clara sold her Chinese cloak to pay for her trip west. She had no heat in her room and told McNaughton: "It is terrifying to try to make a new start. But I feel I should only get poorer and poorer by staying here."[19]

She left Washington in May after having testified before the House of Representatives for woman suffrage eleven times in fifteen years, and under the most adverse circumstances.[20] As she walked down the hallway carrying her leather-belted suitcases, "the tenants of the different rooms stood together in tears at the head of the stairs, as she bade them good-bye to go to the train."[21]

On her way west, Clara stopped in Wisconsin to see relatives and friends, and by July she had rented rooms in Eugene, Oregon. She wrote to a friend on July 12: "I have had special electrical vibration treatment to get a lot of debris out of my system, . . . first a cabinet sweat then vibration massage, then electricity. One does not have to have a doctor to tell that something is wrong. However, I have kept going . . ."[22] She received a crudely written letter from her adopted son Clarence, and she wrote him back: "I am going to stay in this city for awhile, to see if I can make my way. . . . I sent your letter on to Zintka who has always loved you very much. . . . I want . . . to hear from you. . . . Tell me what you are doing to earn your living, and all about yourself. With much love and good wishes, I am your affectionate mother."[23]

The Reverend Olympia Brown, Clara's closest friend, was the only person who knew that Clara was critically ill: "After reading your last letter I felt quite worried about your health. I had supposed your ailments were temporary and that on getting to Oregon the change of scene and improvement of conditions would bring you out all right. . . . [B]eing taken with pneumonia suggests a weakened condition of the system which has been created by the hardships you endured last winter. . . . [G]et the requisite amount of sleep and continue to eat more good foods and rest is what you need."[24] Clara wrote to Olympia admitting: "I do not see how I am going to make it."[25]

The black squirrels in Palo Alto, California, were a slight nuisance to the residents in August 1916, as they sometimes are today. At 758 Waverly Street, in an ordinary frame house with a brick fireplace, Clara's sister Dr. Mary White lived in her home-office. One night Mary got an urgent phone call from her daughter with the news that Clara had suffered a severe relapse of pneumonia. Mary drove to Eugene and nursed Clara for a week, until she felt she could not neglect her own patients in Palo Alto any longer. She bundled Clara into the back seat of her car and drove back to California, arriving about the first of September.

Clara was so weak she was unable to stand or to talk, but she probably made it clear that she would not go to a hospital. Dr. White called in Dr. T. M. Williams, but even with two physicians working over her, she did not rally.

Across the street from Mary's house towered a stately Gothic Revival church, St. Thomas Aquinas. A large gilded cross adorned the tall steeple, with five smaller ones atop the five gables of the sparkling yellow edifice. The 1,500-pound bell sounded "clear and pleasant," and perhaps its joyful tolling comforted Clara if she heard it on Sunday, September 3.

In the shadow of a church named for a great philosopher, theologian, and martyr, and just four years before the women of America received the right to vote, Clara Bewick Colby found perfect peace at 10 P.M., on September 7, 1916.[26]

Annie Kenny, Clara's militant English friend, had faced a similar death in prison, when she prepared to sacrifice her life for the ideals in which she and Clara believed:

> And what is death that it should make me afraid? . . . Some people believe that when death has taken possession of you all is over, and you are just part of the earth. Well, if that is true, there is no need to fear; for in the earth there is quiet and peace—and perhaps you may be a part of the earth which is covered with wild roses in the spring, and wild thyme in the summer. Or near the sea, which thunders and roars in the winter, and comes in softly and gently when the skies are blue, and the sun is warm . . .
>
> Others—of whom I am one—believe that the body returns to the earth, but the spirit lives eternally. If that is true, what have we to fear . . . ?[27]

CHAPTER 24

A Lonely Grave

Mary arranged a brief prayer service for Clara the next morning in her home, and then Clara's body was cremated and the ashes sent home to the peaceful countryside of Wisconsin. To her dying day, Dr. Mary White blamed Leonard Colby for Clara's death. Nor did she approve of Zintka, telling her daughters, "She was never a comfort to anyone."[1] After Clara's death, Zintka may just as well have died with her. She was no longer considered a member of the family; for that reason it is not clear how Zintka found out about Clara's agonizing death, although she may have read about it in the newspaper.

A week later Zintka received a patent in fee, with her land appraised at $3,840.[2] She still did not want to sell the allotment, but the Indian Bureau automatically put the land up for sale.

F. C. Collett of the Indian Board of Co-operation had been Zintka's adviser for some time. She trusted that he represented her best interests.[3] Seven months later, after having taken out three mortgages on the land totaling $1,501.65, Zintka lost her allotment when she could not pay back the debt.[4] It must have devastated her to lose "the only place . . . that I can call my own." Perhaps it was only a coincidence, but the last name of the new owner—Campbell—was the same as that of the agent for the Cheyenne River Reservation. Years later, on February 14, 1928, a federal grand jury demanded a warrant for the arrest of F. C. Collett for allegedly embezzling Indian land and pension funds. Collett's sophisticated "paper organization" had been a convincing front.[5]

By now, the illness for which there was no cure had blinded Zintka in her right eye. She and her husband had been evicted from one hotel after another because they could not find enough work in vaudeville to pay the rent.

In December 1916 and February 1917, the San Francisco Vice Commission closed the brothels in the red-light district of the Barbary Coast, throwing hundreds of women out into the streets.[6] One evening Zintka found a homeless young woman, Pearl Cammack, in a doorway and "was moved by her pathetic story."[7] They told each other about their lives and Pearl showed unusual interest in Zintka's life story.

During her many years of privation and hardship, there is no evidence that Zintka took out her disappointments and anger on her adopted father. But on December 20, 1916, a strange and sensational story appeared on the front page of the *San Francisco Examiner.* The headline read: "SIOUX GETS $100,000 BEQUEST; TO AID TRIBE":

> Zintkalla Anuni [*sic*], a Sioux girl who has been making a living as a lariat thrower and rope spinner in a vaudeville act, received word yesterday at her apartment at 503 Myrtle Street that she had fallen heir to $100,000 through the will of the late Brigadier General Leonard Colby, who adopted and reared her.
>
> The girl is known as "Lost Bird" in her tribe. She is a full-blooded Sioux of the Sitting Bull tribe and was found on a battlefield at Wounded Knee Reservation at the time that General Colby put down an uprising there in 1890.
>
> With the money Miss Anuni hopes to do great things for her tribe in the Dakotas. She will return there, taking with her Miss Pearl Cammack, a girl whom she found destitute and took to live with her recently.[8]

On January 27, Zintka's shocking picture appeared in *The Woman's Home Weekly* magazine. She was almost unrecognizable as the determined, pretty young woman who two years before had posed as Pocahontas for an official photographer at the Panama-Pacific Exposition.[9]

In the photo Zintka's sad-looking face is blotched and her pupil is much smaller in her blind right eye, which is looking in a different direction than her left. Wearing a wide-brimmed cowboy hat and neck scarf, she appeared distressed and on the brink of tears. In the late stages of syphilis, frequent weeping was not unusual, along with "intense stabbing pain [lightning pain] in the legs, lack of insight, and delusions of grandeur," which may have resulted in this case from the news that she had inherited a fortune.[10]

But instead of being thrilled over a solution to her problems, she was clearly a sick and unhappy person. Below Zintka's picture was an inset showing Pearl Cammack, a tight-lipped, hard-looking woman. The headline above the pictures read: "INDIAN GIRL GOING BACK TO TRIBE TO HELP FELLOWS TO BETTER THINGS." The story seemed to focus more on Pearl than on Zintka. It began:

> San Francisco, Cal.—"Lost Bird" is going back to Dakota and the Sioux Indians. And she is going with gold to help them.
>
> And the legacy comes in the nick of time to raise from destitution to

affluence a young vaudeville girl, Miss Pearl Cammack, whom the young Indian woman, despite her own poverty, had befriended.

. . . Pearl Cammack's parents died recently somewhere in the Middle West and left her destitute. The girl tried an engagement with a road show and met with most unfortunate circumstances. Left without any money, she told her story to an actress living in the same hotel.

This girl told Zintkella Anuni [sic] and . . . [s]he insisted that the lonely lass live with her and her husband . . .

"I am glad of the money, of course," she said. "But what I thought of first was the chance to do so much for my people I want to help. I hope to do something permanent on a large scale for the Sioux people. They are in need of help . . ."[11]

Someone in the area, whom Maud Colby later described as "a friend" (possibly Dr. McGillycuddy), sent the article to Leonard Colby, who was still very much alive. In a letter written years later, Maud blamed Zintka for everything, saying that she had "run bills of all sorts on the strength of the fortune that she inherited."[12] She also alluded to the fact that Clara was somehow involved: "All this happened before the death of Mrs. Clara Colby." This was untrue.[13] Whether the alleged inheritance was McGillycuddy's sadistic joke, Pearl's scheme, or Zintka's revenge, the real story may never be known.

The cash raised by all the media attention provided Pearl with the means to escape from the streets of the Barbary Coast, and it gave Zintka a chance to see her homeland once more. According to one written account, Zintka, Dick, and Pearl drove to South Dakota and pulled up in front of Felix Crane Pretty Voice's cabin. Zintka looked so old and drawn that those who saw her thought Pearl was her grown daughter. Felix welcomed Zintka, but Mrs. Pretty Voice "didn't care for her." When Zintka hugged the older woman, she stiffened and scoffed.[14] The guests did not stay long, but before they left, Zintka gave Felix $100.

It is doubtful that Zintka would have missed the chance to visit the mass grave at Wounded Knee. A visitor to the site at that time described the "rickety bridge" at the bottom of the hill, the spring wagons, and the tipis of the small community:

Looking away from the wind-swept hilltop, you see a peaceful, growing, virile country, young, strong, new; war, the roar of guns, bloody ground are worlds away. Worlds away—until you bring your eyes from the flat land beneath you to the top of the rise where you stand. . . . The side of the hill is spotted with army tents; the grass of the plain below is covered with the wreck of other tents and with stiffening, bleeding bodies . . . until they rest upon the white stone pillar at the head of the mound, . . . like a ghost among the graves and read the words cut into its sides: "Cankpe opi el tona wicakte pi qun he cajepi kin, . . . These are the names of those who died at Wounded Knee." And then are carved their names—Big Foot, High Hawk, . . . Lone Bull, and the rest. On another side it says that "this monument was erected by surviving relatives and other Ogalala and Cheyenne River Sioux, in memory of the Chief Big Foot Massacre, December 29, 1890, Colonel Forsyth in command of U. S. troops. Big Foot was a great chief of the Sioux Indians. He often said, 'I will stand in peace until my last day comes.' He did many good and brave deeds for the white man and the red man. Many innocent women and children who knew no wrong died here . . ."[15]

When the money ran out, Zintka and Dick returned to San Francisco (an unlikely place to be if they thought they were in trouble), and Pearl dropped out of sight. Maud wrote later that "when payment was not forthcoming some of her creditors began an investigation."[16] But if criminal charges were filed, they were soon dropped and no mention of the incident appeared in Nebraska papers. Apparently, the debts were paid by someone who wanted the whole thing covered up. The person with the most to lose if the scandal were made public, and the man with enough prestige and money to pay off creditors was General L. W. Colby. He was then director of the Patriotic League of Nebraska, promoting "American Rights—American Ideals—American Honor."[17] There were important speeches scheduled, one of them on June 13, 1917, before the State Legislature at the celebration of the fiftieth anniversary of Nebraska's admission to the Union. The last thing Colby wanted was an embarrassing disclosure, exposing his lack of personal honor and ideals, his moral and financial neglect of his ex-wife, and his seriously ill daughter, whom he repeatedly declared he had adopted for "the citizens of Beatrice."

The expectation of renewed excitement during World War I had lured the seventy-year-old Leonard Colby to an army recruitment office. He had "brushed up on the manual of arms," dyed his hair black, and "gave his age as under forty-six," the oldest age accepted for enlistment.[18] Colby passed the physical examination, but before the swearing in, he was recognized. Disappointed and embarrassed, he complained to Theodore Roosevelt: ". . . [L]oyal, patriotic and efficient men of experience, who are willing and anxious to serve their country in this emergency will have no opportunity to do so. . . . I think it's . . . a grave mistake."[19]

On Maud's birthday, August 24, just a few days before Clara died, Leonard gave his wife a book entitled *When a Man's a Man* by Harold Bell Wright. It begins with:

There is a land where a man, to live, must be a man . . . and a man's freedom must be that freedom which is not bounded by the fences of a too weak and timid conventionalism.

In this land every man is—by divine right—his own king; he is his own jury, his own counsel, his own judge, and—if it must be—his own executioner. And in this land where a man, to live, must be a man, a woman, if she be not a woman, must surely perish.[20]

It was almost a threat. Maud had gained nearly 100 pounds and held herself stiffly erect to support huge, pendulous breasts. Her strut made one citizen remark that "she thought she was an opera star."[21] She wore balloon knickers (knee pants) and drove her new car with the license plate number 1005 (to match her address).[22] Her expensive furs were the talk of lower society, but the more cultivated women saw a "hard, witchy woman with a high pitched voice."[23] Gone, too, were the manners and civilities Clara had tried to teach her. According to Colby's clerk, Maud "swore and talked like a cowboy," and no amount of money would ever change a woman who "opened bottle caps with her teeth."[24] He said Maud had "a throat hold" on the general, and everyone got a chuckle from his teaching a "Business Men's Bible Class." Maud bragged that Leonard's Sunday meetings were the largest in Beatrice and that his church affiliation "reached every corner of our city. His influence brought many into the church that I am sure would never have come in any other way."[25]

Religion was also to play a peripheral role in Zintka's life. In 1918, down on their luck in every way, Dick and Zintka gave up vaudeville and moved back to Hanford to live with Dick's father, William Allen, a staunch Seventh-Day Adventist who accepted Zintka, although neither she nor Dick joined the church. Devout Adventists avoided most theatrical productions, novels, cards, gambling, and ragtime music. They believed in dressing conservatively—no fancy clothes or jewelry—and they did not smoke, eat pork, or drink tea or alcoholic beverages.[26]

Hanford, situated in the fertile San Joaquin Valley, had a population of less than 7,000 people. Its citizens made their living in the stock business or in the meat-packing, cotton, and fruit industries. Few streets were paved. And laws were strict: stealing a bike made front-page news, and using profane language was punishable by a fine of $100 or six months in jail.[27]

But like all small towns, Hanford had its criminals. Police sometimes ignored illegal lotteries, opium dens, and houses of prostitution, until the police chief himself was caught with his hand in the till and resigned.[28]

On November 11, 1918, the citizens of Hanford joyously celebrated the end of World War I: "Every whistle in the city was going . . . full blast so that the pandemonium was deafening. . . . [T]he streets became speed-ways for autos driven by hilarious and jubilant owners . . . banks were closed . . . [and] the parade was at least two miles long."[29]

They desperately needed a celebration. Hanford, like every American community, had been hit hard by what was then called the "Spanish influenza," an international disaster. The disease was so widespread by November 14 that the City Council announced: "All persons while on any public street or in any public place within the limits of the city of Hanford must wear a gauze mask consisting of not less than four layers of gauze, covering the nose and mouth."[30] A man caught disobeying that law was shot by a police officer.[31]

Five hundred thousand deaths were reported nationwide, the worst epidemic in U.S. history.[32] A. A. Hoehling, in *The Great Epidemic*, said that within weeks the influenza "created havoc and carnage for which there had been no precedent," killing 21 million people worldwide—more "than the combined armies . . . had accomplished in four years of fighting."[33]

Doctors were helpless. In a Massachusetts hospital a nurse gave a woman's view of the epidemic:

> One of my cases . . . was a young girl. . . . She was married and about seven months pregnant. The baby was born prematurely and died at birth but I did not dare tell her. . . . She kept begging me to see her baby. . . . She had such a lovely look on her face as she talked about her son and how happy her husband would be . . .
>
> When she died . . . I put the baby into her arms and fixed them so that they seemed only to be sleeping. And so the husband saw them when he came.[34]

When physicians and nurses fell ill and died, women volunteered their services: "There were no qualifications except willingness and courage." It did not matter to which race a woman belonged, for all "social stigmas were forgotten."[35]

The Red Cross issued urgent appeals for volunteers. On February 7, 1920, 395 cases of flu were reported in a second wave of the deadly illness. More volunteers, trained and untrained, were called for duty. Zintka, who had always dreamed of being a nurse, undoubtedly responded by helping Dick's family and friends.

It was overcast and raining on February 9, 1920, when Zintka fell ill. Dr. Charles Foster, the Public Health doctor, was called to the Allen residence at 120 Normandie Avenue, and he rushed over again to see her on February 12. Dr. Foster concluded that Zintka had gotten the flu but complicated by "Endo Carditis, probably of syphilitic origin."[36] There were tremors and rapid breathing, possibly "a feeling of impending doom, that something terrible is happening, that death is imminent." As the days went slowly by, Zintka's mind wandered back to Wounded Knee and her tribal past: "She spent much of her time in searching the back pages of history in an endeavor to find out her real identity."[37] Throughout her life of prejudice, exploitation, poverty, misunderstanding, and disease, she never gave up hope that one day she would find out where she really belonged.

At 3 A.M. on Valentine's Day, February 14, 1920, Zintkala Nuni, the Lost Bird, suffered an intense, bone-crushing pain in her chest and passed away suddenly. "Heart failure was given as the cause of her death."[38] At least she was spared her Lakota mother's piercing wounds and lingering death in the freezing wind, or her adopted mother's slow suffocation from pneumonia.

In the *Hanford Journal* obituary the next day, a kindly article entitled "NOTED INDIAN WOMAN PASSES AT HOME HERE" exaggerated the events and accomplishments of her life:

> ... Her sudden demise puts an end to what might have been the highest career of any living survivor of the American Indians.... Mrs. Allen was known to the world as "Lost Bird." ... The history of her life was a story that would fill many pages and in her travels she had visited all the points of interest in the world ...
>
> She was a graduate of one of the Nebraska universities and a brilliant career was before her.
>
> Her history made her a character of much note and she won world wide fame by travelling with the Buffalo Bill wild west shows.... Some tales say that she was a daughter of the great chief Sitting Bull which however has no foundation.... She was a brilliant woman and her untimely death is a source of sorrow to all who knew her.[39]

There was an official ban on all public funerals during the epidemic, but Adventist pastor Dr. E. C. Bond, his face covered with tight gauze, gave a brief prayer and Zintka was buried by white-masked pallbearers, not beside her mother and father in the blood beneath the Dakota soil, but in a lonely grave far from her native land.

The Lost Bird Comes Home

On the Delta flight carrying Lost Bird's remains to South Dakota, we had to change planes in Salt Lake City. It was the first time I had ever seen Arvol Looking Horse appear nervous. He was standing alone at a large window looking down on the runway and his head and shoulders moved restlessly. Arvol wasn't the only one who was worried. We had all decided that if Lost Bird's coffin didn't make our connecting flight, none of us would board the next plane, even if it meant being stranded. But the airline people were more than kind. They took us down on the runway, and we were able to watch the coffin being loaded onto our plane. None of us knew much about the camcorder we had brought along to video our trip, but Arvol reached down and picked it up. He filmed the coffin as it moved slowly up the baggage elevator and disappeared into our plane. After he put the camcorder carefully back into its case, Arvol looked up shyly and we all smiled at him. The terrible tension was gone.

Delta flight 1196 left the runway and sailed smoothly into the skies. As we flew over the Black Hills, our pilot's voice came over the intercom. "Ladies and gentlemen," he said, "below us is Crazy Horse Mountain, being carved in the likeness of a great Sioux chief." We looked at each other in disbelief. In South Dakota many white people either despise Indians or completely ignore them as if they don't exist. There are racial outrages on both sides. Those who think of the American frontier as a long-lost era of history have never lived in South Dakota.

Indians try to ignore the hurtful prejudice with dignity, but inside there is deep resentment and anger that boils close to the surface, although a Year of Reconciliation in 1990 had been proposed by Tim Giago, the Oglala editor of the *Lakota Times*, among others. Governor George Mickelson went out on a political limb to accept the challenge, despite objections from many white voters. The year passed with definite progress in the school system, but Governor Mickelson died in a tragic plane crash on April 19, 1993, before long-term issues could be resolved.

Even in our airplane flying over South Dakota, it seemed outlandish for a white airline pilot to recognize something Indian like a mountain carved in the likeness of a Lakota chief. We were all puzzled until we deplaned in Rapid City, and out came Pilot Frank Tall Dog Duran to greet us in the terminal. Arvol went over to shake the captain's hand. Ironically, Lost Bird had been flown home by an Oglala Lakota from Pine Ridge. That wasn't the only coincidence: One hundred years earlier, before the Wounded Knee Massacre, there had been a total eclipse of the sun. As we were flying home with Lost Bird's remains, there was another haunting eclipse in midflight.

Ann R. Roberts, Nelson Rockefeller's daughter, was waiting for us at the airport. She had provided funds for Lost Bird's return and showed us support by her gentle, refined presence at the reburial. Also waiting was Joan Indermark, a descendant of the Bewick family, who had driven from Madison, Wisconsin, with her husband, Jerry, to represent Clara's relatives at the ceremonies.

A hearse from the Sioux Funeral Home waited to take Lost Bird to Porcupine Butte, where Chief Big Foot had surrendered in 1890 to the U.S. Seventh Cavalry under a white flag of truce. We left the airport in five cars following the hearse. The trip took an hour and a half through the small towns of Scenic and Rocky Ford, on the edge of the Badlands. Tall rock spires reached up into the sky in variegated shades of pink, chalk white, and yellow. Once past the Badlands, the meadowlarks seemed to sing their names from the rolling hills of waving grass:

> *Tashia gnupa mia yelo.*
> *Tashia gnupa mia yelo.*
> (I am the meadowlark.)
> (I am the meadowlark.)[1]

As we neared Porcupine Butte, a group of mounted Big Foot Memorial Riders waited with an old green dray wagon pulled by two paint horses. Since 1986, during the anniversary of the Wounded Knee Massacre hundreds of Memorial Riders had braved unendurable winter temperatures of 70 degrees below zero, riding and walking the route Chief Big Foot and his band took on their last cold journey to Wounded Knee. Arvol Looking Horse had accompanied them hundreds of miles through icy wind and snow. And now, in the summer sun, Alex White Plume and others waited by the side of the road to take Lost Bird the final five miles home to Wounded Knee.

At Porcupine we stopped and got out of our cars. Someone brought Arvol's spirited horse to him and he was handed an eagle feather staff. He

swung up on the saddle and as he passed I looked up at him and saw victory in his face. He called for six Memorial Rider pallbearers. They dismounted and gently unloaded Lost Bird's plain coffin into the wagon.
Then Arvol raised the memorial staff at arm's length above him. The
sacred black-and-white eagle feathers quilled out in the wind. *"Hoka hey!"*
he called out. I watched as the nineteenth-generation Keeper of the
Sacred Calf Pipe, one of the greatest and most controversial spiritual leaders of the twentieth century, rode out alone in front of the wagon he would
lead to Wounded Knee. Behind the wagon rode the Memorial Riders, and
the rest of us followed slowly in cars.

Two small boys galloped by, one on a white horse with a long eagle
feather attached to his left arm above the elbow. The other boy, about
seven years old, rode bareback with his right arm held high in the air. He
was flying, he was happy, as much a part of the horse as its mane. The boys
galloped up the hills and plunged down—the higher the hill and the
steeper the descent, the better they liked it. They raced each other ahead,
but they never passed in front of the wagon, respectfully turning back to
challenge each other again, dashing up the next hill through grass as high
as their waists, dust from their ponies' hooves raising small clouds behind
them. They laughed and galloped and dared, aware of their incredible riding skills, an example of the proud future of the Lakota Nation.

I looked back and saw that the cortege of cars, pickups, and horse trail-
ers now stretched behind us for more than a mile, and there was no end of
the line in sight.

On the horizon in front of us were more men on horseback, with long,
flowing hair and colorful saddle blankets. As we passed, some rode down
from the hills and others waited by the side of the road to join the riders
behind the wagon for the slow journey. Young couples on horseback rode
double beside us. As I watched the riders, I was seized with a feeling of
great pride and respect.

Ahead was the final hill down into the valley of Wounded Knee Creek,
so long ago the scene of heartbreak and bloody death. In the distance we
could see the hill above Wounded Knee. I could hardly believe my eyes.
Many Lakota lined the road and stood around the mass grave at the top—
the elderly, children, and young couples, silhouettes against the sun. They
watched as the long caravan slowly winded its way toward them. All eyes
were on the wagon carrying Zintkala Nuni—their grandmother, their
aunt, their cousin, their Lost Bird. We parked our car and walked up the
hill to the grave, and by the time we got there, the Memorial Riders had
already placed the coffin on two logs over the open grave. Young men held
large bouquets of flowers nearby.

I was offended by newspaper reporters standing curiously by, and I was embarrassed at their lack of shame. One middle-aged Englishman, with a cumbersome camera hanging heavily around his neck, wore a safari suit and pith helmet. I shuddered. But another, Eric Harrison, an African-American, respectfully kept his distance from what he knew was a sacred ceremony.

At the grave, Avis Little Eagle remembered:

> The procession was greeted by Wounded Knee district chairman Pat Rowland, who said it was a happy occasion because Lost Bird came home to her people. He said community members would be caretakers of the gravesite along with members of the Big Foot Band.
>
> Claudia Iron Hawk, of the Pine Ridge Survivors Association, said it was a sad yet memorable day for the people. "Tunkanshila or Grandfather is looking down on us here," she said, "where one hundred years ago, after gold was discovered, our treaties were broken, and our people slaughtered under a white flag of truce . . ."
>
> Burdell Blue Arm, a member of the Cheyenne River Wounded Knee Survivors, sang a song. Alex White Plume of the Big Foot Riders spoke with deep emotion about the riders' five-year journey to strengthen the people: "What we have done is having a big impact all across Indian country. Our nation has realized we can't make a clear decision with an intoxicated mind. Through sobriety dances, sobriety rides, substance abuse programs, we will become strong again."
>
> Jim Garrett, with the Cheyenne River Big Foot Riders, said the people had to learn that "to bend doesn't mean to break, it means flexibility to survive . . . bend and continue to grow."
>
> Marie Not Help Him told the crowd, "Lost Bird has returned today to the same place she was taken from. This means a new beginning, a process of healing is completed. We can be proud to be a Lakota. To our sacred children, this means a beginning."[2]

As Arvol sang and prayed with the pipe, everywhere I looked I saw people crying. He told the people gathered, "Pray with me; we are all brothers and sisters." Then he sang the four-direction song, and on every verse the people turned in unison to the west, then to the north, to the east, and to the south. A man blew intense, high-pitched sounds through an eagle bone whistle. When the whistle blew, I looked over at Marie's daughter, Summer Thompson, holding up a large photograph of Lost Bird. I remembered the night before we left for California to get Lost Bird's remains, Summer had had a vivid dream: She was at Lost Bird's burial and there were many people standing around the grave. There were elderly men and women crying, and behind these old people were a multitude of ancient ones—spirits—many, many spirits of the ones who had died at Wounded Knee, surrounding the living. Then she knew it would be all right, because the spirits would be there with us to make us strong.

After prayers, men came forward with five young cherry trees. They dug holes and planted the trees around the open grave, and flags of red, black, white, and yellow cloth were tied to them. They attached a small eagle feather to the tree at the head of the grave. The wind came up and a large cloud hovered over, and sheltered us from the hot sun. Just seconds before the coffin was lowered into the grave, Arvol held up a photograph of a smiling woman seated at her desk wearing a feminine Victorian dress, a writing pen poised in her hand. "This is a photograph of Clara Bewick Colby, Lost Bird's adopted mother," Arvol explained. "We are going to put her picture into the grave with Lost Bird." I looked away, tears streaming down my face. They used ropes to lower the coffin. I looked up just as the lavender star quilt disappeared into the earth. A young man sang an honor song and an elderly woman stood tall and gave the trill for bravery, "Li-Li-Li-Li-Li!" Four men began to shovel dirt into the grave, and each load of earth landed with a resounding thump on the coffin below. Every few minutes, each shoveler gave his shovel to another, until twenty men had taken a loving turn filling in her grave. They finished off the mound and placed two large flower arrangements on top. Only one had a note attached. It said: "From the Tribal Chairman and Councilmen." Secured to the arrangement in large gold letters on a long, blood-red ribbon were the words "Lost Bird."

That night a prairie lightning storm kept me restlessly awake. Those of us camped at the bottom of the hill had to take cover in the strongest tents, and many spent the night in cars and pickup trucks.

The storm passed and the next morning dawned beautifully clear and bright. Arvol led a Releasing of the Spirit ceremony with traditional Lakota food offerings in two wooden bowls. He prayed for Zintkala Nuni, prayed that her spirit, tormented by a hundred years of pain, longing, and grief, would now find peace. There was a great tugging on my heart, and I knew she was going. I looked up at her grave and I imagined her spirit rising.

We had a "giveaway" ceremony afterward, with gifts for those who had helped make the return of Lost Bird possible. Marie presented Mrs. Roberts with a beaded white-doeskin pipebag with a small pipe and walnut stem inside. Arvol received a deerskin and two long coils of braided sweetgrass.

After the people had walked down the hill from the gravesite for the community meal in the valley below, I stayed a while longer. I couldn't let her go, even though I knew I had to. I watched Lost Bird's feather flutter-ing in the red-gold sunset, then I bent down and touched the grave, and felt Clara's spirit hovering around me.

"All these years you've been like my own daughter," I told Zintka. "I don't want to have that dream anymore, you sitting all sad on that carousel. You're home now with your people. Good-bye my good girl . . . sleep well." I stood up and reached out my hand to touch her eagle plume fluttering in the wind. My fingers were just inches from the feather when the feeling came to me that I knew it wasn't right to touch a sacred object on an Indian grave. I turned and walked down the hill to join the people at Wounded Knee Creek.

Author's Note

Leonard W. Colby was elected judge of the District Court of Gage and Jefferson counties in 1920. In the summer of 1924, during a strenuous campaign for reelection, Colby became ill and his Beatrice physician recommended that he be seen at once by physicians at the Mayo Clinic. He scoffed at the idea, but the pain became so intense that he went to Rochester, Minnesota, and secretly underwent an exploratory operation. Surgeons found an inoperable stomach tumor that had perforated his liver. After returning to Beatrice, Judge Colby found out that the Mayo Clinic had written his Beatrice physician with the results of the surgery. Colby was furious. He wrote scathing letters to the professionals concerned calling them liars. One of his Beatrice physicians wrote back to the Mayo Clinic explaining that the tirade was probably caused because ". . . the Judge is a candidate for reelection to the bench and . . . feels that if his friends in Beatrice knew his physical condition that he might not receive as much support at the polls as he otherwise would."

Colby's opponent, a man nearly eighty years old, was in good health, which meant that seventy-eight-year-old Colby used age as a campaign strategy, putting on a tremendous show of physical vigor during the campaign. During one outdoor rally on a particularly hot day, his opponent sat down and asked for a glass of water. Seizing the moment, which characterized Colby's entire career, from storming Mobile during the Civil War, to drinking poison to clear a client, to stealing an Indian baby so as to appear a hero, he leaped to the stage, pounded his chest and exclaimed, "My opponent can't take the heat! Elect the younger man!" after which he received a standing ovation. Colby won the election despite constant excruciating pain.

Judge Colby had access to all court records in Beatrice, and possibly with the help of his friend Fordyce Graff, then Register of Deeds, all legal papers pertaining to Zintka were destroyed except her adoption record. Leonard W. Colby did not know that Zintka had died in 1920, nor did he ever bother to find out what had become of her. He died November 15, 1924.

Maud Colby erected an elegant memorial to her late husband in the Beatrice cemetery. The plot was large enough for three graves, and at each corner of the section was embedded a metal marker with the initial "C." A stone bench situated in front of the long tablet detailing all of the general's accomplishments also had the letter "C" on each side.

Colby's widow then squandered all of his money on travel and luxuries. She also spent their son Paul's inheritance. In 1942, she was diagnosed with breast cancer but refused medical help until she was forced into a hospital by county health officials. Maud proved to be a difficult patient. She refused to be bathed, refused a bedpan, and defecated in her bed. Finally, her son Paul was asked to remove his mother from the hospital. He took her home and she died on June 10, 1942.

Paul had been raised to believe he was the son of Thomas Martinez. He attended school away from Beatrice most of his young life and General Colby had little to do with him. When he turned sixteen, Colby insisted Paul should study law, but Paul ran off and joined the Navy instead. He became a heavy drinker, bar fighter, and womanizer and rarely kept a job. After his mother died he was going through her belongings when he found his birth papers. Paul realized that he was Leonard Colby's illegitimate son. Raging against Maud in a drunken fury, he tore into his mother's apartment, threw her furniture into the river, and set her clothing and her personal papers on fire. A woman with him ran to the blaze and recovered the family Bible. She also saved a few pieces of his mother's crystal and jewelry, which Paul later gave to friends before he moved to Oregon. Ironically, he saved all of his father's personal belongings, including a rolltop desk, which he used for the rest of his life. While Maud was alive Paul had a bad reputation and was referred to as a "rounder" and a "good-for-nothing," but after she was gone he changed his life, became a good provider and a loving husband, father, and beloved grandfather. He died in 1965 and his son Wayne inherited the Colby collection.

Zintka's husband, Dick Allen, did not fare as well. After her death in 1920, he joined the Al G. Barnes Circus as a calliope player. In 1930 he clowned with the St. Louis Police Circus. Like so many others during the "Dirty Thirties," he found himself out of work. On May 1, 1937, he borrowed his sister's car to look for a job. In the early morning hours of May 2, he went to sleep in the car near a canal bank on the outskirts of Bakersfield, California. He was assaulted, was thrown or fell into the canal, and then was shot once with a .44 or .45 caliber revolver. Apparently, he tried to climb out of the water and was shot again, this time between the eyes. He was found lying on his back with his feet barely out of the water, his wallet missing. Because Dick had no known enemies, detectives blamed passing tramps for the robbery and murder. The investigation went on for some time and it is not known if the murder was ever solved.

Zintka's first child died at the Milford Industrial Home on April 22, 1908. Her third child, also a boy, died as an infant. His name, date of birth, and location of death are unknown. When Lost Bird was in destitute circumstances in California in 1916, she gave her second child, a boy named Clyde, to an Indian woman. He may yet be alive.

Notes

Abbreviations used in Notes:

SDSHS: South Dakota State Historical Society
SHSW: State Historical Society of Wisconsin
NSHS: Nebraska State Historical Society

PREFACE

1. Linda Roberts Rosene, "A Follow-up Study of Indian Children Adopted by White Families," Ph.D. dissertation, The Fielding Institute, 1983.
2. Ivan Star Comes Out, "The Aftermath of Cross-Cultural Adoption," *Lakota Times* (June 27, 1988). See also the *Denver Post* (April 30, 1993 [no title]): "The Indian suicide rate is four times the national rate."; "Indian Suicide Rate Is Highest," *Montana and the West* (July 6, 1994): "The report by the Health and Human Services Department also found the suicide rate for Indians ages fifteen to twenty-four was higher than for any other ethnic group."; Chuck Hawley, "Child Law Tries to Fathom Tribes," *The Arizona Republic* (April 23, 1988): "The American Academy of Child Psychiatry said in a 1975 report: Indians raised in non-Indian homes tend to have significant social problems in adolescence and adulthood."; Nancy Stancil, "The Baby-Market—The Business of Adoption—Permissive Laws—Big Bucks Make Texas Hot Spot," *The Houston Chronicle* (October 6, 1991).

PROLOGUE

1. Arvol Looking Horse is sometimes criticized by Indian people who believe he should remain at his home at Green Grass, S.D. and should not travel. Arvol says that teaching other nations about world peace is an important reason to travel. In the January 12, 1995 issue of *Indian Country Today,* Arvol says, "My life is not my own. There is a lot of sacrifice and suffering I must go through." (Article by Avis Little Eagle, "Memories of Wounded Knee Marked; Looking Horse to testify at international forum.")
2. Avis Little Eagle, *Lakota Times,* "The Legend of Lost Bird: A Journey to the Spirit World," July 17, 1991. Avis is now managing editor for *Indian Country Today* in Rapid City, South Dakota. The *Lakota Times* changed its name to *Indian Country Today* in October 1992.

1. THE MASSACRE AT WOUNDED KNEE

1. Robert M. Utley, "Guns at Wounded Knee," in the *Westerner's Brand Books,* vol. 15, 71–72.
2. Alice Ghost Horse manuscript. This is the only known Hohwoju Lakota translation of the medicine man's prayer. This refutes the testimony of Philip Wells, whose unreliable interpreting skills are well documented. Philip Wells was a quarter-blood Dakota who spoke in a different dialect than the Hohwoju. He was in a state of panic when he interpreted the prayer and later during investigations he may have had ulterior motives for translating the prayer incorrectly to save himself and Colonel James Forsyth from further prosecution for the atrocities committed at Wounded Knee. Courtesy of Goldie Iron Hawk; see also Merrill J. Mattes, "The Enigma of Wounded Knee," *Plains Anthropologist,* vol. 5, no. 9 (May 1960). He states, "If indeed there was a harangue and a dust-throwing, it must have been an invocation for supernatural aid, which was misunderstood or

distorted by the interpreter (Wells)." Alice Ghost Horse/Kills The Enemy/War Bonnet was born in 1878 and died in 1950. She was thirteen years old at the time of the Wounded Knee Massacre. She escaped with her mother, Alice Her Shawl, and a younger brother aged nine.

Before she died, Alice told her story to her son John War Bonnet. John wrote it down in an old ledger book. The faded pages were passed down to Bill War Bonnet and finally to Goldie Iron Hawk. In 1979 Ms. Iron Hawk allowed Sidney Keith, a Lakota language instructor at Oglala Lakota College, to translate Alice's story into English. Mr. Keith spent two years interviewing elders in order to translate the old Hohwoju dialect. In describing this work he said, "This story sounds horrible as it is written in the Lakota language. White men's words cannot express what she is explaining."

The proper title for the manuscript is "The True Story of What Happened at Wounded Knee (in South Dakota) in December 1890," by Alice Ghost Horse, courtesy of Goldie Iron Hawk.

3. Testimony of Colonel James W. Forsyth in court of inquiry. Wounded Knee File #188, National Archives, Record Group 75, Washington, D.C. See also letter from Colonel James W. Forsyth to Acting Assistant Adjutant General, December 31, 1890, on page 149 of Hearings Before the Committee on the Judiciary, United States Senate, 94th Cong., 2d sess., 1976, S 1147 and S 2900—To Liquidate the Liability of the United States for the Massacre of Sioux Indian Men, Women, and Children at Wounded Knee (February 6, 7, 1976), Government Printing Office, Washington, D.C.

4. *Omaha Bee* (December 8, 1890); see also, "Effect of the Recent Conference," *Yankton Press and Dakotan* (December 11, 1890). Newspaper article cited "one of the striking instances" of mistranslation. "At one time when during the council, Chief Red Willow said to the general, '. . . I was a boy, now I am a man, and have come to listen to you,' Philip Wells translated these words to government agents present. What Red Willow actually said was, 'I am a full-fledged warrior ready to fight you anywhere! What have you got to say about it, anyhow?'"

5. Letters from James McLaughlin to Philip F. Wells, July and August 1884; see James McLaughlin Papers #655, roll 20. Microfilm available from Assumption Abbey Archives, Richardton, N.D.; see also Judge Eli Ricker Collection, interview with Philip F. Wells, series 2, tablet 3-5, Nebraska State Historical Society.

6. Philip F. Wells, "Ninety-six Years Among the Indians of the Northwest: Adventures and Reminiscences of an Indian Scout and Interpreter in the Dakotas," in *North Dakota History*, vol. 15 (January-October, 1948), 279, State Historical Society of North Dakota, Bismarck, N.D.

7. Robert M. Utley, *The Last Days of the Sioux Nation* (New Haven: Yale University Press, 1963), 196.

8. Judge Eli S. Ricker Collection, Nebraska State Historical Society, interview with Joseph Horn Cloud, October 23, 1906; see also *Nebraska History*, vol. 62, no. 2 (Summer 1981), 172.

9. *Nebraska History*, vol. 62, no. 2 (Summer 1981), 172.

10. Ibid., 193.

11. Ibid., 173, 193.

12. Ibid., 192.

13. Ibid., 193

14. Utley, 212; see also Frederic Remington, "The Sioux Outbreak in South Dakota," *Harper's Weekly* (January 24, 1891).

15. Ibid.

16. Alice Ghost Horse manuscript, courtesy of Goldie Iron Hawk.

17. Ibid.

18. Holy Rosary Mission Records, series 7, box 13, folder 6, letter from John Jutz, S.J., entitled "Historic Data on the Causes of Dissatisfaction Among the Sioux Indians in 1890," Marquette University Archives.

19. Passim, Donald E. Carr, *The Forgotten Senses* (Garden City, N.Y.: Doubleday and Company, 1972).

20. John G. Neihardt, *Black Elk Speaks: Being a Life Story of a Holy Man of the Oglala Sioux* (New York: Morrow, 1932), 6.

21. Curtis, Natalie, *The Indian's Book* (New York: Harper and Row Publishers, Bonanza Books, 1935), 45.

22. According to Dr. Martin BrokenLeg, Lakota scholar, an extended family or tiospaye, can mean as many as 300 people. Interview with Dr. BrokenLeg, Augustana College, Sioux Falls, S.D. 1992.

23. Alice Ghost Horse manuscript, courtesy of Goldie Iron Hawk.

24. "Indians Who Read," *Daily Capital Journal*, Pierre, S.D. (November 1890). Exact date illegible on original; see also "Indians Read," *Boston Morning Journal* (January 31, 1891).

25. Ella C. Deloria, *Waterlily* (Lincoln: University of Nebraska Press, 1988), 41.

26. Alice Ghost Horse manuscript, courtesy of Goldie Iron Hawk.
27. Unpublished manuscript entitled "The Arrest and Killing of Sitting Bull," told by John Loneman, one of the Indian police ordered to arrest the chief; see Walter S. Campbell (Stanley Vestal) papers, the Western History Collections, University of Oklahoma, Norman.
28. Alice Ghost Horse manuscript, courtesy of Goldie Iron Hawk.
29. Marie Not Help Him, in interview recounting Dewey Beard Story, July 1990.
30. Ibid., Marie Not Help Him.
31. Alice Ghost Horse manuscript, courtesy of Goldie Iron Hawk.
32. "Someone smuggled a ten-gallon keg of whiskey into the soldier's camp and by the next day had consumed the greater part of this whiskey," George E. Bartlett said in an interview for an article, "Babe Survives Fierce Battle," Salt Lake Herald (January 2, 1903). Bartlett says about the massacre at Wounded Knee: "The matter was hushed up as much as possible, and the world was given an account of the battle . . . as it did not occur." See also Robert M. Utley, The Last Days of the Sioux Nation, 199; Judge Eli Ricker collection, Nebraska History, vol. 62, no. 2 (Summer 1981), 222.
33. The Association of the Graduates of the United States Military Academy Annual Report (June 12, 1917), 111. William Wallace Robinson, Jr., letter from GPT. George Eaton, instructor, Department of History, West Point, to author (April 11, 1991). "Robinson was transferred to 7 Cav. on 26 June (the day after the battle)."
34. Robert M. Utley, The Last Days of the Sioux Nation, 199.
35. Judge Eli Ricker collection, Nebraska History, vol. 62, no. 2, 222.
36. Unpublished manuscript of Hobart Keith. Elaine Melior collection, Spokane, Wash.
37. Wounded Knee Memorial and Historic Site, Little Big Horn National Monument Battlefield, S. HRG.101-1184, Hearing Before the Select Committee on Indian Affairs, United States Senate 101st Cong., 2nd sess.—To Establish Wounded Knee Memorial and Historic Site and Proposal to Establish Monument Commemorating Indian Participants of the Little Big Horn and to Redesignate Name of Monument from Custer Battlefield to Little Big Horn National Monument Battlefield (September 25, 1990), Washington D.C., U.S. Government Printing Office, 78, statement of Celene (Beard) Not Help Him, descendant of Wounded Knee survivor.
38. Ibid., 79.
39. Alice Ghost Horse manuscript, courtesy of Goldie Iron Hawk.
40. J. W. Powell, Fourteenth Annual Report of the Bureau of Ethnology, 1892–93, Part 2, 54th Cong., 2nd Sess. House of Representatives, doc. no. 230, "The Ghost-Dance Religion and the Sioux Outbreak of 1890" by James Mooney, 1069. Portion of a Ghost Dance song was "composed by a woman, who had evidently met her dead child in the spirit world."
41. Alice Ghost Horse manuscript, courtesy of Goldie Iron Hawk.
42. Nebraska History, summer 1981, vol. 62, no. 2, 172, Judge Eli Ricker interviews Joseph Horn Cloud, Oct. 23, 1906 in article entitled "The Wounded Knee Interviews of Eli S. Ricker," edited by Donald F. Danker.
43. Henry Davenport Northrup, Indian Horrors or Massacres by the Red Men (Philadelphia: National Publishing Company, 1891), 549–50. Account of a private in the Seventh Cavalry written from Pine Ridge to his brother in Philadelphia. Also Elaine Goodale Eastman, "The Ghost Dance and Wounded Knee 1890–91," Nebraska History, vol. 26, 1945, 26–42. Also Kent-Baldwin Report, Record Group 393, Military Division of the Missouri, Letters Received 1891, Box 126–127. Also C. G. Seymour and J. C. Gresham, Harper's Weekly, vol. 35 (February 7, 1891), 106–109.
44. Northrup. Letter from Private Eugene Caldwell to his father and mother in Philadelphia, 542–45.
45. Robert M. Utley, The Last Days of the Sioux Nation, 221–22; see W. F. Beyer and O. F. Keydel (eds.), Deeds of Valor (Detroit: 1907), vol. 2, 316; see also Harry L. Hawthorne, "The Sioux Campaign of 1890–91," Journal of the Military Service Institution of the United States, 29 (1896), 185–87.
46. Medal of Honor Recipients 1863–1978, 96th Cong., 1st Sess., 1979, Senate Committee Print No. 3, prepared by the Committee on Veterans Affairs, United States Senate (February 14, 1979).
47. The Wounded Knee interviews of Eli S. Ricker, edited by Donald F. Danker, in Nebraska State Historical Society, vol. 62, no. 2, summer 1981, 195.
48. Testimony of Lieutenant Sedgwick Rice, 2nd Lt., Seventh Cavalry, Troop E, for the Subcommittee of Indian Affairs, House of Representatives, 124, Wounded Knee Investigation Report #188, National Archives, Record Group 75, 124. Hearings before the Committee on the Judiciary, U.S. Senate, 94th Congress, 2nd session on S 1147 and S 2900—to liquidate the liability of the United States for the massacre of Sioux men, women, and children at Wounded Knee. February 6–7, 1976, Government Printing Office, Washington, D.C.

49. Alice Ghost Horse manuscript, courtesy of Goldie Iron Hawk.
50. J. W. Powell, Fourteenth Annual Report of the Bureau of Ethnology, 1892–93, Part 2, 54th Cong., 2nd sess., 1890, House of Representatives, doc. no. 230, "The Ghost Dance Religion and the Sioux Outbreak of 1890," by James Mooney, 1073.
51. Alice Ghost Horse manuscript, courtesy of Goldie Iron Hawk.
52. Ibid.
53. Ibid. This was the camp of Short Bull. He warmly greeted the survivors, fed, and clothed them.
54. "Horrors of the Frontier," *Sunday Indianapolis Sentinel* (February 8, 1891). See also Wounded Knee Special Investigation Report #188, National Archives, Record Group 75.
55. Letter from Captain Frank D. Baldwin to the Assistant Adjutant General, Headquarters Division of the Missouri, Pine Ridge, S.D., 140, of Hearings Before the Committee on the United States Senate, 94th Cong., 2nd Sess., 1976, S 1147 and S 2900—To Liquidate the Liability of the United States for the Massacre of Sioux Indian Men, Women, and Children at Wounded Knee (February 5, 6, 1976), Government Printing Office, Washington, D.C.
56. Charles W. Allen interview with Eli Ricker, Aug 21, 1907, 227, *Nebraska History*, summer 1981, vol. 62, no. 2. A Lieutenant snatched a gun from the hands of a soldier and shot her in the back as she ran to her father.
57. Hearing before the Select Committee on Indian Affairs, United States Senate, 101st Congress, 2nd Sess., 1991, S. HRG. 101–1184 (September 25, 1990), Washington, D.C. Dora High Whiteman made a tape recording of her remembrances of Wounded Knee prior to her death on June 16, 1964, at the age of eighty-three. It is translated by Marie Not Help Him. Spotted Elk was Chief Big Foot's name.
58. Testimony from Dr. Charles A. Eastman. See Wounded Knee Special Investigation Report #188, National Archives, Record Group 75.

2. THE LOST BIRD

1. Two 1990 interviews with Sam Eaglestaff, a member of the Cheyenne River Sioux tribe and president of the Cheyenne River Wounded Knee Survivors Association. He was also a tribal councilman. Mr. Eaglestaff, along with tribal Attorney General Steve Emery, a graduate of Harvard Law School, obtained Lost Bird's official tribal records.
2. John G. Neihardt, *Black Elk Speaks: Being the Life Story of a Holy Man of the Oglala Sioux* (Lincoln: University of Nebraska Press, 1961), 270. Black Elk was twenty-seven years old in December 1890. He became furious after seeing the bodies of women and children after the massacre. On the day following the massacre, Black Elk was badly wounded in the abdomen during the Drexel Mission Fight, but he survived.
3. Ibid., 262.
4. The name of the creek where White Eyes and her band camped for the night has not survived in the oral Lakota tradition. The area between French Creek and Battle Creek is the probable location of the Buffalo Gap Ambush. The Lakota refer to the ambush as Buffalo Gap, which points to the origin of the hostility, not the location of the ambush. From numerous newspaper accounts, the date of the massacre was December 10, 1890. There was no mention of children killed in the attack, and the name of the rancher at Buffalo Gap is not remembered.
   Big Foot's main village was located on the south side of the Belle Fourche and Cheyenne rivers. White Eyes was living in a cabin, not a tipi, in Big Foot's village. Her journey back to her village and then to Wounded Knee Creek may be estimated at more than 250 miles, covering a period of approximately twenty-two days. She was a young woman familiar with the terrain, and except for the last days of her ordeal, the weather was unseasonably mild compared to other years. From late December until the end of March 1891, colder and often frigid temperatures prevailed.
5. Letter to the Hon. Commissioner of Indian Affairs, from Agent Perain P. Palmer at Cheyenne River Agency (March 2, 1891), National Archives (hereinafter NA), Record Group (hereinafter RG) 75, Special Report #188, Reel 1; also interview with Oliver Bradford (August 24, 1990), Rapid City, S.D. Bradford's uncle, Everett J. Bradford, and grandfather, Esra James Bradford, were hired by a couple of ranchers to watch several ranches while the men were riding with the Home Guard. They witnessed "white renegades" raiding and looting ranches. These depredations were blamed on the Ghost Dancers. The so-called "Indian depredations" were later paid by the United States Government.
   Also: Bert L. Hall, "Old Cowboy Blames Cattlemen for Scare," in *Roundup Years: Old Muddy to*

Black Hills (Pierre, S.D.: The Reminder, Inc., 1954), 51. "Robert Davis, an old-time cowboy, said, 'Big cattle operators were to blame for the historic Indian Scare of 1890.' Davis recalls that the cattlemen . . . were considerably upset by the ever-increasing number of settlers who were breaking . . . up range land.' He said, 'The cattlemen tried to scare the settlers out . . .' " This interview originally appeared in the *Rapid City Daily Journal* (December 7, 1952). See Don Huls, *The Winter of 1890: What Happened at Wounded Knee* (Chadron, Nebraska: *The Chadron Record*, 1974), 76; see also Herbert S. Schell, *History of South Dakota* (Lincoln: University of Nebraska Press, 1961), 326–328.

6. The oral traditional remembrance of the Buffalo Gap Ambush on December 10, 1890, came from interviews in 1990–93 with Victoria Siers, Verna Hultgren, Linda and Marty Two Bulls, and Richard Garnier. Josephine Rooks, or Goes After Her Horses, was interviewed at a nursing home in Martin, S.D., on November 15, 1990, and again on January 3, 1991. Marie Not Help Him provided invaluable advice and Lakota language interpretation; see also *Omaha Morning Bee,* which published a story written on December 9, 1890: "At daylight tomorrow morning [Dec. 10] a large party of armed cowboys will leave Buffalo [Gap] and will kill and capture what Indian hostiles they may find"; also "A Battle Possible" in *Yankton Press and Dakotan* (December 10, 1890); also "Warlike Preparations" in *Omaha Morning Bee* (December 11, 1890): "No word has been received up to this hour from the party of armed ranchers and cowboys who went out to defend the outlying ranches and to punish the depredating Sioux"; also *Rapid City Journal* (December 13, 1890): "General Carr had received a dispatch stating that ever so many Indians and whites had been killed in the ensanguined encounter."

7. Passim, Margaret Lemley Warren, *The Badlands Fox,* edited by Renee Sansom Flood (Rapid City, S.D.: Fenske Printing, 1991).

8. "Rapid City to Organize," *Rapid City Journal* (December 5, 1890).

9. Clipping entitled "The Governor Half Starved—South Dakota hunters lose their way and wander several days without food," Governor Arthur C. Mellette Papers, 1890–91 correspondence, University of South Dakota Archives, Vermillion, S.D.

10. J. B. McCloud Papers, #H76-15, Box 3664A, South Dakota State Historical Society, Pierre, S.D.; see also The Wounded Knee Survivors Association Archives, Claudia Iron Hawk Sully of Wounded Knee, President, and Marie Not Help Him, Secretary, Pine Ridge, S.D. The following is a signed, notarized list of men who were members of Colonel M. H. Day's Home Guard in December 1890: Dan Galligher, William F. McClelland, Paul McClelland, Francis M. Roush, Royal E. Coats, Harvey Reynolds, Thomas Roush, John Wilson, A. W. Hollenbeck, Frank Kelley, John Gilpin, Daniel N. Phinney, Halley G. Wise, John Haley, Jr., John McCrea, Arthur N. Smith, La Grange Fowler, William Cromwell, Sam Twining, Frank Stanton, Frank Spring, R. B. Carter, Fred Simpson, B. J. Williams, Pinkney Ayers, Ed Ayers, P. F. McMahan, James Bothwell, James Furgason, J. B. McCloud, Gene Akin, Frawley Sprague, H. S. Sprague, Joe Burkenbine, Dave Simpson, W. L. Hughes, E. Elliott, D. W. House, George M. Tarbox, W. A. Brisbine, Pete Richards, Nelse Torkelson, G. A. Bartholomew, M. Kelley, Frank Graham, Fred Graves, Uriah Shott, Chester Mills, Paul Geary, Charley McCrory, Joseph W. Bobier, Orin Surlock, Burton V. Robertson, C. W. Gorsuch, Jr., William T. Gorsuch, Perry Cox, Allen Cox, Ernest Johnsandt, J. R. Bobier, John H. Bobier, Arnel Hernard, Bob Beatty, Evert Allen, William Shorter, S. Davis, A. C. Toute, John Burl, George G. Cosgrove, J. W. Craft, Thomas Thompson, George W. Wilson, Ed Peterson, George B. Hyde, John Belson, Frank J. Blacknich, Levi Martial Hoisington, Harry Watkins, Harry M. Shearn, Lewis J. Ervin, L. Parnick, Frank Lockhart, Riley Miller, Will Arbuckle, Charles Smith, George F. Frink, William C. Fay, William J. Rogers, J. H. Boyden, Frank Golhan, G. H. Sanders, J. B. Chase, H. A. Stevens, E. L. Keyes, C. G. Parrish, Harry Hall, Al Smith, and D. O. Chase; for information about individuals on this list, see *Our Yesterdays,* compiled by the Eastern Custer County Historical Society (Marceline, Missouri: Pischel Yearbooks, Inc., 1970).

11. South Dakota State Historical Collection, vol. 6, 1912, 426; for Mellette's involvement in war buildup, see *Rapid City Journal* (December 5, 1890); for history of Mellette's terms as governor, see S.D. Historical Collections and *South Dakota Magazine* (September 1985), 14–18; see also *Historical Society Quarterly,* vol. 19, no. 1 (Spring 1989).

12. "The Indian Situation," *Rapid City Journal* (December 17, 1890); see also "The Indian Problem" (December 18, 1890).

13. "The Indian Problem," *Rapid City Journal* (December 18, 1890). For biography of John Richard Brennan, see George W. Kingsbury, *History of Dakota Territory, South Dakota, Its History and Its People* (Chicago: S. J. Clarke Publishing Company, 1915), 1162–1164. John R. Brennan was born in Kilkenny, Ireland on May 22, 1848. "He was brought to America at the age of three and was educated in various schools, choosing the hotel business as his profession. He came to the Black

Hills in November 1875, and was one of the founders of Rapid City. He was prominent in civic affairs, serving as president of the first city council, first postmaster and Board President of the Dakota School of Mines. He built The American House Hotel and later the Harney Hotel. He was a large stockholder in the First National Bank of Rapid City and served as its vice president in the 1890s. He was also first Superintendent of Schools of Pennington County, Chief of the Rapid City Fire Department and President of the Black Hills Firemen's Association. On November 1, 1900, he became U.S. Indian Agent, superintendent, and special disbursing agent for the Pine Ridge Indian Reservation, a position he held for many years. At one time he had as many as seven thousand Oglala Lakota under his charge." As a pillar in his community and a strong Catholic, Brennan nonetheless thought an Indian scalp a prized trophy in December of 1890. The *Rapid City Journal* (December 17, 1890) reports that Brennan wrote a note to the newspaper telling of the killing of Dead Arm at the Cole Ranch: "They are keeping the body at the ranch so that all the neighbors and Indian fighters can gaze on a good Indian." The *Rapid City Journal*'s "News from the Cheyenne" stated on December 18, 1890, that the nephew of Kicking Bear was shot in the left temple and that Brennan secured his scalp for Tom Sweeney (an Indian artifact collector and store owner in Rapid City).

14. Ibid., and *Hermosa Pilot* (December 19, 1890).
15. Ibid. The Home Guard Militia also called themselves the Big Flat Guards and the Mountain Rangers.
16. J. B. McCloud Papers, #H76–15, Box 3664A, South Dakota State Historical Society, Pierre, S.D.
17. Ibid. See also South Dakota Oral History Project #018, interview with Dr. Ray Lemley (March 24, 1970). During this interview Dr. Lemley says, "They scalped those Indians." See also interview with Archie Cosgrove #969 (July 20, 1973). Mr. Cosgrove's father, Captain George Cosgrove, was under Colonel Day during the militia raids. Interview states that George Cosgrove's wife "burned several Indian scalps Father had possibly from the fight at the ranch near the Cheyenne River." See also interview with Oliver Bradford (August 24, 1990), who remembered seeing several scalps in a trunk owned by Smokey Thomas. Smokey may be Thomas Thompson, a member of the militia.
18. J. B. McCloud Papers, #H76–15, Box 3664A, South Dakota State Historical Society, Pierre, S.D. Dead Arm was identified by Dr. Valentine McGillycuddy as a nephew of Kicking Bear and close relative of Sitting Bull. It is therefore likely that Kicking Bear family members were among the singers; see "Sioux on the Warpath," *The Illustrated American* (January 10, 1891), 269; "Sitting Bull's death has not caused the excitement that the shooting of the young man by the cowboys has"; for documentation on Warren Cole's Store, see *The Late Military Invasion of the Home of the Sioux*, edited by T. A. Bland (Washington, D.C.: National Indian Defense Association, 1891), 9: "A party of young men from [Chief] Two Strike's camp visited a trader's store on the Cheyenne River, where some cowboys fired on them, killing one of their number. This had a bad effect."
19. Interview with Pete Lemley (February 12, 1959), number 542. American Indian Research Project, South Dakota Oral History Center, University of South Dakota, Vermillion.
20. Ibid.
21. Ibid.
22. Ibid. See also "Indian Battles Galore," *Hermosa Pilot* (December 19, 1890): "On Tuesday eight of the big flat guards went across the river looking for some stolen horses, and as might be expected, ran across some Indians and got into a little scrap with them. About sixty Indians came pell mell after the men, shooting as they came. The men got out of the way as rapidly as possible, but kept up a pretty steady fire . . . and report says there were some Indians sent to the happy hunting ground upon this occasion. See also *Omaha Morning Bee* (December 19, 1890): "The opinion is freely expressed here among ranchmen that many Indians have bit the dust during the past week."
23. The approximate location of the Home Guard Ambush is Quad Heutmacher Table-T4, south range 12E, Section 17, SW 1/4 Section 8, SE 1/4 Section 7. The Big Corral Draw rises between Cuny Table (the Stronghold) and Goat Ridge extending northwest and opens onto the Cheyenne River. The Little Corral Draw is twelve miles from the Big Corral Draw, across a flat. The Little Corral Draw is located southwest of Heutmacher Table. According to Dr. Ray Lemley, the location of the Home Guard Ambush: ". . . There's some evergreens on a Butte there between Little Corral Draw and Big Corral Draw just southwest of Heutmacher Table, about three miles . . . right by the butte . . ."
24. Pete Lemley interview, SDOHC, AIRP #542.
25. *Rapid City Journal* (December 31, 1890).
26. Ranchers wasted no time putting in for so-called Indian depredation claims. By December 19, 1890, the *Hermosa Pilot* reported: "Since it is known to be a fact that thousands of dollars worth of

stock and other property have been stolen by the Sioux Indians recently, it seems to us that it would be a wise plan for this congress to authorize the appointment of a commission whose duty it shall be to make a thorough canvass and inventory of all property so destroyed, and to make an estimate of such loss. This should be done in justice to the settlers whom the government has invited to free homes, many of whom have lost nearly all they possessed at the hands of the villainous Sioux. . . . We hope South Dakota representatives will take action upon the matter at once, as it is of vital importance to a goodly number of their constituency in this section of the state." A bill asking for the adjudication and payment of Indian depredation claims was submitted to Congress shortly thereafter. Articles appeared in the *Yankton Press and Dakotan* on January 12, 1891, and January 28, 1891. On January 23, 1891: "A good many people on the Nebraska and Dakota frontiers are sending to Washington their claims against the government for losses incurred as a result of the Indian outbreak. They are calling for immediate action upon them, which is not possible until Congress shall make provision for their payment. The general government is . . . liable for every dollar of loss that can be traced to the action of the Indians. This statement applies not only to property stolen and destroyed by the redskins, but also to stock that may have been lost as a result of the panic caused by the uprising. The government must also return to the states money expended by them in defending their citizens." The number and amount of depredation claims submitted by the settlers was so large, including thousands of cattle, that an investigation was called. South Dakota Senator Moody introduced the bill and worked tirelessly on it for a year. After the claims were paid, the Assistant Attorney General of the United States, General Leonard Wright Colby, testified, "I believe most of these depredations were depredations of white men; that they took advantage of those troubles to steal cattle and take them off and charge it up to the Indians." For this quote see U.S. Congressional Hearings Supplement (SS 52B) Select Committee on Indian Depredations, 1893, 25–26 (February 7–8, 1893). Microfiche available from the Edmun Low Library Microform Archives, Oklahoma State University, Stillwater, Okla.

27. Merritt H. Day was born at Markasan, Green Lake County, Wisconsin, in 1844. He served in Company I, Eleventh Infantry Regiment, Wisconsin Volunteers, during the Civil War. Day was described on muster roll as a farmer having light hair, light complexion, and a height of five feet four inches at age eighteen on October 12, 1861. He was absent due to sickness several times and was wounded May 1, 1863. He was promoted to corporal June 15, 1863, but in October was reduced in rank to private. In 1865 he was again promoted to corporal and was ordered, under General Order 33, to remain in Alabama. Day was mustered out on September 4, 1865. He first shows up in South Dakota in the early 1870s as a freighter and Indian trader in Brule County. By 1879 he was living in Springfield, Dakota Territory. There he met Arthur C. Mellette, who later became the first governor of the state of South Dakota. See Official Records of the Union and Confederate Armies in the War of the Rebellion (Washington: Government Printing Office, 1901); see also *Rapid City Journal* (November 3, 1901); see also L. G. Ochsenreiter, *History of Day County from 1873 to 1926* (Mitchell, S.D.: Educator Supply Company, 1975), 34. Day moved to the Black Hills in 1880 with his wife and three children. He served in the upper house of the Legislature in 1878, and from 1884 to 1888 was the national Democratic chairman for Dakota Territory. See also Eka Parkinson, *Rapid City Pioneers of the Nineteenth Century* (Rapid City: Rapid City Society For Genealogical Research, 1989), entry 57. See also *Yankton Press and Dakotan* (January 1891–April 1891) for embezzlement charges against Day. He disappeared with funds allocated for the Home Guard in December 1890. He had in fact gone to Chicago, where he blamed missionaries for the Wounded Knee Massacre (*Yankton Press and Dakotan,* January 9, 1891). It is interesting to note that Riley Miller, Day's sharpshooter, was also in Chicago at the same time, setting up the Kohl and Middleton Museum exhibit, which contained hundreds of Indian artifacts taken from murdered Lakota during the Home Guard attacks, including fresh scalps. See *Rapid City Republican* (March 5, 1891). Few of the hundreds of rifles allocated for the use of the Home Guard were ever recovered. Governor Mellette then came under heavy criticism for allowing Day access to state monies. During the investigation, the February 18, 1991, *Yankton Press and Dakotan* reported that Colonel Day was denounced in the State Legislature by Representative Harrison, saying, "I believe this man Day to be a common swindler; that his reputation in Pennington County, in Bon Homme County, in Douglas County and other parts of the state is the same." The investigation continued as Governor Mellette wired Colonel Day in Chicago that he should return immediately to South Dakota, as he was on the verge of an indictment. Day finally responded to Governor Mellette's worried telegrams on March 3, 1891: "Leave for Pierre this morning. Hold everything until I arrive."

On March 4, Day showed up in Pierre as mysteriously as he had left. By March 5, Day had paid off his debt and was exonerated in the local newspapers (see *Rapid City Journal,* March 4–5, 1891). On March 12, 1891, the *Rapid City Journal* reports that Day was talking about yet another threatened Indian uprising at Pine Ridge, saying the Sioux were planning to attack when "the grass is green." This time, his attempts to cause trouble were ignored. Governor Mellette continued doing business with Colonel Day, as his correspondence includes a letter from Colonel Day written from New York on March 2, 1892: "I am now closing out a big RR deal that will give you bbl [bundle?] of money."

During the last years of his life, Merritt H. Day invested heavily in two gold mines, the Gilt Edge Mine and the Specie Payment Gold Mining Company. (For Mellette-Day letters see Arthur C. Mellette Collection, #H74.188, Correspondence File, 1890–91, and Miscellaneous File, University of South Dakota Archives, Vermillion, S.D.); see also John Brennan Papers, Scrapbook 5–932, Department of the Interior, United States Indian Service, SDSHS: letter from Sen. D. H. Clark, February 26, 1891, to John Brennan regarding Mellette's anger that Colonel Day had not returned to South Dakota to face charges. He reports that if Day does not return, Mellette "would authorize the Attorney General to commence proceedings against him. . . . [H]e had enough of Day. . . ."

28. Miller worked as a meat hunter for mining camps in the Black Hills. See "Riley Miller Killed 56 Antelope," *Rapid City Journal* (November 12, 1886); "Riley Miller Killed Bald Eagle for Dealer," *Rapid City Journal* (November 22, 1889); "Killed 53 Deer," *Rapid City Journal* (November 23, 1888); "Returned from Powder River-Riley Miller Killed 64 Deer and 16 Grey Wolves," *Rapid City Journal* (November 15, 1895).

29. Nebraska State Historical Society, Lincoln. Charles D. Bristol (stage name "Omaha Charlie"). Letter to author from Gail DeBuse Potter, Museum Collections Director at NSHS (March 16, 1991): "In 1906 Bristol loaned his entire collection to the Nebraska State Historical Society and in 1935 the collection was purchased by the Historical Society. Since 1906 various portions of the collection have been displayed and several objects are currently on display at the Museum of Nebraska History."

30. Ibid. The Bristol collection includes posters showing the mummified child. It is unknown whether the historical society still has the mummified remains.

31. The following information comes from the Riley Miller Collection, owned by Miller's great-grandson, Jim Ross. On September 21, 1977, Ada Miller Adams, Riley's daughter, wrote about her father for her family records called "What I Remember About My Father, Riley Miller": "As a small child I recall he was seldom at home. We lived on a ranch near Rapid City, S. Dak. My two older brothers run the ranch & (with my Mother's help) raised his 8 children. He did no work or in any way contributed to their support. To me, as a child, he was more like a 'Santa Claus,' as he would bring me little gifts & some times write a letter to me. I still have one written in 1894. Some where along the line, he became a Captain in some Indian War, but I do not know where or when. And there, from the Battlefield, he gathered a large collection of Indian Relics. He brought them home once so we all saw them. With these he joined the Cody show & was known as Capt. Riley Miller. Cody is buried on Lookout Mt. just outside Denver, Colo. & a small museum where I found a group picture and recognized my father in it. Thru the years he traveled far and wide & often we did not know where he was. When I was 9 yrs. old was the last time I saw him. He came by the ranch & stopped for about 20 min. to tell my Mother & me that he was on his way to Alaska to make a lot of money. He always had some get rich quick scheme, but they never came out that way. We knew he only had one lung when he started & were surprised to learn he was one, of only a few, who made it thru the Chilicoot Pass. You already have the data on his death. To go back to the War days. I remember very well a picture he showed us of the Andersonville Prison & described the horrors of his stay there. Said when they were releasing a small group, he crawled on the ground, along side the others, & slipped thru without them seeing him. He was more dead than alive when he escaped. In one Affidavit you sent I recognized his handwriting. He wrote a beautiful hand, & when he was home he would write calling cards for the neighbors. He was a wonderful artist. When on hunting trips he would make a pencil sketch of things he would see, then come back & make a painting of it." Riley Miller died in Valdez, Alaska, in 1899.

32. South Dakota Historical Collections, vol. 6, 1912; see also House Executive Documents, vol. 2, 1st Cong., 1891–92, Report of the Secretary of War 1891, 180: "There had been since April, 1890, two troops, A and B of the Eighth Cavalry, from the garrison of Fort Meade, South Dakota, Capt. Almond B. Wells, Eighth Cavalry, commanding, in camp at Oelrichs, South Dakota, a short distance west of the Cheyenne Indians of the Pine Ridge Reservation . . ."

33. Frederic Remington, "Lieutenant Casey's Last Scout," *Harper's Weekly* (January 31, 1891). Lieutenant Joseph Charles Byron saw brief action in the Spanish-American War and was wounded at Hormiqueros, Puerto Rico, on August 10, 1898. He later joined the China Relief Expedition where he was promoted to Major during the Boxer Uprising. He resigned from active military service in 1902 and became a lawyer in Williamsport, Maryland. He became a pillar in his community, served as president of the county school board and served on the YMCA committee. During World War I he worked on the Council of National Defense in Washington and became the chairman of the War Industries Board. Interestingly, at the same time he maintained a large leather company whose major purchaser was the United States Army. After fifteen years he was awarded the Distinguished Service Medal. This gained him promotion to the rank of colonel. In later life he went into banking and trust companies, and when he died on February 5, 1932, at Hagerstown, Maryland, he was one of two honorary members of the Hagerstown Rotary Club. They claimed "his life exemplified their motto of 'Service Above Self.'" See the United States Military Academy Association of Graduates in the Annual Reunion 1932, United States Military Academy Library, West Point, N.Y.; see also House Documents, vol. 97, number 446, and Historical Register and Dictionary of Army, 17-89-1903, vol. 2, 57th Cong., 2nd Sess., 1902–1903.

34. Ibid.

35. Ed Lemmon, *Boss Cowman: The Recollections of Ed Lemmon, 1857–1946,* ed. by Nellie Snyder Yost (Lincoln: University of Nebraska Press, 1969), 150.

36. Ibid., 151.

37. Interview with Robert G. Hanson (September 15, 1990), Vermillion, S.D. The man who recovered and sold the guns was afraid that if his name was published, he would be charged with dealing in stolen government arms and he would have to release the name of his great-uncle. For these reasons his name will not be published. For military records see Records of the United States Army, RG 98, #75-772M, 1 Reel, South Dakota State Historical Society, Pierre, S.D.

38. Frederic Remington, "Lieutenant Casey's Last Scout," *Harper's Weekly*, January 31, 1891.

39. *Hermosa Pilot* (December 19, 1890). General Miles was unpopular in the Black Hills because non-Indians felt they had to protect themselves while troops sat in Rapid City supposedly with nothing to do. See also John A. Stanley, *From Here Until Now,* (s.l., s.n., 1948), 52: "Delays in action toward protecting the alarmed citizens on the part of General Miles' troops aroused considerable indignation, many thinking he should without delay have moved to the seat of trouble. . . . This delay increased the general dissatisfaction among the settlers. The displeasure over General Miles' course resulted in a mass meeting of Black Hills citizens at Hermosa on January 14, 1891, when they passed resolutions of "indignation and chagrin" and appointed a committee to prepare an appropriate medal to present to the general. When the committee was about to send the result of its action to the general at Pine Ridge they publicly announced that the medal was "unique and suggestive, about five inches in diameter, bound with red tape, ornamented with a white feather, and that on its face, "In commemoration of the masterly inactivity of the commanding general in the field during the Indian War of 1890–91, this beautiful leather medal is dedicated to Major General Nelson A. Miles by disgusted residents of the Black Hills, at Hermosa, S.D. January 14, 1891." At the beginning were the Latin words *"Veni Vidi Vici, Brutum Fulmen,"* and at the end, *"Bones Nocet Quis Quis Pepercerit Malis."*

40. Special Wounded Knee Investigation Report #188, National Archives, Record Group 75.

41. Ricker Collection, Wounded Knee interviews. Philip F. Wells asked Judge Eli Ricker to correct his statement about what happened: "He wants the clubroom incident dropped." In series two, tablet 5, Ricker made the notation "caution here." Thereafter at least eighteen pages of the Wells interview are mysteriously missing—pages 126–44. NSHS.

42. Philip F. Wells, "Ninety-six Years Among the Indians of the Northwest," *North Dakota History,* vol. 15 (1948), 295.

43. Ibid., 295.

44. Ibid., 295.

45. Ibid., passim.

46. Article entitled "An Indian Doll," from *Harper's Weekly* (n.d.), John R. Brennan scrapbook, South Dakota State Historical Society, Pierre.

47. Ibid.

48. Unpublished autobiography of Private August Hettinger, "Personal Recollections of the Messiah Craze Campaign." Hettinger was a private in Company H of the Eighth U.S. Infantry. A copy of this manuscript can be found in the Gage County Historical Society in Beatrice, Nebr.

49. Ibid.

50. Brennan scrapbook, SDSHS.
51. Plate and description XCIII in James Mooney, Fourteenth Annual Report of the Bureau of Ethnology 1892–93.
52. Article by W. J. Bordeaux entitled "Battle of Wounded Knee, 47 Years Ago Wednesday, Declared Massacre." Found in Brennan scrapbook, South Dakota State Historical Society, Pierre, S.D.
53. Yellow Bird's legs show the deterioration of a man who had lain for some time facing down. The blood had clotted under the skin in that position before he was turned over. His arms and face are flattened as well, showing a facedown position. Obviously, the propped gun could not have been placed there by the dead man. This was a staged photograph.
54. The author's research and interviews with three artifact collectors who do not wish their names revealed.
55. Hearings before the Committee on the Judiciary, United States Senate, 94th Cong., 2nd Sess., 1976, S 1147 and S 2900—February 5, 6, 1976 (Washington, D.C.: Government Printing Office, 1976), 94.
56. Charles A. Eastman, See Wounded Knee Special Investigation #188, N.A., R.G. 75.
57. G. E. Bartlett interviewed in the Salt Lake Herald (January 2, 1903). See letter from Bartlett to Clara Colby (March 7, 1904). Clara Colby Collection, State Historical Society of Wisconsin, Madison. Hereinafter SHSW.
58. John Neihardt, Black Elk Speaks: Being a Life Story of a Holy Man of the Oglala Sioux (New York: Morrow, 1932), 270.
59. Interview with Hazel Cuny, Rapid City, S.D. (April 5, 1991).
60. Hazel Cuny interview.
61. Ibid.
62. Ibid.
63. Special Wounded Knee Investigation Report #188, N.A., R.G. 75.
64. Bartlett in Salt Lake Herald (January 2, 1903).
65. Letters to Clara Bewick Colby regarding her adopted daughter Lost Bird. See Clara B. Colby Collection, Historical Society of Wisconsin, Madison, Wisconsin.
66. Testimony of Chester White Butterfly taken in 1902. See N.A. R.G. Records of the Bureau of Indian Affairs, Letters Received 1881–1907, 48184–1901, Land Records 27474-1902.
67. Interview with Jeanette Yellow Bird, Rapid City, S.D. (August 12, 1993).
68. Ibid.
69. See Woman's Tribune (December and January, 1890–91), Clara Colby Collection, the Historical Society of Wisconsin, Madison.
70. Ibid.
71. Interview with Jeanette Yellow Bird, August 12, 1993.

3. A TROPHY OF WAR

1. Report of Brigadier General L. W. Colby (Commanding the Nebraska National Guard in the Indian Campaign of 1890–91) "The Sioux Indian War of 1890–91" in Transactions and Reports of the Nebraska State Historical Society, vol. 3 (Hammond Bros. Printers, 1892), 161.
2. Report of Brigadier General L. W. Colby [Commanding the Nebraska National Guard in the Indian Campaign of 1890–91] to the Adjutant General, Lincoln, Nebr. (Calhoun and Woodruff Printers, 1891), 14; see also Mead Cockrell Family Papers, Box 1, fl-5.2, "Pipe of Peace at Pine Ridge," Nebraska State Historical Society, Lincoln.
3. Transactions and Reports, Colby, 163; see also Philip F. Wells, Ninety-Six Years Among the Indians.
4. "Disgraceful Row," Boston Evening Journal (January 9, 1891).
5. "It Is Red Hot," Beatrice Daily Expresss (January 8, 1891).
6. "Exciting Scenes in the Nebraska Legislature," New York Times (January 9, 1891).
7. Colby's report to Adjutant General.
8. Transactions and Reports of the Nebraska State Historical Society, vol. 3, "The Sioux Indian War of 1890–91," by Brig. General L. W. Colby, 161.
9. "Gone to the Front," Beatrice Daily Express (January 5, 1891).
10. Ibid.
11. Ibid.
12. Charley O'Kieffe, Western Story: The Recollections of Charley O'Kieffe, 1884–1898 (Lincoln: University of Nebraska Press, 1960), 214.

13. See "Need of Assistance," *Yankton Press and Dakotan* (December 6, 1890) for details of the suffering in Nebraska as a result of the shortage of crops: "Almost total failure of crops in twelve counties . . . 10,000 families are in need of assistance."

14. From Helen Colby, West Linn, Ore. General Colby's sword, epaulets, and tassels are still in the Colby family collection, as is his medal for service during the Wounded Knee Campaign and many other personal belongings.

15. James W. Colby, *History of the Colby Family* (Waltham, Mass., 1895), 21.

16. "General Leonard Wright Colby's Civil War History," handwritten by his wife Maud Miller Colby (October 7, 1933). Helen Colby collection, West Linn, Ore.

17. Ibid.

18. See Helen Colby collection, West Linn, Ore.; also *The National Cyclopedia of American Biography* (New York: James T. White and Company, 1922), 399. See also passim, Gene Smith, *Maximilian and Carlota* (New York: William Morrow and Company, Inc., 1973).

19. Ibid., Colby's service record.

20. Letter from L. W. Colby (1917) to his nephew, David Colby, regarding David's possible service in World War I. Renee S. Flood collection.

21. Undated Letter from Thomas Reynolds in Clara B. Colby Collection, State Historical Society of Wisconsin, Madison.

22. *Who's Who in America, 1914–1915* (Chicago: A. N. Marquis Co., 1916); see also Helen Colby Collection, West Linn, Ore.

23. Colby, *History of the Colby Family*. Book in Helen Colby Collection, West Linn, Oregon.

24. Ibid.

25. Maud Miller Colby's history of Leonard W. Colby's life. Helen Colby Collection, West Linn, Ore.

26. Ibid.

27. Ibid.

28. Ibid.

29. Ibid.

30. "The Boys in Camp," *Beatrice Daily Express* (January 8, 1891).

31. Lieutenant Wm. R. Hamilton, United States Army, *Outing Magazine* (July 1896), 317. Found in the E. S. Watson Papers, Newberry Library, Chicago. See also Dale Higgins scrapbook, Beatrice, Nebr.

32. "Nebraska's National Guard in the Sioux War," Hamilton.

33. B. J. Petersen, *The Battle of Wounded Knee* (Sheridan County Historical Society, 1941), 16.

34. For Buffalo Bill's involvement with the Nebraska National Guard, see General L. W. Colby, "The Sioux Indian War of 1890–91."

35. Oral remembrance of Leonard Colby's son, Paul, who tried this stunt on his own and got thrown in jail. When General Colby was told to come down to the jail and get his son, he remarked; "I don't have a son!" From Helen Colby, West Linn, Ore.

36. "Sioux on the Warpath" [From our special correspondent], *The Illustrated American* (January 10, 1891), 263–270.

37. Colby, "The Sioux Indian War of 1890–91," 176.

38. Although Frank D. Baldwin submitted a full report contained in Special Wounded Knee Investigation (Kent-Baldwin) #188, N.A., R.G. 75, Mrs. Baldwin did not mention her husband's presence at Wounded Knee in Baldwin, Alice B. *Memoirs of the Late Frank D. Baldwin*, ed. by Brigadier General W. C. Brown, Col. C. C. Smith, and E. C. Brininstool (Los Angeles: Wetzel Publishing Company, Inc., 1949).

39. President Benjamin Harrison Papers, Series 1, 1890, Reel 30, Library of Congress, letter dated February 11, 1891, to Commissioner of Indian Affairs from Chief of Education Division.

40. Letter to Bob Lee from Florence Joint (February 26, 1954), Wounded Knee File, South Dakota Historical Society, Pierre, S.D. Mrs. Joint quotes from a letter written by her grandmother Mrs. Royer, the agent's widow. Mrs. Royer was still living at this time and was ninety-two years old. See "Doctors to Answer: State Medical Board Cites Seventeen for Violation of Laws (*Los Angeles Examiner*, September 29, 1927). Dr. Daniel F. Royer was the agent at Pine Ridge during the Wounded Knee Massacre. Many blamed Dr. Royer's weak and erratic behavior for the massacre. Royer was then removed as agent and he left South Dakota. He moved to California and was later cited for the misuse of narcotics, including morphine, to which he became addicted to such a degree that he could no longer attend to his medical practice. See also article in the same newspaper entitled "Doctor Wins Battle to Keep License with Story of Life's Battle on Disease, Epidemic and Plague" (October 19, 1927). Dr. Royer appeared before the Board of Medical

Examiners with a pitiful tale of having endured severe hardships in South Dakota. He began to use narcotics, he said, "to keep me up." He begged the board not to revoke his license, promising to clean himself up. The board believed his story and Royer kept his medical license. The extent to which Dr. Royer's drug addiction kept him from performing his duties properly while agent at Pine Ridge can only be surmised. Dr. Valentine McGillycuddy knew of Dr. Royer's addiction. (See letter from McGillycuddy to Mr. William Garnett in *The Killing of Chief Crazy Horse*, ed. by Robert A. Clark, 127.)

41. *Chicago Tribune* (August 23, 1885): "E. G. Asay, Jr., Creditors of the Durham House Drainage hope he will not be given a government position."

42. *Chicago Tribune* (Sept. [exact date illegible] 1885).

43. Books to read on Buffalo Bill include: John Burke, *The Noblest Whiteskin* (New York: G. P. Putnam's Sons, 1973); Don Russell, *The Lives and Legends of Buffalo Bill* (Norman: University of Oklahoma Press, 1960); and biography told by Buffalo Bill's sister Helen C. Wetmore, *Last of the Great Scouts* (Lincoln: University of Nebraska Press, 1899); also Nellie Snyder Yost, *Buffalo Bill: His Family, Friends, Fame, Failures and Fortunes* (Columbus, Ohio: Swallow, 1979).

44. Many citizens of Rushville, Nebr. were treated to an open display of affection between Mrs. Asay and William F. ("Buffalo Bill") Cody. May Asay wore a four-carat diamond ring. People speculated that Buffalo Bill had given it to her. In her will May left the ring to her niece, Mrs. Jennie Bishop of Detroit.

May married James F. Asay in December 1881, and they had no children, although they raised a boy and girl. James died October 26, 1906. May's name was often linked with male suitors over the years, and she was involved in at least one other love affair with a married man, which again brought scandal. She died August 16, 1943.

When Buffalo Bill died in 1917, his devoted wife of many years was in attendance at his funeral. During the burial ceremonies, a heavily veiled woman in black came up to the graveside and lingered at the open grave. Spectators were aghast as she turned and disappeared into the crowd. Was the woman in black Mrs. Margaret Asay, Buffalo Bill's longtime love?

45. O'Keiffe, per note 12, 111.

46. "Reception at Nailors," *Washington Post* (January 5, 1891). See also Charles A. Eastman, in Special Wounded Knee Investigation #188, N.A., R.G. 75; also *Woman's Tribune* (January 10, 1891), and *The Winter of 1890* by Don Huls, *Chadron* (Nebr.) *Record*, 1974, 49. Huls says Zintka was christened on January 4, 1891. Major Burke also adopted a small boy named No Neck.

47. Ibid.

48. Michael Paul Rogin, *Fathers and Children: Andrew Jackson and the Subjection of the American Indian* (New York: Alfred A. Knopf, 1975), 188–89. Jackson wrote to his wife Rachael: "Keep Lincoyer in the house, he is a savage"; see also Eaton, *The Autobiography of Peggy Eaton* (New York: Charles Scribner's Sons, 1932), 167ff. Eaton was the wife of Jackson's secretary of war. She also adopted a Creek Indian after the Redstick Wars. The adoption lasted only three years and was unsuccessful because "Johnny" rebelled against trying to be a white boy. Mrs. Eaton explained, "I had him dressed as nicely as any child in Washington and sent him to school; but . . . if there was a feather afloat in the air . . . or if there was a scrap of red ribbon astray, John would appropriate it; and sometimes came home befeathered . . . in the most ridiculous manner; he always showed the savage. . . . He was now about ten years of age, and we were going to Nashville. While ascending the river I thought there was something curious in John's appearance and mentioned it to my husband. All at once we heard a splash, and John struck for the shore. . . . [W]hen he saw John in the water, he said, 'Let him go. Let him go.' John went. I never saw him afterwards; but we heard of him. . . . John had found his own people and made good his escape. He was a beautiful boy and . . . a perfect Indian." The child was a relative of John Ross. Also consulted: Gelett Burgess, "The Keepsake," *Atlantic Monthly*, vol. 98 (n. d.), 837.

49. Ibid., passim.

50. Burgess, per note 48. See also Sherry C. Smith, *The View from Officers' Row* (Tucson: University of Arizona Press, 1990), 72–78.

51. Interview with Jeanette Yellow Bird, Rapid City, S.D. (August 12, 1993).

52. Interviews with Helen Colby (1989), West Linn, Ore.

53. "The Waif of Wounded Knee," *Beatrice Daily Express* (January 19, 1891).

54. In 1892, Colby gave his supervisor, the Attorney General of the United States, an Arabian colt. See Clara Bewick Colby Collection, Historical Society of Wisconsin, Madison. He also gave two Saint Bernards to a judge.

55. Burgess, "The Keepsake," *Atlantic Monthly* (n.d.), vol. 98, 837.

56. "General Colby's Capture," *Nebraska State Journal* (January 18, 1891). Annie's Indian name was Hinhanwin, or Owl Woman. According to Holy Cross Episcopal Mission Record Book #2, Baptisms, Pine Ridge 1881–1891, 320, Annie had a baby boy in May 1891.

57. Ibid.

58. Ibid.; See also "The Waif of Wounded Knee," *Beatrice Daily Express* (January 18, 19, and 20, 1891).

59. "Zintka Lanuni," *Woman's Tribune* (Sept. 12, 1891).

60. Special Wounded Knee Investigation Report #188, N.A., R.G. 75.

61. Jeanette Yellow Bird interview. For a time Annie hid in a cave.

62. "Zintka Lanuni," *Woman's Tribune* (Sept. 12, 1891).

63. Robert M. Utley, *The Last Days of the Sioux Nation* (New Haven: Yale University Press, 1963), 257.

64. Ibid., 258

65. *Rapid City Journal* (January 8, 1891) and *New York Times* (January 8 and 9, 1891).

66. Newspapers in the East referred to Lost Bird as "the infant heroine" because she had survived the massacre as well as the three-day blizzard that tore down buildings and halted railroad trains from South Dakota all the way to Kansas City, Missouri, down to Abilene, Texas. For details see "The Western Blizzard," *Boston Morning Journal* (January 3, 1891).

67. "Drank Poison to Save His Client," in Dawson Scrapbook, Book 35, page 49, Colorado State Historical Society, Denver.

68. Ibid. This story is well known by the residents of Beatrice, Nebr.

69. "Nebraska Militia Officer and Lawyer Figured in a Strange Court Scene," in Dawson Scrapbook, Book 35, page 49, Colorado State Historical Society.

70. Ibid.

71. Ibid., "Stomach Pump Was Ready."

72. Ibid., "After swallowing deadly dose he walked to office, where poison was brought out—client was acquitted."

73. Report of Brigadier General L. W. Colby (Commanding the Nebraska National Guard in the Indian Campaign of 1890–91) to the Adjutant General, Lincoln, Nebraska, 1891, 19.

74. Special Wounded Knee Investigation Report #188, N.A., R.G. 75.

75. Transactions, Colby, 169.

76. Portion of a February 1891 edition of *Illustrated American* found in the Elaine Goodale Eastman Papers, Smith College Library, Northampton, Mass.

77. Capt. W. E. Dougherty, "The Recent Messiah Craze," Journal of the Military Service Institution of the United States, 12 (1891), 577.

78. Interview with Fordyce Graff, Beatrice, Nebraska, 1985. Graff worked for Colby and often heard this story.

79. "The Waif of Wounded Knee," *Beatrice Daily Express* (Jan. 19, 1891). Colby said, "A peculiar thing in connection with securing the infant was the remarkable reluctance with which the Indians surrendered it. Everyone . . . claimed to be its father or mother and all had a warm, loving interest in its welfare."

80. "Zintka Lanuni," *Woman's Tribune* (Sept. 12, 1891).

81. "Looking Backward 26 Years," *Norton Champion* (April 10, 1930). Quote from Leonard Colby at the Dewey Murder Trial in which he stated that his grandmother was a full-blood Seneca Indian and that when he found Lost Bird after Wounded Knee, she looked like a "frozen frog." For more information see 1903, "Three killed and two injured as Dewey-Berry feud breaks into warfare in northwest Kansas." Reprinted in *Norton Daily Telegram* (September 9, 1963). Copies of Leonard W. Colby's biography and duties during this trial can be found at the Norton Public Library, Norton, Kans.

82. Philip F. Wells, *Ninety-Six Years Among the Indians of the Northwest*, 295.

83. Thomas Henry Tribbles, *Buckskin and Blanket Days* (Garden City, N.Y.: Doubleday and Company, 1957), 327–328.

84. Pat Locke, Lakota educator, has contributed numerous columns about Lakota culture for the *Lakota Times*, now *Indian Country Today*, printed in Rapid City, S.D. It is the largest Indian-owned weekly in the United States. Tim Giago, an Oglala Lakota, is the founder and publisher.

85. Manuel P. Guerrero, "A response to the threat to Indian children caused by foster and adoptive placements of Indian children," in *American Indian Law Review* 7 (1979), 51–77; also Philip A. May, "Suicide Among American Indian Youth: A Look at the Issues," in *Children Today* (July-August 1987), 22; also Joseph Westermeyer, M.D., "Cross-racial Foster Home Placement Among Native American Psychiatric Patients," in *Journal of the National Medical Association* 69 (1977), 231–236;

also Troy R. Johnson, ed., *The Indian Child Welfare Act: Indian Homes for Indian Children* (Los Angeles: American Indian Studies Center, UCLA, 1991); also Marc Mannes, *Family Preservation and Indian Child Welfare* (Albuquerque: American Indian Law Center, Inc., 1990); also Joseph A. Meyers, ed. *They Are Young Once but Indian Forever* (Oakland, Calif.: American Indian Lawyer Training Program, 1981); also Steven Unger, ed, *The Destruction of American Indian Families* (New York: Association on American Indian Affairs, 1977); also Joseph Westermeyer, M.D. "The Ravage of Indian Families in Crisis," in *The Destruction of Indian Family Life,* ed. by Steven Unger (New York: Association of American Indian Affairs, 1976); also Edwin McDowell, "The Indian Adoption Problem," in *Wall Street Journal* (July 12, 1974); also "Indian Suicide Rate Is Highest," *Montana and the West* (July 6, 1994); also Joan Smith, "Baby-Snatchers, How White Americans Steal Indian Children," *San Francisco Examiner* (July 3, 1988); also Chuck Hawley, "Child Law Tries to Fathom Tribes," *Arizona Republic* (April 23, 1988). Quote from this last article: "The American Academy of Child Psychiatry said in a 1975 report: Indians raised in non-Indian homes tend to have significant social problems in adolescence and adulthood. Also Nancy Stancill, "The Baby Market: The Business of Adoption—Permissive Laws—Big Bucks Make Texas Hot Spot," *Houston Chronicle* (October 6, 1991); also Ivan Star Comes Out, "The Aftermath of Cross-Adoption," *Lakota Times* (June 27, 1988). Quote: "The common practice of removing unfortunate children from their homes at an early age and adopting them out to non-Indian families has accomplished . . . what bullets during the 1800s failed to do: the destruction of the American Indian family, language and culture." Also Linda Roberts Rosene, "A Follow-up study of Indian Children Adopted by White Families (Transracial Identity, Adolescent)," Ph.D. dissertation, The Fielding Institute, 1983. Quote: "Children would have been better off raised in an Indian family instead." Also Avis Little Eagle "A Mother and Child Reunion," *Lakota Times* (September 5, 1989).

86. Yellow Bird testimony, Pine Ridge (June 14, 1902). Felix Crane Pretty Voice testimony (January 3, 1925). Yellow Bird's statement can be found in correspondence between John R. Brennan and A. C. Towner, Acting Commissioner, National Archives, Land 42053-1901 and Land 27474-1902, Dept. of the Interior, Office of Indian Affairs. See also Wounded Knee file, Lost Bird, Nebraska State Historical Society, Lincoln; also Marguerite Elizabeth Allen file, Cheyenne River Sioux Tribe, Eagle Butte, S.D. Felix Crane Pretty Voice statements can be found in the Allen file, Cheyenne River Sioux tribe. See also Records of the Bureau of Indian Affairs Cheyenne River Agency, 1869–1961 Reg. 6; also Index to Correspondence received from the office of Indian Affairs, Indian Warehouses and Special Agents 1896-1906, REG. 6. Felix Crane Pretty Voice gave sworn testimony on January 3, 1925 that he doubted he was the father of Lost Bird and that Colby had given him $50 to purchase clothing. See Cheyenne River Files.

87. Ibid.

88. *Beatrice Daily Sun* 1957 Centennial Edition; see B6, "General Colby Reared Indian Girl."

89. Gage County Court Records, Beatrice, Nebr. Adoption Record of Marguerite Elizabeth Colby (January 19, 1891).

90. Box of Colby hieroglyphics and Arabian pedigrees—Helen Colby Collection, West Linn, Ore.

91. Letter from Lea to Leonard W. Colby, December 15, 1892. Albert T. Lea Collection, Gilcrease Museum Archives, Tulsa, Okla.

92. Ibid. Letter from Colby to Lea (December 27, 1892).

93. Ibid.

94. Bureau of Catholic Indian Missions Records, Series 1, Box 25, Folder 12, letter to Rev. J. A. Stephan from Father M. J. Craft, in Marquette University Archives, Milwaukee. Also Special Wounded Knee File #188, N.A., R.G. 75; also W. Fletcher Johnson, *Life of Sitting Bull and History of the Indian War of 1890–91* (Edgewood Publishing Company, 1891), 468; also Charles Percival Jordan Papers, FB-43, South Dakota State Historical Society, Pierre, S.D.

95. Ibid., Charles Percival Jordan Papers. SDSHS.

96. St. Francis Mission Records, Series 7, Box 7, Folder 14, vol. 2, Fr. Emil Perrig diary (February 21, 1891), 15, Marquette University Archives, Milwaukee.

97. Memorial Petition to the 55th United States Congress, 1st Sess., 1897. Red Cloud petitioned to ask that James Asay be barred from coming onto the Pine Ridge Reservation. This report can be found in Senate Documents, vol. 5, 55th Cong., 1st Sess., 1897.

98. B. J. Petersen, *The Battle of Wounded Knee*, published in Gordon, Nebraska, 1941. Copy can be found at the Nebraska State Historical Society Reading Room in Lincoln. Article entitled "Sixteen Years Later" by W. A. Luke.

99. *Pen and Sunlight Sketches of Lincoln, Nebraska* (Chicago: Phoenix Publishing Company, 1893), 118–120 (n.a.).

100. "The Waif of Wounded Knee," *Beatrice Daily Express;* also "General Colby's Capture," *Nebraska State Journal* (January 18, 1891).

101. *Beatrice Daily Express* (January 18, 19, and 20, 1891).

102. "Zintka Lanuni," *Woman's Tribune* (Sept. 12, 1891).

103. "Nebraska's Guard," *Beatrice Daily Express* (January 20, 1891).

104. Ibid.

105. Interview with Fordyce Graff, 1985. Mr. Graff worked for General Colby and knew him well.

106. "Nebraska's Guard," *Beatrice Daily Express* (January 20, 1891).

107. Ibid.

108. "Notes," *Beatrice Daily Express* (January 20, 1891).

109. "Notes," *Beatrice Daily Express* (January 20 and 21, 1891).

110. Clara Bewick Colby Collection, State Historical Society of Wisconsin, Madison.

111. The *Woman's Tribune,* published and edited by Clara Bewick Colby, shows Clara's work in Washington during December 1890 and January 1891. Clara did not know her husband had adopted Lost Bird until the third week of January, when she received a letter from him. General Colby put her name on the adoption papers as though she were present.

4. THE SUFFRAGE MOTHER

1. Adoption records, Gage County Court House, Beatrice, Nebr.

2. Olympia Brown, *Democratic Ideals: A memorial sketch of Clara B. Colby* (Washington, D.C. Federal Suffrage Association), xi and xii.

3. Winona Evans Reeves, ed., *The Blue Book of Nebraska Women* (1916), 36–38; also Elizabeth Cady Stanton, *History of Woman Suffrage,* vols. 3 and 5 (1886–1902); also Ida H. Harper, *The Life and Work of Susan B. Anthony,* vols. 1–2 (1898).

4. Letter from Elizabeth Cady Stanton to Clara B. Colby (June 11, 1889). This letter can be found in the Papers of Elizabeth Cady Stanton, Library of Congress, Manuscript Division, Washington, D.C.

5. From a tribute read by Clara B. Colby at memorial gathering for Susan B. Anthony after her death in 1906. Original handwritten text at SHSW.

6. Birth record from General Register Office, Somerset House, London.

7. Diary entry (March 8, 1866), SHSW.

8. Thomas Bewick, Clara B. Colby's father, was born April 25, 1822, in Durham County, England, and died at Windsor, Wisconsin. See Stephenson Chilton L. Bewick, *The Bewick Family* (July 1923), 156, SHSW.

9. Quote from Clara's article "English Yuletide Means Giving, Not Getting," SHSW.

10. S. C. L. Bewick, Colby Family History, 160, SHSW.

11. S. C. L. Bewick, Recollections of Pioneer Life in Wisconsin, C-1, SHSW.

12. Ibid.

13. Ibid., 2–3.

14. Clara B. Colby, essay entitled "Trip to America," University of Wisconsin, Oct. 14, 1867. SHSW.

15. Clara's notes regarding her mother's agonizing death in childbirth on August 18, 1855. Clara Willingham was born July 17, 1821, in England and died at the age of thirty-four in Windsor, Wisconsin. She was of very slight build and delicate constitution. This would have been her tenth pregnancy in fifteen years of marriage. SHSW.

16. Bewick Family History, C-6, SHSW.

17. Handwritten notes by Clara B. Colby regarding her mother's untimely death in childbirth, SHSW.

18. S. C. L. Bewick, Recollections of Pioneer Life in Wisconsin, C-2, SHSW.

19. Bewick Family Supplement, C-7, SHSW.

20. Ibid, C-10, SHSW.

21. Excerpt from Clara's diary (April 15, 1868). SHSW.

22. Bewick Family History, C-12, SHSW.

23. Grandmother Chilton blamed Thomas Bewick for her daughter's death. She was critical of his choice for a new bride, and didn't approve of the woman's children; see also letter to Clara from grandmother Chilton (March 11, 1874), SHSW.

24. Clara's letter to her grandparents (April 14, 1867), SHSW.

25. Letter to her grandparents (August 31, 1867), SHSW.

26. Letter from Clara to a suitor named John Kelly, May 1867.

27. Alden Whitman, ed., *American Reformers* (New York: H. W. Wilson Company, 1985), 180.

28. Amy Hague, "Give Us a Little Time to Find Our Places: University of Wisconsin Alumnae, Classes 1875–1900," Master's thesis in history (1983), 15.

29. Clara B. Colby's valedictory essay read at her graduation from the University of Wisconsin (1869), SHSW.

30. Letter from Clara B. Colby to the "Gentlemen of the Executive Committee" (September 30, 1870), SHSW.

31. The female members of the Bewick family were advised to "make it your first and principal business . . . to please and gratify your husband." Letter to "my dear sister Mary" from William Medhurst (October 20, 1821), SHSW; see also Deborah Gorham, The Victorian Girl and the Feminine Ideal (Bloomington: Indiana University Press, 1982), 102.

32. Grandmother Chilton was a devout Christian, although there is evidence that in her youth she did as she pleased. If anyone crossed her, she let that person have it verbally, and in no uncertain terms. She raised Clara as her own daughter and doted on her. After Grandmother's death, her grandson William said that, up to the last, she had been a fighter and "only gave up because she was too weak to argue her point." Letter to Clara (October 15, 1879), SHSW.

33. Brown, Democratic Ideals, 16.

34. Letter from Clara to "Gentlemen of the Executive Committee."

35. Letter to Clara from J. W. Sterling (November 7, 1870), SHSW.

36. Letter to Clara from N. B. VanSlyke (November 10, 1870), SHSW.

37. Hugh J. Dobbs, History of Gage County, Nebraska (Lincoln: Western Publishing and Engraving Company, 1918), 493–99.

38–43. Clara B. Colby Papers, SHSW.

44. Handwritten poem (no date), SHSW.

45. Letter from Grandmother Chilton to Clara at Fort Atkinson (February 15, 1871), SHSW.

46. Letter from William Bewick to his sister Clara (February 24, 1871), SHSW.

47. Ibid.

48. Letter from Grandmother Chilton to Clara at Fort Atkinson (March 17, 1871), SHSW.

49. Letter from Grandmother Chilton to Clara (March 17, 1871), SHSW.

50. Letter from Grandmother Chilton to Clara (May 21, 1872), SHSW.

51. Letter from Reverend Richards to Clara (May 29, 1871), SHSW.

52. Wedding announcement in the Freeport (Ill.) Bulletin, (June 24, 1971), in Abigail Colby's scrapbook, Helen Colby collection, West Linn, Ore.

53. Bewick Family History, 18, SHSW.

54. Clara Bewick Colby, "Concerning Farmers' Wives," paper read before the Association for the Advancement of Women at its annual congress in Boston (1880); later published by New England Publishing Co. (1881), SHSW.

5. THE NEBRASKA FRONTIER

1. Letter from Clara to her grandparents in Wisconsin (October 11, 1871), SHSW.

2. Letter from Clara to her grandparents (October 13, 1871), SHSW.

3. Olympia Brown, Democratic Ideals: A Memorial Sketch of Clara B. Colby (Washington, D.C.: Federal Suffrage Association, 1917), 56.

4. Letter from Clara to her grandfather (October 24, 1872), SHSW.

5. Ibid.

6. Clara sends her grandparents local newspaper clippings (undated, probably November 1872).

7. Letter from Clara to her grandparents (November 6, 1872).

8. Mrs. Clara Medhurst Chilton died October 7, 1879, at the age of seventy-nine years. Her obituary appeared in the local Beatrice newspaper, and Clara pasted it in her scrapbook, page 100. SHSW.

9. Clara's letter to grandparents (October 12, 1871).

10. Letter to her grandparents (December 28, 1872).

11. Renée Sansom Flood, Lessons from Chouteau Creek: Yankton Memories of Dakota Territorial Intrigue (Sioux Falls, S.D.: The Center for Western Studies, Augustana College, 1986), 36.

12. Ibid. 37.

13. Passim, Frederick K. Hoxie, ed. Indians in American History (Arlington Heights, Ill.: D'Arcy McNickle Center for the History of the American Indian, The Newberry Library, Harlan Davidson, Inc., 1988).

14. Brown, *Democratic Ideals*, 20–29.

15. *Beatrice Express* (January 23, 1873).

16. Ibid. (February 27, 1873).

17. *Who Was Who in America*, vol. 1 (1897–1942), 241.

18. Jefferson Hunsaker Broady Papers, scrapbook, box 2 (undated newspaper article), Nebraska State Historical Society, Lincoln.

19. Jefferson Hunsaker Broady papers, scrapbook, box 2, in *Johnson County Journal* (October 12, 1883).

20. Broady Papers, letter from Leonard Colby to Judge Broady (October 16, 1883), Nebraska State Historical Society, Lincoln.

21. On June 25, 1875, Leonard Colby and Alexander W. Conley organized the Paddock Guards in honor of United States senator Algernon Sidney Paddock.

22. Letters dated June 1875, SHSW. Colby often sent pressed flowers to Clara.

23. Undated letter from Elizabeth Cady Stanton to Clara B. Colby, SHSW. (Many of Mrs. Stanton's letters are undated.)

24. Letter from Susan B. Anthony to Clara B. Colby (November 2, 1877), SHSW. This was one of the first letters (four pages) that Clara received from Miss Anthony. Their friendship, despite Anthony's constant admonishments, lasted until Anthony's death in 1906. There are perhaps 200 letters from Anthony to Clara Colby in the Huntington Library and the State Historical Society of Wisconsin, Madison.

25. Margaret Truman, *Women of Courage: From Revolutionary Times to the Present* (New York: William Morrow and Company Inc., 1976), 151

26. Memorial tribute given after Susan B. Anthony's death by Clara B. Colby (1906), SHSW.

27. A portion of Clara B. Colby speech reprinted in the *Woman's Tribune* (November 9, 1903).

28. Reprinted many times in *Woman's Tribune* starting in February 1891, SHSW.

29. Passim, Miriam Z. Langsam, *Children West: A History of the Placing-Out System of the New York Children's Aid Society, 1853–1890* (Madison: The State Historical Society of Wisconsin, 1964).

30. Letter to Clara B. Colby from Susan B. Anthony (November 2, 1964), SHSW.

31. One of Clara's reasons for deciding against Miss Anthony's advice not to accept the Lost Bird may well have been because she had no daughter of her own to carry on the suffragist cause. Many of her friends in the movement had daughters, including Stanton, Antoinette Brown Blackwell, Lucy Stone, Harriet Robinson, Mary Livermore, Matilda Joslyn Gage, Belva Lockwood, and many more. See Harriet J. H. Robinson and Harriette L. R. Shattuck Papers, Series 9, H.R.S. Scrapbook—Reel no. 77–16, Schlesinger Library, Radcliffe (Harvard University).

32. During 1889 and 1890, Clara was Susan B. Anthony's right hand in the suffrage movement. She was seated next to Miss Anthony at major functions and was lauded in the press. See *Washington Evening Star* (January 21, 1889); regarding Miss Anthony's collapse on January 24, 1891, letter to author from Patricia G. Holland, editor of the Papers of Elizabeth Cady Stanton and Susan B. Anthony, University of Massachusetts, Amherst (March 26, 1992): "Dear Renee, . . . [N]o diary entries [for Anthony] exist after Dec. 15, 1890, nor of course for 1891. . . . A letter of 12-29-90 says she will leave the next day to be settled in Washington, D.C., 'in a few days,' (Clara was in Washington). . . . [T]he 12-27-90 issue of the *Woman's Tribune* says she and Colby will receive [guests] at Riggs House [Hotel] on Jan. 1st." This shows that Clara and Miss Anthony were visiting the week Miss Anthony collapsed on Jan. 24, 1891, one day after Clara received the letter from her husband about Lost Bird.

See also Ida Husted Harper *The Life and Work of Susan B. Anthony*, vol. 2 (Indianapolis: Bowen-Merrill Company, 1898), 701: ". . . Wm. Lloyd Garrison came at once and took her [Anthony] to his hospitable home . . . and a most fortunate thing it was. Since leaving South Dakota [six months before?], she had been fighting off what seemed to be a persistent form of La Grippe and the next morning (Jan. 24, 1891) she collapsed utterly. . . . [S]he was obliged to keep [to] her room for a week." It is interesting to note that if Miss Anthony was upset with Clara for agreeing to adopt Lost Bird, that may explain why neither Clara nor Miss Anthony attended the Fortieth Anniversary of the First National Woman's Rights Convention in Boston on January 27 and 28, 1891. It was announced that Miss Anthony was ill and could not attend.

33. Ida Husted Harper, *The Life and Work of Susan B. Anthony*, vol. 2, 701.

34. No diary for 1891 has been found.

35. Letter from Patricia Holland to author: "She [Anthony] did uncharacteristically ease off over the summer [1891] perhaps because she wasn't feeling well."

The year 1891 marked the first time in over forty years that Miss Anthony wasn't constantly on the road. She did, however, take time in March to speak at a Woman Suffrage League dinner in honor of Clara B. Colby in New York City. Clara had decided not to hurry home to Nebraska to see the infant, but would stay in Washington for Susan B. Anthony's birthday in February 1891. See also Harper, vol. II, op. cit.

36. Charles A. Eastman was a Dakota who became a physician and renowned author of such works as *From the Deep Woods to Civilization* (New York: Little, Brown and Company, 1916).
37. Editor's note in the *Woman's Tribune* (January 31, 1891), SHSW.
38. *Woman's Tribune* (December 5, 1891), SHSW.

6. THE LION OF THE PARTY

1. *Woman's Tribune* (May 9, 1891), SHSW. On her way to Beatrice, Clara gave several lectures and attended the Woman Suffrage Convention at Englewood, Ill. She did not arrive in Beatrice until May 1, 1891.
2. Interview with Fordyce Graff (August 2, 1985) in Beatrice. Graff recalled that Maud walked "like a prairie chicken, all puffed up."
3. *Woman's Tribune* (October 1888), Clara Colby Scrapbook, Huntington Library, San Marino, Calif., 20
4. Ibid.
5. Undated Nebraska newspaper clipping in Clara B. Colby collection, SHSW.
6. Ibid.
7. Handwritten notes entitled "Nebraska Days," probably by Mary White's daughter Sadie, in Clara Colby Collection, SHSW. The list: "Pinafores, needlepoint, white shoes, morning glories, left alone at night, picket fence, plate of tarts, white dress sash, reading 'Hiawatha' by Uncle Leon, church bells, train, frosty morning sidewalks, sliding and skating, archery and croquet, lawn cherry trees, peacocks, old Black John and the white horses."
8. Ibid.
9. Ibid.
10. *Woman's Tribune* (February 21, 1891).
11. Ibid.
12. Ibid.
13. Iapi Oaye—The Word Carrier (June 1891), vol. 20, no. 6. "So strange that the Indians don't like milk!"
14. This is the philosophy of most present-day social workers, clergymen (and -women), and physicians in Indian country. The key word here is *comfortable*. What may be comfortable for the majority of Americans may be very uncomfortable for Indians. The eagle does not feel at home in the nest of a swan.
15. *Woman's Tribune* (March, 1892), SHSW.
16. Lucie Fursenberg Huger, "Dr. Mary Edwards Walker, The Little Lady in Pants," *Society of the Daughters of the American Revolution Magazine* (December 1989), vol. 123, no. 10. Lucie Huger is a member of the Cornelia Greene chapter of the DAR in St. Louis. Dr. Walker was also a member of this DAR chapter. Her Congressional Medal of Honor was restored to her in 1977 after her grandniece, Helen Hay Wilson, lobbied in Washington on her behalf.
17. Ibid.
18. Ibid.
19. Remembrance of Dr. Mary White's daughter, Mary M. Matthes, who lived in the Colby Home in Washington, SHSW.
20. U.S. National Museum Smithsonian Institution Accession Card 31021, Acc. No 24052, dated Feb. 2, 1891. "Fossils presented by L. W. Colby of Beatrice, Neb." Colby's land was northwest of Orlando.
21. Letter to Clara from Leonard Colby (February 12, 1891), SHSW. Colby was involved in similar land deals in at least ten states.
22. Article reprinted four times in *Woman's Tribune* (1891 and 1892).
23. Ibid.
24. *Woman's Tribune* (January 10, 1891), SHSW
25. *Washington Post* (January 11, 1891). The article mentioned Clara's testimonial to Miss Anthony.
26. Ralph K. Andrist, ed., *The American Heritage History of the Confident Years: 1865–1916* (New York: Bonanza Books, 1987), 251. "Banks, railroads, silver, gold mines, oil, utilities, all claimed

their proxy seats in the Senate until by the close of the century over two dozen industrial millionaires were sitting in the upper chamber."

27. L. W. Colby's boss in the attorney general's office was W. H. H. Miller. Miller's wife was Mrs. Carrie Harrison's intimate friend in Washington, and it was Mrs. Miller who introduced Clara to Mrs. Benjamin Harrison. They remained good friends until Mrs. Harrison's untimely death in late October 1891. See *New York Times* (October 26–27, 1891); see also Index to the Presidential Papers of Benjamin Harrison, letter from Carrie (May 2, 1890), Library of Congress, Washington, D.C.
28. John W. Noble resigned in March 1891. Benjamin Harrison asked him to stay on, although Noble's credibility in the handling of the Wounded Knee tragedy was seen as a disaster.
29. Clara used her considerable clout with political wives to gain support for her husband. Mrs. William Kent, wife of a U.S. representative from California; Mrs. Miles Poindexter, wife of the lawyer and political leader; and many more lobbied on Clara's behalf.
30. See letter book from William H. H. Miller's office (April 1890–February 1893), National Archives, Washington D.C. Letter from Judge George H. Hastings, George A. Murphy, and replies (dated April 14, 1891 and June 2, 1891).
31. "By the Woman's Suffrage League," *New York Times* (March 20, 1891)
32. Ibid.
33. "Editor's Notes," *Woman's Tribune* (May 9, 1891).
34. Ibid.
35. Alma Lutz, *Susan B. Anthony: Rebel, Crusader, Humanitarian* (Boston: Beacon Press, 1959), 213.
36. General L. W. Colby's official appointment records, Helen Colby Collection, West Linn, Ore.
37. Passim, Sean Dennis Cashman, *America in the Gilded Age* (New York: New York University Press, 1984); also L. de Hegermann-Lindencrone, *The Sunny Side of Diplomatic Life, 1875–1912* (New York: Harper and Bros., 1914); also J. Kirkpatrick Flack, *Desideratum in Washington: The Intellectual Community in the Capital City, 1870–1900* (Cambridge, Mass.: Schenkman Pub., 1975); also Eleanor Flexner, *Century of Struggle: The Woman's Rights Movement in the United States* (Cambridge, Mass.: Belknap Press of Harvard University Press, 1959); and Constance M. Green, *Washington, Capital City 1879–1950* (Princeton, N.J.: Princeton University Press, 1963); also Benjamin Harrison, *Views of an Ex-president*, edited by Mary Lord Harrison (Indianapolis: The Bowen-Merrill Company Publishers, 1901); also Irwin Hood Hoover, *Forty-two Years in the White House* (New York: Houghton Mifflin Company, 1934); also Richard Hofstadter, *The Age of Reform* (New York: Vintage Books/Alfred A. Knopf/Random House, Inc., 1955).
38. Anonymous letter to Leonard Colby (June 15, 1891). SHSW.
39. Ibid.
40. *Woman's Tribune* (September 6, 1891).
41. Ibid., (September 20, 1891).
42. Ibid.
43. *Woman's Tribune* (August 29, 1891).
44. Ibid.
45. Ibid.
46. Interview with Leonard Colby's nephew, David Colby (1988), Ashland, Ore.
47. "Premium Pictures," *Woman's Tribune* (January 9, 1892).

7. KICKING BEAR'S PRAYER

1. "A Visit to the Woman's Tribune," *Woman's Tribune* (May 17, 1890), SHSW.
2. Letter from Miss Anthony to Harriet Taylor Upton (March 14, 1892). The Papers of Susan B. Anthony and Elizabeth Cady Stanton, edited by Patricia Holland, University of Massachusetts, Amherst.
3. Clara Colby's correspondence for NAWSA can be found at the Historical Society of Wisconsin and the Huntington Library, San Marino, Calif.
4. Ibid.; see also the Susan B. Anthony Collection, University of Rochester, N.Y.
5. "Dear Friend," undated letter from Clara Colby saying she is sorry if she offended the woman, but she did so after a remark was made about her child, SHSW. See also Olympia Brown Papers, Reel 8, letter to Brown from Ida H. Harper (June 17, 1917), Schlesinger Library, Radcliffe (Harvard University) Cambridge, Mass. Harper called Zintka "that unspeakable Indian child."
6. Mrs. Stanton and her husband, Henry B. Stanton, an abolitionist, had a large family. Susan B.

Anthony often took care of their children while Mrs. Stanton prepared suffrage lectures; see Elisabeth Griffith. *In Her Own Right: The Life of Elizabeth Cady Stanton* (New Oxford University Press, 1985); see also William O'Neill, *Everyone Was Brave: A History of Feminism in America* (New York: Quadrangle, 1969); see also Andrew Rosen, *Rise Up Women! The Militant Campaign of the Women's Social and Political Union, 1903–1914* (London: Routledge and Kegan, Paul, 1974); see also Elizabeth Cady Stanton, *Eighty Years and More: Reminiscences, 1815–1897*, edited by Theodore Stanton and Harriot Stanton Blatch, vols. 1 and 2 (New York: Arno, 1969).

7. Letter from Mrs. Stanton to Clara (February 21, 1889), SHSW.

8. Undated letter from Elizabeth Cady Stanton to Clara, SHSW.

9. Undated letter from Elizabeth C. Stanton to Susan B. Anthony. See the Papers of Susan B. Anthony and Elizabeth Cady Stanton, University of Massachusetts, Amherst.

10. Undated clipping from the *New Decatur:* "Will Fight Side By Side," SHSW.

11. Clara and Leonard took a ten-week vacation over the summer of 1888. They toured Idaho, Colorado, Wyoming, Oregon, and Washington. That fall Clara described her adventures in the *Woman's Tribune.* Her scrapbook with travel articles can be found in the Huntington Library, San Marino, Calif. (pp. 171–73). Clara's readers enjoyed the travel items. Many women wrote saying they were so poor or overburdened with children that they could not travel and only through Clara's writings did they have the chance to learn about U.S. and world travel.

12. Undated letter from Elizabeth Cady Stanton to Clara Colby, SHSW; see also the Papers of Susan B. Anthony and Elizabeth Cady Stanton, University of Massachusetts, Amherst.

13. Undated letter from Elizabeth Cady Stanton to Clara Colby, SHSW. With Stanton's permission, Clara gave the famous woman's signature as a premium to new subscribers. There is no record of how many Stanton letters were destroyed in this way, for no partial letters without signature were found in Clara's personal files.

14. Ibid.

15. Mary Matthes donated her collection of Colby memorabilia to the State Historical Society of Wisconsin, Madison. This included her remembrances about her stay in the Colby home in Washington, D.C.

16. Ibid.

17. Interview with Fordyce Graff in Beatrice, Nebr. (1985).

18. *Woman's Tribune* (April 1892), SHSW.

19. Ibid.

20. Ibid.

21. See Leonard Wright Colby, Indian Depredation Trials—Hearings Before the U.S. Senate in Relation to Indian Depredation Cases in the Court of Claims, Testimony of Special Agent Cooper to Asay's Involvement, Indian file 2138, New York State Library, Albany; see also Report of the Attorney General 1894, House Executive Documents, 53rd Cong., 3rd Sess., vol. 27. 11–25; see also Act of Congress, March 3, 1891 (26 stat. 851); see also Preliminary Inventories, number 163, Records of the Bureau of Indian Affairs, vol. 1, compiled by Edward E. Hill, National Archives and Records Service, General Services Administration, Washington, D.C. (1965), 199–200.

22. "Pine Ridge Depredation Claims," *New York Evening Post,* Sept. 21, 1891; see also Act of Congress, March 3, 1891 (26 stat. 851); also House Executive Documents 7 (52-1) 2942, 52nd Cong., 1st Sess., 1891–92, vol. 22; see also 52nd Cong., 2nd Sess., vol. 21.

23. The medals were made in Washington by S. D. Childs & Company; see also invoice no. 58960, which shows sixty-five "Sioux Medals" purchased by L. W. Colby from his own pocket on January 9, 1892, Leonard W. Colby Collection, NSHS.

24. Undated letter from Rowell Colby to Clara B. Colby, SHSW; see letter to the author from Leonard Colby's nephew, David Colby (March 10, 1988). Mr. Colby says, "None of the Colbys I ever knew or heard of was part Indian, and definitely not on his mother's side." David Colby knew his uncle well. Renee Sansom Flood collection.

25. Interview with Reverend James W. Garvie's daughter Elaine Melior (August 1989). Mrs. Melior is compiling documentation for a biography of her father, which should prove valuable to historians. See Renee Sansom Flood, Shirley A. Bernie, and Leonard R. Bruguier, *Remember Your Relatives: Yankton Sioux Images, 1865 to 1915,* Yankton Sioux Tribe, vol. 2 (1989), 69–71.

26. *Woman's Tribune* (March 28, 1896), SHSW.

27. When lawyers in various states were needed to take depositions regarding depredation cases, Colby notified his friends. It is interesting that despite published position openings, Colby's friends got the jobs. See Court of Claims, Indian Depredations, Letters Received, March 1891–June 1892, N.A., R.G. 205.

28. "Indian Depredation Claims," *Woman's Tribune* (April 1, 1893), SHSW.

29. Franklin Willey, ed., *State Builders: An Illustrated Historical and Biographical Record of the State of New Hampshire at the Beginning of the Twentieth Century* (Manchester: New Hampshire Publishing Corporation, 1992).

30. Charles Robert Corning diary entry (December 31, 1890), Concord Public Library, Concord, N.H.

31. Ibid. (April 30, 1892).

32. Ibid. (June 7, 1892).

33. Ibid. (May 20, 1892).

34. Ibid. (June 14, 1892).

35. Ibid. (Oct. 17, 1892).

36. Leon Burr Richardson, *William E. Chandler: Republican* (New York: Dodd, Mead and Company, 1940), 734–43; see also William E. Chandler Papers, Library of Congress, Washington, D.C.; also William E. Chandler Papers in the New Hampshire Historical Society, Concord, N.H.

37. Ibid.

38. Corning diary (November 16, 1892).

39. Ibid. (October 24, 1892).

40. *Woman's Tribune* (April 1, 1893), SHSW.

41. Ibid. Testimony Before Senate Select Committee, Depredation Hearings.

42. The Indian depredation bill passed in Congress on February 19, 1891, as reported in the *Boston Morning Journal* (February 20, 1891).

43. Letters from Leonard W. Colby to R. S. Bibb (March 1893), Nebraska State Historical Society, Lincoln; see also Homer Kidd Papers, NSHS.

44. Letter from President Benjamin Harrison to Leonard W. Colby (January 11, 1892), SHSW.

45. *New York Times* (October 26–28, 1892).

46. W. H. H. Miller Collection (letter book), Indiana State Library, Indianapolis, letter from Miller to Colby (September 25, 1895) and Miller to Colby (May 8, 1894).

47. Indian Depredations, Letters Received, March 1891–June 1892, N.A., R.G. 205, E72. Mr. Howry asks Corning to go to Pine Ridge as special agent to investigate Colby (January 20, 1894). Corning's diary entry for that date says, "Ye Gods! My abhorrence of cold weather is exceedingly brisk & no place can be colder than Pine Ridge & Rosebud at this time of year."

48. Letter from Corning to Senator Chandler (September 11, 1894); see also letter from Corning to Senator Chandler (July 9, 1894); also letter from Corning at Rosebud Agency to Senator Chandler (June 15, 1894), New Hampshire Historical Society, Concord, N.H.

49. Thomas Flood, a Rosebud Lakota, was born May 17, 1864, and died April 6, 1907. Corning hired Flood as interpreter to find evidence of fraud in the Indian depredation cases involving Colby. The plan was to turn Indians against each other as a way to uncover damaging information. Once Flood found out that Corning was a government spy, the special investigator never had a chance. He left Rosebud a year later without uncovering anything. Corning's wife stayed on the reservation to teach school after he lost his job. Thomas Flood's closest living relative, Bernard G. Flood, Jr., lives at O'Kreek, S.D.; see also Corning diary (1892–94).

50. Letter from Corning to Senator Chandler (June 15, 1894), William E. Chandler Papers, Box 31, NHHS; see also letter from the Assistant Attorney General of the United State Charles B. Howry to Corning (April 27, 1894), Corning Papers, NHHS; also Court of Claims, Indian Depredations, Letters Received, March 1891–June 1892, N.A., R.G. 205-E71.

51. Letter from Charles B. Howry to Senator Chandler (June 15, 1894), NHHS.

52. Annual Report of the Assistant Attorney General of the United States (1892), N.A., R.G. 205.

53. Corning diary (February 29, 1896), Concord Public Library, Concord, Mass.; see also letter from Horace S. Cummings to Corning (December 20, 1897).

54. "Employing an Attorney for the Nation," *Muskogee Phoenix* (November 9, 1893); see also Leonard W. Colby's certification to act as attorney for the Cherokee Nation (February 5, 1894) and his earlier certification to act as attorney (December 19, 1893); see also Contract of the Otoe & Missouri Indians with Leonard W. Colby to act as attorney (1893), McFarlin Library, Cherokee Records, University of Tulsa, Okla; see also "Creek Council," *Muskogee Phoenix* (November 9, 1893); also Colby's contract to represent the Creek Nation, Litton Creek Papers (1870–1930), Oklahoma Historical Society, Oklahoma City.

55. "Advice from the Indian Department," *Muskogee Phoenix* (July 27, 1893).

56. "The Cherokee Outlet," *Sioux Falls Argus Leader* (April 10, 1893); see also Angie Debo, *And Still the Waters Run* (Princeton, N.J.: Princeton University Press, 1940); see also Angie Debo, *The Road*

to Disappearance: A History of the Creek Indians (Norman: University of Oklahoma Press, 1941), 354–56.

57. Passim, Debo, *And Still the Waters Run.*

58. "Indian Land Lawyers," *Outlook Magazine,* vol. 95 (August 27, 1910), 911–12.

59. *Indian Journal* (July 13, 1894).

60. "Gen. Colby at Tahlequah," *Indian Chieftain* (Dec. 13, 1894).

61. Undated *Muskogee Phoenix* article (probably January 1895), microform available at the Oklahoma Historical Society.

62. Undated letter from Leonard Colby to Clara Colby (probably 1893), written from Oklahoma, SHSW.

63. Mary Matthes, remembrances of Lost Bird, SHSW.

64. *Woman's Tribune* (February 5, 1896), SHSW.

8. THE HEART WOUND

1. Passim, Allan Nevins, *Grover Cleveland: A Study in Courage* (New York: Dodd, Mead & Company, 1933).

2. Passim, Sean Dennis Cashman, *America in the Gilded Age* (New York: New York University Press, 1984).

3. Interview with Helen Bewick (1989), Madison, Wisc.

4. Gertrude M. McDowell, "Suffrage in Nebraska," in Nebraska Society of the Daughters of the American Revolution, *Collections of Nebraska Pioneer Reminiscences* (Cedar Rapids, Iowa: Torch Press, 1916).

5. J. Sterling Morton and Albert Watkins, *History of Nebraska* (Lincoln: Western Publishing and Engraving Company, 1918).

6. Letter from Elizabeth Cady Stanton to Clara B. Colby (August 21, 1889), SHSW.

7. Moeller family genealogy can be found in the Helen Colby collection, West Linn, Ore.

8. Court of Claims Section, Indian Depredations, Letters Received, Letter from Charles B. Howry to Leonard Colby (January 2, 1894), N.A., R.G. 205-E72.

9. "How to Make Children Brave," *Woman's Tribune* (May 5, 1894).

10. Letter from Maud Miller to Clara Colby (June 8, 1893), SHSW.

11. Letters from Clara Colby to Maud Miller (June 1893–September 19, 1893), SHSW.

12. "Sacrifice," an essay by Clara B. Colby, SHSW.

13. Letter from Maud Miller to Clara Colby (June 20, 1893), SHSW.

14. The *Woman's Tribune* often reflected Clara's outrage toward her husband, although she never printed his name. In 1889 she had given a speech entitled "Women in Marriage" at the Twenty-first Annual Convention of NAWSA. She now added to that essay and began printing it in the *Tribune.* The speech was reprinted three times in 1893.

15. Olympia Brown, *Democratic Ideals: A Memorial Sketch of Clara B. Colby* (Washington, D.C.: Federal Suffrage Association, 1917), 48.

16. Ibid.

17. *Woman's Tribune* (August 5, 1893), SHSW

18. Note found in Clara Colby Collection with pressed flower, SHSW.

19. Nevins; see also Ralph K. Andrist, *The American Heritage History of the Confident Years* (New York: Bonanza Books, 1987), 295–296.

20. Passim, Nevins, *Grover Cleveland.*

21. *Woman's Tribune* (May 15–September 1893); see also Joel Cook, *The World's Fair at Chicago* (Chicago: Rand, McNally & Company, 1891); see also Ernest L. Bogart, *The Modern Commonwealth: 1893–1918* (Chicago: A. C. McClurg & Co., 1922); for details of women suffrage at the World's Columbian Expo, see "World's Columbian Exposition—Interior of Woman's Building," *Scientific American* (September 9, 1893), 171.

22. Ida Husted Harper, *The Life and Work of Susan B. Anthony,* vol. 2 (Indianapolis: The Bowen-Merrill Company, 1898), 737–54; see also Steven Longstreet, *Chicago: 1860–1919* (New York: David McKay Company, Inc., 1973).

23. Passim, George E. Hyde, *Spotted Tail's Folk: A History of the Brule Sioux* (Norman: University of Oklahoma Press, 1976).

24. *Woman's Tribune* (October 14, 1893), SHSW

25. Letter from Susan B. Anthony to Clara B. Colby (May 12, 1893), SHSW.

26. Letter from Mrs. Skinner to Clara B. Colby (May 28, 1893), SHSW.

27. Ibid.

28. Letter from Leonard Colby to his wife, Clara (June 12, 1893), SHSW.

29. Ibid.

30. Letter from Grandmother Chilton to Clara and Leonard (March 29, 1874), SHSW.

31. Clara often used the term "Heart Wound." In the *Woman's Tribune* (February 27, 1892): "A heart-wound is generally concealed from the public gaze."

32. Martha Vicinus, ed., *A Widening Sphere: Changing Roles of Victorian Women* (Bloomington: Indiana University Press, 1977), 163–81.

33. Note found in Clara B. Colby Collection in her handwriting says she wrote down how terrible she felt and then destroyed the pages, SHSW.

34. Letter from Mrs. Skinner to Clara B. Colby (June 3, 1893), SHSW.

35. Interview with Helen Colby, Paul Colby's daughter-in-law (1989), West Linn, Ore.

36. Passim, Francis F. Beirne, *Baltimore: A Picture History 1858–1958* (New York: Hastings House, 1957).

37. Letter from Maud Miller to Clara B. Colby (June 8, 1893), SHSW.

38. Letter from Leonard Colby to Clara B. Colby (June 12, 1893), SHSW.

39. See envelope postmarked June 12, 1893, SHSW.

40. Letter from Leonard Colby to his wife Clara B. Colby (June 15, 1893), SHSW.

41. Letter from Leonard Colby to Clara B. Colby (June 15, 1893), SHSW.

42. Letter from Maud Miller to Clara B. Colby (June 20, 1893), SHSW.

43. Letters from Susan B. Anthony to Clara B. Colby (April 4, 1893, and April 9, 1896).

44. Letter from Clara B. Colby to Maude Miller (September 19, 1893), SHSW.

45. A copy of this essay can be found in the Clara B. Colby Collection, SHSW.

9. BACK ALLEYS

1. *Woman's Tribune* (December 16, 1893), SHSW.

2. Letter from Maud Miller to Clara B. Colby (September 11, 1893), SHSW.

3. Letter from Maud Miller to Clara B. Colby (September 28, 1893), SHSW.

4. Letters from Leonard W. Colby to his wife (June 12 and 15, 1893), SHSW.

5. Harriett L. Coolidge, "Zintka Lanuni—Lost Bird," *Trained Motherhood* (January 1898), 15–19.

6. W. H. Babcock, *American Anthropologist, 1888–89*, vols. 1–2, 267–68.

7. Passim, Peter Gammond, *Scott Joplin and the Ragtime Era* (New York: St. Martin's Press, 1975); see also Edward Berlin, *Ragtime: A Musical and Cultural History* (Berkeley: University of California Press, 1980).

8. Ibid. Passim. Edward Berlin. *Ragtime: A Musical and Cultural History* (Berkeley: University of California Press, 1980).

9. Ibid. Passim, Peter Gammon. *Scott Joplin and the Ragtime Era* (New York: St. Martin's Press, 1975).

10. For Clara's version of the incident, see "Zintka Lanuni's Corner," *Woman's Tribune* (June 13, 1896).

11. Barbara Hilkert Andolsen, "Racism in the Nineteenth- and Twentieth-Century Women's Movement: An Ethical Appraisal," Ph.D. dissertation, Vanderbilt University, Nashville, Tenn., 1981. Susan B. Anthony asked Frederick Douglass not to attend the annual NAWSA convention in 1894 because she did not want to antagonize southern women. Anna Shaw said, "Never before in the history of the world have men made former slaves the political masters of their former mistresses"; see Shaw, *Story of a Pioneer*, 312.

    Stanton had a tendency to refer to nonwhite Americans as "Sambo" and "Dinah." Stanton feared the enfranchisement of black men (without the accompanying full female suffrage) because she viewed "degraded" black men as even more prone to oppress women than were white men; see also Wilmer A. Linkugel, "The Speeches of Anna Howard Shaw (collected and edited with introduction and notes)," Ph.D. dissertation, University of Wisconsin, 1961.

    Andolsen writes: "The moral irony of the American woman suffrage movement is that the suffragists committed the very sin for which they called others to task." See also Thomas Gossett, *Race: The History of an Idea in America* (Dallas: Southern Methodist University Press, 1963), 311; see also Calvin Hernton, *Sex and Racism in America* (New York: Grove Press, 1965), 123–28; also "Indians Versus Women," *Woman's Tribune* (May 9, 1891).

12. *Woman's Tribune* (May 16, 1896). Clara often published articles about Sojourner Truth, the first

black woman to speak against slavery; see Victoria Ortiz, *Sojourner Truth, A Self-Made Woman* (New York: Lippincott, 1974); also Hertha Pauli, *Her Name Was Sojourner Truth* (New York: Avon, 1976).

13. "About Washington," *Woman's Tribune* (March 14, 1891), see also Ida Husted Harper, *The History of Woman Suffrage*, vol. 4, 247.

14. "Zintka Lanuni's Corner," *Woman's Tribune* (June 13, 1896).

15. Passim, Constance McLaughlin Green, *Washington: Capital City, 1879–1950* (Princeton, N.J.: Princeton University Press, 1963).

16. "A Dark Little Stranger," *Freeport (Nebr.) Daily Bulletin* (November 17, 1894). The article goes on to say that Zintka's "ideas of her race are very vague."

17. From Clara's list of Zintka's baby sayings. This was a Christmas list given "to Florence and her papa" (probably 1895), SHSW.

18. *Woman's Tribune* (June 12, 1894), SHSW.

19. Letter from Leo Tolstoy to Clara B. Colby (October 17, 1894), SHSW.

20. Letter from Maud Miller to Clara B. Colby (January 15, 1894), SHSW.

21. Ibid.

22. Loose ledger note on which Clara has added up all of Leonard's expenses with regard to Maud Miller, SHSW.

23. Letter from Mary H. Watson to Clara B. Colby (March 2, 1894), SHSW.

24. Letter from Mary H. Watson to Clara B. Colby (March 15, 1894), SHSW.

25. Letter from Clara B. Colby to Maud Miller (February 28, 1894), SHSW.

26. Letter from Maud Miller to Clara B. Colby (March 2, 1894), SHSW.

27. Letter to Clara B. Colby from Maud Miller (undated), SHSW.

28. Letter from Clara B. Colby to Maud Miller (March 20, 1894), SHSW.

29. Letter from Maud Miller to Clara B. Colby (n.d.), SHSW.

30. Letter from Maud Miller to Clara B. Colby (n.d.), SHSW.

31. Letter from Maud Miller to Clara B. Colby (n.d.), SHSW.

32. Interview with Zoa Worden (1985) in Beatrice, Nebr.; also interview with Fordyce Graff (1985) in Beatrice.

10. SCANDAL

1. "Can Find No Fraud," *Nebraska State Journal* (December 16, 1894).

2. Angie Debo, *The Road to Disappearance: A History of the Creek Indians* (Norman: University of Oklahoma Press, 1941), 354.

3. *Muskogee Phoenix* (November 2, 1893).

4. Ibid.

5. Ibid, see also "Creek Council," *Muskogee Phoenix* (November 9, 1893). Colby was appropriated $12,000. See also Litton Creek Papers, 1870–1930, CRN-17, Oklahoma Historical Society, Oklahoma City.

6. "Employing an Attorney for the Nation," *Muskogee Phoenix* (November 9, 1893).

7. Cherokee Nation Records, Box 20, Folder 4, 1894; Contract to Represent the Cherokee Nation, Dept. of Special Collections, McFarlin Library, University of Tulsa, Okla; see also Otoe and Missouri Contract (1893).

8. *Territorial News* (November 24, 1892). Beck tried to get a job with his tribe but was not successful, so he took a position as editor of the *Wagoner Record*, an Oklahoma newspaper.

9. Angie Debo, *The Road to Disappearance*, 354, 355, 356; see also Creek Tribal Records 29030 FF, 29227, 33171, 35607; also *Muskogee Phoenix* (November 2, 1893); also United States Court of Claims Records 716, 1752, 3141, 3584; also National Archives, Depredation Claims 3373, 3978, 4008, 7079.

10. Ibid.

11. Angie Debo, *The Road to Disappearance*, 355.

12. "The Creek Muddle," *Muskogee Phoenix* (July 25, 1895); see also "Trouble at Okmulgee" (May 29, 1895). The Cherokee Strip equaled the combined land area of Rhode Island, Delaware, and Connecticut.

13. *Muskogee Phoenix* (July 25, 1895).

14. Ibid.

15. Cherokee National Records, Indian Archives Division. Letters Sent and Received, Cherokee

(Tahlequah)—Strip (Jan. 1, 1894–Dec. 16, 1899), Oklahoma Historical Society, Oklahoma City.

16. Angie Debo, *The Road to Disappearance*, 354–60.
17. Ibid.
18. *Muskogee Phoenix* (February 24, 1895).
19. See the Angie Debo Papers, Edmun Low Library Special Collections, Oklahoma State University, Stillwater.

Barnard handled over 18,000 cases of graft in a short time. In 1910 she intervened in nearly 200 cases of orphaned Indian children who had lost their land to unscrupulous land grabbers. Her salary was inadequate and her duties increased as the years went by. Oftentimes she caught a swindler, but the Indians had been threatened beforehand and were generally afraid to testify.

Kate put up a magnificent fight against grafters, but soon she uncovered fraudulent contracts signed by government politicians. The powerful men in Oklahoma politics drove Barnard to a nervous collapse. Her health ruined, she retired from public life. See also Edward T. James, W. Janel, and Paul S. Boyer, eds., *Notable American Women, 1607–1950* (Cambridge, Mass.: The Bellnap Press of Harvard University, 1971), vol. 1., 90–92.
20. Wm. W. Cook, Sr., interview (1988). Maud bragged to a banker in Beatrice that she had a male loan officer friend who would do anything she asked.

Among the items found in the Leonard Colby Collection were letters from the Painseville (Ohio) Lake County Savings & Loan Company called Tuttle & Hubbard. Maud therefore may have been referring to Martin Tuttle, who died in 1949. See Morley Library, Painseville, Ohio. See also Helen Colby Collection, West Linn, Ore.
21. "Coxey's Indian Ally," *Woman's Tribune* (May 12, 1894), SHSW.
22. Passim, Luther Standing Bear, *My People, the Sioux* (Lincoln: University of Nebraska Press, 1975).
23. *Woman's Tribune* (March 21, 1893), SHSW.
24. "Nobody's Kitty," *Woman's Tribune* (April 6, 1895), SHSW.
25. "Zintka's Corner," *Woman's Tribune* (May 25, 1895), SHSW.
26. "The Bird That Would Sing," *Woman's Tribune* (January 18, 1896), SHSW.
27. Ibid.
28. *Woman's Tribune* (November 3, 1894), SHSW.
29. Letter from Clara to Harriet Miller (July 7, 1894), Sophia Smith Collection, Smith College Archives, Northampton, Mass; see also *Woman's Tribune* (June 23, 1894).
30. *Woman's Tribune* (September 22, 1894), SHSW.
31. *Woman's Tribune* (June 23, 1894), SHSW.
32. *Woman's Tribune* (July 28, 1894), SHSW.
33. Letter from Susan B. Anthony to Clara B. Colby (May 26, 1894); see Clara B. Colby Collection, Huntington Library, San Marino, Calif.
34. *Woman's Tribune* (November 3, 1894), SHSW.
35. Letter from Susan B. Anthony to Elizabeth Cady Stanton (July 24, 1895); see Papers of Susan B. Anthony and Elizabeth Cady Stanton, University of Massachusetts, Amherst.
36. Interview with Fordyce Graff (1985).
37. "The Governor's New Staff," *Wahoo New Era* (June 6, 1895).
38. Letter from Norma Kidd Green to Edward T. James (January 31, 1962). James was the editor of *Notable American Women: A Biographical Dictionary*, a work sponsored by Radcliffe College. This letter was given to the author, Renee Sansom Flood, by Mrs. Green's daughter, Mrs. Elizabeth Green Davis of Newark, Del., on June 23, 1990.
39. *Woman's Tribune* (May 5, 1894, and May 25, 1895), SHSW.
40. "Little Lost Bird's Story," *Evening World Herald* (February 9, 1897); see the John R. Brennan Scrapbook, Wounded Knee File, South Dakota State Historical Society.
41. Interview with Helen Bewick (1988), in Madison, Wisc.
42. *Woman's Tribune* (September 14, 1895), SHSW.
43. Letter from Dr. Mary White to her sister, Clara B. Colby (May 10, 1895), SHSW.

11. WHITES ONLY

1. "Zintka's Corner," *Woman's Tribune* (August 17, 1895), SHSW.
2. *Freeport Daily Bulletin* (n.d. 1897), Helen Colby Collection, West Linn, Ore.

3. Ibid.
4. Ibid.
5. For information about anthropologist Alice Fletcher, see Joan Mark, *A Stranger in Her Native Land: Alice Fletcher and the American Indians* (Lincoln: University of Nebraska Press, 1988). Elaine Goodale Eastman was the wife of Dakota physician Charles A. Eastman. For more information about Mrs. Eastman, see Kay Graber, *Sister to the Sioux: The Memoirs of Elaine Goodale Eastman, 1885–1891* (Lincoln: University of Nebraska Press, 1978).
6. Letter from Elizabeth Cady Stanton to Clara B. Colby (May 19, 1888), SHSW.
7. "Announcement," letter to the *Woman's Tribune* (December 7, 1895), SHSW.
8. Letter from Elizabeth C. Stanton to Clara B. Colby (n.d.), SHSW.
9. "Zintka Lanuni's Corner," *Woman's Tribune* (September 4, 1897), SHSW.
10. For a list of Clara's lectures, see her collection in SHSW; see also Olympia Brown, *Democratic Ideals: A Memorial Sketch of Clara B. Colby* (Washington, D.C.: Federal Suffrage Association, 1917), 105–108.
11. Letter from Susan B. Anthony to Clara B. Colby (December 13, 1895 and December 18, 1895), Clara B. Colby Collection, Huntington Library, San Marino, Calif.
12. *Woman's Tribune* (February 22, 1896), SHSW.
13. Letter from Elizabeth Cady Stanton to Clara B. Colby (n.d.), SHSW.
14. Letter from Susan B. Anthony to Elizabeth C. Stanton (February 1896), Susan B. Anthony Papers, Huntington Library, San Marino, Calif. For *Woman's Bible,* see Stanton, "Something Remains to Dare," Introduction to *The Woman's Bible* (New York, Arno Press, 1974).
15. Ida Husted Harper, *The Life and Work of Susan B. Anthony,* vol. 2 (Indianapolis: The Bowen-Merrill Company, 1898), 856.
16. *Woman's Tribune* (February 8, 1896), SHSW.
17. Eleanor Claire Jerry, "Clara Bewick Colby and the Woman's Tribune: Strategies of a Freelance Movement Leader," Ph.D. dissertation, University of Kansas (1986), 112.
18. Letter from Susan B. Anthony to Clara Colby (March 25, 1895), Clara B. Colby Collection, Huntington Library, San Marino, Calif.
19. Letter from Susan B. Anthony to Clara B. Colby (January 13, 1896), Clara B. Colby Collection, Huntington Library, San Marino, Calif.
20. Letter from Ida Husted Harper to Reverend Olympia Brown (April 11, 1919); see Olympia Brown Papers, Reel 8, Schlesinger Library, Radcliffe (Harvard University), Cambridge, Mass.
21. Letter from Edw. G. Mauger (undated, 1897), Brooklyn, N.Y., SHSW.
22. Letter from Edw. G. Mauger to Clara B. Colby (August 26, 1897), SHSW.
23. Brown, *Democratic Ideals,* 88–102.
24. Obituary for Thomas Bewick, *Wisconsin State Journal* (April 17, 1897). The obituary states that he died April 16 from an "attack of the grippe."
25. "Mrs. Besant on Hypnotism," *Woman's Tribune* (May 29, 1897); also "Elizabeth Lyle Saxon on Psychic Experiences" (May 1, 1897), SHSW.
26. Letter from Susan B. Anthony to Clara B. Colby (June 25, 1897), Clara B. Colby Collection, Huntington Library, San Marino, Calif.
27. "Miss Anthony in Berkshire," *Rochester Democrat & Chronicle* (July 30, 1897); see the Susan B. Anthony Collection, Berkshire County Historical Society, Rochester, N.Y.
28. Ida Husted Harper, *The Life and Work of Susan B. Anthony,* vol. 2 (Indianapolis: Bowen-Merrill Company, 1898), chapter 50, 942-B.

12. CUBA LIBRE!

1. Henry Houghton Beck, *Cuba's Fight for Freedom and the War with Spain* (Philadelphia: Globe Bible Publishing Company, 1898), 215.
2. Beck, *Cuba's Fight,* 295.
3. Hugh J. Dobbs, *History of Gage County, Nebraska* (Lincoln: Western Publishing and Engraving Company, 1918), 494. Not one local newspaper reported that Colby or anyone else organized forces for Cuba in or around Matamoros, Mexico. American and Mexican historical societies in that area have nothing to show that this occurred. No oral traditional stories exist in the border towns about a buildup of men such as Leonard Colby stated.
4. The original photograph of Zintka and Leonard Colby was given to the author in 1991 by Helen Colby, West Linn, Oregon.

5. Letter from R. F. Pettigrew, Chairman of the Committee on Indian Affairs, to Clara B. Colby (May 30, 1898), SHSW.
6. By April 30, 1898, the *Woman's Tribune* is full of war articles. Influenced by her husband, Clara's remarks are far from her usual anti-war views.
7. *Woman's Tribune* (March 19, 1899, and April 21, 1898), SHSW.
8. Letter from Clara B. Colby to Susan B. Anthony, n.d., 1898, SHSW. See also The Huntington Library, Susan B. Anthony and Clara Colby Papers, San Marino, Calif.
9. Letter from Susan B. Anthony to Clara B. Colby, April 20, 1898, SHSW.
10. Ibid., May 10, 1898, SHSW.
11. Letter from Elizabeth Cady Stanton to Clara Colby, July 20, 1898, SHSW.
12. *Woman's Tribune* (July 9, 1898), SHSW.
13. Ibid. March 11, 1898, SHSW.
14. Ibid. June 25, 1898, SHSW.
15. *Woman's Tribune* (May 28, 1989), SHSW.
16. For original War Correspondent's Pass see Clara B. Colby Collection, SHSW.
17. "Zintka Lanuni's Corner," *Woman's Tribune* (August 20, 1898).
18. Letter from Susan B. Anthony to "Miss White," July 17, 1989, SHSW.
19. *Woman's Tribune* (August 6, 1898), SHSW.
20. "Letter from the Editor," *Woman's Tribune* (August 20, 1889).
21. Ibid.
22. Letter from L. W. Colby to his law partners in Beatrice, Griggs, Rinaker & Bibb, December 10, 1898. Leonard W. Colby Collection, NSHS.
23. *Woman's Tribune* (September 13, 1898), SHSW.
24. Ibid.
25. *Woman's Tribune* (September 10, 1898), SHSW.
26. Ibid. October 8, 1878, SHSW.
27. *Woman's Tribune* (October 15, 1898), SHSW.
28. Ibid. October 29, 1898, SHSW.
29. Letter from Clara B. Colby to Nellie Richardson, February 4, 1906, SHSW.
30. In 1933, Maud wrote about her then lover (Gen. Colby) and his mission to Cuba. The "secret mission" was not a military order, but a clandestine rendezvous for the purpose of bilking nearly half a million dollars from the U.S. government in war claims. Copy in Helen Colby Collection, West Linn, Oregon.
31. Passim, Beck, *Cuba's Fight for Freedom and the War with Spain*.
32. *Nebraska State Journal*, June 9, 1906. "Secures Large Estate." See also the *Chicago Inter-Ocean*, April 15, 1906, "Claim By Nebraska Woman."
33. Beck, 77–79.
34. Ibid, 80.
35. *The Beatrice Daily Sun*, March 19, 1961. Article about General Leonard W. Colby coming home from Cuba a "local hero" (February 1899).
36. For proof of Maud's sudden fortune see 57th Congress, 1st Session, Senate, House Executive Document No. 299. "List of Claims Before the Spanish Treaty Claim Commission." Letter from the Acting Attorney General. This list shows that Maud put in a claim (the largest before the commission) for destroyed property including "houses, sugar factory, locomotive cars, electric plants and sugar cane plantations named Diana and Destino."

13. THE TRIP ABROAD

1. Trachoma is viral conjunctivitis affecting both the upper and lower eyelids and the cornea of the eye. Antibiotic therapy and sulfonamides are used today as treatment for trachoma.
2. Letter from Susan B. Anthony to Clara B. Colby, May 17, 1899. Clara B. Colby Papers, The Huntington Library. Anthony wasn't the only suffragist to warn Clara not to go. Elizabeth C. Stanton wrote to Clara, "Above all things, do not take a child with you. . . . I have been in families for days without seeing one of the children under sixteen. They are considered a nuisance unless very beautiful. . . . If they had children they would be afraid of your child's sore eyes as they are contagious. Her . . . appearance would be against her. . . . leave her at home. . . . I advise you as I would my own daughter *stay at home*." Undated letter, SHSW.
3. "Editor's Notes," *Woman's Tribune* (June 3, 1899), SHSW.

4. *Woman's Tribune* (July 15, 1899), SHSW.

5. Ibid.

6. Ibid.

7. *Woman's Tribune* (August 12, 1899), SHSW.

8. Ibid. "Editorial Journeyings."

9. Ibid. See also *Woman's Tribune* (March 9, 1901), SHSW.

10. *Woman's Tribune* (October 21, 1899), SHSW. Clara took many photographs with her "Kodak" on the trip, but the author was unable to locate them. Zintka seems to have enjoyed the trip and spoke of it often during her life. Clara wanted Zintka to see the world.

11. Ibid.

12. *Woman's Tribune* (November 4, 1899), SHSW. Wind Cave is located north of present-day Hot Springs, South Dakota. It is the site of the Lakota creation story in the sacred Black Hills.

13. *Woman's Tribune* (October 21, 1899), SHSW.

14. *Woman's Tribune* (August 12, 1899), SHSW.

15. Ibid.

16. Ibid.

17. Letter from Susan B. Anthony to Clara B. Colby, November 20, 1899, SHSW.

18. Letter from Susan B. Anthony to Clara B. Colby, December 22, 1899, SHSW.

19. Letter from Clara B. Colby to her husband, Leonard W. Colby, December 31, 1899, SHSW.

14. THE MISSING BOND

1. When Miss Anthony wanted something of Clara she gushed, "Be a good girl," and signed her letters "Devoted" or "Lovingly yours." On January 10, 1900, Anthony wrote: "Your letter shows that the new year finds you with as many irons in the fire as you had all through the last year. Your attempt at keeping roomers and boarders seems to me just the added ounce that broke the camel's back. . . . You are not a successful *financier*—that you have proved, but you are a splendid writer."

2. Books belonging to Leonard and Maud are in the Helen Colby Collection, West Linn, Oregon.

3. Clara reviewed publications, and if she liked them, she advertised the books in her paper. In 1900 every issue contained at least three book reviews.

4. Letter from Elizabeth C. Stanton to Clara B. Colby, March 6, 1900, SHSW. Earlier Stanton had written: "No. No, if you are determined to stick we shall also. We shall not desert you. I shall send you all the items I find in my reading and write you something each week. . . . If I were you, dear Clara, I would give up the *Tribune* and be foot-free to lecture, to get rid of so much mechanical work as you have to do and the constant wearing anxiety as to finances. You have a fine mind, a great education, and as you can afford it, take your time now for self improvement, for reading, thought, and meditation. There is such a thing as being too active, living too full a life. Most reformers fail at this point." December 8, 1898.

5. "The Pan-American," *Woman's Tribune* (October 5, 1901), SHSW.

6. Ibid.

7. Joseph Iron Eye Dudley, *Choteau Creek: A Sioux Reminiscence* (Lincoln: University of Nebraska Press, 1992). Dudley is an Ihanktonwan Dakota (Yankton). This is a perceptive look at his Indian childhood and his grandparents' role in child rearing.

8. *Woman's Tribune* (October 5, 1901), SHSW.

9. Interviews with Ben Gullikson (Yankton), Leonard R. Bruguier (Yankton), and Robert Stead (Rosebud), 1985–1992.

10. Letter from Anna Pope to Clara B. Colby, March 22, 19__, SHSW.

11. Interviews with the Pope family, 1989.

12. Ibid.

13. *Woman's Tribune* (July 8, 1900), SHSW.

14. Pope family remembrances, 1992.

15. Ibid.

16. *Woman's Tribune* (August 11, 1900), SHSW.

17. Pope family remembrances, 1992.

18. *Woman's Tribune* (July 30, 1900), SHSW.

19. Pope family remembrances, 1992.

20. Ibid.

21. Ibid.

22. Letter from Clara B. Colby to Clara McNaughton, May 29, 1901. See Clara McNaughton Papers, University of San Francisco Archives.
23. Undated poem found in Clara's Papers, SHSW.

15. "MY HEART'S BLOOD"

1. See National Archives, Record Group 75, Bureau of Indian Affairs. Letters Received, Northern Cheyenne Agency, 1881–1907. See also Richmond L. Clow, "The Lakota Ghost Dance After 1890," *South Dakota History* (Winter 1990), vol. 20, no. 4, 323–33.
2. Interview with Helen Bewick, Madison, Wisconsin, 1989.
3. See Sandy K. Warteie and Cindy L. Miller-Perrin, *Preventing Child Sexual Abuse* (Lincoln: University of Nebraska Press, 1992); Florence Rush, *The Best Kept Secret: Sexual Abuse of Children* (Englewood Cliffs, N.J.: Prentice-Hall, 1980); Wayne Kritsberg, *The Invisible Wound* (N.Y.: Bantam Books, 1993).
4. Letter from Clara B. Colby to Captain Richard H. Pratt, Oct. 17, 1902. ". . . she seemed to think it would be delightful to go and live among the Indians . . ."
5. In January 1891, Clara wrote in the *Tribune*: ". . . the editor of the *Tribune* will state that, for *herself*, she rejoices in this opportunity, by the care and education of this child, to join in expiating . . . the wrongs of our race against hers."
6. Letter from A. C. Towner to U.S. Indian Agent John R. Brennan at Pine Ridge, August 7, 1901. N.A., R.G. 75, Records of the Bureau of Indian Affairs, Letters Received, 1881–1907.
7. Letter from A. C. Towner to U.S. Agent Ira A. Hatch, Cheyenne River Sioux Agency, April 6, 1901. N.A., R.G. 75, Records of the Bureau of Indian Affairs, Letters Received, 1881–1907.
8. Hatch to Towner, July 29, 1901.
9. Brennan to Towner, August 7, 1901, 48184-1901.
10. Ibid.
11. Brennan to Towner, August 29, 1901, 48184-1901.
12. Hatch to Towner, July 29, 1901.
13. Ibid.
14. Letter from George E. Bartlett to Clara, March 7, 1904, SHSW.
15. Ibid.
16. Brennan to Towner, June 14, 1902.
17. Ibid.
18. Brennan to Towner, July 1, 1902.
19. Towner to Brennan, July 25, 1902.
20. Wilson I. Austin of Norfolk, Nebraska, asked for information about Lost Bird in December 1925. Felix Crane Pretty Voice and James Ax gave testimony January 3, 1925. Austin wrote again on January 14, 1925, asking for more details of Lost Bird's life story.
21. See Lost Bird's file at Cheyenne River Sioux Tribe, Eagle Butte, South Dakota.
22. Ibid. Interview with James Ax or Brown Sinew, 1925.
23. Interview with Fordyce Graff, 1985, Beatrice, Nebraska.
24. Ibid.
25. Interview with Helen Colby, 1989, West Linn, Oregon.
26. Interview with David Colby, 1985, Ashland, Oregon.
27. Ibid.
28. Interview with Fordyce Graff, 1985. Interview with David Colby, 1985.
29. Interview with David Colby, 1985.
30. Interview with Albert J. Allgier, 1989.
31. "Westward Wanderings," *Woman's Tribune* (Setpember 20, 1902), SHSW.
32. *Woman's Tribune* (July 26, 1902), SHSW.
33. *Woman's Tribune* (August 30, 1902), SHSW.
34. *Woman's Tribune* (September 20, 1902), SHSW.
35. Interview with Helen Bewick, 1989, Madison, Wisconsin.
36. Letter from Clara B. Colby to Susan B. Anthony, October 9, 1902, SHSW.
37. L. G. Moses and Raymond Wilson (eds.), *Indian Lives: Essays on Nineteenth and Twentieth Century Native American Leaders* (Albuquerque: University of New Mexico Press, 1985), 145.
38. Letter from Clara B. Colby to Captain Richard H. Pratt, October 14, 1902. See Richard H. Pratt Papers, Beineke Rare Book and Manuscript Library, Yale University Library, New Haven, Conn.

39. Pratt to Colby, October 15, 1902.

40. Colby to Pratt, October 17, 1902.

41. Letter from J. H. Clewell, Principal, Salem Academy and College, Winston-Salem, N.C., to Clara B. Colby, December 11, 1902, SHSW.

42. Ibid. January 8, 1903, SHSW.

43. Ibid. January 19, 1903, SHSW.

44. Ibid. For good overview of boarding schools, see Frederick E. Hoxie, *Indians in American History*. D'Arcy McNickle Center for the History of the American Indian. The Newberry Library, Arlington Heights, Illinois, 1988.

45. Letter from Sister M.———, Principal, to Clara B. Colby, August 16, 1903, SHSW. See also letter from Rev. C. G. Vardell, President, Red Springs Seminary for Young Ladies, Red Springs, N.C., September 2, 1903, to Clara B. Colby, SHSW.

46. Letter from Leonard Colby to his wife Clara B. Colby, March 7, 1903, SHSW. Clara wanted at least $420 a year for alimony and child support.

47. *Beatrice Daily Express* (December 11, 1903). See also *Beatrice Morning Sun* (December 11, 1903).

48. Letter from Clara B. Colby to herself, written August 11, 1903, SHSW.

49. Letter from Dr. Mary White to her sister, Clara B. Colby, August 1903, SHSW.

50. Letter from Leonard Colby to Clara B. Colby, August 16, 1903, SHSW.

51. Letter from Clara B. Colby to Leonard Colby, August 22, 1903, SHSW.

52. Ibid.

53. Letter from Leonard Colby to Clara B. Colby, September 30, 1903, SHSW.

54. Letter from Leonard Colby to Clara B. Colby, December 1, 1903, SHSW.

55. Letter from Clara B. Colby to Leonard Colby, November 11, 1903, SHSW.

56. Letter from Leonard Colby to Clara B. Colby, November 20, 1903, SHSW.

57. "The Story of an Indian Girl Kindness Could not Tame," *St. Louis Post-Dispatch* (February 28, 1904).

58. "Looking Backward 26 Years—The Dewey Murder Trial Under Judge Geiger," *Norton Champion*, Norton, Kansas (April 10, 1930).

59. Ibid.

16. BOARDING SCHOOL

1. Letter from Lost Bird to Clara B. Colby, January 10, 1904, SHSW.

2. Letter from Helen Peabody at All Saints School to Clara B. Colby, January 14, 1904, SHSW.

3. Ibid. January 27, 1904, SHSW.

4. Letter from L. W. Colby to Clara B. Colby, January 31, 1904, SHSW.

5. Letter from Helen Peabody to Clara B. Colby, February 15, 1904.

6. Letter from George E. Bartlett to Clara B. Colby, March 7, 1904, SHSW.

7. Leonard Colby brought a cradleboard with him when he returned from Wounded Knee with the infant, Lost Bird. He told Clara she was found in it. None of the men who found her (in the search party) mentioned a cradleboard or "postant." If she had been in a cradleboard, it would have been heavily soiled with urine, feces, and blood. More than likely, Leonard Colby bought the postant or Annie Yellow Bird made it for Lost Bird. No cradleboard has been found, although a pair of Lost Bird's baby moccasins are still in the Helen Colby Collection, West Linn, Oregon.

8. Letter from Lost Bird to Clara B. Colby, March 17, 1904, SHSW.

9. Interview with Bertha Ree Santee, 1986–1987, Springfield, South Dakota.

10. Letter from Lost Bird to Clara B. Colby, March 24, 1904, SHSW.

11. Letter from Lost Bird to Clara B. Colby, March 26, 1904, SHSW.

12. Letter from Helen Peabody to Clara B. Colby, April 14, 1904, SHSW.

13. *Woman's Tribune* (March 19, 1904), SHSW.

14. Letter from Clara B. Colby to Leonard W. Colby, May 6, 1904, SHSW.

15. Letter from L. W. Colby to Clara B. Colby, June 1, 1904, SHSW. Zintka was transferred from All Saints School in Sioux Falls, South Dakota to the all Indian girls' school, Hope School, located on the Missouri River at Springfield. There is no indication that Clara knew about this change. For Zintka's enrollment record see N.A., R.G. 75. Register of Pupils, Hope School, Springfield, South Dakota Bureau of Indian Affairs, Series E 725, Reference Books 1882–1909. Zintka Colby's term began September 21, 1904, and she "was returned home May 4, 1905 at personal expense."

16. Letter from Helen Peabody to Clara B. Colby, May 30, 1904, SHSW. For an excellent book on Indian boarding schools see Szasz, Margaret Connell, *Education and the American Indian: The Road to Self-Determination 1928–1973* (Albuquerque: University of New Mexico Press, 1974).

17. William Bewick to his sister Clara B. Colby, June 2, 1904, SHSW.

18. Letter from Mr. Mauger to Clara B. Colby, August 14, 1904, SHSW.

19. Letter from Clara B. Colby to Leonard Colby, August 11, 1904, SHSW. On September 17, 1904, Clara wrote to her dear friend, Dr. Clara McNaughton, "I am going without everything that is possible for a human being to go without." Dr. Clara McNaughton Papers, University of San Francisco Archives.

20. Interview with Fordyce Graff, 1985, Beatrice, Nebraska.

21. Two undated articles from the *Freeport Daily Bulletin* pasted into Clara B. Colby's scrapbook, SHSW. Mrs. Abigail Livingston Colby was a gifted seamstress. She made lovely knitted, tatted, and embroidered fancywork. Her handiwork is still appreciated in the Helen Colby Collection, West Linn, Oregon. Abigail Colby died February 27, 1905. Leonard Colby does not seem to have done much to protect his mother.

22. Letter from Clara B. Colby to Leonard Colby, February 27, 1905, SHSW.

23. Letter from Clara B. Colby to Leonard Colby, October 11, 1904, SHSW.

24. Maud moved to Lincoln, Nebraska, in order to see other men. It was a ploy that worked. See *Beatrice Daily Express*, June 14, 1906, SHSW.

25. Letter from Zintka to Clara B. Colby, November 4, 1904, SHSW.

26. Letter from Clara B. Colby to Leonard Colby, November 22, 1904, SHSW.

27. Letter from Zintka to Clara B. Colby, January 16, 1905, SHSW.

28. Annual Reports of the Department of the Interior, June 30, 1904 (Washington, D.C.: Government Printing Office, 1904), 453–454.

29. Ibid.

30. Ibid.

31. Letter from Mrs. Annie Flinn to Clara B. Colby, November 9, 1904, SHSW.

32. Ibid. April 4, 1905, SHSW.

33. Letter from John Flinn to Clara B. Colby, April 30, 1905, SHSW.

34. Letter from Clara B. Colby to Leonard Colby, August 17, 1905, SHSW. See also letter from Clara B. Colby to Mrs. Theisz, October 16, 1906, SHSW.

17. "CHI"

1. Passim, John Bakeless, *The Journals of Lewis and Clark* (New York: NAL Penguin, Inc., 1964).

2. This is the classic inconsistency that confuses and threatens the Indian child being raised in a non-Indian home. On the one hand the "Noble Indian" in native dress is lauded as a hero or heroine, such as Sacajawea or Pocahontus, and then when the child wants to wear moccasins, or her hair in braids, the non-Indian parents do not approve because they are threatened. The bottom line is that parents, of whatever nationality or race, want their child to be an extension of themselves, a carbon copy of their manners, philosophy of life, morals, and value judgements. Clara allowed Zintka her Indian name, she played with Indian dolls and went to Indian exhibitions, but she was *not* allowed to transfer the Indian image to her everyday life.

If non-Indian parents do not allow the child to read books about Indians or learn about Indian culture, the results are the same—an unhealthy identity crisis. It is a tragedy not only for the child, but also for the well-meaning white parents who ask themselves what they have done wrong. See also William Feigelman and Arnold Silverman, *Chosen Children* (New York: Praeger, 1983).

3. Letter from Clara B. Colby to Dr. Clara McNaughton, a close personal friend, January 1, 1905. Clara McNaughton Papers, University of San Francisco Archives.

4. Letter from Carrie Chapman Catt to Clara B. Colby, December 14, 1908, SHSW. In this letter Catt said, "The kind of militant suffrage which is needed most in Oregon . . . would be . . . (to) knock out those who stand in the way of better organization and of a higher type of work."

5. *The Oregonian*, November 4, 1906. "Mrs. Duniway Is Chosen." See Abigail Scott Duniway Scrapbook, vol. 1, Clyde A. Duniway Papers, David C. Duniway, Custodian, Salem, Oregon.

6. Ibid.

7. Letter from Abigail Scott Duniway to "Miss Blackwell," Duniway Papers, Suffrage Correspondence, 1905–1906. See also letter from Duniway to Rev. Anna Shaw, September 18, 1906. David C. Duniway, Custodian, Salem, Oregon.

8. *Woman's Tribune* (August–September, 1905), SHSW.
9. Letter from Clara B. Colby to Clara McNaughton, June 1, 1905. Clara McNaughton Papers, University of San Francisco Archives.
10. Lewis and Clark Journal, vol. 3, no. 6, June 1905, "Hit the Trail." See Abigail Scott Duniway Papers.
11. Letter from Clara B. Colby to Clara McNaughton, June 1, 1905. Clara McNaughton Papers, University of San Francisco Archives.
12. Lewis and Clark Journal, vol. 3, no. 2, February 1905. Abigail Scott Duniway Papers.
13. Letter from Clara B. Colby to Clara McNaughton, June 15, 1905. Clara McNaughton Papers, University of San Francisco Archives.
14. Letter from Carl Montgomery to Clara B. Colby, July 22, 1905, SHSW.
15. Letter from Zintka to Clara B. Colby, August 7, 1905, SHSW.
16. Letter from Isabella Beecher Hooker to Clara B. Colby, August 16, 1905, SHSW.
17. Letter from Clara B. Colby to Carl Montgomery, July 26, 1905, SHSW.
18. Letter from Clara B. Colby to Carl Montgomery, August 26, 1905, SHSW.
19. Letter from Zintka to a friend, September 9, 1905, SHSW.
20. Letter from Zintka to Clara B. Colby, September 18, 1905, SHSW. She signs the letter "Zintkala N. Colby."
21. Letter from E. Chalecraft to Clara B. Colby, October 6, 1906, SHSW.
22. Passim, Robert Gessner. *Massacre: A Survey of Today's American Indian* (New York: Jonathan Cape and Harrison Smith, 1931). Feminist and Dakota activist Gertrude Bonnin said, "One of the boys had a ball & chain locked unto his leg and was locked to the bed at night," 109.
23. Ibid.
24. Interviews with Bill Flood, Warren Flood, and Celene Not Help Him.
25. Letter from Zintka to Clara B. Colby, September 22, 1905, SHSW.
26. Letter from Zintka to Clara B. Colby, September 30, 1905, SHSW.
27. Letter from Clara B. Colby to Leonard W. Colby, December 2, 1905, SHSW.
28. Letter from Leonard W. Colby to Clara B. Colby, December 20, 1905, SHSW.
29. Letter from Zintka to Clara B. Colby, January 9, 1906, SHSW.
30. Letter from Carl Montgomery to Clara B. Colby, January 27, 1906, SHSW.
31. Letter from Clara B. Colby to Carl Montgomery, February 6, 1906, SHSW.
32. Letter from Clara B. Colby to Leonard W. Colby, February 12, 1906, SHSW.
33. Letter from Carl Montgomery to Clara B. Colby, April 3, 1906, SHSW.
34. Ibid.
35. Letter from Rev. Anna Shaw to Ida Husted Harper, Summer 1906. See Ida Husted Harper Collection, HM-10712, The Huntington Library. Carrie Chapman Catt and Rev. Anna Shaw did not like Clara B. Colby and tried to turn Susan B. Anthony against her. When Anthony died, Catt and Shaw took over the leadership of the suffrage movement. They made sure that Clara was not invited to speak at conventions after 1906. This hampered Clara but it did not stop her. Rev. Shaw was especially prejudiced against Indians and was totally disgusted with Clara for having adopted Zintka.
36. Elizabeth C. Stanton, Susan B. Anthony, Matilda J. Gage, *History of Woman Suffrage*, vol. 5, 191–92. Not long before she died, Anthony said, "I shall work to the end of my time and when I am called home, if there exist an immortal spirit, mine will still be with you, watching and inspiring you."

18. "NO ONE NEED EVER KNOW"

1. Letter from Edwin Chalecraft to Clara B. Colby, April 20, 1906, SHSW.
2. Letter from Miss Theisz to Clara B. Colby, September 28, 1906, SHSW.
3. L. I. Sudlow, "Homestead Years 1908–1968," *The Bison* (S.D.) *Courier,* 1968.
4. Interview with Helen Culbertson, September 26, 1990, Rapid City, S.D. See also the *Perkins County Signal,* September 20, 1911: "Indian Pete Visits Lemmon."
5. Interview with Helen Culbertson, September 26, 1990, Rapid City, S.D.
6. Ibid. For collection of photos of the Culbertson Wild West show, see Mrs. T. O. Bramble file, Lemmon Public Library, Lemmon, S.D.
7. *Perkins County Signal,* September 20, 1911. See also *Faith Country Heritage 1910–1985* (Faith, S.D., Faith Historical Committee, 1985), 192–193. See also L. I. Sudlow, "Homestead Years 1908–1968," *The Bison Courier,* 1968.

8. Foghorn Clancy, *My Fifty Years in Rodeo* (San Antonio: The Naylor Company, 1952); see also an excellent autobiography by Vera McGinnis, *Rodeo Road: My Life as a Pioneer Cowgirl* (New York: Hastings House, 1974); Gil Robinson, *Old Wagon Show Days* (Cincinnati: Brockwell Company Publishers, 1925); Cleo Tom Terry and Osie Wilson, *The Rawhide Tree: The Story of Florence Reynolds in Rodeo* (Clarendon, Texas: Clarendon Press, 1957).

9. Ibid., *Rodeo Road*.

10. L. I. Sudlow, "Homestead Years: 1908–1968," *The Bison Courier*, 1968.

11. Annual Reports of the Department of the Interior, June 30, 1906, Washington, Government Printing Office, 1906.

12. Passim, Ella Cara Deloria, *Waterlily* (Lincoln: University of Nebraska Press, 1988). See also Mary Lou Hultgren and Paulette Fairbanks Molin, *To Lead and To Serve: American Indian Education at Hampton Institute 1878–1923*. Virginia Foundation for the Humanities and Public Policy, 1989.

13. Ibid., *To Lead and To Serve*, 33. "There was no happy gathering of family and friends, as I had so fondly dreamed there might be. Instead of being eager to learn new ideas I had to teach them, they gave me to understand very plainly that they did not approve of me. I had no real home to go to and my relatives did not welcome my presence."

14. Ibid.

15. Interview with Fordyce Graff, 1985, Beatrice, Nebr.

16. Ed Lemmon, edited by Nellie Snyder Yost. *Boss Cowman: The Recollections of Ed Lemmon 1857–1946* (Lincoln: University of Nebraska Press, 1969), 159.

17. Robert M. Utley, *The Last Days of the Sioux Nation* (New Haven: Yale University, 1963), 226, 267.

18. Interview with Helen Culbertson, September 26, 1990.

19. Ed Lemmon, *Boss Cowman*. p. 159.

20. Ibid.

21. *The Woman's Home Weekly*, January 27, 1917, "Indian Girl Going Back to Tribe to Help Fellows to Better Things."

22. Interview with Sam Eaglestaff, 1991, Vermillion, S.D.

23. *Beatrice Daily Sun* (June 15, 1906), SHSW.

24. "Marie Martinez Gets Half Million," *Nebraska State Journal* (June 1906), SHSW.

25. *Beatrice Daily Express*, June 15, 1906. "Indian Chief Wants Gen. Colby's Pappoose."

26. Letter from Inspector James McLaughlin to Hon. Cato Sells, Commissioner of Indian Affairs, Washington, D.C., 16. The Wounded Knee Survivors Association Archives, Pine Ridge, S.D.

27. *Beatrice Daily Express*, June 15, 1906.

28. Letter from Clara B. Colby to Leonard Colby. January 1, 1907, SHSW.

29. Interview with Phil Cook, 1986, Beatrice, Nebraska.

30. Interview with Fordyce Graff, 1985, Beatrice, Nebraska.

31. Interview with Tom Damrow, 1986, Beatrice, Nebraska.

32. Interview with Maxine Hill, 1986, Fordyce Graff, 1985, Florence Lock, 1988, Hazel Tucker, 1989, Virginia Vette, 1989, Beatrice, Nebraska.

33. Ibid. and interview with Jane Leech, 1988–1990, William Lenhart, 1988, Henry Scott, 1986, Beatrice, Nebraska.

34. Interview with Fordyce Graff, 1985.

35. Ibid.

36. Letter from Clara B. Colby to Leonard Colby, June 25, 1907, SHSW.

37. Letter from Clara B. Colby to Leonard Colby, December 22, 1907, SHSW.

38. Letter from Leonard Colby to Clara Colby, December 26, 1907, SHSW.

39. Letter from Leonard Colby to Superintendent, Haskell Indian School, November 8, 1907. Helen Colby Collection, West Linn, Oregon.

40. Letter from Clara B. Colby to Belva Lockwood, December 26, 1907, SHSW.

41. Letter from Clara B. Colby to her sister, Dr. Mary White, February 21, 1908, SHSW.

42. Letter from Clara B. Colby to Zintka, January 2, 1908, SHSW.

43. Letter from Leonard Colby to Haskell Superintendent, April 7, 1908. Helen Colby Collection, West Linn, Oregon.

44. Milford Industrial Home Records of Zintka's Placement. Helen Colby Collection, West Linn, Oregon. See also Irene Ficke, *History of Milford, Nebraska 1920–1930*. Southeast Community College. Milford Campus, 1992.

45. Betty Stevens, "Maternity Home Fades into History," no. 29, 1987. *Lincoln Star Journal*.

46. Ibid.

47. Interview with Floyd Miller, 1992, Seward, Nebraska. Mr. Miller worked at the Milford Home. He found a straitjacket in the attic discipline room.
48. The author visited the Milford Industrial Home in 1989 and 1991. Interviews with Tim Stauffer, owner, Milford, Nebraska.
49. *The Lincoln Star Journal* said the high temperature on April 21, 1908, was 81 degrees. *The Sioux Falls Argus Leader* noted the temperature at 86 degrees.
50. See Milford Industrial Home Records, Helen Colby Collection, West Linn, Oregon.
51. Interview with staff at the Lauber Funeral Home, 1990. The Blue Mound Cemetery is two miles southwest of the home.
52. *Woman's Tribune* (May 9, 1908, and August 8, 1908), SHSW.
53. *Woman's Tribune* (August 8, 1908), SHSW. "On Platform Seven."
54. *Woman's Tribune* (May 9, 1908, and August 8, 1908), SHSW.
55. Letter from Zintka to Clara B. Colby, August 8, 1908, SHSW.
56. Letter from Clara B. Colby to Leonard W. Colby, November 18, 1908, SHSW.
57. Ibid.
58. Colby stationery in the Helen Colby Collection, West Linn, Oregon.
59. Interview with William Lenhart, 1988, Beatrice, Nebraska.
60. Letter from Leonard W. Colby to Haskell Superintendent, August 12, 1908. See Haskell Institute Records, 1908. Helen Colby Collection, West Linn, Oregon.
61. Letter from Haskell Superintendent to Leonard Colby, August 20, 1908. Haskell Institute Records. Helen Colby Collection, West Linn, Oregon.
62. Letter from Zintka to Clara B. Colby, December 28, 1908, SHSW.
63. Letter from Clara B. Colby to Leonard Colby, January 18, 1909, SHSW.
64. Howard B. Woolston, *Prostitution in the United States* (New York: The Century Co., 1921), vol. 1, 253.

19. THE BRIDE'S GIFT

1. Clara B. Colby diary, January to March 1909, SHSW.
2. Ibid., February 19, 1909, SHSW.
3. Ibid., January 23, 1909, SHSW.
4. Ibid., February 27, 1909, SHSW.
5. Letter from Clara B. Colby to Lilian Whiting, January 17, 1909, SHSW.
6. Clara's diary, January 12, 1909, SHSW.
7. Letter from Clara B. Colby to Monsieur and Madame Chalivat, April 28, 1909, SHSW.
8. Clara's diary, January 12, 1909, SHSW.
9. Ibid., January 21, 1909, SHSW.
10. Ibid., January 26, 1909, SHSW.
11. Ibid. March 3, 1909, SHSW.
12. Ibid., March 5, 1909, SHSW.
13. Ibid., March 12, 1909, SHSW.
14. Letter from Clara B. Colby to Ida Husted Harper, March 26, 1910, SHSW.
15. Letter from Clara B. Colby to M. Chalivat, Paris, France, n.d., 1910, SHSW.
16. Ibid.
17. Ibid.
18. *Beatrice Daily Sun* (May 4, 1909), SHSW.
19. Letter from Clara B. Colby to the Chalivats, April 28, 1909, SHSW.
20. *Beatrice Daily Sun* (May 4, 1909), SHSW.
21. Ibid.
22. Letter from Clara B. Colby to Leonard W. Colby, May 6, 1909, SHSW.
23. Ibid.
24. Letter from Clara B. Colby to Mr. Callahan, May 16, 1909, SHSW.
25. *Beatrice Daily Sun* (May 22, 1909), SHSW.
26. Letter from Clara B. Colby to M. Chalivat, April 28, 1909, SHSW.
27. Letter from Clara B. Colby to Dr. Ernest Barton, December 23, 1909, SHSW.
28. Letter from Clara B. Colby to M. Chalivat, n.d., 1910, SHSW.
29. Letter from Clara B. Colby to Nellie Richardson, May 16, 1909, SHSW.
30. Letter from Olympia Brown to Clara B. Colby, May 29, 1909, SHSW.

31. Ibid. June 15, 1909, SHSW.

32. *Yellow Star*, by Elaine G. Eastman, can be found in the Smith College Library, Northampton, Massachusetts.

33. Ibid.

34. Elaine Eastman, *Yellow Star* (Boston: Little, Brown & Company, 1911), 269.

35. Letter from Clara B. Colby to Dr. Ernest Barton, December 23, 1909, SHSW.

36. Interview with Fordyce Graff, 1985.

37. Ibid.

38. Ibid.

39. This prayer, entitled "An Evening Prayer," was found in Maud Colby's papers. See Helen Colby Collection, West Linn, Oregon.

20. THE NATION OF THE LAKOTAH

1. Letter from Cora Smith Eaton to Clara B. Colby, March 8, 1910, SHSW.

2. Letter from Clara B. Colby to Cora Smith Eaton, March 9, 1910, SHSW.

3. Letter from Clara B. Colby to Ida Husted Harper, March 26, 1910, SHSW.

4. Letter from Clara B. Colby to Mrs. Wardall, April 1, 1910, SHSW.

5. Letter from Clara B. Colby to Mr. Joseph Fels, March 21, 1910, SHSW.

6. The postal card is in Clara B. Colby's 1910 file, SHSW.

7. Ibid.

8. Letter from Zintka to Clara B. Colby, May 10, 1910, SHSW.

9. Ibid.

10. Letter from Clara B. Colby to Zintka, May 30, 1910, SHSW.

11. Letter from Clara B. Colby to "El Camancho," Mr. W. S. Phillips, May 30, 1910, SHSW.

12. Letter from W. S. Phillips to Clara B. Colby, June 1, 1910, SHSW.

13. Letter from Clara B. Colby to Lilla Hill, June 8, 1910, SHSW.

14. Letter from Clara B. Colby to Dr. Clara McNaughton, September 13, 1910, SHSW.

15. Eastman, *Yellow Star*, 205.

16. Interview with Dora Shoots Off Bruguier, 1990, Eagle Butte, S.D.

17. Frederick E. Hoxie, "From Prison to Homeland: The Cheyenne River Indian Reservation Before WW1." *South Dakota History*, vol. 10, no. 1, winter 1979, 1–24.

18. Ibid.

19. Telephone interview with Fred Hoxie, 1992, Vermillion, S.D.; also interview with Marilyn Runs After, 1992; Felix Crane Pretty Voice testimony, 1925. Cheyenne River Sioux file on Marguerite (Colby) Allen, Eagle Butte, S.D.

20. Dora Shoots Off Bruguier, 1992. Eagle Butte, S.D.

21. Ibid.

22. Eastman, *Yellow Star*, 221.

23. Passim, Ella Cara Deloria, *Waterlily*.

24. Letter found in Brennan Scrapbook, Wounded Knee File, SDSHS, from Ellen In The Woods. See also *Waterlily* by Ella Cara Deloria.

25. Ibid., *Waterlily*.

26. Interview with Marilyn Runs After, 1992.

27. Interview with Marilyn Runs After. She remembers Olney telling about Zintka.

28. Dr. Fred Hoxie interview with Olney Runs After at Cherry Creek, August 25, 1977. Copy of tape recording given to author. Hoxie is at the Newberry Library, Chicago.

29. Telephone interview with Fred Hoxie, 1992.

30. Interview with Marilyn Runs After, 1992, Cheyenne River Reservation.

21. MOVIES AND MILITANTS

1. Passim, Scott Eyman, *Mary Pickford: America's Sweetheart* (New York: Douglas F. Fine, Inc., 1990). See also Paul O'Neil (ed.), *The End and the Myth* (Alexandria, Virginia: Time-Life Books, 1979). See also Leo C. Rosten, *Hollywood: The Movie Colony, the Movie Makers* (New York: Harcourt, Brace and Company, 1941).

2. Ibid.

3. Ibid. *The End and the Myth.* See also letter from Frank W. Mauger to Clara B. Colby, July 27, 1912, SHSW; *Catalogue of Motion Pictures* (New York: Pathé Exchange, Inc., 1923); Moving Picture World, N.A. "The Great Works of Pathé Frères," March 19, 1917; Moving Picture World, "Charles Pathé, Film Producer," November 14, 1914.

4. Cleo Tom Terry and Osie Wilson, *The Rawhide Tree* (New York: Clarendon Press, 1957), 27. See also Paul O'Neil (ed.), *The End and the Myth*; Joyce Gibson Roach, *The Cowgirls.* C.L. Sonnichen. n.d.

5. "Indian Maid in Poverty," October 2, 1913. Unnamed San Diego newspaper clipping, SHSW.

6. Ibid.

7. Passim. Paul O'Neil (ed.), *The End and the Myth.*

8. Paul O'Neil (ed.), *The End and the Myth,* 201.

9. Ibid., 202.

10. Letter from Clara B. Colby to Zintka, "My Dearie Girlie," May 26, 1913, SHSW.

11. California State Board of Health, Bureau of Vital Records, Certificate of Marriage, Orange County, California, May 31, 1913.

12. A Santa Ana, California newspaper clipping, October 4, 1913. "Indian Girl's Story Has Strange Features." Helen Colby Collection, West Linn, Oregon.

13. Ibid.

14. Clara B. Colby diary, 1913–1914, SHSW.

15. Olympia Brown, *Democratic Ideals,* 49.

16. *New York Times,* January 31, 1912. "Women Make Plea for the Right to Vote."

17. Letter from Clara B. Colby to Mr. Hawkes, January 1, 1913, SHSW.

18. Passim, Olympia Brown, *Democratic Ideals.*

19. Correspondence pertaining to Clara B. Colby's sponsor, the American Peace Society, in Clara B. Colby's Papers, SHSW.

20. *Woman's Tribune.* See also Frank Moxon, *What Forcible Feeding Means* (London: The Woman's Press, 1914); *The Suffragette,* "Cat and Mouse," edited by Christobel Pankhurst, August 1, 1913, vol. 1, no. 42. This can be found in the Woman Suffrage file in the Sophia Smith Collection, Smith College Archives, Northampton, Mass.

21. Ibid.

22. Letter from Clara B. Colby to Clara McNaughton, August 4, 1913, SHSW.

23. Ibid.

24. *The Suffragette,* August 22, 1913, 787. See Woman Suffrage, Sophia Smith Collection, Smith College Archives, Northampton, Massachusetts.

25. Letter from Clara B. Colby to "Eva," September 19, 1913, SHSW.

26. Letter from Clara B. Colby to Olympia Brown, April 16, 1915, SHSW.

27. Ibid.

28. Letter from Clara B. Colby to Clara McNaughton, October 17, 1913. Clara McNaughton Papers, University of San Francisco Archives.

22. THE BARBARY COAST

1. *Who's Who in America 1914–1915* (Chicago: A. N. Marquis Co., 1915), 480–481.

2. Clara B. Colby diary, March 15, 1914, SHSW.

3. S. L. A. Marshall, *World War I* (Boston: Houghton Mifflin Company, 1964), passim

4. Letter from Clara B. Colby to her sister, Mary White, August 14, 1914, SHSW.

5. Sells-Floto Circus Records, Circus World Museum, Baraboo, Wisconsin. See also John Burke, *The Noblest Whiteskin* (New York: G. P. Putnam's Sons, 1973), 273; *Buffalo Bill Wild West Route, 1883–1916,* McCracken Research Library, Buffalo Bill Historical Center, Cody, Wyoming; *Bandwagon* magazine Nov.–Dec. 1975, "Sells-Floto Circus 1914–1915," by Gordon M. Carver.

6. Ibid.

7. Seventh-Day Adventist Records for Hanford, California, show that Ernest Cornelius Allen's brothers and sisters belonged to the church, but Ernest's name is missing.

8. M. H. Welsh Circus Records at Circus World Museum archives, Baraboo, Wisconsin. The correct name was Col. M. H. Welsh's Great American One Ring Circus. See also *Billboard,* July 10, 1909, 18; Ringling Bros. Circus Ledger, 1912.

9. Gordon M. Carver, *Bandwagon.* "Sells-Floto Circus, 1914–1915." Nov.–Dec. 1975, 22–30.

10. Clara B. Colby diary, August 5, 1914, SHSW.

11. Ibid., August 16, 1914, SHSW.
12. *Buffalo Bill Wild West Route 1883–1916*, McCracken Research Library, Buffalo Bill Historical Center, Cody, Wyoming.
13. Interview with Helen Bewick, 1989, Madison, Wisconsin.
14. Ibid.
15. See archives, Circus World Museum, Baraboo, Wisconsin, *Billboard* magazine. See also David L. Hammanstrom, *Big Top Boss: John Ringling North and the Circus* (Urbana: University of Illinois Press, 1992), 12.
16. *Buffalo Bill Wild West Route 1883–1916.*
17. Letter from Clara B. Colby to Belva Lockwood, January 12, 1915, SHSW.
18. Clara B. Colby diary, November 9, 1915, SHSW.
19. Letter from Clara B. Colby to P. J. Green, February 15, 1915, SHSW.
20. Letter from Clara B. Colby to Mrs. Tuttle, March 31, 1915, SHSW.
21. Letter from Commissioner of Indian Affairs to the agent at Cheyenne River Agency, February 1915. N.A., R.G. 75, Records of the Bureau of Indian Affairs, Central Classified File, 1907–1939, 15148-1915.
22. Letter from Zintka to Clara B. Colby, April 14, 1916, SHSW.
23. *The Argonaut*, January 1, 1916. See San Francisco Library, vaudeville magazines and literature.
24. Richard M. Ketchum, *Will Rogers, His Life and Times* (New York.: American Heritage Publishing Company, Inc., McGraw-Hill Company, 1973), 108–110.
25. Ibid.
26. Passim. George Burns, *All My Best Friends* (New York: G. P. Putnam's Sons, 1989), 40–41.
27. Ibid., 35–45.
28. Ibid., 43.
29. Letter from Zintka to Robt. G. Valentine, February 2, 1915. N.A., R.G. 75. Records of the Bureau of Indian Affairs, Central Classified File, 1907–1939, 15148-1915.
30. Herbert Asbury, *The Barbary Coast* (New York: Garden City Publishing Company, Inc., 1933), 242, 258–259.
31. Passim, George Jackson, *History of Centennials, Expositions and World Fairs,* (Lincoln: Wekesser Brinkman Co., 1959).
32. Olympia Brown, *Democratic Ideals,* 83–84.
33. Letter from Zintka to Clara B. Colby, August 3, 1915, SHSW.
34. Clara B. Colby diary, August, 1915, SHSW.
35. Clara B. Colby diary, November 13, 1915.
36. Letter from Ida Husted Harper to Olympia Brown, June 17, 1917. Olympia Brown Papers, Ca. 1849–1963, Reel 8, Series 3, Folders 129–142. Schlesinger Library, Radcliffe College, Cambridge, Mass. See also letter from Clara B. Colby to Olympia Brown. November 21, 1915, SHSW.
37. Letter from Clara B. Colby to Jennie Cox, October 6, 1916, SHSW.
38. Ibid.
39. Letter from Zintka to Robert G. Valentine, November 29, 1915. N.A., R.G. 75. Records of the Bureau of Indian Affairs, Central Classified File, 1907–1939, 131583-1915.
40. San Francisco City and County Court Records, City and County of San Francisco. See also San Francisco Police Records.
41. Pamphlet entitled "The San Francisco City Hall," from the Public Affairs Department, Office of the Mayor, San Francisco City Hall.

23. THE VOICE OF THE SPIRIT

1. N.A., R.G. 75, Records of the Bureau of Indian Affairs, Central Classified File, 1907–1939. Kiowa Agency. 1915–1916.
2. Letter from Agent F. C. Campbell to Zintka, December 16, 1915. N.A., R.G. 75. Records of the Bureau of Indian Affairs. Central Classified File, 1907–1939. 21366-1916.
3. McLaughlin tried to bribe Sitting Bull with liquor when bullying did not work (One Bull, Box 105, item 41, Walter S. Campbell Papers, Western History Collection, University of Oklahoma). He also tried to exploit Sitting Bull in tourist attraction schemes. When the spiritual leader refused and later accepted Buffalo Bill's offer for a season with the Wild West Show, McLaughlin was furious. See James McLaughlin Papers, #655, Roll 20, August 1884. Assumption Abbey Archives, Richardson, N.D.

4. Letter from Clara B. Colby to Olympia Brown, December 28, 1915, SHSW.
5. Letter from Clara B. Colby to Clara McNaughton, January 26, 1916. University of San Francisco Archives, Clara McNaughton Papers.
6. Letter from Clara B. Colby to Olympia Brown, February 21, 1916, SHSW.
7. Letter from Zintka to Clara B. Colby, January 22, 1916, SHSW.
8. Clara B. Colby diary, February 27, 1916, SHSW.
9. Ibid.
10. Clara's typed New Thought Reading was found among her papers, SHSW.
11. Letter from Zintka to Clara B. Colby, February 17, 1916, SHSW.
12. Letter from Clara B. Colby to Olympia Brown, March 3, 1916, SHSW.
13. Letter from Dr. Valentine McGillycuddy to Clara B. Colby, March 4, 1916, SHSW.
14. McGillycuddy was either a totally honest individual or a genius at deception. He was the object of constant fraud complaints from white employees during his tenure as agent. For one investigation, among others, see the *Chicago Tribune,* July 27, 1885, "Investigating McGillycuddy." Chief Red Cloud had his men watch McGillycuddy at all times. At one point he wrote a letter to the President saying that if the Chief Executive did not remove McGillycuddy, "I, Red Cloud, will." The agent was finally removed for insubordination. He then moved to Rapid City, built a large home, and became president of a bank and president of the South Dakota School of Mines. He served a term as mayor and then retired to California a wealthy man. Zintka probably met McGillycuddy at Buffalo Bill's Wild West Shows, as McGillycuddy was a frequent visitor there. The wily doctor was assigned to Fort Robinson in 1877 and was the attending physician with Crazy Horse when the War Chief died. He gave Crazy Horse morphine to ease the pain. He was also known to administer cannabis to his patients. See Robert A. Clark, *The Killing of Chief Crazy Horse* (Glendale, Calif.: The Arthur H. Clark Company, 1976). For the wife's biased biography of an adored husband, see *McGillycuddy, Agent,* Julia B. McGillycuddy (Palo Alto: Stanford University Press, 1941).
15. Letter from Clara B. Colby to Zintka, March 9, 1916, SHSW.
16. Letter from Clara B. Colby to Dr. Valentine McGillycuddy, March 9, 1916, SHSW.
17. Letter from Zintka to E. B. Merritt, Acting Commissioner, March 13, 1916. N.A., R.G. 75. Records of the Bureau of Indian Affairs, Central Classified File, 1907–1939. 29566-1916.
18. Ibid. Letter from Zintka to Chief Clerk, Department of the Interior, April 4, 1916.
19. Letter from Clara B. Colby to Clara McNaughton, Clara McNaughton Papers, University of San Francisco Archives.
20. Before 1902, Clara testified in numerous hearings. For her hearing record of testimony after 1902, see CIS US Congress Committee Hearings, Index, Part 1, 23rd Congress–64th Congress, Dec. 1833–March 1917. Reference Bibliography H.S. 25-A-(64) SJ-1. Congressional Information Service, Inc., Washington, D.C.
21. Letter from Clara B. Colby to Clara McNaughton, May 15, 1916. Clara McNaughton Papers, University of San Francisco Archives.
22. Letter from Clara B. Colby to "Rachel," July 12, 1916, SHSW.
23. Letter from Clara B. Colby to Clarence Colby, July 14, 1916, SHSW.
24. Letter from Olympia Brown to Clara B. Colby, August 8, 1916, SHSW.
25. Letter from Clara B. Colby to Olympia Brown, July 17, 1916, SHSW.
26. "Clara B. Colby, Noted Suffrage Leader, Dead," *Madison Democrat* (September 12, 1916).
27. "What Is There to Fear?" *The Suffragette* (July 25, 1913). See Woman Suffrage, England. Smith College Archives, Sophia Smith Collection, Northampton, Mass.

24. A LONELY GRAVE

1. Interview with Mrs. Carl McDowell, Mary White's granddaughter, 1989. Palo Alto, CA.
2. Letter from Cato Sells, Commissioner, to Fred C. Campbell, July 31, 1916. N.A., R.G. 75. Records of the Bureau of Indian Affairs, Central Classified File 1907–1939. Land Sales 60945-16. The 320 acres includes the south half of section 22 in township 16 north of range 24 east of the Black Hills meridian, South Dakota.
3. Mr. F. C. Collett advised Zintka to sell her land. He told her the land was too far away and that South Dakota weather was too harsh. He probably advised many Indians to sell their land. When she refused to sell, he then advised her to mortgage her land for the cash. See Register of Deeds, Timberlake, S.D. Special Agent James McLaughlin also advised Indians at the Cheyenne River

Agency to sell their land; this type of advice was typical all over the United States to the lasting detriment of the tribes and the generations to follow.

4. Zintka lost her allotment on April 4, 1917, to D. E. Campbell and B. A. Walton when she could not pay back her mortgage debt.

5. F. G. Collett was indicted for "using the mails to defraud." Collett's methods were fully referred to in the 42nd Annual Report of the Indian Rights Association, Philadelphia, Pa. See also *Indian Truth*, April 1928, vol. 5, no. 4, published by the Indian Rights Association, Inc., Philadelphia, Pa. The *Indian Truth* can be found at the Bancroft Library, University of California, Berkeley, Calif.

6. *San Francisco Chronicle*, December to February, 1916–17. See "Pack Rink to Assist War on Vice," January 26, 1917. Prostitutes were advised to beg families to take them in, remain homeless, or leave the state.

7. Zintka often helped homeless people with food and shelter. Pearl Commack, a woman down on her luck, was undoubtedly one of the prostitutes thrown out on the street. When she met Zintka she gave her a good story. By that time Zintka was ill, depressed, and almost penniless. It is unlikely, considering her state of health, that she was the mastermind behind a scheme to defraud. Years later, Maud Colby wrote that "someone" had tipped General Colby of the scheme. The only person known to have a grudge against Zintka in the area was Dr. Valentine McGillycuddy, who must have read about her on the front page of the *Examiner*, December 20, 1916, and then notified the general. McGillycuddy, known to exact revenge, may have invented the cruel hoax from the beginning. Knowing Mrs. Colby was dead, he had a clear route to revenge.

8. Ibid. If Zintka had spoken to the reporter, he might not have misspelled her name. Pearl Commack's name and facts about her life were correct, however.

9. The photo clearly showed the ravages of the disease Zintka's first husband had given her.

10. Interview with Frank Brady, M.D., University of South Dakota, Health Sciences/School of Medicine, 1992. He recommended books on the subject including Robert Berkow, M.D. (ed.), *The Merck Manual, 1992* (Rahway, New Jersey: Merck Research Laboratories, 1992).

11. *The Woman's Home Weekly*, January 27, 1917. "Indian Girl Going Back to Tribe to Help Fellows to Better Things."

12. Letter from Maud Colby to Mr. S. C. L. Bewick, January 6, 1925, SHSW.

13. Ibid.

14. Letter from Ms. In The Woods found in the Brennan Scrapbook, Wounded Knee File. SDSHS.

15. The memorial is still standing at Wounded Knee.

16. Letter from Maud Colby to Mr. S. C. L. Bewick, January 6, 1925, SHSW.

17. "Home Front Organizations Formed for World War I," *Beatrice Daily Sun*, 50th Anniversary Edition, 1902–1952.

18. Address written by Maud Colby in 1933 for the presentation of General Colby's sword to the State of Nebraska.

19. Letter from Leonard W. Colby to Hon. Theodore Roosevelt, July 4, 1917. See Index to the Presidential Papers of Theodore Roosevelt, Series 1, Reel 239, Oklahoma State University, Edmun Low Library, Stillwater, Okla.

20. Harold Bell Wright, *When a Man's a Man* (Chicago: The Book Supply Company Publishers, 1916), 12.

21. Interview with Fordyce Graff, 1985, Beatrice, Nebraska.

22. Interview with William Lenhart, 1988, Beatrice, Nebraska.

23. Interview with Zoa Worden, 1985, Beatrice, Nebraska.

24. Interview with Fordyce Graff, 1985, Beatrice, Nebraska.

25. Letter from Maud Colby to S. C. L. Bewick, January 6, 1925, SHSW.

26. See the *Adventist Review*, edited by Kenneth H. Wood, vol. 155, no. 18, May 4, 1978; see also the *Adventist Review*, vol. 158. no. 31. "What Seventh-day Adventists Believe."

27. *Hanford Daily Sentinel*, One Hundredth Anniversary Edition, 1886–1986, April 26, 1986. See Hanford Historical Society.

28. Ibid.

29. Ibid.

30. "Masks Must Be Worn," *Hanford Morning Journal* (January 22, 1919).

31. "Council Tackles Corruption . . ." *Hanford Daily Journal*, 100th Year Edition.

32. Passim. A. D. Hoeling, *The Great Epidemic* (Boston: Little Brown and Company, 1961).

33. Ibid.

34. Ibid.

35. Ibid.

36. California State Board of Health, Bureau of Vital Statistics, Standard Certificate of Death, February 14, 1920.
37. "Noted Indian Woman Passes at Home Here," *Hanford Journal* (February 17, 1920).
38. Death Certificate signed by Dr. E. C. Foster, February 14, 1920.
39. *Hanford Journal,* February 17, 1920.

EPILOGUE

1. Moses Nelson Big Crow, *A Legend from Crazy Horse Clan,* edited by Renée Sansom Flood (Chamberlain, SD: Tipi Press, 1987), 27. *Tashia gnupa* is a Siouan onomatopoeia for the song of the lark.
2. Avis Little Eagle, "A Journey to the Spirit World," *Lakota Times* (July 17, 1991).

Bibliography

BOOKS

Allen, Albert H., ed. *Dakota Imprints 1858-1889*. New York: R.R. Bowker Company, 1947.

Anberg, George. *The New York Times Film Previews 1913-1970*. Vol. I. New York: Arno Press, 1971.

Andrews, Ralph W. *Indians As the Westerners Saw Them*. Seattle: Superior Publishing Company, 1963.

Andrist, Ralph K. *The Long Death*. New York: Macmillan Company, 1964.

————. *The American Heritage History of the Confident Years*. New York: Bonanza Books, distributed by Crown Publishers, Inc., 1987.

Anthony, Katharine. *Susan B. Anthony, Her Personal History and Her Era*. Garden City, N.Y.: Doubleday & Company, Inc., 1954.

Armitage, Susan, and Elizabeth Jameson, eds. *The Women's West*. Norman: University of Oklahoma Press, 1987.

Asbury, Herbert. *The Barbary Coast*. Garden City, N.Y.: Garden City Publishing Company, Inc., 1933.

Bakeless, John. *The Journals of Lewis and Clark*. New York: NAL Penguin Inc., 1964.

Baldwin, Alice Blackwood. *Memoirs of the Late Frank D. Baldwin*. Edited by Brigadier General W. C. Brown, Colonel C. C. Smith, and E. A. Brininstool. Los Angeles: Wetzel Publishing Company, Inc., 1929.

Barsh, Russel Lawrence, and James Youngblood Henderson. *The Road: Indian Tribes and Political Liberty*. Berkeley: University of California Press, 1980.

Beck, Henry Houghton. *Cuba's Fight for Freedom and the War with Spain*. Philadelphia: Globe Bible Publishing Company, 1898.

Beirne, Frances F. *Baltimore, A Picture History 1858-1958*. New York: Hastings House, 1957.

Bennet, Estelline. *Old Deadwood Days*. New York: Grosset & Dunlap, 1908.

Berkow, Robert, M.D., ed. *The Merck Manual 1992*. Rahway, New Jersey: Merck Research Laboratories, 1992.

————. *The Merck Manual of Diagnosis and Therapy*. Rahway, New Jersey: Merck, Sharp & Dohme Research Laboratories, 1982.

Berlin, Edward. *Ragtime, a Musical and Cultural History*. Berkeley: University of California Press, 1980.

Beyer, W. F,. and O. F. Keydel. *Deeds of Valor: How America's Heroes Won the Medal of Honor. II*. Detroit: The Perrien-Keydel Company, 1903.

Billington, Ray Allen. *The Protestant Crusade, 1800-1860: A Study of the Origins of American Nativism*. New York: The Macmillan Company, 1938.

Bland, Thomas A., ed. *The Late Military Invasion of the Home of the Sioux*. Washington, D.C.: The National Defense Association, 1891.

Blasingame, Ike. *My Life in the Old Days*. New York: G.P. Putnam's Sons, 1958.

Bogart, Ernest Ludlow, and John Mabry Mathews. *The Centennial History of Illinois: The Modern Commonwealth 1893-1918*. V. Chicago: A.C. McClurg & Co., 1922.

Bowlby, John, ed. *Maternal Care and Mental Health*. New York: Schocken Books, 1951.

Brendtro, Larry K., Martin Brokenleg, and Steve Van Bockern. *Reclaiming Youth at Risk*. Bloomington, Indiana: National Educational Service, 1990.

Bronson, Edgar Beecher. *Cowboy Life on the Western Plains*. New York: Grosset & Dunlap, 1908.

Brown, Gene, ed. *The New York Times Encyclopedia of Film 1896-1928*. New York: Times Books, 1984.

Brown, Rev. Olympia. *Democratic Ideals: A Memorial Sketch of Clara B. Colby*. Washington, D.C.: Federal Suffrage Association, 1917.

Brininstool, E. A. *Crazy Horse: The Invincible Ogalala Sioux Chief*. Los Angeles: Wetzel Publishing Company, Inc., 1949.

Burdick, Usher L. *The Last Days of Sitting Bull, Sioux Medicine Chief*. Baltimore: Wirth Brothers, 1941.

Burke, John M. *Buffalo Bill: From Prairie to Palace, An Authentic History of the Wild West*. Chicago: Rand, McNally & Company Publishers, 1893.

Burke, John. *The Noblest Whiteskin*. New York: G. P. Putnam's Sons, 1973.

Burns, George. *All My Best Friends*. New York: G. P. Putnam's Sons, 1989.

———. *Gracie: A Love Story*. New York: G. P. Putnam's Sons, 1988.

Cahn, Edgar S., ed. *Our Brother's Keeper: The Indian in White America*. Washington, D.C.: New Community Press, 1969.

Carr, Donald E. *The Forgotten Senses*. Garden City, N.Y.: Doubleday & Company, Inc., 1972.

Cashman, Sean Dennis. *America in the Gilded Age: From the Death of Lincoln to the Rise of Theodore Roosevelt*. New York: New York University Press, 1984.

Clancy, Foghorn. *My Fifty Years in Rodeo*. San Antonio: The Naylor Company, 1952.

Clark, Robert A., ed. *The Killing of Chief Crazy Horse*. Glendale: The Arthur H. Clark Company, 1976.

Clay, John. *My Life on the Range*. New York: Antiquarian Press, Ltd., 1961. (1st printing was a private printing in Chicago, 1924.)

Colby, James W. *History of the Colby Family*. Waltham, Massachusetts: n.p. 1895.

Collections of Nebraska Pioneer Reminiscence, Nebraska Society of the Daughters of the American Revolution. Cedar Rapids, Iowa: The Torch Press, 1916.

Commager, Henry Steele, ed. *The American Destiny*. Vol. 8. Danbury: The Danbury Press, Grolier Enterprises Inc., 1976.

Connelly, Mark Thomas. *The Response to Prostitution in the Progressive Era*. Chapel Hill: The University of North Carolina Press, 1980.

Cook, James H. *Fifty Years on the Old Frontier as Cowboy, Hunter, Guide, Scout, and Ranchman*. New Haven: Yale University Press, 1923.

Cook, Joel. *The World's Fair at Chicago*. Chicago: Rand, McNally & Company, 1891.

Crawford, Lewis F. *Ranching Days in Dakota and Custer's Black Hills Expedition of 1874*. Baltimore: Wirth Brothers, 1950.

Creigh, Dorothy Weyer. *Nebraska, Where Dreams Grow*. Lincoln, Nebr.: Miller & Paine, Inc., 1980.

Curti, Merle, and Vernon Carstensen. *The University of Wisconsin, A History, 1848-1925*. Madison: University of Wisconsin Press, 1949.

Curtis, Natalie. *The Indians' Book*. New York: Dover Publications, Inc., 1907.

Debo, Angie. *And Still the Waters Run*. Princeton, N.J.: Princeton University Press, 1940.

———. *The Rise and Fall of the Choctaw Republic*. Norman: University of Oklahoma Press, 1934.

———. *The Road to Disappearance, A History of the Creek Indians*. Norman: University of Oklahoma Press, 1941.

de-Hegermann-Lindencrone, L. *The Sunny Side of Diplomatic Life, 1875-1912*. New York: Harper and Bros., 1914.

Deloria, Ella Cara. *Waterlily*. Lincoln: University of Nebraska Press, 1988.

Dobbs, Hugh J. *History of Gage County, Nebraska*. Lincoln: Nebraska Western Publishing and Engraving Co., 1918.

Downey, Fairfax Davis. *Colonel Eugene A. Carr: Indian- Fighting Army*. New York: Charles Scribner's Sons, 1941.

Dudley, Joseph Iron Eye. *Chouteau Creek: A Sioux Reminiscence*. Lincoln: University of Nebraska Press, 1992.

Duncan, Kunigunde. *Blue Star: The Story of Corabelle Fellows, Teacher at Dakota Missions 1884-1888*. St. Paul: Minnesota Historical Society Press, 1990.

Duniway, Abigail Scott. *Pathbreaking*. Portland, Ore.: James, Kerns & Abbott Co., 1914.

Eastern Custer County Historical Society. *Our Yesterdays*. Marceline: Pischel Yearbooks Inc., 1970.

Eastman, Charles A. *From the Deep Woods to Civilization*. Little Brown and Company, 1916.

Eastman, Elaine Goodale. *Yellow Star*. Boston: Little Brown & Company, 1911.

Eaton, Peggy. *The Autobiography of Peggy Eaton*. New York: Charles Scribner's Sons, 1932.

Edey, Maitland A., ed. *This Fabulous Century 1900-1910*. New York: Time-Life Books, 1969

Ellis, Edward S. *The Indian Wars of the United States*. Grand Rapids, Mic.: P.D. Farrell & Co., 1892.

Ellison, Mary. *The Adopted Child*. London: Victor Gollancz Ltd., 1958.

Eyman, Scott. *Mary Pickford: America's Sweetheart*. New York: Douglas F. Fine, Inc., 1990.

Faith Country Heritage, 1910-1985. Pierre, S.D.: Faith Historical Committee, n.d. Printed by the State Publishing Co., 1985

Feigelman, William, and Arnold R. Silverman. *Chosen Children: New Patterns of Adoptive Relationships*. New York: Praeger Publishers, 1983.

Ficke, Irene. *History of Milford, Nebraska 1920-1930*. Milford: Southeast Community College, 1992.

Flack, J. Kirkpatrick. *Desideratum in Washington: The Intellectual Community in the Capital City, 1870-1900*. Cambridge, Mass.: Schenkman Publishing, 1975.

Flood, Renée Sansom, and Shirley A. Bernie. Edited by Leonard R. Bruguier. *Remember Your Relatives: Yankton Sioux Images, 1851 to 1904*. Vol. I. Marty, S. D.: Marty Indian School, 1985.

Flood, Renée Sansom. *Lessons from Chouteau Creek: Yankton Memories of Dakota Territorial Intrigue*. Sioux Falls, S.D.: The Center for Western Studies at Augustana College, 1986.

Flood, Renée Sansom, Shirley A. Bernie, and Leonard R. Bruguier. *Remember Your Relatives: Yankton Sioux Images, 1865 to 1915*. Vol. II. Marty, S.D.: Yankton Sioux Advisory Board, 1989.

Flexner, Eleanor. *Century of Struggle: The Woman's Rights Movement in the United States*. Cambridge, Mass.: Belknap Press of Harvard University Press, 1959.

Fraser, Antonia. *The Wives of Henry VIII*. New York: Alfred A. Knopf, 1992.

French, Emily. *Emily: The Diary of a Hard-Worked Woman*. Edited by Janet Lecompte. Lincoln, Nebr.: University of Nebraska Press, 1987.

Freud, Anna, and Dorothy T. Burlingham. *War and Children*. New York: International University Press, 1944.

Gammond, Peter. *Scott Joplin and the Ragtime Era*. New York: St. Martin's Press, 1975.

Gerhardt, Alfred C. P. *1665-1965: Three Hundred Years of Missionary Work Among the Sioux Indians, A Chronology*. Dunmore, Pennsylvania: F. Pane Offset Printing Col, 1969.

Gessner, Robert. *Massacre: A Survey of Today's American Indian*. New York: J. Cape and H. Smith, 1931.

Gorham, Deborah. *The Victorian Girl and the Feminine Ideal*. Bloomington: Indiana University Press, 1982.

Gossett, Thomas. *Race: The History of an Idea in America*. Dallas: Southern Methodist University Press, 1963.

Graber, Kay., ed. *Sister to the Sioux: The Memoirs of Elaine Goodale Eastman 1885-1891*. Lincoln, Nebr.: University of Nebraska Press, 1978.

Green, Constance McLaughlin. *Washington: Capital City, 1879–1950*. Princeton, N.J.: Princeton University Press, 1963.

———. *The Secret City: A History of Race Relations in the National Capital*. Princeton: Princeton University Press, 1967.

Hall, Bert L. *Roundup Years, Old Muddy to Black Hills*. Pierre: The Reminder, Inc., 1954.

Hall, C. L. *Biographical Manual of the Members and Officers of the Twentieth Legislature of Nebraska*. Lincoln: Journal Company, State Printers, 1887.

Hammarstrom, David L. *Big Top Boss: John Ringling North and the Circus*. Urbana: University of Illinois Press, 1992.

Hammond, Paul. *Marvellous Méliés*. New York: St. Martin's Press. 1975.

Harper, Ida Husted. *The Life and Work of Susan B. Anthony*. 2 vols. Indianapolis: The Bowen-Merrill Company, 1898.

Harrison, Benjamin. *Views of an Ex-President*. Edited by Mary Lord Harrison. Indianapolis: The Bowen-Merrill Company Publishers, 1901.

Hasse, John Edward, ed. *Ragtime: Its History, Composers and Music*. New York: Schirmer Books, 1985.

Heitman, Francis B. *Historical Register and Dictionary of the U.S. Army, From its Organization Sept. 29, 1789, to March 2, 1903*. Washington, D.C.: Government Printing Office, 1903.

Hernton, Calvin. *Sex and Racism in America*. New York: Grove Press, 1965.

Hesnard, Douglas B., ed. *Hermosa 1886-1986: Railroads, Cowboys and Memories*. Hermosa, S.D.: The Hermosa Centennial Committee, 1986.

History of Pennington County, South Dakota. Dallas: Taylor Publishing Co., 1986.

Hoehling, A. D. *The Great Epidemic*. Boston: Little, Brown and Company, 1961.

Hofstadter, Richard. *The Age of Reform*. New York: Vintage Books, published by Alfred A. Knopf, Inc., and Random House Inc., 1955.

Hoover, Irwin Hood. *Forty-two Years in the White House*. New York: Houghton Mifflin Company, 1934.

Hoxie, Frederick E., ed. *Indians in American History*. Arlington Heights, Illinois: D'Arcy McNickle Center for the History of the American Indian. The Newberry Library. Harlan Davidson, Inc., 1988.

Hoxie, Frederick E. *A Final Promise: The Campaign to Assimilate the Indians, 1880-1920*. Lincoln: University of Nebraska Press, 1984.

Hughes, Richard B. *Pioneer Years in the Black Hills*. Edited by Agnes Wright Spring. Glendale, Calif.: The Arthur H. Clark Company, 1957.

Huls, Don., ed. *The Winter of 1890*. Chadron, Nebraska: The Chadron Record, 1974.

Hultgren, Mary Lou, and Paulette Fairbanks Molin. *To Lead and to Serve: American Indian Education at Hampton Institute, 1878-1923*. Hampton: Virginia Foundation for the Humanities and Public Policy, 1989.

Hyde, George. *Spotted Tail's Folk: A History of the Brule Sioux*. Norman: University of Oklahoma Press, 1976.

Iverson, Peter, ed. *The Plains Indians of the Twentieth Century*. Norman: University of Oklahoma Press, 1985.

Jabobs, Wilbur R. *Dispossessing the American Indian*. Norman: University of Oklahoma Press, 1972.

Jackson, George. *History of Centennials, Expositions and World Fairs*. Lincoln: Wekesser-Brinkman Co., 1959.

Jackson, Helen Hunt. *A Century of Dishonor*. New York: Harper & Brothers, 1881.

James, Edward, and Janel W. and Paul S. Boyer, eds. *Notable American Women 1607-1950: A Biographical Dictionary*. 3 volumes. Cambridge, Mass.: The Bellnap Press of Harvard University, 1971.

James, Marquis. *The Life of Andrew Jackson*. New York: Garden City Publishing Co., Inc., 1940.

Johnson, Troy R., ed. *The Indian Child Welfare Act: Indian Homes for Indian Children*. Los Angeles: American Indian Studies Center, UCLA, 1991.

Johnson, Virginia W. *The Unregimented General*. Boston: Houghton Mifflin Company, 1962.

Johnson, W. Fletcher. *Life of Sitting Bull and History of the Indian War of 1890-91*. Edgewood Publishing Company, 1891.

Jones, Eugene H. *Native Americans as Shown on the Stage 1753-1916*. Metuchen, N.J.: Scarecrow Press, 1988.

Jordan, Teresa. *Cowgirls, Women of the American West*. Garden City, N.Y.: Anchor Press, Doubleday & Company, Inc., 1982.

Kaye, Dena. *The Traveling Woman*. Garden City, N.Y.: Doubleday & Company, Inc., 1980.

Kelley, Peggy A. V. *Women of Nebraska Hall of Fame*. Lincoln: Nebraska International Woman's Year Coalition, Arbor Printing Co., 1976.

Kelley, William Fitch. *Pine Ridge, 1890*. Edited by Alexander Kelley and Pierre Bovis. San Francisco: Pierre Bovis, 1971.

Ketchum, Richard M. *Will Rogers: His Life and Times*. New York: American Heritage Publishing Company, Inc., 1973.

Kevles, Daniel J. *In the Name of Eugenics*. New York: Alfred A. Knopf, 1985.

King, James T. *War Eagle: A Life of General Eugene A. Carr*. Lincoln: University of Nebraska Press, 1963.

Kingsbury, George W. *History of Dakota Territory: South Dakota, Its History and Its People*. Volumes III & IV. Chicago: The S. J. Clarke Publishing Company, 1915.

Kirk, David. *Adoptive Kinship: A Modern Institution in Need of Reform*. Canada: Butterworth & Co., Ltd., 1981.

Kirkland, Edward C. *Business in the Gilded Age*. Madison: University of Wisconsin Press, 1952.

———. *The Gilded Age: The Conservatives' Balance Sheet*. Madison: University of Wisconsin Press, 1952.

Kolbenschlag, George R. *A Whirlwind Passes: News Correspondents and the Sioux Indian Disturbances of 1890-1891*. Vermillion: University of South Dakota Press, 1990.

Kraditor, Aileen. *The Ideas of the Woman Suffrage Movement 1890-1920*. New York: Columbia University Press, 1965.

Kriebel, Robert C. *Where the Saints Have Trod: The Life of Helen Cougar*. West Lafayette, Indiana: Purdue University Press, 1932.

Kritsberg, Wayne. *The Invisible Wound*. New York: Bantam Books, 1993.

Kvasnicka, Robert M., and Herman J. Viola, eds. *The Commissioners of Indian Affairs, 1824-1977*. Lincoln: University of Nebraska Press, 1979.

Lang, Lincoln A. *Ranching with Roosevelt*. Philadelphia: J. B. Lippincott Company, 1926.

Langsam, Miriam Z. *Children West: A History of the Placing-Out System of the New York Children's Aid Society, 1853-1890*. Madison: The State Historical Society of Wisconsin, 1964.

Leedy, Carl H. *Golden Days in the Black Hills*. Rapid City, S.D.: Holmgren's Inc., 1961.

———. *Black Hills Pioneer Stories*. Edited by Mildred Fielder. Lead, S.D.: Bonanza Trails Publications, 1973.

Lemmon, Edward. *The Recollections of Ed Lemmon 1857-1946*. Edited by Nellie Snyder Yost. Lincoln: University of Nebraska Press, 1969.

Lewis, Lt. Colonel George G. *History of Prisoner of War Utilization by the United States Army 1776-1945*. Washington, D.C.: Center of Military History, United States Army, 1982.

Lindblom, Elizabeth, and Dick Cheatham, eds. *Tragedy at Wounded Knee*. Mitchell, S.D.: Friends of the Middle Border Museum, Dakota Wesleyan University, 1966.

Logan, Mrs. John A. *Thirty Years in Washington; or, Life and Scenes in our National Capital*. Washington, D.C.: A.D. Worthington, 1902.

Longstreet, Stephen. *Chicago 1860-1919*. New York: David McKay Company, Inc., 1973.

Lutz, Alma. *Elizabeth Cady Stanton*. New York: The John Day Company, 1940.

———. *Susan B. Anthony: Rebel, Crusader, Humanitarian*. Boston: Beacon Press, 1959.

Mannes, Marc. *Family Preservation and Indian Child Welfare*. Albuquerque: American Indian Law Center, Inc., 1990.

Mark, Joan. *A Stranger in Her Native Land: Alice Fletcher and the American Indians*. Lincoln: University of Nebraska Press, 1988.

Marshall, S. L. A. *World War I*. Boston: Houghton Mifflin Company, 1964.

Metcalf, Henry Harrison, ed. *One Thousand New Hampshire Notables*. Concord, N.H.: The Rumford Printing Co., 1919.

McConnell, Jane and Burt. *First Ladies: From Martha Washington to Mamie Eisenhower*. New York: Thomas Y. Crowell Company, 1953.

McGillycuddy, Julia B. *McGillycuddy: Agent*. Palo Alto, Calif.: Stanford University Press, 1941.

McGinnis, Vera. *Rodeo Road, My Life as a Pioneer Cowgirl*. New York: Hastings House Publishers, 1974.

McGregor, James H. *The Wounded Knee Massacre from the Viewpoint of the Sioux*. Minneapolis: Minnesota Lund Press, 1940.

McLaughlin, James. *My Friend the Indian*. Boston: Houghton Mifflin Company, 1910.

McNickle, D'Arcy. *Native American Tribalism: Indian Survivals and Renewals*. New York: Oxford University Press, 1973.

McReynolds, Robert. *Thirty Years on the Frontier*. Colorado Springs: El Paso Publishing Co., 1906.

Miller, David Humphreys. *Ghost Dance*. New York: Duell, Sloan and Pearce, 1959.

Miller, Benjamin F. (M.D.), and Claire B. Keane. *Encyclopedia and Dictionary of Medicine, Nursing and Allied Health*. Philadelphia: W.B. Saunders Company, 1987.

Mooney, James. *The Ghost-Dance Religion and the Sioux Outbreak of 1890*. Fourteenth Annual Report of the Bureau of American Ethnology, 1892-93. Part II. Washington, D.C., 1896.

Morey, Sylvester M., and Olivia L. Gilliam, eds. *Respect for Life: The Traditional Upbringing of American Indian Children*. Garden City, N.Y.: Waldorf Press, 1974.

Morrison, Dorothy N. *Ladies Were Not Expected: Abigail Scott Duniway and Women's Rights*. New York: Atheneum, 1977.

Morton, Sterling J., and Albert Watkins. *History of Nebraska*. Lincoln, Nebr.: Western Publishing and Engraving Company, 1918.

Moses, George H., ed. *New Hampshire Men*. Concord, N.H.: The New Hampshire Publishing Company, 1893.

Moses, L. G., and Raymond Wilson, eds. *Indian Lives: Essays on Nineteenth and Twentieth Century Native American Leaders*. Albuquerque: University of New Mexico Press, 1985.

Moynihan, Ruth Barnes. *Rebel for Rights: Abigail Scott Duniway*. New Haven: Yale University Press, 1983.

Moxon, Frank. *What Forcible Feeding Means*. London: The Woman's Press, 1914.

Myres, Sandra L. *Westering Women and the Frontier Experience 1800-1915*. Albuquerque: University of New Mexico Press, 1982.

National Cyclopedia of American Biography. New York: James T. White & Company, 1922.

Nebraska Blue Book, 1915. Lincoln: Nebraska Legislative Council, n.d.

Neihardt, John G. *Black Elk Speaks: Being a Life Story of a Holy Man of the Oglala Sioux*. New York: Morrow, 1932.

Nevins, Allan. *Grover Cleveland: A Study in Courage*. New York: Dodd, Mead & Company, 1933.

Northrop, Henry Davenport. *Indian Horrors*. Augusta, Maine: J. F. Hill Publishers, 1891.

Ochsenreiter, L. G. *History of Day County From 1873 to 1926*. Mitchell, South Dakota: Education Supply Company, 1975.

O'Kieffe, Charley. *Western Story: The Recollections of Charles O'Kieffe 1884-1989*. Lincoln: University of Nebraska Press, 1960.

O'Neil, Paul, ed. *The End and the Myth*. Alexandria, Virginia: Time-life Books, 1979.

O'Neil, William L. *Everyone Was Brave: A History of Feminism in America*. New York: Quadrangle, 1969.

————. *The Woman's Movement: Feminism in the United States and England*. New York: Barnes and Noble, Inc., 1969.

Ortiz, Victoria. *Sojourner Truth: A Self-Made Woman*. New York: Lippincott, 1974.

n.a. *Our Yesterdays*. Hermosa, S.D.: Eastern Custer County Historical Society, 1970.

Parkison, Eka. *Rapid City Pioneers of the Nineteenth Century*. Rapid City, S.D.: Rapid City Society for Genealogical Research, 1989.

n.a. *Pathé Exchange, Inc. Catalogue of Motion Pictures*. New York: Pathé Exchange, Inc., 1923.

Pauli, Hertha. *Her Name Was Sojourner Truth*. New York: Avon, 1976.

Peck, Mary Gray. *Carrie Chapman Catt*. New York: The H. W. Wilson Company, 1944.

n.a. *Pen and Sunlight Sketches of Lincoln*. Chicago: Phoenix Publishing Co., 1893.

Pennington County History Book Committee. *A History of Pennington County, South Dakota*. Dallas: Taylor Publishing Co., 1986.

Petersen, B. J. *The Battle of Wounded Knee*. Gordon, Nebraska: News Publishing, 1941.

Pevar, Stephen L. *The Rights of Indians and Tribes*. Toronto: Bantam Books, 1983.

Pohanka, Brian C., edited in collaboration with John M. Carroll. *Nelson A. Miles: A Documentary Biography of His Military Career 1861-1903*. Glendale, Calif.: The Arthur H. Clark Company, 1985.

Pratt, Richard H. *Battlefield and Classroom: Four Decades with the American Indian 1867-1904*. Edited by Robert M. Utley. Lincoln, Nebr.: University of Nebraska Press, 1987.

Red Horse, John, August Shattuck, and Fred Hoffman, eds. *The American Indian Family: Strengths and Stresses*. Isleta, New Mexico: American Indian Social Research and Development Associates, Inc., 1980.

Reeves, Winona Evans, ed. *The Blue Book of Nebraska Women through the Years 1867-1967*. Lincoln, Nebr.: Johnsen Publishing Co., 1967.

Remington, Frederic. *Pony Tracks*. New York: Harper & Brothers Publishers, 1895.

Richardson, Leon Burr. *William E. Chandler, Republican*. New York: Dodd, Mead & Co., 1940.

Riegel, Robert E. *American Feminists*. Lawrence: University of Kansas Press, 1963.

Robinson, Doane. *History of South Dakota*. Volume I, Chicago: The American Historical Society, Inc., 1930.

————. *A History of the Dakota or Sioux Indians*. Minneapolis: Ross & Haines Inc., 1904.

Robinson, Gil. *Old Wagon Show Days*. Cincinnati: Brockwell Company Publishers, 1925

Robinson, Josephine De Mott. *The Circus Lady*. New York: Thomas Y. Crowell Company Publishers, 1925.

Rogin, Michael Paul. *Fathers and Children: Andrew Jackson and the Subjection of the American Indian*. New York: Alfred A. Knopf, 1975.

Rosen, Andrew. *Rise Up Women! The Militant Campaign of the Women's Social and Political Union, 1903-1914*. London: Routledge and Kegan Paul, 1974.

Rosen, Ruth. *The Lost Sisterhood: Prostitution in America 1900-1918*. Baltimore: The Johns Hopkins University Press, 1960.

Rosten, Leo C. *Hollywood: The Movie Colony. The Movie Makers*. New York: Harcourt, Brace and Company, 1941.

Rush, Florence. *The Best Kept Secret: Sexual Abuse of Children*. Englewood Cliffs, N.J.: Prentice-Hall, 1980.

Russell, Don. *The Lives & Legends of Buffalo Bill*. Norman: University of Oklahoma Press, 1960.

Schell, Herbert S. *History of South Dakota*. Lincoln: University of Nebraska Press, 1961.

Scott, John Anthony. *Woman Against Slavery: The Story of Harriet Beecher Stowe*. New York: Thomas Y. Crowell Company, 1978.

Seawell, Molly Elliot. *The Ladies' Battle*. New York: The Macmillan Company, 1913.

Seymour, Flora Warren. *Indian Agents of the Old Frontier*. New York: Appleton-Century Company, 1941.

Shaw, Anna Howard. *A Story of a Pioneer*. New York: Harper & Brothers Publishers, 1915.

Shengold, Leonard, M.D. *Soul Murder*. New Haven: Yale University Press, 1989.

Sherr, Lynn. *Failure Is Impossible*. New York: Time-Life Books, 1995.

Sievers, Harry J. *Benjamin Harrison, Hoosier President: The White House and After*. Indianapolis: Bobbs Merrill, Inc., 1968.

Sinkler, George. *The Racial Attitudes of American Presidents: From Abraham Lincoln to Theodore Roosevelt*. Garden City, N.Y.: Doubleday & Co., Inc., 1971.

Slayden, Ellen Maury. *Washington Wife: Journal of Ellen Maury Slayden from 1897-1919*. New York: Harper and Row, 1962.

Smith, Gene. *Maximilian and Carlota*. New York: William Morrow & Company, Inc., 1973.

Smith, Sherry L. *The View from Officers' Row*. Tucson: University of Arizona Press, 1990.

Solomon, Barbara Miller. *In the Company of Educated Women: A History of Women in Higher Education in America*. New Haven: Yale University Press, 1985.

Spear, Allen H. *Black Chicago 1890-1920*. Chicago: University of Chicago Press, 1967.

Spindler, Will H. *Tragedy Strikes at Wounded Knee*. Gordon, Nebraska: Gordon Journal Publishing Co., 1955.

Spindler, Will H. *Yesterday's Trails*. Gordon, Nebraska: Gordon Publishing Company, 1942.

Sproat, John G. *The Best Men: Liberal Reformers in the Gilded Age*. New York: Oxford University Press, 1968.

Stanton, Elizabeth Cady. *Suffrage: A Natural Right*. Chicago: The Open Court Publishing Company, 1894.

———. *The Woman's Bible*. Volumes I and II. New York: European Publishing Company, 1895.

———, Susan B. Anthony, and Matilda Joselyn Gage. *History of Woman Suffrage 1876-1885*. Volumes 3, 4, and 5. New York: Charles Mann, 1887.

———. *Eighty Years and More: Reminiscences, 1815-1897*. Volumes I and II. Edited by Theodore Stanton and Harriot Stanton Blatch. New York: Arno, 1969.

Strain, David F. *Black Hills Hay Camp, Images and Perspectives of Early Rapid City*. Rapid City, S.D.: Dakota West Books & Fenske Printing Inc., 1989.

Sudlow, Adria Blackburn. *Homestead Years 1908-1968*. Bison, S.D.: Bison Courier, 1968

Sweet, William Warren. *Religion on the American Frontier: The Baptists 1783-1830*. Chicago: University of Chicago Press, 1931.

Szasz, Margaret Connell. *Education and the American Indian: The Road to Self-Determination 1928-1973*. Albuquerque: University of New Mexico Press, 1974.

Terry, Cleo Tom, and Osie Wilson. *The Rawhide Tree: The Story of Florence Reynolds in Rodeo*. Clarendon, Texas: Clarendon Press, 1957.

Thornton, Russell. *We Shall Live Again: The 1870-1890 Ghost Dance Movements as Demographic Revitalization*. London: Cambridge University Press, 1986.

Tibbles, Thomas. *Buckskin and Blanket Days*. Garden City, N.Y.: Doubleday & Company, Inc., 1957.

Transactions and Reports of the Nebraska State Historical Society. Volume III. Fremont, Nebraska: Nebraska State Historical Society, Hammond Brothers Printers, 1892.

Truman, Margaret. *Women of Courage: From Revolutionary Times to the Present*. New York: William Morrow & Company, Inc., 1976.

Unger, Steven, ed. *The Destruction of American Indian Families*. New York: Association on American Indian Affairs, 1977.

Note: The following is a chapter from the above book: Red Bird, Aileen, and Patrick Melendy, "Indian Child Welfare in Oregon," pp. 43–46.

Unger, Steven, ed. *The Destruction of Indian Family Life*. New York: Association of American Indian Affairs, 1976. Note: See the following chapter in this book: Westermeyer, Joseph, M.D. "The Ravage of Indian Families in Crisis," pp. 47–56

Utley, Robert M. *The Last Days of the Sioux Nation*. New Haven: Yale University Press, 1963.

Vestal, Stanley. *Sitting Bull, Champion of the Sioux*. Norman: University of Oklahoma Press, 1952.

Vicinus, Martha, ed. *A Widening Sphere: Changing Roles of Victorian Women*. Bloomington: Indiana University Press, 1977.

Walker, James R. *Lakota Belief and Ritual*. Edited by Raymond J. DeMallie and Elaine A. Jahner. Lincoln: University of Nebraska Press, 1980.

Walston, Howard B. *Prostitution in the United States*. New York: The Century Co., 1921.

Ward, John W. *Andrew Jackson: Symbol for an Age*. New York: Oxford University Press, 1953

Warren, Margaret Lemley. *The Badlands Fox*. Edited by Renée Sansom Flood. Rapid City, S.D.: Fenske Printing Inc., 1991.

Warteje, Sandy K., and Cindy L. Miller-Perrin. *Preventing Child Sexual Abuse*. Lincoln: University of Nebraska Press, 1992.

Weeks, Philip, ed. *The American Indian Experience: A Profile*. Arlington Heights: Forum Press, Inc., 1988.

Wellman, Paul I. *Death on Horseback: Seventy Years of War for the American West*. Philadelphia: J. B. Lippincott Company, 1934.

White, Lonnie J. *Hostiles and Horse Soldiers*. Boulder, Colo.: Pruett Publishing Company, 1972.
Whitman, Alden, ed. *American Reformers*. New York: The H.W. Wilson Company, 1985.
Who's Who in America, 1914-1915. Chicago: A.N. Marquis Co., 1915.
Who Was Who in America, 1887-1942. Vol. I. Chicago: A.N. Marquis Co., 1943.
Wiebe, Robert H. *The Search for Order 1877-1920*. New York: Hill and Wang, 1967.
Wilcox, Virginia Lee. *Comprehensive Index to Westerners Brand Books 1944-1961*. Denver: The Denver Posse of the Westerners, 1962.
Willey, George Franklin, ed. *State Builders: An Illustrated Historical and Biographical Record of the State of New Hampshire at the Beginning of the Twentieth Century*. Manchester, N.H.: The New Hampshire Publishing Corporation, 1902.
Wilson, James J. *Valor and Honor in Defense of Country*. Rapid City, S.D.: Little Warrior Publishing Company, 1983.
Wissler, Clark. *Indian Cavalcade or Life on the Old-Time Indian Reservations*. New York: Sheridan House, 1938.
Woman's Who's Who of America. New York: The American Commonwealth Co., 1914.
Woodward, C. Vann. *The Strange Career of Jim Crow*. New York: Oxford University Press, 1974.
Wordon, Zoa Ann. *Queen City of the Blue*. Beatrice, Nebraska: Gage County Historical Society, 1976.
Wright, Harold Bell. *When a Man's a Man*. Chicago: The Book Supply Company Publishers, 1916.
Yost, Nellie Snyder. *Buffalo Bill, His Family, Friends, Fame, Failures and Fortunes*. Chicago: Sage Books, 1979.

JOURNAL AND MAGAZINE ARTICLES

Abbott, O. A. "Recollections of a Pioneer Lawyer." *Nebraska History Magazine* 3(July–September 1928).
Attneave, C. L. "An Analysis of Therapeutic Roles in Tribal Settings and Urban Network Intervention." *Family Process* 8(1969):192–210.
Babcock, W. H. (no title) *American Anthropologist* 1–2(1888–1889):267–68.
Barbour, Fannie C. W. "Overland by the Southern Pacific." *Chautauquan* 15(July 1892): 391–401.
Beach, Rex. "Wounded Knee." *Appleton's Booklovers Magazine* 7(June 1906):731.
Berlin, Irving N. "Suicide Among American Indian Adolescents: An Overview." *Suicide and Life-Threatening Behavior* 17(1987):225-26.
Billings, Elden E. "Social and Economic Life in Washington in the 1890s." *Records of the Columbia Historical Society* (1966).
Blanchard, Joseph D. and Evelyn, and Samuel Roll. "A Psychological Autopsy of an Indian Adolescent Suicide with Implications for Community Services." *Suicide and Life-Threatening Behavior* 6(1976):3–10.
Blanchard, Evelyn and Russel Lawrence Barsh. "What is best for Tribal Children?" *White Cloud Journal* (1980):350–357.
Boggs, Stephen T. "Culture Change and the Personality of Ojibwa Children." *American Anthropologist* 60(1953):47–58.
Bordeaux, W. J. "Battle of Wounded Knee, 47 Years Ago Wednesday, Declared Massacre." *Harper's Weekly* (1937) n.p.
Bosma, Boyd. "An Interview with Jim Mesteth." *The Indian Historian* 11(1978):18–21.
———. "An Interview with Jim Mesteth." *The Indian Historian* 11(1978):18–21.
Burgess, Gelett. "The Keepsake." *Atlantic Monthly* 98(December 1906):837.
Buthod, Therese. "An Analysis of Cases Decided Pursuant to the Indian Child Welfare Act of 1978." *American Indian Law Review* 10(1982):311–31.
Carver, Gordon. "Sells-Floto Circus 1914–1915." *Bandwagon* (November–December):22.
Cash, Joseph H. "Prelude to Tragedy: The Indians and the Military in Dakota in 1889." *South Dakota Historical Collections* 35(1970):59–68.
Cayton, Anne H. "The Ghost Dance of 1870 in South Central California." *University of California Publications in Archaeology and Ethnology* 28(1930):n.p.
Chestang, L. "The Dilemma of Biracial Adoption." *Social Work* 17(1972):100–105.
Clow, Richmond L. "The Lakota Ghost Dance After 1890." *South Dakota History* 20(Winter 1990):323–333.
Colby, Clara B. "Elizabeth Cady Stanton." *Arena* 29(1903):152–160.

———. " What Glasgow Is Doing for Her People." *Arena* 33(1905):361–9.

———. "Nell Gwynne." *Overland Monthly* 5(November 1901): 21.

———. "Flowers and Perfume in Sentiment and Commerce." *Today's Magazine*. n.d. n.p.

———. "Stirring Scenes." n.d.(1913)n.p.

Colby, L. W. "The Ghost Songs of the Dakota." *Nebraska State Historical Society*. Series 2(1895):n.p.

———. "The Sioux Indian War of 1890–91." *Transactions and Reports of the Nebraska State Historical Society* 3(1892):144–190.

———. "Indian Depredation Claims." *Lend a Hand* 11(1893):337–345.

———. "Wanagi Olowon Kin, the Ghost Songs of the Dakotas." *Proceedings and Collections of the Nebraska State Historical Society* 1(1895):131–150.

———. "Zintka Lanuni." *The Illustrated American* 10(1892):34.

Coolidge, Harriet Lincoln. "Zintka Lanuni—Lost Bird." *Trained Motherhood* 2(January 1898):15–19.

Daddario, Wilma A. "They Get Milk Practically Every Day, the Genoa Indian Industrial School, 1884–1934." *Nebraska History* (1992):2–11.

Danker, Donald F. (ed.). "The Wounded Knee Interviews of Eli S. Ricker." *Nebraska History* 62(1981):151–243.

de Forest, Katharine. "Education for Girls in France." *Scribner's Magazine* 14(1893):633.

DeMallie, Raymond J. "The Lakota Ghost Dance: An Ethnohistorical Account." *Pacific Historical Review* 51(1982):385–405.

Dougherty, Capt. W. E. "The Recent Messiah Craze," *Journal of the Military Service Institution of the United States* 12(1891):577

Eastman, Elaine Goodale. "The Ghost Dance and the Wounded Knee Massacre of 1890–91." *Nebraska History* 26(1945):26–42.

Frink, Maurice M. "Died Here Innocent." *Outing* 65(1915):549–554.

Gephart, Ronald M. "Politicians, Soldiers and Strikes: The Reorganization of the Nebraska Militia and the Omaha Strike of 1882." *Nebraska History* 46(1965):89–120.

Geyer, Alan. "Wounded Knee and My Lai." *Christian Century* 88(1971):59.

Glascow, O. M. and Hugh McGinnis. "I Was There." *True West* 8(1961):6.

Goodluck, Charlotte Tsoi and Florence Eckstein. "American Indian Adoption Program: An Ethnic Approach to Child Welfare." *White Cloud Journal* 2(1982).

Greene, Jerome A. "The Sioux Land Commission of 1889." *South Dakota History* 1(1970):62.

Guerrero, Manuel P. "A Response to the Threat to Indian Children Caused by Foster and Adoptive Placements of Indian Children." *American Indian Law Review* 7(1979):51–77.

Hamilton, W. R. "Nebraska's National Guard in the Sioux War." *Outing* 28(1896):317.

Hillis, Newell. "Just Christmas." *Cosmopolitan* 48(1910):185.

Hoxie, Frederick E. "From Prison to Homeland: The Cheyenne River Indian Reservation Before WWI." *South Dakota History* 10(1979):1–24.

Huger, Lucie Furstenberg. "Dr. Mary Edward Walker, The Little Lady in Pants." *Society of the Daughters of the American Revolution* (1989):813.

Hunt, Burl. "Lost Bird of Wounded Knee." *Golden West* (May 1969):11.

Hutchin, George L. "Hit the Trail." *Lewis and Clark Journal* 3(1905):48–54.

n.a. "An Indian Doll." *Harper's Weekly*, n.d.

n.a. "Indian Land Lawyers." *Outlook* 95(1910):911–912.

Johnson, John J., and Edith Red Buffalo. "Helping Services for Indian People." *Concepts* (1977):1–4. (Published by the Lewis and Clark Mental Health Center, Yankton, South Dakota.)

Kalstrom, J. "Our First Governor's Watertown Mansion: The House, Like the Man, Faced Some Unhappy Times." *South Dakota Magazine* (Sept. 1985):14–18.

Lamar, R. Howard. "Perspectives on Statehood: South Dakota's First Quarter Century 1889–1914." *South Dakota History* 19(1989):2–25.

Larson, Cedric. "Censorship of Army News During the World War, 1917–1918." *Journalism Quarterly* 4(1940):313

Lathrop, Alan K. "Another View of Wounded Knee." *South Dakota History* 16(1986):249–268.

Lee, Bob. "Messiah War on Cheyenne River." *The Wi-iyohi Bulletin of the South Dakota Historical Society* 8(1963):1–8.

Lesser, A. A. "Cultural Significance of the Ghost Dance." *American Anthropologist* 35(1933):108–115.

Ley, Beth. "Sour News About Milk." *Muscle and Fitness* (May 1993):211

Limprecht, Jane. "The Indian Child Welfare Act: Tribal Self-Determination Through Participation in Child Custody Proceedings." *Wisconsin Law Review* 19(1979):1202–27.

Low, Maurice A. "Washington: The City of Leisure." *Atlantic Monthly* 86(1900):767–78.

Marousek, Linda A. "The Indian Child Welfare Act of 1978: Provisions and Policy." *South Dakota Law Review* 25(1980):98–115.

Mattes, Merrill, J. "The Enigma of Wounded Knee." *Plains Anthropologist* 5 (May 1960):1–11.

May, Philip A. "Suicide Among American Indian Youth: A Look at the Issues." *Children Today* (July–August 1989):22.

Mead, Margaret. "Cultural Discontinuities and Personality Transformation." *Journal of Social Issues* 8(1954):3–16.

Medicine, Bea. "The Changing Dakota Family and the Stresses Therein." *Pine Ridge Research Bulletin* 9(1969):1–20.

Merrick, Frank L. "Woman's Part at the Centennial." *Lewis and Clark Journal* 3(February 1905):25.

McGinnis, Hugh, and Olive Glasgow. "I Took Part in the Wounded Knee Massacre." *Real West* (January 1966):31–34.

McMullen, Mary C. "Preserving the Indian Family." *Children's Legal Rights Review* 2(1981):36–37.

Miles, Nelson A. "Rounding Up the Redmen." *The Cosmopolitan* 51(June 1911):522–529.

———. "The War with the Messiah." *The Cosmopolitan* 51(September 1911):522–529.

Moorehead, Warren K. "Masking the Frauds." *The Illustrated American* 5(1891):544.

Morris, Michele, "Intensive Care for Families in Crisis." *Woman's Day* (February 2, 1993):58–60.

Morrow, Prince A., M.D. "The Relations of Social Diseases to the Family." *American Journal of Sociology* 14(1909):622–635.

Moses, L. G. "Wild West Shows, Reformers and the Image of the American Indian 1887–1914." *South Dakota History* 14(Fall 1984):193.

Quarles, Benjamin. "Frederick Douglass and the Woman's Rights Movement." *Journal of Negro History* 25(1940):35–44.

Remington, Frederic. "The Art of War and Newspapermen." *Harper's Weekly* 34(1890):947.

———. "Lt. Casey's Last Scout." *Harper's Weekly* 35(1891):85–91.

Richardson, W. P. "Some Observations Upon the Sioux Campaign of 1890–91." *Journal of the Military Service Institution of the United States* 18(1896):512–31.

Ruger, T. H. "Department News, at the Front." *Army and Navy Journal* (December 1890):279.

Scott, E. D. "Wounded Knee, a Look Back at the Record." *The Field Artillery Journal* 29(1939):5–94.

Seymour, C. G. and J. C. Gresham. "Sioux Rebellion or the Story of Wounded Knee." *Harper's Weekly* 35(February 1891):106–109.

Seymour, Forrest W. "A Look Back at Wounded Knee." *Proceedings of the American Antiquarian Society*. Volume 84.

Sievers, Harry J. "The Catholic Indian School Issue and the Presidential Election of 1892." 2(July 1952):129–155.

n.a. "Sioux on the War-Path." *The Illustrated American* (1891):269.

Standing Bear, Luther. "The Tragedy of the Sioux." *American Mercury* 24(1931):278.

Steinman, Marion. "Fighting the Genetic Odds." *Life* 71(1971):19–25.

Traub, Peter E. "The First Act of the Last Sioux Campaign." *Armor* (April 1905): 872–879.

Venables, Robert W. "Looking Back at Wounded Knee 1890." *Northeast Indian Quarterly* (Spring 1990):36–37.

Watson, Elmo Scott. "Pine Ridge 1890–1891." *The Westerner's Brand Book* 1(March 1945).

———. "The Last Indian War, 1890–91—A Study of Newspaper Jingoism." *Journalism Quarterly* 20(1943):205–219.

Westermeyer, Joseph, M.D. "The Apple Syndrome: The Effects of Racial Discontinuity." *Journal of Operational Psychiatry* 10(1979):134–140.

———. "Disorganization: Its Role in Indian Suicide Rates." *American Journal of Psychiatry* 128(1971):123.

———. "A Review of the Relationship Between Dysphoria, Pleasure and Human Bonding." *Journal of Clinical Psychiatry* 39(1978):415–424. Quote: "Psychological studies of motherhood have ignored the bonding of mother and child." p. 416.

———. "Ethnic Identity Problems Among Ten Indian Psychiatric Patients." *International Journal of Social Psychiatry* 25(1979):188–197.

———. "Cross-Racial Foster Home Placement Among Native American Psychiatric Patients." *Journal of the National Medical Association* 69(1977):231–236.

n.a. "Westerners Fight Again the Ghost Dance 'War' and the 'Battle' of Wounded Knee." *The Westerners Brand Book* 1 (January 1945).

Wier, Jeanne Elizabeth. "Diary (1908)." *Nevada Historical Society Quarterly* 4(1961):1–21.

Wilson, George. "The Sioux War." *The Nation* 52(1891):29–30.

Wood, Kenneth H., ed. "People Who Know Why They Believe as They Do." *Adventist Review* 155(May 1978):2.

———. "Christian Behavior." *Adventist Review* 158(1981):1.

n.a. "Zintkala Nuni." *Sunset* (October 1915).

GOVERNMENT DOCUMENTS

United States Senate. Hearings Before the Committee on the Judiciary, 94th Congress, 2nd Session on S1147 and S2900, to Liquidate the Liability of the United States for the Massacre of Sioux Indian Men, Women, and Children at Wounded Knee, February 5, 6, 7, 1976, Government Printing Office, Washington, D.C., 1976.

Wounded Knee Memorial and Historic Site, Little Big Horn National Monument Battlefield, S.HRG.101-1184, Hearing Before the Select Committee on Indian Affairs, United States Senate, 101st Congress, 2nd Session on To Establish Wounded Knee Memorial and Historic Site and Proposal to Establish Monument Commemorating Indian Participants of the Little Big Horn and to Redesignate Name of Monument from Custer Battlefield to Little Big Horn National Monument Battlefield, September 25, 1990, Washington, D.C., U.S. Government Printing Office, Washington, 1991.

Medal of Honor Recipients 1863–1978, 96th Congress, 1st Session, Senate Committee Print No. 3, Prepared by the Committee on Veteran's Affairs, United States Senate, February 14, 1979.

U.S. Congressional Hearings Supplement (SS52B), Select Committee on Indian Depredations, Feb. 7 & 8, 1893, Government Printing Office, Washington, D.C., 1893.

House Executive Documents, 1st Session, 52nd Congress, Volume 2, 1891–92. Report of the Secretary of War, United States Government Printing Office, Washington, D.C., 1892.

House Documents Volume 97, Number 446, Historical Register and Dictionary of Army 1789–1903, Volume 2, 57th Congress, 2nd Session, United States Government Printing Office, Washington, D.C., 1903.

U.S. Senate Documents Volume 5, 55th Congress, 1st Session, Memorial Petition to the 55th United States Congress, May 13, 1897. United States Government Printing Office, Washington, D.C., 1897.

House Executive Documents, 3rd Session, 53rd Congress, Report of the Attorney General of the United States, Volume 27, United States Government Printing Office, Washington, D.C., 1891.

Preliminary Inventories, Number 163, Records of the Bureau of Indian Affairs, Volume 1, The National Archives and Records Service, General Services Administration, Washington, D.C., 1965.

House Executive Documents 7(52-1), 1st Session, 52nd Congress, 1891–92, Volume 22, Government Printing Office, Washington, D.C., 1892.

Act of Congress March 3, 1891 (26 Stat. 851), Government Printing Office, Washington, D.C., 1891.

National Archives, Record Group 205, E72, Indian Depredations March 1891–June 1892, Washington, D.C.

National Archives, Record Group 205, Annual Report of the Assistant Attorney General of the United States, Washington, D.C., 1892.

House Executive Document No. 299, 57th Congress, 1st Session, "List of Claims Before the Spanish Treaty Claim Commission," Government Printing Office, Washington, D.C., 1906.

National Archives, Record Group 75, Bureau of Indian Affairs, Letters Received, Northern Cheyenne Agency, Montana 1881–1907.

National Archives, Records Group 75, Register of Pupils, Hope School, Springfield, South Dakota, Bureau of Indian Affairs, Series E725, Reference Books 1882–1909.

Annual Reports of the Department of the Interior, June 30, 1904. Washington, D.C.: Government Printing Office, 1904.

Annual Reports of the Department of the Interior, June 30, 1906. Washington, D.C.: Government Printing Office, 1906.

National Archives, Record Group 75, Records of the Bureau of Indian Affairs, Central Classified File—1907–1939, Washington, D.C.

CIS. United States Congress Committee Hearings, Index, Part 1, 23rd Congress, 64th Congress, Reference Bibliography H.S. 25-A-(64)SJ-1. Congressional Information Service, Inc., Washington, D.C., December 1833–March 1917.

House Executive Documents, 1st Session, 52nd Congress, Volume Two, 1891–92. Report to the Inspector-General, U.S. Army, Government Printing Office, Washington, D.C., 1892.

United States Congress, Senate, Select Committee on Indian Affairs, Committee on Interior and Insular Affairs, Problems that American Indian Families Face in Raising Their Children and How These Problems are Affected by Federal Action or Inaction, Hearings before a Subcommittee of the Committee on Interior and Insular Affairs, 93rd Congress, 2nd Session, 1974.

United States War Department Official Records of the Union and Confederate Armies in the War of the Rebellion, Washington, D.C., Government Printing Office, 1901.

House Executive Documents, 2nd Session, 53rd Congress, Volume 21, 1893–94, No. 1, Part 8, Nos. 4, 7, 23. Reports of the Assistant Attorney General of the United States.

House Executive Documents, 1st Session, 54th Congress, 1895–96. Report of Charles B. Howry, Assistant Attorney General of the United States.

National Archives, Record Group 98, Colonel E. Carr, Records of the United States Army (H75.77sM), Report Relative to the Sioux Campaign 1890–92, 6th Cavalry Regimental Returns.

Executive Documents No. 127, Creek Tribal Records, United States Statutes at Large XXVI, 25th Congress, 2nd Session, Government Printing Office, Washington, D.C.

Historical Register and Dictionary of Army House Documents No. 446 17–89-1903, Volume Two, 57th Congress, 2nd Session, 1902–1903. Government Printing Office, Washington, D.C.

National Archives, Record Group 75, Special Case #188-Wounded Knee File. Note: On December 11, 1890, General Nelson A. Miles wrote to Brigadier General John R. Brooke. This letter is proof that General Miles knew of the bloodshed and the ambushes against the Lakota in the month prior to the Wounded Knee Massacre.

U.S. Congress. Senate. Claims of Friendly Indians for Depredations Committed during the Pine Ridge Disturbances, 52nd Congress, 2nd Session (S.exdoc. 93), Washington, D.C., U.S. Government Printing Office, 1893–94.

National Archives, Record Group 305, Court of Claims, Indian Depredations, Letters Received, March–August 1893.

House Executive Documents, 53rd Congress, 3rd Session, 1894–95, Volume 27, "War Claim Cases." Report of the Assistant Attorney General of the United States Charles B. Howry. Note: Howry wrote that investigating Leonard Colby was like "chasing phantoms."

MANUSCRIPT COLLECTIONS

Assumption Abbey Archives, Richardton, North Dakota: James McLaughlin Papers.

Bakersfield Historical Society, Bakersfield, California: Ernest C. Allen File.

Bancroft Library, University of California, Berkeley: The California Indian Herald, Panama Pacific Exhibition records.

Beatrice Public Library, Beatrice, Nebraska: Clara B. Colby Papers, Beatrice Daily Express, Woman Suffrage Collection.

Beinecke Rare Book and Manuscript Library, Yale University, New Haven, Connecticut: Richard Henry Pratt Papers, U.S. Army and Navy Journal.

Berkshire County Historical Society, Adams, Massachusetts: Susan B. Anthony Collection.

Brigham Young University Library, Provo, Utah: Walter Camp Papers.

Brown University Library, Providence, Rhode Island: Lester Frank Ward Papers, Harriet Coolidge Papers.

Buffalo Bill Home and Museum, North Platte, Nebraska: Buffalo Bill (William F. Cody) records.

Buffalo Bill (William F. Cody) Historical Center, Cody, Wyoming: Buffalo Bill Wild West Show tour schedules and photographs.

Buffalo Bill Memorial Museum and Gravesite, Lookout Mountain, Golden, Colorado: Leonard W. Colby Correspondence; Wild West Show schedules; photographs and museum collections.

California Department of Health and Vital Records, Sacramento, California: Birth, marriage and death records.

California Historical Society, San Francisco: San Francisco Chronicle, Woman Suffrage Papers, The Municipal Clinic Papers, Overland Monthly Records.

Center for Western Studies, Augustana College, Sioux Falls, South Dakota: Archives of the Episcopal Church in South Dakota, Bishop William Hobart Hare Papers, The Word Carrier, All Saints School records, Private collections and photographs.

The Cherokee Nation Records, Okmulgee, Oklahoma: Enrollment records.

Cheyenne River Sioux Tribe, Eagle Butte, South Dakota: Enrollment and allotment records.

Circus World Museum, Baraboo, Wisconsin: Ringling Brothers Records, Sells–Floto Records, Numerous small circus records such as M.H. Welsh's Great American One Ring Circus, Al G. Barnes Circus, St. Louis Police Circus.

Colorado Historical Society, Denver, Colorado: Thomas F. Dawson scrapbooks, Wild West records.

Columbia Historical Society, Washington, D.C.: Unpublished records and manuscripts about Washington's social and economic past.

Concord Public Library, Concord, New Hampshire: The Charles Robert Corning diaries and William E. Chandler Collection.

Dakota Wesleyan University Library, Mitchell, South Dakota: Leonard Jennewein papers.

Denver Public Library, Denver, Colorado: Wounded Knee collection, Buffalo Bill Papers, Western photo archives.

Freeport Public Library, Freeport, Illinois: Rowel Colby papers.

Friends of the Middle Border Museum, Mitchell, South Dakota: Leonard Jennewein Papers.

Gage County Historical Society, Beatrice, Nebraska: Leonard W. and Clara B. Colby Papers, August Hettinger Manuscript, Beatrice history.

Genoa Boarding School Museum, Genoa, Nebraska: Boarding school records.

Gilcrease Museum, Tulsa, Oklahoma: Wounded Knee Collection, A.T. Lea Papers.

Haskell Indian Junior College, Haskell, Kansas: Enrollment records and correspondence (restricted to family members).

Hampton University Archives, Hampton, Virginia: Enrollment records.

Hanford Kings County Library, Hanford, California: Hanford Daily Journal, Hanford Historical Archives.

Michael and Margaret B. Harrison Western Research Center, Fair Oaks, California: Rare books and manuscript archives.

Henry E. Huntington Memorial Library, San Marino, California: Susan B. Anthony papers, Clara B. Colby papers, Elizabeth Boynton Harbert papers.

I.D. Weeks Library, University of South Dakota, Vermillion: Chilson Collection, Western History Archives, South Dakota newspapers.

Indiana State Library, Indianapolis, Indiana: Benjamin Harrison Collection, William Henry Harrison Miller papers.

Institute of American Indian Studies, University of South Dakota, Vermillion: South Dakota Oral History Center, American Indian Research Project.

Kings County Department of Judicial Administration, Seattle, Washington: Criminal and Court Records.

Lauber and Moore Funeral Home, Milford, Nebraska: Blue Mound Cemetery Records.

Lemmon Public Library, Lemmon, South Dakota: Perkins County Signal, Bamble papers, Indian Pete Culbertson collection.

Library of Congress, Washington, D.C.: Leonard Wood Papers, Charles D. Rhodes Papers, Edward S. Godfrey Papers, Richard Olney Papers, Harriot Stanton Blatch papers, Elizabeth Cady Stanton Papers, Susan B. Anthony Papers, Clara B. Colby Papers.

Marquette University Archives, Milwaukee, Wisconsin: Bureau of Catholic Indian Mission Records, Holy Rosary Mission Records, Wounded Knee Collection.

Miami University Library, Oxford, Ohio: Walter Havinghurst Papers, Burton L. French Papers.

Minnesota State Historical Society, St. Paul, MN: T.H. Beaulieu Papers, Clement H. Beaulieu Papers.

Morley Library, Painesville, Ohio: Martin Tuttle and William M. Hubbard Genealogical Records, Lake County Savings and Loan Papers.

National Archives, Washington, D.C.: W.H.H. Miller letterbooks, Attorney General of the United States, 1891–1893; Hope School Records, Records of the Bureau of Indian Affairs, Classified Files, U.S. War Department Archives, Woman Suffrage Archives, President William McKinley Papers, Records of Congressional Hearings, House Executive Documents.

Nebraska State Historical Society, Lincoln, Nebraska: Wounded Knee Collection; Leonard W. Colby Papers; John D. Bratt Papers; Nathan Kirk Griggs Papers; John Thayer Papers; Norma Kidd Green Papers; Griggs, Rinaker and Bibb Papers; Jefferson Hunsaker Broady Papers; E.A. Brininstool Papers; Eli S. Ricker Collection; D. Charles Bristol Papers; James E. Boyd Papers; Hazlett and Jack Papers; Mead-Cockrell Family Papers; Joseph J. Imhoff Papers; Charles W. Allen Papers; Erasmus M. Correll Papers; Archibald J. Weaver Papers; Thomas Jefferson Majors Papers; Mari Sandoz Collection.

Newberry Library, D'Arcy McNickle Center for the History of the American Indian, Chicago, Illinois: Edward E. Ayer Collection, Elmo Scott Watson Papers.

New Hampshire Historical Society, Concord, New Hampshire: Charles R. Corning Papers, William E. Chandler Papers.

New York City Public Library: The Pathé Frères Silent Film File.

Oglala Lakota College Archives, Kyle, South Dakota: The Jeanne Smith Collection of Pine Ridge Reservation Families and Community Histories.

Oklahoma Historical Society, Oklahoma City, Oklahoma: The Creek Nation Records, The Cherokee Nation Records.

Oklahoma State University, Edmun Low Library, Stillwater, Oklahoma: Angie Debo Collection.

Pioneer Woman Museum, Ponca City, Oklahoma: 101 Wild West Show Collection.

Radcliffe College, The Arthur and Elizabeth Schlesinger Library on the History of Women in America, Cambridge, Massachusetts: Harriette Robinson Shattuck Papers, Anna Howard Shaw Papers, Mary Earhart Dillon Papers, Harriot Stanton Blatch Papers, Olympia Brown Papers, Susan B. Anthony Papers, Maltilda E. Joslyn Gage Papers, Elizabeth Cady Stanton Papers, Lucy Stone Papers, Isabella Beecher Hooker Papers, Julia Ward Howe Papers, Belva A. Lockwood Papers, May Wright Sewall Papers, Susan B. Anthony Papers, Harriet Taylor Upton Papers, Carrie Chapman Catt Papers, Elizabeth Boynton Harbert Papers, Alma Lutz Papers, Grace Richardson Papers.

Red Cloud Mission Records, Pine Ridge, South Dakota: Holy Rosary Mission Records.

San Francisco Public Library: Vaudeville Collection.

State Historical Society of Wisconsin, Madison, Wisconsin: Clara Bewick Colby Collection.

University of San Francisco: Dr. Clara McNaughton Papers.

Smith College Library, Northampton, Massachusetts: Sophia Smith Collection, Elaine Goodale Eastman Papers, Woman Suffrage Collection, Susan B. Anthony Papers.

DISSERTATIONS

Andolsen, Barbara Hilkert. "Racism in the Nineteenth and Twentieth Century Women's Movements: An Ethical Appraisal." Ph.D. dissertation, Vanderbilt University, 1981.

Carroll, J.F. "The Acceptance or Rejection of Differences between Adoptive and Biological Parenthood by Adoptive Applicants as Related to Various Indices of Adjustment/Maladjustment." Ph.D. dissertation, Temple University, 1968.

Elam, Pamela Lynn "How Long Must Women Wait for Liberty?': Perceptions of the Militant Woman Suffrage Movement in the United States, 1916–1920." Masters Thesis, Sarah Lawrence College, 1980.

Evans, Eola Adel ne. "Activity of Black Women in the Woman Suffrage Movement 1900–1920". Master's thesis, Lanmar University, 1987.

Ford, Linda G. 'American Militants: An Analysis of the National Woman's Party, 1913–1919," Ph.D. dissertation Syracuse University, 1984.

Hague, Amy "Give Us a Little Time to Find Our Places: University of Wisconsin Alumnae Classes of 1875–1900." Master's thesis. University of Wisconsin, 1983.

Jerry, Eleanor Claire. "Clara Bewick Colby and the Woman's Tribune: Strategies of a Free Lance Movement Leader." Ph.D. dissertation, University of Kansas, 1986.

Johnson, Troy Rollen. "Status of Adoption and Foster Home Placement of Indian Children under the Indian Child Welfare Act." Master's thesis, University of California, 1988.

Linkugel, Wilmer A. "The Speeches of Anna Howard Shaw." Ph.D. dissertation, University of Wisconsin, 1961.

Ogden, Florence Ruth. "Charles Fletcher Lummis: His Life and Works," Master's thesis, University of Texas, 1940.

Pyle, Prosper Dee. "An Early History of Beatrice, Nebraska," Master's thesis, University of Nebraska, 1941.

Robertson, Diana Conway. "Parental Socialization Patterns in Interracial Adoption," Ph.D. dissertation, University of California, 1974.

Rockefeller, Alfred Jr. "The Sioux Troubles of 1890–1891." Ph.D. dissertation, Northwestern University, 1949.

Rosene, Linda Roberts. "A Follow-up Study of Indian Children Adopted by White Families (Transracial identity, Adolescent)," Ph.D dissertation, The fielding Institute, 1983.

Wood, Katharine Valeda. "The Life of the Pioneer Woman on the Kansas-Nebraska Frontier." Master's thesis, University of Nebraska, 1940.

UNPUBLISHED MANUSCRIPTS AND COLLECTIONS

Alice Ghost Horse manuscript, private collection of Sidney Keith, Rapid City, South Dakota, and Goldie Iron Hawk, Cheyenne River Reservation.

"The Arrest and Killing of Sitting Bull." Walter S. Campbell Papers, The Western History Collections, University of Oklahoma, Norman.

Hobart Keith's Remembrance of the Wounded Knee Massacre, Elaine Melior Collection, Spokane, Washington.

Riley Miller Collection, Jim Ross, Belle Fourche, South Dakota.

Unpublished Autobiography of Private August Hettinger, Gage County Historical Society, Beatrice, Nebraska.

General Leonard W. Colby family collection, Helen Colby, West Linn, Oregon.

Clara B. Colby family genealogy and photographs, Joan Indermark, Madison, Wisconsin.

Abigail Scott Duniway Collection, David Duniway curator, Salem, Oregon.

Colby family photographs, David C. Colby, curator, Ashland, Oregon.

Kate Barnard papers, see Angie Debo Collection, Edmun Low Library, Special Collections, Oklahoma State University, Stillwater, Oklahoma.

Jean Waddell papers, Beatrice, Nebraska.

Margaret Benson photographs, Gordon, Nebraska.

Helen Bewick family records, Madison, Wisconsin.

Mrs. William Davis collection (Norma Kidd Green Papers), Newark, Delaware.

Jane Kadlecek photographs, Hay Springs, Nebraska

INTERVIEWS

Allgier, Albert J. Omaha, Neb., 5/89.
Anderson, LaVerne. Beatrice, Neb., 1990.
Angel, JoAnn. Vermillion, S.D., 6/92–94.
Arms, Ruth. Oklahoma City, Okla., 1990–1993.
Arnold, Tim. Hanford, Calif., 1990–1991.

Ball, Gladys. Beatrice, Neb., 1988.
Barnard, Roy. Beatrice, Neb., 9/88.
Bausch, Roy. Beatrice, Neb., 9/88.
Bazemore, Beth Todd. Vermillion, S.D., 1992–1994.
Bear, Gertrude. Rushville, Neb., 10/89.
Benson, Margaret. Gordon, Neb., 2/93.
Bernie, Shirley. Lake Andes, S.D., 1978–1995.
Bewick, Helen. Madison, Wisc., 1989–1993.
Bewick, Tom L. Tarpon Springs, Fla., 1989.
Bishop, Lydia S. Norton, Kan., 9/91.
Blue Arm, Burdell. Vermillion, S.D., 1992.
Bradford, Oliver. Rapid City, S.D., 10/90–91.
Brady, Frank, M.D. Vermillion, S.D., 12/92.
Breslauer, Max R. Calumet City, Ill., 1989–93.
Brietigam, Nelda. Lemoore, Calif., 1989–91.
Broken Leg, Martin. Sioux Falls, S.D., 4/91.
Bruguier, Dora Shoots Off. Eagle Butte, S.D., 1990–1994.
Buchan, Bob. Rushville, Neb., 10/89.
Bunge, Robert. Vermillion, S.D., 1992.

Caldwell, Sandy. Asbury Park, N.J., 11/92.
Carroll, Curtis. Eagle Butte, S.D., 1990–1992.
Chandler, Arthur. Urbanna, Va.
Clow, Rich. Missoula, Mont., 1992.
Colby, David. Ashland, Ore., 1987–1989.
Colby, Delmar H. Shingleton, Calif., 1988.

Colby, Helen. West Linn, Ore., 1989–1995.
Cook, J. Frank. Beatrice, Neb., 7/89.
Cook, Phil. Beatrice, Neb., 1986.
Cook, William Wilson, Sr. Beatrice, Neb., 1988.
Culbertson, Helen. Rapid City, S.D., 9/90.
Cuny, Hazel. Rapid City, S.D., 4/5/91.

Damro, Tom. Beatrice, Neb., 1986.
Davis, Bill. Beatrice, Neb., 7/89.
Davis, Elizabeth Green. Del., 1990.
Dillon, Harold and Irene. Hanford, Calif., 1987–1992.
Duniway, David C. Salem, Ore., 1989–1990.

Eagle Staff, Sam. Vermillion, S.D., 1992.
Eaton, George (Capt.). West Point, N.Y., 1991.
Emery, Steve. Eagle Butte, S.D., 1991–1993.
Everett, Naomi. Thermopolis, Wyo., 1987–1990.

Figueras, Tony, M.D. Los Angeles, Calif., 1985–1995.
Flood, Bernard. O'Kreek, S.D., 1992.
Flood, Bill. Marty, S.D., 1977–1995.
Flood, Warren. Marty, S.D., 1977–1995.
Freund, Elma. Hanford, Calif., 9/87.

Gannon, Verna. Rapid City, S.D., 1992–1995.
Garnier, Richard. Wounded Knee, S.D., 1990.
Gibson, Judy. Beatrice, Neb., 1992.
Gillihan, Jim. Dekalb, Ill., 1984–1994.
Goes After Her Horses on Josephine Rooks. Martin, S.D., 1990–91.
Gonzalez, Mario. Black Hawk, S.D., 1989–1995.

Gorman, Frank. Woodbine, Ind., 1992.
Graff, Fordyce. Beatrice, Neb., 1985–1986.
Gullickson, Ben. Ravinia, S.D., 1985.

Hail, Sadie. 1991.
Hanson, Kathy. Yankton, S.D., 1984–1994.
Hanson, Robert G. Yankton, S.D., 1986–1994.
Heart, Carol Anne. Bismarck, N.D., 1978–1995.
Hevelone, Dorothy. Beatrice, Neb., 1986.
Higgins, Mr. and Mrs. Dale W. Beatrice, Neb., 1986.
Hill, Maxine T. Beatrice, Neb., 1986.
Hines, Susan. Chadron, Neb., 1991–1992.
Hogan, Michael and Eleanor. Seattle, WA, 1989–1993.
Holland, Patricia. Amherst, Mass., 1987–1993.
Hoxie, Frederick E. Chicago, Ill., 1992–1995.
Hultgren, Verna. Rapid City, S.D., 1990–1991.

Indermark, Joan and Jerry. Madison, Wisc., 1989–1995.
Iron Hawk, Goldie. Cheyenne River Reservation, S.D., 1991.

Kadlecek, Jane. Hay Springs, Neb., 2/93.
Keith, Sidney. Rapid City, S.D., 1991–1992.
Kendall, Bea. Yankton, S.D., 1984–1994.
Kilpatrick, Mrs. George. Beatrice, Neb., 9/88.
Kilpatrick, Bill. Beatrice, Neb., 9/88.
Kuhms, Berniece. Virginia, Neb., 1988.

Leech, Jane. Beatrice, Neb., 1988–1990.
Lenhart, William. Beatrice, Neb., 1988.
Little Eagle, Avis. Rapid City, S.D., 1990–1995.
Lock, Florence. Beatrice, Neb., 1988.
Looking Horse, Arvol. Green Grass, S.D., 1989–1994.
Lux, Julius. Beatrice, Neb., 1988.

Mannas, Mark. Las Cruces, N.M., 1992.
Manternach, Josie C. Concord, N.H., 2/89 and 6/91.
McDowell, Berniece. Palo Alto, Calif., 1987–12/89.
McGaa, Nona. Walnut Grove, Calif., 1990–1992.
Melior, Elaine. Spokane, Wash., 1989–1991.
Miller, Mr. and Mrs. Floyd. Seward, Neb., 11/92.
Muir, JoAnn. Rapid City, S.D., 1990–1995.

Necklace, Danny. Vermillion, S.D., 1990–1994.
Necklace, Martina. Vermillion, S.D., 1990–1994.
Necklace, Parnel and Grace. Vermillion, S.D., 1990–1994.
Necklace, Samuel. Vermillion, S.D., 1990–1994.
Nelson, Elizabeth. Beatrice, Neb., 9/91.

Nickeson, P. T. Beatrice, Neb., 9/88.
Niece, Marian. Boise, Idaho, 10/92.
Noble, L. Beatrice, Neb., 9/88.
Norder, Sue. Watseka, Ill., 7/93.
Not Help Him, Celene. Pine Ridge, S.D., 1989–1995.
Not Help Him, Marie. Pine Ridge, S.D., 1989–1995.

Papik, Barbara. Vermillion, S.D., 1992–1994.
Polley, Doris Robertson. Hanford, Calif., 1991–1995.
Pope, Arthur. Verona, Wisc., 1989.
Pope, Henry. Mandan, N.D., 10/92.
Pope, Lucille. Bozeman, Mont., 1989.
Pope, Tom. Mandan, N.D., 1992.

Quinn, Ellen. Marty, S.D., 1977–1979.

Rackby, Mabel Burke. Fresno, Calif., 1992.
Reinhart, Ruth. Painesville, Ohio, 1990.
Riedesel, Laureen. Beatrice, Neb., 1988–1994.
Runnels, Vic. Hill City, S.D., 1993–1995.
Runs After. Marilyn, S.D., 1992.

Schiel, Richard and Juanita. Suigun, Calif., 1989.
Scott, Henry. Beatrice, Neb., 1986.
Shangreaux, Frances. Pine Ridge, S.D., 7/89.
Short Bull, Lisa (Gerth). Vermillion, S.D., 1991–1993.
Siers, Victoria. Rapid City, S.D., 9/10/90.
Smith, Bobbie. Hanford, Calif., 1992.
Snyder, Marlene, 1986–1990.
Somen, Georgina. Westminster, Calif., 1988.
Sones, Kathleen. Gordon, Neb., 12/93.
Sorenson, Bill and Betty. Filly, Neb., 1990.
Spindler, Tim. Baraboo, Wisc., 1992.
Stauffer, Tim. Milford, Neb., 1991.
Stead, Robert. Rosebud, S.D., 1977–1992.
Stevens, Mike. Portland, Ore., 1989.
Stuhlmacher, Charlene. Yankton, S.D., 1980–1994.
Stutzman, Irvin Gene. Escondido, Calif., 12/92.
Sully, Claura Iron Hawk. Wounded Knee, S.D., 1989–1993.

Tate, Jerrod. Cleveland, Ohio, 1993–1995.
Tate, Patricia. Laramie, Wyo., 1993–1995.
Taylor, Chauncey. Hermosa, S.D., 1991–1992.
Taylor, Rev. Robert. Hanford, Calif., 12/92.
Thompson, Summer. Pine Ridge, S.D., 1989–1994.
Tucker, Hazel. Beatrice, Neb., 1989.
Two Bulls, Linda. Rapid City, S.D., 1991–1994.
Two Bulls, Marty. Rapid City, S.D., 1991–1994.

Viele, Bernice. Harrison, Neb., 3/93.
Vette, Virginia. Beatrice, Neb., 1989.

Wadell, Jean R. Beatrice, Neb., 1988–1990.
Ward, Wayne. Guthrie, Okla., 1988.
Warren, Margaret L. Hermosa, S.D., 1990–1995.
Weeks, Marjorie. Vermillion, S.D., 1990–1995.
Weesner, Jean. Hanford, Calif., 7/92.

White Plume, Alex. Kyle, S.D., 1991–1993.
Willis, Christine. Holstein, Ind., 1989.
Wordon, Zoa Ann. Beatrice, Neb., 1986.

Yeackley, Jackie. Salt Lake City, Utah, 9/91.
Young Bear, Seibert. Pine Ridge, S.D., 1989.

NEWSPAPER SOURCES

Arizona Republic

Hawley, Chuck.
"Child Law Tries to Fathom Tribes"
April 23, 1988.

Beatrice Daily Express

"The Seventh Cavalry and the Indians"
December 30, 1890

"Gone to the Front"
January 5, 1891

"It is Red Hot!"
January 8, 1891

"The Waif of Wounded Knee"
January 19, 1891

"Nebraska's Guard, the Banquet and Reception
    to Company K an Ovation"
January 20, 1891
See also same date an article entitled "Notes"

"Return of the 7th"
January 26, 1891

"Soldiers took firewater"
January 27, 1891

"Clara Colby is free"
 March 31, 1906

"Secures Large Estate—Mrs. Marie C. Martinez
    is awarded half a million dollars"
June 9, 1906

"Martinez-Colby" [marriage announcement]
June 14, 1906

"Indian Chief Wants General Colby's
    Pappoose"
June 15, 1906

Beatrice Daily Sun

"Defense Council Organized"
May 13,1916

"Patriotic League of Nebraska, General Colby Director"
April 28, 1917

"National Guard Reserve Militia"
August 22, 1917

"Legislative Reunion"
June 13, 1917

"Signing of Armistice Blasts Hopes of General Colby"
November, 1918

"Out of the Past"
May 4, 1939

"The Upper Room"
March 19, 1961

"The Upper Room"
February 3, 1966

"Independence Day"
July 2, 1976

"General Colby Reared Indian Girl"
1957 Centennial Edition

Beatrice Republican

October 11, 1883

"General Colby's Capture"
January 18, 1891

"Colby's Indian Papoose"
January 24, 1891

Black Hills Weekly Journal

"Colonel M. H. Day purchased Land in the
    Black Hills of South Dakota"
September 21, 1888

"Day Locates near Rapid City"
December 14, 1888

"Day was 'appointed Lt. Colonel of the Dakota
    Militia.'"
December 12, 1890

"Losses to Indians"
December 12, 1890

"Plans to go to California to Live"
September 29, 1893

"Day arrested for embezzlement."
May 27, 1896

Day's Obituary
May 11, 1900

Boston Morning Journal

"The Border Conflict"
January 1, 1891

"Unmitigated Falsehoods"
January 6, 1891

"The Nebraska Muddle"
January 10, 1891

"The Indians"
January 15, 1891

"The Hostile Indians"
January 15, 1891

"A Blizzard in Nebraska and Kansas"
January 3, 1891

"Miles Orders Civilians out"
January 16, 1891

"The Battle of Wounded Knee"
January 17, 1891

"The Indian Troubles"
January 19, 1891

"Indians Read Newspapers"
January 31, 1891

"Dr. Charles A. Eastman's Pathetic
    Description"
January 8, 1891

"A Terrific Blizzard Raging"
January 1, 1891

"Father Craft and the Indians"
January 3, 1891

"Depredation Bill Passes Congress"
February 19, 1891

"The Nebraska Muddle"
January 9, 1891

"Food to Indians"
January 14, 1891

The Brownville Republican

"Colby's Base Habits"
November, 1883

The Centerville [Neb.] *Journal*

"Albert Moore Close to Wounded Knee
    Battle"
March 9, 1873

Chadron [Neb.] *Democrat*

"Nebraska Legislature"
January 15, 1891

"The War Department Aroused"
November 22, 1890

"Pine Ridge Petrified Club"
January 15, 1891

The Cherokee Advocate

"The Life-long friend of Indians"
December 2, 1894

The Chicago Inter-Ocean

"Pine Ridge"
November 24, 1890

The Crawford [Neb.] *Clipper*

"Tales along the Sidney Trail"
Summer, 1986

The Denver Post

"Drank Poison to Save His Client"
n.d

"Ghost Dance at the Battle of Wounded
    Knee"
May 12, 1929

"The Great Whitewash"
December 31, 1950

Miniclier, Kit
"Lost Bird Comes Home to Wounded
    Knee"
July 14, 1991

"Injustice to Indians"
January 6, 1891

The Freeport [Ill.] *Daily Bulletin*

"Gen. Colby's Waif"
January 28, 1891

"A Dark Little Stranger"
November 17, 1894

"Visit for Lost Bird"
1897 [no exact date]

"Old Lady Ill Treated"
n. d

Green Bay [Wisc.] *Press Gazette*

MacFarlan, Joynes W
"Crandon man, Hugh McGinnis, Among
   Last of Indian Fighters"
1964 [no exact date]

Hanford Morning Journal

"Spanish Flu Quarantine Law"
January 1, 1919

"Sells-Floto and Buffalo Bill"
May 1, 1914

"Noted Indian Woman Passes at Home
   Here"
February 15, 1920

"Flu Ban Lifted"
February 25, 1920

"Obsequies Held for Mrs. E. C. Allen"
February 17, 1920

"Population"
January 7, 1920

"Ban on all public gatherings in city—
   theatres, schools, pool halls, no
   public funerals or gatherings of any
   kind"
February 4, 1920

"Women Make Plea for the Right to
   Vote"
January 31, 1913

Harper's Weekly

"Lieutenant Casey's Last Scout"
January 31, 1891

"The Sioux Rebellion
February 7, 1891

"The New Messiah"
December 6, 1890

"The Art of War and Newspaper Men"
December 6, 1890

"The Story of Wounded Knee"
February 7, 1891

Harper's Monthly

Burgess, Gelett
"The Keepsake"
98 (December 1906): 837

Hermosa [S.D.] *Pilot*

"Will the Military Help Protect?"
"Ye Gods!"
December 19, 1890

"General Miles Unpopular"
December 19, 1890

"Disgusted Residents"
January 14, 1891

"Photos"
April 3, 1891

"Indian Battles Galore"
December 19, 1890

"Sitting Bull's Dream"
March 6, 1891

"South Dakota and the World's Fair"
March 20, 1891

Houston Chronicle

Stancill, Nancy
"The Baby Market—The Business of
   Adoption—Permissive Laws, Big Bucks
   Make Texas Hot Spot"
October 6, 1991

The Indian Chieftain

"Indian Lands"
April 12, 1894

"General Colby at Tahlequah"
December 13, 1894

The Indianapolis Sentinel

"Horrors of the Frontier"
February 8, 1891

The Indian Journal

"Captain Grayson and General Colby were Robbed in their Hotel Room"
July 13, 1894

Johnson County [Neb.] *Journal*

"Colby a Candidate"
October 12, 1883

Indian Country Today

Little Eagle, Avis
"Memories of Wounded Knee Marked."
January 12, 1995

The Lakota Times

Byrd, Sid
"The Betrayal at Wounded Knee"
December 26, 1989

Cook-Lynn, Elizabeth
"The Broken Cord: Death of a Race"
January 16, 1990

Cudmore, Patrick
"The Great American Holocaust"
January 8, 1991

Cook, Mary
"Sidney Keith Keeping Lakota Language Alive"
October 3, 1989

Cook, Mary
"Lakota Grandmother Fights State for Custody of her Takojas [grandchildren]"
October 3, 1989

Giago, Tim
"Indigenous Culture Could Be the Last Hope for Survival"
October 3, 1989

Giago, Tim
"Wounded Knee Remembered 1980–1990"
"Wounds Still Fester After 100 Years"
January 8, 1991

Lone Eagle, Julia
"Wounded Knee Remembered"
December 27, 1988

Little Eagle, Avis
"Lost Bird's Final Journey Set"
June 12, 1991

Little Eagle, Avis
"Lost Bird Society Helps to Find Roots"
April 10, 1991

Little Eagle, Avis
"Mending the Sacred Hoop"
January 8, 1991

Little Eagle, Avis
"Zintkala Nuni: The Only Living Trophy of the Massacre"
January 8, 1991

Little Eagle, Avis
"Lost Bird Soon to Return Home"
February 12, 1991

Little Eagle, Avis
"Lost Bird: 30-Year Quest for Missing Daughters"
March 30, 1994

Little Eagle, Avis
"Woman Seeks Twin"
June 27, 1989

Little Eagle, Avis
"The Legend of Lost Bird: A Journey to the Spirit World"
July 17, 1991

Martin, John
"Hostage Crisis Brings Back Memories of Boarding School"
August 15, 1989

Not Help Him, Celene
"A Descendant Relates her Grandfather's Version"
January 8, 1991

Reynolds, Jerry
"A Mother and Child Reunion"
September 5, 1989

Star Comes out, Ivan
"The Aftermath of Cross-Adoption"
June 27, 1988

Star Comes Out, Ivan
"Adopting out"
June 27, 1989

Stillman, Pamela
"Iowa Court Ignores Child Welfare Act"
August 7, 1991

Wisecarver, Charmaine
"Vigilance at Wounded Knee—Big Foot Riders Finish Fourth Year"
January 9, 1990

White Plume, Debra
"The Dream"
January 8, 1991

Lincoln Star Journal

Stevens, Betty
"Former Social Worker Follows Story of Lost
    Bird Adoption"
December 25, 1990

Stevens, Betty
"Maternity Home Fading into History"
November 29, 1987

Lincoln Daily Evening News

"Weather"
April 21, 1908

"Weather"
April 22, 1908

Los Angeles Examiner

"Doctors to Answer—State Medical
    Board Cites Seventeen for Violation of
    Laws"
September 29, 1927

"Aged Doctor Wins Battle to Keep License
    with Story of Life's Battle on Disease,
    Epidemic and Plague"
October 19, 1927

Harrison, Eric
"After Century, Lost Bird Rejoins Flock"
July 12, 1991

Harrison, Eric
"A Girl called 'Lost Bird' Is Finally at Rest"
July 13, 1991

Madison [Wisc.] *Democrat*

"Clara B. Colby, Noted Suffrage Leader,
    Dead"
September 12, 1916

The Milford [Neb.] *Times*

"Unwed mothers get new start"
July 18, 1984

Milwaukee Journal

"Battle of Wounded Knee"
"I ordered my men to fire."
May 18, 1963

Minneapolis Journal

Torrey, Edwin C.
"Cattle Thieves"
August 7, 1929

Montana and the West

"Indian suicide rate is highest"
July 6, 1994

Muskogee Phoenix

"Seven Million Dollars"
December 8, 1892

"Sharks"
February 23, 1893

"Advice from the Indian Department"
July 27, 1893

"Council Notes—Visitors to Okmulgee"
November 2, 1893

"Employing an attorney for the nation—Creek
    under council"
November 9, 1893

"Cherokee Strip"
February 15, 1894

"Senate Report"
"Patience means pudding"
May 24, 1894

"Creek News"
November 7, 1894

"Personal"
"General Colby with the Indians"
November 24, 1894

"Fraud in Indian Payments"
December 12, 1894

"Eufaula Special Session"
May 22, 1895

"Trouble at Okmulgee"
May 25, 1895

"The Creek Muddle"
July 25, 1895

The Nebraska City Press

"Senator Colby's Bill"
January 3, 1887

The Nebraska Farmer

"Lindentree purchased by Colby"
June 12, 1888

Nebraska State Journal

"Marie Martinez gets Half Million"
June 9, 1906

"Can Find no Fraud, Complete Vindication of
General Colby of Nebraska"
December 16, 1894

The New York Times

"The Militia Desert Thayer"
January 11, 1891

"The Two Who Are Responsible"
January 11, 1891

"Throngs at the Reception"
January 14, 1891

"General Howard's opinions: The government
treatment of Indians a series of mistakes"
January 11, 1891

"Indians' Depredation Claims Manner of
Settling Criticized"
February 29, 1892

"The Nebraska Muddle—Thayer to Retire"
January 16, 1891

"By the Woman's Suffrage League"
March 20, 1891

The Norton [Kan.] *Champion*

"The Dewey Murder Trial—Looking Backward
26 Years"
April 10, 1930

Omaha Morning Bee

"Warlike Preparations"
"The Indian situation here is hourly growing
more threatening."
December 11, 1890

"Indians"
"250 Armed citizens left Rapid City yesterday
for the badlands."
December 11, 1890

"Indian Problem"
December 19, 1890

"Pierced by Cowboy Bullets"
December 14, 1890

"More Skirmishes Reported"
December 19, 1890

Omaha-World Herald

"Leonard W. Colby"
May 8, 1899

"Zintka, General Colby's Protégé, Waif of
Wounded Knee"
January 20, 1901

Hollis, Limprecht
"Reporter Tibbles Provided Truth in Stories
of Battle at Wounded Knee"
March 17, 1985

Bliss, Ronald G
"Galloping Nebraskan"
February 14, 1965

Palo Alto Times

"Dr. Mary White's Sister Passes Away"
September 8, 1916

Pawnee Interprise

"Mr. Colby fought the battles of the Liquor
men"
November 1883

Perkins County [S.D.] *Signal*

"Indian Pete Visits Lemmon"
September 20, 1911

Portland Oregonian

"Mrs. Colby Gets Divorce"
March 31, 1906

Rapid City Journal

(In chronological Sequence Showing Buildup of
Violence against the Lakota Before
Wounded Knee)

"Rapid City to Organize"
December 5, 1890

"All Quiet Along the Cheyenne"
December 6, 1890

"Rumors"
December 7, 1890

"Several Raids Reported"
December 7, 1890

"The Deserted Ranches on Lower Spring and
     Battle Creeks Raided"
December 9, 1897

"Arming the Settlers"
December 9, 1890

"More Arms"
December 9, 1890

"The Indians"
December 11, 1890

"Startling Rumors of Battles and Bloodshed
     Prevalent."
December 12, 1890

"From the Front"
December 14, 1890

"The Indians"
December 16, 1980

"The Indian Situation"
December 17, 1890

"The Indian Problem"
December 18, 1890

"Colonel Day's Battle"
December 18, 1890

"Colonel Day's Return, His Experience and fights
     with the Indians—At least twenty Dead Braves"
December 19, 1890

"Three More Good Indians"
December 20, 1890

"From the Reservation"
December 20, 1890

"Left for the Front"
December 21, 1890

"At the Front"
December 24, 1890

"Has His Eyes Open"
December 31, 1890

*Rapid City Journal articles regarding
the sharpshooter Riley Miller:*

"Riley Miller killed 8 buffalo"
March 14, 1884

"Riley Miller killed 56 antelope"
November 12, 1886

"Riley Miller killed bald eagle for dealer"
November 22, 1889

"Killed 53 deer"
November 23, 1888

"Killed 52 deer"
November 22, 1889

"Exhibition of Indian Relics"
December 11, 1891

"Returned from Powder River"
November 15, 1895

"Trophy Displayed"
n.d

"Photo"
"W.J. Collins took photo of Riley Miller with
     Wounded Knee collection."
n.d

"Wounded Knee Survivors"
"Old Cowboy Blames Cattlemen for Scare"
August 18, 1947

Yankton [S.D.] *Press and Dakotan*

"Indian youth suffer from social problems"
March 25, 1992

"A Battle Probable"
December 12, 1890

Rochester Democrat and Chronicle

"Miss Anthony in Berkshire"
July 30, 1897

"Miss Anthony at Her Old Home"
August 1, 1897

San Francisco Examiner

"Navajo Leaders Criticize Media on Child
     Custody Battle"
April 20, 1988

Smith, Joan
"Young once, Indian Forever"
July 3, 1988

"Sioux Gets $100,000 Bequest; to Aid
     Tribe"
December 20, 1916

St. Louis Post Dispatch

"Bidka: The story of an Indian Girl kindness
    could not tame"
February 28, 1904

St. Paul Dispatch

"Child of battlefield goes into girls'
    seminary"
"Little Zintka clung to her with sobs and
    declared that she would not stay more
    than a week among strangers."
January 13, 1904

The Sacramento Bee

"Doctor Wins Battle to Keep License"
October 19, 1927

no title—San Diego Newspaper
"Longs for Hills and Plains"
October, 1913

San Francisco Chronicle

"1978 Indian Child Law Evolved from a
    Horrible Situation"
April 21, 1988

Sioux City [Iowa] *Journal*

"The Chief of Indian Scouts, P.F. Wells,
    Gives Some Interesting News about the
    Reds"
May 5, 1891

"To Aid Sitting Bull's Daughter"
October 3, 1912

Sioux Falls Argus Leader

"Telling Stories with art"
March 12, 1993

"The Weather"
April 21, 1908

"Wounded Knee, 100 Years Later"
March 25, 26, 1990

Mollison, Chris
"In Shock: Two friends find they are
    sisters"

The Suffragette [London]

"What is there to fear?"
July 25, 1913

Pankhurst, Christabel
"A Woman's Question"
August 8, 1913

"Cat and Mouse Victims"
August 8, 1913

Pankhurst, Sylvia
"A Prisoner in Bow"
August 22, 1913

"Many Haystacks In Flames"
August 22, 1913

"Prison News"
August 22, 1913

Territorial News [Okla.]

"Lawyers"
November 24, 1892

USA Today

Keen, Judy
"Sioux Symbol's Remains Returned to Tribal
    Land"
July 11, 1991

The Wahoo New Era [Neb.]

no title
"General Colby was not elected Brigadier Gen-
    eral. Col. C. J. Bills of Fairbury got the posi-
    tion."
April 16, 1896

Washington Post

"General Miles will make a great mistake
    if he fails to disarm the newspaper
    correspondents."
January 13, 1891

"Wimbidausis"
"Susan B. Anthony is called 'Saint
    Susan'"
January 11, 1891

The Woman's Tribune

"The editor calls for February 15, 1890 to be
    regarded as a 'Holy Day.'" [Susan B.
    Anthony's birthday]
January 4, 1890

"A Visit to the Woman's Tribune"
May 17, 1890

"A Novel Spectacle"
June 21, 1890

"Editor's note"
January 31, 1891

"The Indian Baby"
January 10, 1891

"Editor's Note"
January 1891

"Editor's Notes"
February 14, 1891

"Home Again"
May 9, 1891

"Editorial Trip"
August 29, 1891

"Zintka Lanuni" [sic]
September 12, 1891

"Zintka lanuni [sic], the Waif of Wounded
    Knee"
February 21, 1891

"Lost Bird—The Message from the Sea" (poem
    by Isabel Darling)
January 9, 1892

"Indian Depredation Claims"
April 1, 1893

"How to Make Children Brave"
May 5, 1894

"Editor's Notes"
March 19, 1904

"Editorial"
September 9, 1905

"For Better, For Worse"
September 23, 1905

"The Exhibition"
May 7, 1907

"Suffragists Grand March"
July 11, 1908

"On Platform Seven"
July 11, 1908

"A-foot with my Vision, Welcome for Released
    Prisoners"
December 12, 1908

"A-foot with my Vision"
May 23, 1908

IAPI OAYE—The Word Carrier

"Depredations"
March, 1891

"Friendlies"
March, 1891

"It was a blessing"
January, 1891

"Sitting Bull's Death"
December, 1890

Yankton Press and Dakotan

"Ten Thousand in Need of Family Assistance."
December 6, 1890

"Under a Flag of Truce"
December 11, 1890

"A Battle Probable"
December 12, 1890

"Nearing a Crisis"
December 13, 1890

"Sitting Bull's Blood"
December 16, 1890

"Paragraphic Eulogy on the Death of that
    Venerable Devil Taurus Recumbent"
December 18, 1890

"The Missionaries to Blame"
January 9, 1981

"Depredation Claims"
January 12, 1891

"Indian Depredation Claims"
January 23, 1891

"M. H. Day thoroughly roasted in the
    House"
February 18, 1891

"From Pierre to-day"
February 19, 1891

"Investigation"
March 5, 1891

"M. H. Day"
March 6, 1891

"Day again predicts another outbreak"
March 12, 1891
"Depredation Bill"
February 25, 1891

"Damages by Indians"
February 26, 1891

Lunner, Chet
"Study Shows Indian Youth at Higher Risk for Suicide"
March 25, 1992

Giago, Tim
"Indian Beliefs Merit Honor"
May 18, 1992

Index